ULRICH REINHARDT

SHAPING GERMANY'S FUTURE

STRENGTHENING TRUST
SHARING RESPONSIBILITY
LIVING COOPERATION

Die Deutsche Bibliothek – CIP Einheitsaufnahme:

Shaping Germany's Future
Strengthening trust
Sharing responsibility
Living cooperation

CH. GOETZ VERLAG, Tegernsee 2025
ISBN 978-3-947140-14-5

Prof. Dr. Ulrich Reinhardt,
Foundation for Future Studies – an Initiative of BAT,
in cooperation with the WEIMER MEDIA GROUP GmbH

Assisted by Ayaan Güls and Angela Reinhardt

Layout: Matthias Erhardt, WEIMER MEDIA GROUP GmbH
Print and binding: Westermann Druck Zwickau GmbH

Printed in Germany

ULRICH REINHARDT

SHAPING GERMANY'S FUTURE

STRENGTHENING TRUST
SHARING RESPONSIBILITY
LIVING COOPERATION

LUDWIG ERHARD GIPFEL
TEGERNSEE SUMMIT

Stiftung für Zukunftsfragen
Eine Initiative von BAT

CH. GOETZ VERLAG

CONTENT

CONTENT

COOPERATION

QUESTIONS ABOUT THE FUTURE

USMAN ZAHUR

General Manager, BAT Germany

At a time when Germany faces challenges on a number of fronts – demographic change, the digital transformation and the need for sustainable economic activity – it is clear that shaping our future must be a joint undertaking. A collective approach is needed: one where responsibility is shared, trust is strengthened and cooperation is active.

The BAT Stiftung für Zukunftsfragen (BAT Foundation for Future Studies) has made it its mission to contribute to making our society more sustainable. By initiating scientific analysis of issues concerning the future and proposing sustainable solutions, it addresses the challenges ahead in a responsible manner. Its guiding principle is "The world in change – people at the center".

Societal commitment has always been integral to the corporate philosophy of BAT Germany. The BAT Stiftung für Zukunftsfragen and such milestones as this book testify to our endeavours to take responsibility and create positive impetus for society. Our purpose is to build A Better Tomorrow™.

This book makes an important contribution towards these ends. It provides comprehensive analysis of current social currents and reveals how positive changes can be brought about through collective action. The perspectives and proposed solutions presented in this work encourage dialogue, thinking outside the box and active involvement in shaping our shared future.

As Scientific Director of the BAT Stiftung für Zukunftsfragen, Professor Dr. Ulrich Reinhardt, puts it, "We are optimistic about the future and see the myriad opportunities that lie ahead. Let's work together on a future in which trust, responsibility and cooperation are not merely buzzwords but are the lived reality. The groundwork has been done – it's now up to all of us to make that future a reality and take it further."

May this book be a source of inspiration and help to constructively drive forward the conversation about Germany's future. It calls on us all to share responsibility, to strengthen trust and to actively cooperate – for the sake of a sustainable Germany.

Usman Zahur

FOREWORD

CHRISTIANE GOETZ-WEIMER, WOLFRAM WEIMER

Publisher WEIMER MEDIA GROUP

'The time is out of joint' is a literary quote from Shakespeare's world-famous play Hamlet (1623), which has been translated to us in German in a slightly modified form as **'die Welt ist aus den Fugen geraten' ('the world is out of joint').** Frank-Walter Steinmeier, when he was still Foreign Minister, and Angela Merkel, when she was Chancellor, both liked to use this flowery phrase in their speeches to emphasise the urgency of the world's situation dramatically, not to say theatrically.

And the current German Chancellor Friedrich Merz could easily incorporate this quote into his speeches – he would be hitting the nail on the head, because global crises will still be numerous in 2025, from Ukraine to the Middle East to China: the shocks emanating from them can be felt worldwide, not least in Germany, which is trying hard to guard its flanks. But if, as William Butler Yeats wrote in The Second Coming ,'Things fall apart; the centre cannot hold', then all efforts will seem to be in vain. Even supposedly old allies on the other side of the Atlantic no longer seem to be reliable when they present Germany with hitherto unprecedented economic hurdles and political challenges. If we then consider the menacing rise of extremes on both sides of the political spectrum and the increasingly overwhelming climate change, the future of our country seems less than encouraging. The diagnosis is shockingly sobering, the symptoms are unmistakable: Germany is afflicted by a dangerous malaise that is otherwise only known as a fin-de-siècle mood.

These are difficult times, and the question of where Germany stands in these turbulent times is as valid as it is vital. How can Germany reposition itself in this rapidly changing world in order to safeguard its future? And above all: What tools can Germany use to avoid being swept away by the tide of time and history and becoming a victim, rather than the shaper of its own future? These are not easy questions, but they demand answers and bold solutions.

The publication of the first highly acclaimed volume in this series, German Mut statt German Angst (2023), ('German Courage Instead of German Fear'), showed that the other side of fear is courage. And the greatest form of courage is despair overcome. That is the courage of true heroes. One needs this courage not only to act, but also to think.

So this year, we have once again embarked on a search for clues, together with twenty authors from different socially relevant areas. Despite their differences, they are united by their youth and, above all, their willingness to provide us with bold answers to our questions. After all, who better than the young, the beacon of hope for the future, could muster the necessary courage to provide answers to the questions that concern us?

Three crucial keywords, which are also contained in the title of this third edition, served as a guide for our authors to discuss the prerequisites for sustainable, positive change in view of the current situation. Even if, as Professor Ulrich Reinhardt rightly points out, the relationship between our three concepts should be understood as being circular and reciprocal rather than linear, the concept of trust seems to be the starting point. So, trust is the basis, because without trust, a society cannot function; without trust, it loses its cohesion. Trust, as Francis Fukuyama writes in his book Trust: The Social Virtues and the Creation of Prosperity (1995), has a significant influence on the economic and social success of a country. The question thus arises as to how trust, as the foundation of our society, can be strengthened. However, trust alone is not enough to make a difference. It also takes the courage to assume responsibility: A wise population trusts and relies on its elites — by which no special social class is meant, but all who are ready to assume responsibility for others and to take a chance: for thinking and acting are never without risk. This shows once again the reciprocity of the terms that we use, as emphasised by Professor Reinhardt. It is therefore a question of

FOREWORD

exploring the relationship between the freedom of the individual and the willingness to assume responsibility for society. Not least, the concept of cooperation between civil society actors and policy-makers must take centre stage, because thinking without acting leads nowhere and acting without thinking is mere noise. This is where society and politics complement each other in their natural functions to form a powerful joint force that is capable of bringing about positive change.

Unlike the past, the future has not yet been written. The future is being shaped at this very moment. With trust, responsibility and cooperation as the basis of our thought and action, this future — as described by our young authors — will succeed.

We wish you an exciting, encouraging and future-oriented read.

Christiane Goetz-Weimer and Dr. Wolfram Weimer

FOREWORD

ULRICH REINHARDT

Scientific Head of "Foundation for Future Studies – an Initiative of BAT"

Many citizens are increasingly seeking a sense of direction in a world that is changing at an ever-faster pace and confronting challenges such as social and political division, demographic shifts, the climate crisis, migration, and global conflicts. There is a growing desire to find meaningful ways of responding to these complex issues in a sustainable manner. This pursuit often goes beyond personal values or individual life plans. Rather, there is a widespread longing to identify shared foundations, foster trust, and shape the future collaboratively.

Meeting these demands requires an openness to change and a willingness to reassess established routines. Each individual is called upon to reflect on fundamental questions so as to find their own answers: Which values truly matter to me? How much responsibility am I prepared to shoulder? And what vision do I hold for my own future? While such questions can be a source of inspiration and promote innovation and personal development, they can also provoke uncertainty – feelings of being overwhelmed or isolated, for instance. What is, therefore, needed are conditions in which individual needs and collective demands are brought into harmony.

Society, in this regard, is not only a driving force but is itself significantly shaped by the evolving structures and developments. Financial and personnel strains on the healthcare system, shortages of skilled professionals, the energy transition, delays in digital transformation, infrastructure deficits, social and political polarisation, housing scarcity, and security concerns – these are but a few of the pressing issues that reflect the breadth of current challenges. Accordingly, traditional models must be re-evaluated and financial priorities rebalanced. The more complex these challenges become, the greater the need for public and private institutions to rely on the strength of societal cohesion.

For this societal transformation to succeed, citizens' trust in the necessary measures and the changing structures is required. Equally important is their willingness to assume responsibility and to view all societal actors as equal partners in a spirit of cooperation - rather than as opponents or rivals.

The good news is: The foundations for this already exist among the vast majority of citizens. Despite the multitude of crises and uncertainties, the overwhelming majority of Germans look to the future with (surprisingly) optimistic eyes - an attitude that inspires confidence and can serve as a basis for collective action.

Does trust prevail?

Out of every 100 respondents, the following number
agree with the statement:
'I have a positive attitude towards life and I'm optimistic about the future.'

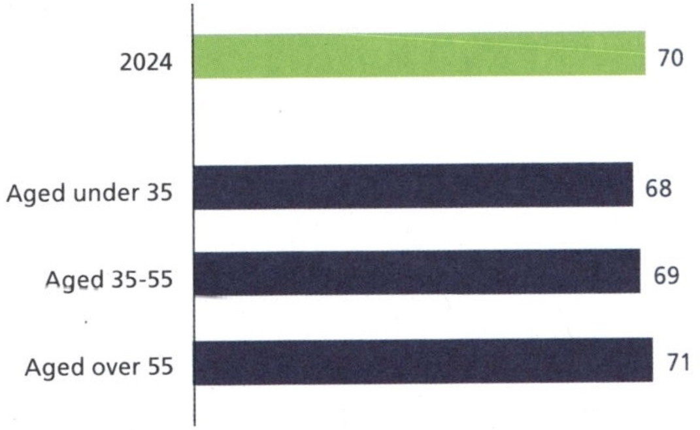

INTRODUCTION

More than two-thirds of citizens state that they have a positive outlook on life and look to the years ahead with optimism and confidence. This figure reveals that - contrary to common clichés - Germans do not view the world solely through a lens of negativity. On the contrary, while they recognise the challenges, they choose to concentrate on encouraging trends and signs of progress. Notably, there is little variation across generations: Both younger and older citizens show similar values.

Optimism can be characterised as a positive attitude towards life that is characterised by the conviction that general developments will change for the better in the long term—regardless of the specific circumstances or content. Various factors, including family and school influences, financial resources, stable interpersonal relationships, the public mood, and media influence this fundamental attitude significantly. A high level of inner trust also plays a key role, enabling individuals to hope for a positive future in uncertain or difficult times.

Numerous successful and inspiring projects also help to promote this optimistic outlook. Advances in science and technology, locally implemented sustainability initiatives, and innovative social concepts are developments that encourage and promote active participation. These successes act as motivation and invite people to become part of a positive dynamic and contribute to shaping a better future.

In a private context, optimism contributes significantly to strengthening mental and emotional health by promoting a sense of hope and confidence. This positive attitude leads to a greater focus on opportunities and possibilities, while obstacles and rejections become less important. Positive thinking proves to be particularly helpful in everyday challenges as well as in extraordinary events or crises—such as illness, conflict, loss or failure. It not only supports the reduction of stress, but also coping with setbacks by focusing on solutions and potential opportunities.

INTRODUCTION

Comparable effects can be observed in the social context. Optimism helps to overcome resistance, accept challenges and focus less on annoyances, grievances and problems. Instead, it promotes active participation in shaping social life as well as confident and supportive behaviour. This includes a reduction in criticism, more tolerant behaviour and greater recognition and promotion of positive developments. In the interpersonal sphere, citizens expect this attitude to lead to a stronger community, greater cohesion and reduced selfish behaviour. Optimism transcends the individual level and unfolds its social significance. It is not interpreted as a denial of problems but as a conscious decision to focus on opportunities and possibilities. In short: Optimism is contagious.

The second part of the publication presents interviews conducted in the form of three questions, and 20 personalities from politics and business were interviewed. From different perspectives and with varying emphases, they comment on the possibilities of building trust in political and economic structures, the relationship between individual freedom and social responsibility, and the need for cooperation beyond particular interests. A kaleidoscope of inspiring perspectives becomes visible.

TRUST

Trust is currently the subject of almost every societal debate. However, the positive expectations inherent in this term are rarely expressed. Rather, we mostly come across a loss of trust that can be observed everywhere, be it towards political parties, the media and corporations or generally towards other citizens or even democracy. In order to counter this development, it is first necessary to take a closer look at the characteristics, prerequisites and forms of trust. Thus, questions arise as to what it means to trust, what is necessary in order to trust someone and when trust is particularly important. In examining these questions, it is possible to identify a number of reasons for this waning of trust.

Etymology

Trust is a concept of ideological and ethical thought and expresses a relationship of reciprocity. The German word for trust ('Vertrauen') is derived from the Old High German verb 'gitrouwen' (or 'trauwen'). Its origin lies in the Indo-European word stem 'dreu-' and, according to historical interpretation, means being 'firm' or 'faithful' in one's beliefs and hopes. The Greek word for this is 'pistis' (faith), and in Latin it is 'fiducia' (self-confidence) or 'fides' (loyalty). In ancient and medieval usage, the term found itself in the contested field between loyalty and faith (e.g. Democritus advocated that we should not trust everyone, but only the well-proven). Since the 13th century, the German word stem 'trauen' (to trust) also meant 'to get married'. In the 16th century, the common Old High German words 'hoffen' (to hope) and 'glauben' (to believe) developed into 'vertrauen' (to trust) in the sense of trusting in the abilities of others, loyalty and reliability. This reflects a development from an expression of general hope to a more specific, interpersonal concept of trust . Since the beginning of the modern era, the noun 'Vertrauen' (trust) has increasingly come to mean confidence in one's own abilities (as in 'Selbstvertrauen': 'self-confidence'). Today, trust is a term used in everyday speech that permeates all areas of life and comes into play in different concepts of action and types of relationship. This applies, for example, to the family, group processes, school, media, the world of work, politics and economic and financial systems.

Scientific classification

Trust cannot be assigned to any one discipline, but is instead an interdisciplinary phenomenon, and research into the subject was long left to theologians and philosophers. However, since the early 1990s at the latest, the topic of trust has also been an important field of research in disciplines such as sociology, psychology, economics and political science. Due to a multitude of theories, it is difficult to arrive at a universally valid definition. Thus, for example, dispositional theories are based on the assumption that trust is acquired through early childhood attachments and socialisation processes, while identity-based approaches focus on the development of trust through significant commonalities and similarities. Conversely, the reputation-based approach cites certain qualities as being a prerequisite for trustworthiness, while the interactionist approach is based on the assumption that trust can only develop through repeated positive experiences and contact. Finally, institutionalism is based on the far-reaching effects of political structures that guarantee a certain stability, routine and predictability and thus create a social climate of trust. Despite their differences, most approaches see trust as a social attitude that has a mental (reason, reflection), emotional and action-influencing (routine, regularity) component. Another feature is the declaration of positive expectations and the elimination of uncertainty. Every act of trust also involves a moment of uncertainty. Without uncertainty, trust would be unnecessary as one could always precisely predict the behaviour of the other. Accordingly, the giver of trust can never be completely sure that they will not be disappointed, since none of the possible behaviours of the other nor their probability can really be known. In order to be able to trust despite this, the giver of trust must be clearly aware of the uncertainty, yet able to put it to one side.

People thus build trust by giving greater weight to their positive expectations regarding the behaviour of others than to uncertainty about their actual intentions.

Significance for the individual and for society

For every citizen, trust is the basis of their ability to relate and act. This initially applies to a person's family ties in particular and, later on, their interactions with their social environment, working environment, living environment and their relationship with institutions. The strongest trust is usually placed in people who have similar experiences and provide support (bonding relationships). In this type of identification-based trust, there is a strong emotional bond between the participants. Characteristics include for example close cooperation, regular communication and interaction, identification with each other's values and goals, and mutual liking. These relationships of trust are primarily found within the circle of family and friends.

Individuals enter into more loose relationships (bridging relationships) with groups with which they can exchange ideas and pursue specific group interests. In this context, trust is given on the basis of a situation or attributes and is based on certain characteristics or attributes of a person or organisation. These are expressed above all in terms of competence, integrity and goodwill. Competence can relate to expertise, skills or experience, integrity to moral values and ethical standards such as honesty and reliability, and goodwill to an optimistic, balanced and open attitude. This type of trust is often found in the work environment and in associations, as well as in client relationships.

Linking relationships establish a connection with institutions. In this case, the degree of uncertainty about the behaviour of the other or of institutions is greater than in the case of family ties or friendships. In their behaviour, the individual weighs up whether or not it is worth trusting the other person. Linking relationships are often based on situation-based or attribute-based trust. The former type of relationship often arises spontaneously and is heavily shaped by external factors. It is established for the duration of a particular situation, or more specifically is only temporary. Trust is based less on a deep, interpersonal relationship than on the expectation or necessity born of a situation. This applies, for example, to crisis situations or spontaneous political cooperation. Since situational trust is not 'real' trust, those involved must be convinced of the added value of the cooperation. In the longer term, this kind of trust can act as the basis for deeper forms of trust. Attribute-based trust is based on certain characteristics of a person, system or organisation rather than on a personal relationship or previous interactions. These characteristics do not necessarily have to be of a human nature, but may also include technical or organisational attributes, such as certain security certificates (software), authorisations (lawyers or doctors) or prescribed standards (organisations).

What are the consequences of the different types of trusting behaviour for an individual? An individual can develop an optimistic attitude, gain new experiences from which they can learn and build new relationships. They can confidently enter into cooperations and achieve common goals. By socialising with people from different backgrounds, an individual can learn to develop trust across groups and reduce prejudices. With regard to linking relationships, the growth of trust in the state can be fostered if the state enables participation in societal and political decision-making processes. At the same time, trust can have a burden-relieving function, especially in complex communities. Citizens can set priorities without having to constantly question everything and instead 'blindly' trust certain processes, people or institutions. This strengthens their ability to act.

In terms of society as a whole, the trusting relationships between citizens form an indispensable social capital for the stability, prosperity and cohesion of a society.

They are the basis for civic engagement, promote identification with the community and foster supportive behaviour. A wide variety of areas benefit from this. In the economic

TRUST

sector or within financial systems, for example, trust forms a central basis for a functioning market and for trade. In the political system, it ensures legitimacy for its representatives, while within the judiciary, in administration or within the police force, it guarantees justice and security. Trust in a society is therefore a sign of how stable and open interpersonal relationships are, how strongly these people trust institutions and how robust democratic structures are.

Loss of trust

Despite the multifaceted potential and possibilities inherent in trustful awareness and behaviour, the public debate tends to be dominated by its opposite: the loss of trust. Mistrust cannot simply be understood as the opposite of trust, but represents a state of its own. Doubts and uncertainties are deliberately emphasised here. And even if the current loss of trust is primarily focused on the political sphere, other institutions are also affected – from companies, churches and the media to the police and courts. There is also evidence of increasing mistrust towards other countries, minorities and religious groups.

Wherever trust dwindles, differences are no longer seen as enrichments that can be accepted with respect, but as irreconcilable differences that must be subordinated to the majority opinion.

As a result, sympathetic coexistence becomes hardly possible and the division within society becomes entrenched. A loss of trust among the younger generation can have particularly far-reaching consequences. If young citizens have few trustworthy experiences, if they are often disappointed or rejected even though they have placed their trust in others or if they feel that they are not taken seriously by decision-makers, they can develop increasing mistrust and become susceptible to populist positions. These processes are reinforced by an increase in – not always reputable – (online) sources of information and an erosion of traditional media, so that the uncertain and the temporary are further intensified. A longing for trust remains, and often finds its fulfilment in communities or associations that offer simple but identity-forming explanations and apparent certainties.

TRUST

The much-cited loss of trust in political parties involves a combination of different aspects. For instance, many citizens feel insecure, especially in times of economic uncertainty, political tensions and rapid technological change. They increasingly ask themselves whether the democratic system still recognises their concerns and is responding appropriately to the challenges of our time – be it global or national. In addition, they sense a lack of transparency, weak positioning of the popular parties and a gulf or alienation between politicians and the population. Combined with mistrust in other state bodies, such as the police, judiciary or even independent media, this can lead to a diminishing sense of security and stability. As a result, political polarisation increases, linked to a growing hostility between different political camps and a decline in societal consensus and in trust in compromise and democratic discourse. The rise of populist movements is both a consequence and an amplifier of the loss of trust.

Measures for building trust

The basis for a more trusting relationship in the interpersonal sphere is the establishment of a stable, empathetic and respectful relationship. Starting with family structures, school institutions, club structures or other social networks are later responsible for promoting this and thus strengthening social capital. This requires a local infrastructure with meeting places that appeal to broad societal groups, as well as targeted support for intercultural initiatives and programmes. It is important to engage in regular dialogue, also and especially with groups that think differently, in order to promote respect, tolerance and reflection and to create a long-term basis for understanding and cooperation. Other trust-building measures may include the development of bridging projects, diversity programmes, exchange programmes and a culture of extracurricular participation and civic engagement.

In order to overcome the mistrust between citizens and institutions, greater transparency, clear communication, access to reliable information and open decision-making processes are a sort of basic prerequisite. When these are fulfilled, even unpopular government measures will be more likely to be supported by citizens, as they will serve not only individual interests, but the common good.

TRUST

Participatory structures are of great importance for greater civil participation in political processes. These include, for example, municipal participation formats, citizens' forums, round tables and referendums. In addition, measures for more civic engagement promote trust in institutions and in the community.

A conglomerate of attitudes, behaviours, decisions and interactions that counter uncertainty with pragmatic solutions, combine material security with a sense of justice and maintain a positive view of the future, despite knowing about the need for change in the face of numerous challenges, has proven to be particularly sustainable.

Best practice examples

1. Transparency in government

In Scandinavian countries, citizens have access to government documents. For example, the 'Offentlighetsprincipen', the right of public access which has been enshrined in the constitution since 1766, allows citizens to view almost all documents and information from authorities and public offices, including emails, interview notes and even investigation files. The principle of transparency is the rule in Sweden, while secrecy is the exception and may only be applied under strict legal conditions.

Advantages: Regular reporting, open data platforms and citizen participation in political decisions. A reduced risk of corruption and mismanagement. Decision-making processes that can be tracked more easily.

TRUST

2. Integrity and ethical behaviour in companies

Companies certified under the B Corporation Standard are committed to social and environmental goals, added societal value and ecological sustainability. This transparency and responsibility towards society strengthens the trust of customers and citizens in the company. One example is the Dutch chocolate company Tony's Chocolonely. It not only pursues social and ecological standards, but is also actively committed to fair and sustainable cocoa production in order to end modern slavery and exploitation in the supply chain.

Advantages: Companies gain the trust of society through ethical business practices, sustainability initiatives and transparent communication and increase their long-term reputation and profits.

3. Social inclusion and integration

Canada has one of the most inclusive immigration systems in the world. Immigrants are seen as an asset and their integration is actively promoted through education and employment programmes. Through these measures, the country has achieved a high level of social trust and integration and has strengthened interpersonal relationships and understanding for one another.

Advantages: Measures that include minorities and disadvantaged groups, as well as initiatives to promote social cohesion, such as language and integration courses, contribute both to strengthening trust within society and to constructively tackling economic challenges (e.g. skilled labour shortages).

4. Strengthening the community and civil society in the area of security

In numerous cities in the USA, including New York, the police have introduced the practice of 'community policing', in which police officers work closely with local authorities and the public. The aim is to identify problems better and preventively and develop solutions together. This measure has strengthened citizens' diminished trust in the police and demonstrably reduced the crime rate.

Advantages: Building community organisations that rely on trust and cooperation between institutions and citizens can strengthen the sense of security as well as the sense of community.

5. Digital education and participation

Estonia is considered a pioneer in the field of digital education and participation. Back in the 1990s, the country began building a comprehensive e-government system and a digital infrastructure that enables all citizens to access government services online. Schools are digitised across the board and pupils learn to use digital technologies at an early age. The 'ProgeTiiger' programme promotes the digital competence of children and young people from an early age by teaching them programming and other IT skills.

Advantages: Trust in digital systems is strengthened as citizens learn early on how to use technology safely and competently. In addition, access to digital resources promotes equal opportunities and social participation, which increases trust in the education system and the government.

TRUST

How does trust develop?

Out of every 100 respondents, the following number agree with the statement:
'You can trust most of your fellow citizens.'

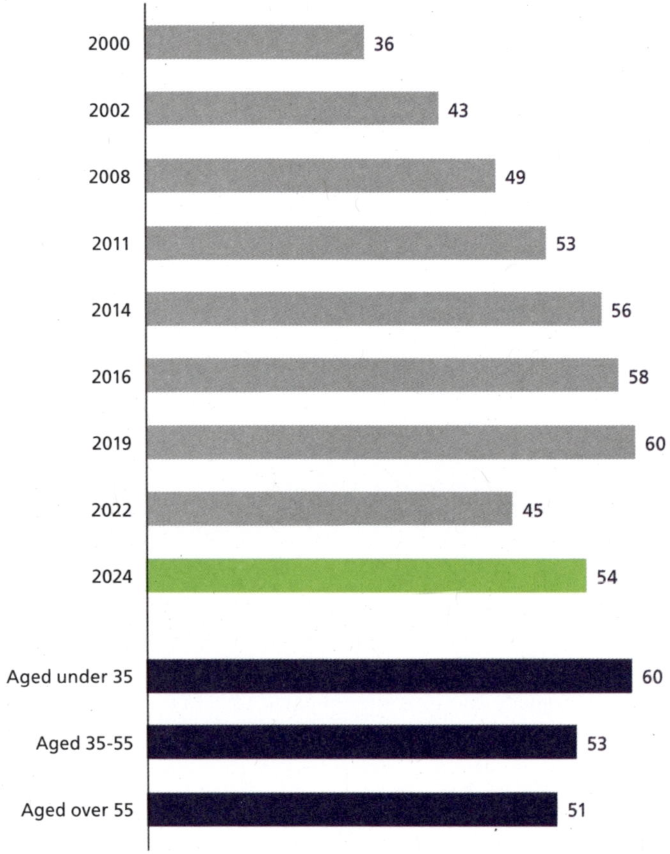

Renaissance of trust

A MAJORITY AGAIN BELIEVE IN THE RELIABILITY OF OTHERS

Results

Trust forms an essential basis for societal coexistence. Currently, a slim majority of the population trust most of their fellow citizens. At 60 percent, the proportion of under 35-year-olds is higher than that of older generations, of whom only around one in two express trust in their fellow human beings.

A look at the development over the years shows a changeable dynamic. In 2000, the share was just 36 percent, rising steadily to a high of 60 percent in 2019. This was followed by a decline to 45 percent in 2022, before the figure recovered to its current level of 54 percent.

Reasons

For the individual, trust forms the basis of their ability to relate and act. At first, this mainly concerns the individual's family ties, and later on their interactions with their social environment, working environment and fellow citizens. The greatest trust is generally placed in people who share similar experiences and identities and who offer support or are in a comparable social environment.

The increase in trust between 2000 and 2019 must be viewed primarily in the context of societal and economic developments. These include, for example, a relatively stable economic situation with low unemployment over the entire period as well as the sustained trust that emerged even after the 2008/2009 financial crisis. The experience of surviving these times of crisis unscathed had a profound influence on people's social trust in each other. It promoted a sense of security and stability and thus strengthened trust in society in general and in fellow human beings.

In addition, other societal challenges were overcome, such as the promotion of equal rights and diversity, the improvement of crime control and measures to combat climate change. All of these aspects contributed to a growing sense of community, which was reflected, among other things, in the increased amount of volunteer work carried out by the general public – be it in the form of neighbourhood help, participation in sports clubs or in aid organisations.

The close connection between the perception of societal stability and a personal willingness to trust was clearly demonstrated in 2022, when the trust of Germany's citizens not only in institutions and political actors, but also towards citizens fell by a total of 15 percent. This decline can be explained, among other things, by the effects of the coronavirus pandemic and also by frustration with sometimes non-transparent political measures and contradictions. In addition, other developments included the war in Ukraine, with its economic and social uncertainties, the energy crisis, rising inflation and the higher cost of living, increasing dissatisfaction with political decisions (e.g. energy policy, arms supplies), growing societal inequality (e.g. energy price cap or gas levy), societal divisions, the rise of populist forces and the spread of fake news and disinformation.

In comparison, trust between German citizens has again increased by almost 10 percent, to 54 percent, as of 2024. This can be explained, among other things, by citizens drawing closer together in times of perceived uncertainty. This can be seen, for example, in increasing neighbourhood help, community actions, offers of help for Ukrainian refugees and swap fairs. Experiences during the coronavirus pandemic in particular, including isolation, a lack of social contact and societal polarisation, prompted many citizens to network more intensively in person again, actively combat social division and seek out social interaction more consciously. Similarly, the war in Ukraine has strengthened the willingness of citizens to reflect on common values, to appreciate societal stability and to get more involved. As a result, interpersonal relationships as a whole have become the focus of a new sense of appreciation, which has ultimately also led to an increase in mutual trust.

The differences between younger and older citizens reveal different realities in their lives. Younger people show a higher level of trust in their fellow human beings, which is promoted by greater networking and openness to social contact. Digital platforms enable this age group to build diverse relationships and gain positive experiences. The phase of life also plays a decisive role: younger people feel at home in an environment that is more geared towards cooperation and exchange, for example at school, university or when starting a career. In addition, they tend to have an optimistic and idealistic attitude, are more open to new things, are often integrated in social communities and are in constant exchange with others. These factors lead to an increased willingness to trust. As younger citizens have less economic responsibility and are less likely to be confronted with difficult decisions, their mistrust of others is lower.

The middle and older generations, on the other hand, are more frequently exposed to professional, financial or personal challenges and consequently experience more interpersonal disappointments. These experiences foster restraint and greater foresight in dealing with others. Negative societal developments, such as polarisation and insecurity, further reinforce this attitude.

The reasons why some citizens currently have no trust in their fellow citizens are also important. The reasons for this often lie in personal disappointments or negative experiences, such as a lack of willingness to help or conflicts in everyday life. Societal factors, such as societal division, economic insecurity or the influence of disinformation, further reinforce this mistrust. A climate like this makes it difficult for many citizens to approach others and fosters isolation and reservations. The perception of inequality also plays a role: citizens who feel disadvantaged or have the impression of being treated unfairly are more likely to develop mistrust in others. A decline in community activities, such as extracurricular work or neighbourhood projects, and increasing anonymity in urban areas also contribute to this, as personal contacts become rarer and the feeling of community fades.

TRUST

Prognosis

A high level of trust in others is a key resource for living together. Trust facilitates cooperation, reduces conflicts and strengthens social cohesion. Societies with a high level of trust are characterised by greater stability and resilience, as citizens are willing to take responsibility and actively participate in community projects. The willingness to approach others and develop joint solutions to problems also increases with growing trust.

It is important to utilise this diverse potential of trust in the future.

Younger generations in particular offer potential for building a trusting society due to their higher level of trust. Their stronger networking and openness towards new contacts can help to build bridges between different social groups. Digital platforms enable them to build relationships across geographical and cultural boundaries. This networking should be specifically used to promote dialogue and dismantle prejudices. Younger people are also often in phases of life that are characterised by cooperation, such as education, starting a career or starting a family. These environments offer ideal conditions for establishing trust as the basis for long-term social bonds.

A decline in trust, on the other hand, harbours considerable risks for the social fabric. Mistrust makes it difficult to build social relationships and fosters isolation and polarisation. In a society with low trust, the willingness to work together decreases, which has a negative impact on both social and economic life. In addition, a climate of mistrust reinforces social divisions and reduces the willingness of citizens to engage.

Promoting trust requires targeted measures at an individual and societal level. Encounters between different social groups create opportunities to dismantle prejudices and promote mutual understanding. Community projects and neighbourhood initiatives offer spaces for positive interaction and strengthen the feeling of belonging. Educational institutions can lay the foundations for trusting relationships at an early stage through programmes to promote social skills and intercultural sensitivity. Politics could also strengthen trust in institutions through greater transparency in decision-making processes and improved communication, which in turn would have a positive effect on interpersonal trust.

It is therefore important to create structures that facilitate encounters and guarantee social stability and security. A future society with a high level of trust would not only be more stable, but also better equipped to jointly overcome future challenges . The promotion of trust should be understood as a continuous process that requires both individual efforts and institutional support.

TRUST

How much do you trust your family and friends?

Out of every 100 respondents, the following number agree with the statement:
'I trust that my friends and family will be there for me in difficult times.'

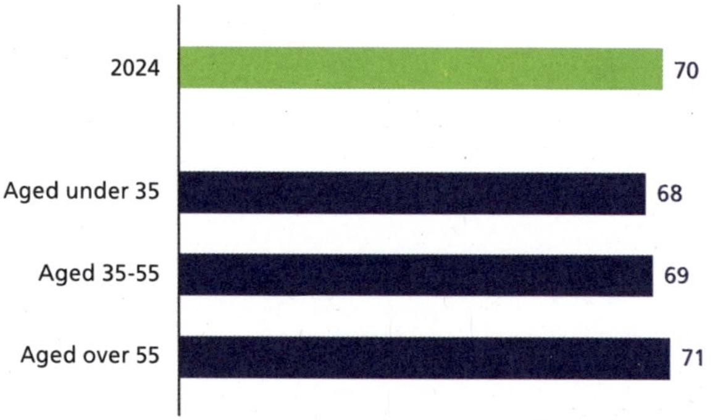

Family and friends as an anchor

SOLIDARITY IN TIMES OF CRISIS

Results

Of all social networks, your own family is the most stable. It not only has an important meaning for the individual, and shapes and protects them, but also plays a central role in fostering cohesion within society.

Eight out of ten citizens continue to trust their family even in times of crisis, with citizens over the age of 55 expressing a significantly above-average level of agreement.

TRUST

Reasons

Family relationships play a central role throughout a child's development, creating a sense of security and trust. A loving environment helps to achieve emotional security and self-confidence and to develop one's personality. In addition, the family is the place where children first learn moral values, norms, behaviour and social skills. In later years, the narrow core area expands and friends take on an important role. Their close bond is based above all on shared experiences and peers of the same age. Even in adulthood, the vast majority of citizens rely on long-standing relationships or their closest social environment and rely on them trustingly.

The importance of close social relationships is particularly evident in times of crisis: for example, in the case of problems looking for a job, in further training or studies, in the case of path-defining decision-making, relationship problems, bullying or exclusion, financial worries, identity crises or disorientation. In such cases, not only family but also friends offer a safe haven where you can be sure of emotional support, comfort, encouragement, appreciation, guidance and support in decision-making. Over the course of life, crises then manifest themselves above all in the area of transitions – children moving out, separations, entry into retirement – but also in terms of health issues and deaths, and in connection with isolation and loneliness. In addition, external crises can sometimes also give rise to an internal conflict. This can include, for example, political and social tensions, experiences of violence, natural disasters and pandemics, the effects of fleeing and migration or economic crises with high inflation and recession.

Through stable personal connections and positive experiences, citizens also develop greater trust in their fellow citizens and institutions, thereby strengthening the social capital of society. As a result, this fosters solidarity, a sense of responsibility, the ability to cooperate and the resilience of the community as a whole, as citizens with stable social connections recover more quickly from personal setbacks in times of crisis. In addition, the family also provides practical help by helping to reduce the burden on societal institutions or social services, for example, in education, at work, in childcare, in the event of illness or in the event of temporary financial difficulties.

Other reasons for the high level of agreement with this statement include familiarity due to the often long-term connections, the feeling of unconditional support and loyalty (this is less common in other social networks), similar values and norms or the feeling of family as a safe haven where you are protected from external pressures and receive support at the same time.

The generation over 55 shows higher levels of trust in the family, as their social environment often becomes smaller with increasing age and close friendships become rarer. At the same time, there is a growing need for emotional and practical security, which is primarily provided by the family. Health restrictions sometimes make family support indispensable, be it regarding care, everyday life or emotional support. In addition, many older people gradually withdraw from professional and societal obligations and focus more on their private sphere. The family thus becomes the centre point for stability, support and security.

Prognosis

The future of trust in the family as well as friends presents a hopeful picture. In a world characterised by social, economic and political upheaval, the importance of personal relationships will continue to increase. The family thereby remains a kind of indispensable anchor that offers citizens stability and security in all situations in life. In future, the family will offer emotional support even more than at present, as well as orientation and concrete help.

The certainty of always having the support of one's closest social circle remains a decisive factor for personal well-being and societal cohesion. The family will continue to diversify in its structure without losing its central function. Patchwork families, multi-generational households and chosen families are increasingly being accepted and valued (again). This diversity enables people to feel at home in different relationship constellations and to form flexible social bonds.

The importance of personal relationships is also increasing in society as a whole. Because the more that flexibility, individuality and unreliability increase in a society that offers multiple options, the greater becomes the need for reliability, solidarity and a sense of community – qualities that are increasingly valued. In the long term, trust in the family will play a key role in the resilience of modern societies. Personal bonds not only create individual security, but also help in overcoming societal challenges together. It is therefore important to continuously expand the high level of trust within family structures.

TRUST

How high is the level of trust in institutions?

Out of every 100 respondents, the following number agree with the statement:
'Trust in institutions (e.g. parliaments, courts, media) is an important basis for a stable society.'

Support for democracy

TRUST IN INSTITUTIONS REMAINS INDISPENSABLE

Results

Trust in institutions forms the foundation of a stable society. It enables key institutions such as parliaments, courts and the media to fulfil their tasks effectively. Over three quarters of citizens share this conviction. Differences between the age groups are only slight. Older citizens attach slightly greater importance to trust, while the younger generation shows a somewhat more reserved attitude. Overall, however, there is a broad consensus that emphasises the essential role of trust for societal stability and peaceful coexistence.

TRUST

Reasons

In recent years, the public debate has often been characterised by a loss of trust in institutions such as political parties, academia and the media. Various causes and developments have contributed to this situation, for example political polarisation, populist movements, a lack of transparency, poor crisis management, misleading communication and disinformation. Despite all these mistakes and criticism, trust in institutions remains essential for the majority of citizens in order to enable secure coexistence.

Trust thus forms the basis for legitimising and accepting decisions, even if they do not correspond to one's own ideas. It creates the trust that conflicts can be resolved peacefully and that basic needs such as education, healthcare or pension security can be guaranteed. Without trust, there is not only the threat of an erosion of democracy and social cohesion, but also economic stagnation and reduced innovative strength.

Older citizens attach slightly greater importance to trust in institutions than younger generations. Their experiences with times of crisis have taught them to value stable structures. For them, institutions stand for security, stability and prudent behaviour. With increasing age, the direct dependence on functioning systems, for example in the area of healthcare or pensions, also increases. The socialisation of this generation took place at a time when institutions were equated with authority and were widely respected. This has led to older citizens being less suspicious of state structures. Their lower affinity for digital media also protects them from the scepticism and criticism that is often spread there.

In contrast, the younger generation has grown up in a world of digitalisation and sees itself more as part of a globalised world, in which local or national institutions are less important in shaping their lives. In addition, authorities and traditionalties to state institutions play a lesser role in their lives. This is also evident in their emphasis on self-determination and self-realisation as well as their stronger rejection of institutional regulations and guidelines, by which they often feel restricted.

TRUST

Prognosis

Trust in institutions will play a central role in the stability of democracy and society in the coming years. The development of this trust depends to a large extent on how political representatives respond to challenges such as migration and economic uncertainties. Parties that convince people by displaying effective crisis management will gain in prestige. At the same time, there is a risk that inefficient action or a lack of transparency will further undermine existing trust. Past experience shows how quickly trust can be lost if decisions are perceived as inadequate or contradictory.

Technological developments, such as the use of artificial intelligence, will also shape the relationship of trust between citizens and institutions. Missing or unclear regulations will foster mistrust, especially when technologies make mistakes or contribute to the spread of disinformation. Institutions that set ethical standards and organise innovation transparently, on the other hand, will be perceived as more trustworthy.

Another decisive factor will be the ability of institutions to organise their work in a traceable and transparent way. Social media plays a dual role here: On the one hand, it can increase mistrust; on the other, it opens up new opportunities for dialogue between citizens and decision-makers. In the long term, time will tell whether institutions just want to achieve short-term success ('thinking in terms of legislative periods', 'thinking about the headline/circulation/click figures'), or instead want to credibly overcome complex challenges.

Trust will therefore remain a key resource for the legitimacy of government measures and the stability of democratic structures in the future.

TRUST

TRUST

How high is trust in politicians?

Out of every 100 respondents, the following number agree with the statement:
'Trust in politicians is crucial for the functioning of a society.'

Credibility of politicians

TRUST IS INDISPENSABLE

Results

A society can only function if its citizens trust the country's state decision-makers. Seven out of ten citizens agree with this view.

Reasons

The importance of trust in politicians for the functioning of a society is rated so highly by most citizens because for them, trust is a central basis for societal cohesion. Through them, the elected representatives of the people receive legitimisation for their ability to decide and act. This is particularly important in areas that affect the everyday lives of citizens (education, health, security), crisis management (natural disasters, economic crises, pandemics) and global challenges (security, diplomacy, climate protection). In these areas, citizens expect political leaders to put all party interests aside and focus on solutions that are responsible, socially just, effective and sustainable.

They see further characteristics or prerequisites for an open relationship of reliability as comprehensible, honest and transparent communication, citizen-centred design and management processes (especially at the municipal level), independence and realistic election promises (instead of short-term populism), expertise and professional competence, a willingness to make courageous (and unpopular) decisions and the ability to develop positive visions for the future.

An important characteristic of trust can also be seen in the desire for political role models. As elected representatives at various levels, politicians not only represent the interests of their own party, but are also committed to general political decision-making and shaping policies for the good of society. As public figures, they are watched closely by citizens, who often place high demands on their behaviour. Ideally, they are people of integrity who are characterised by authenticity, prudence, goal orientation and trustworthiness. Their function as role models is referred to above all in connection with the above-mentioned social challenges and uncertain crisis situations. The citizens want role models who inspire the general public with their foresight, conviction, confidence and drive thanks to their behaviour, and who point out possible solutions. In terms of their public impact, political role models should not only be exemplary in their private lives, but also send a signal to the whole of society.

If there is fundamental trust in socially just, efficient and sustainable measures and concepts, implementation is much more likely to be supported. As a result, citizens also emphasise the far-reaching positive effects of a trusting relationship, for example with regard to coexistence with others, the feeling of community cohesion and the willingness to actively participate in societal life. This also includes the fear that dwindling trust in politics will increase the popularity of populist movements that promise simple solutions to complex problems.

Despite all the arguments in favour of trusting politicians and the high level of agreement on this point among the general public, we must not forget those who see things differently. Almost one in three citizens sees other mechanisms as being responsible for the stability of a society (e.g. media, governance structures, civic engagement), has a pragmatic view (trust is not as important as control mechanisms) or harbours fundamental mistrust or even rejection of political representatives.

Prognosis

The future development of political trust will be strongly characterised by societal and global changes. In the face of growing challenges, the ability of governments to ensure long-term stability and justice will be crucial. Citizens increasingly expect policy that does not simply react to crises, but that primarily offers proactive solutions to fundamental problems.

A central focus will be on strengthening the dialogue between citizens and policy makers. Transparent communication and genuine opportunities to help shape societywill increase the sense of belonging and responsibility within society. Political leaders who are characterised by authenticity, integrity, orientation and a clear vision will be trusted.

In the future, governments will not only manage, but also shape things – with foresight, confidence and a clear focus on the needs of citizens. Only through this approach will it be possible to create and maintain a stable foundation for societal cohesion.

TRUST

TRUST

Do politicians act in the interests of citizens?

Out of every 100 respondents, the following number agree with the statement:
'I trust elected politicians to act in the best interests of citizens.'

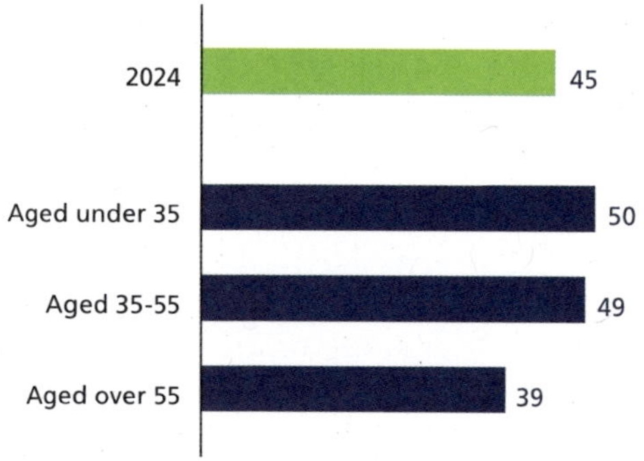

Politics without citizens' interests

A MAJORITY MISTRUST THE PEOPLE'S REPRESENTATIVES

Results

In recent years, societal discussions about citizens' trust in politicians have primarily centred on the loss of trust. The lack of role model function, revelations of corruption or moral misconduct, lack of clarity and commitment, a lack of proximity to citizens and non-transparent decision-making processes are all subjects of public debate.. The general public are divided on the issue. A narrow majority do not trust the people's representatives to act in the best interests of the citizens. The young generation still has the greatest trust in their elected representatives, while only two in five older people still feel they can rely on their actions.

TRUST

Reasons

One major reason for the mistrust of many citizens is the perception that political actors often pursue their own interests and place party political goals or the interests of specific groups above the common good. This view is further reinforced by a lack of transparency in decision-making processes. As a result, many citizens doubt the neutrality and independence of political decisions.

Another factor in mistrust is the perception of inefficient crisis management. In challenging situations in particular, citizens expect decisive action and clear strategies. Delays, contradictory measures or obviously wrong decisions, on the other hand, give the impression of a lack of competence and decision-making ability.

The role of the media also makes a significant contribution to building or losing trust. Reporting that focuses heavily on bad behaviour and problems reinforces negative perceptions. While critical analyses of political processes are necessary, a one-sided presentation leads to less awareness of positive developments and further cements existing prejudices.

The increasing polarisation within society is another major reason for the loss of trust. Populist movements specifically exploit the existing mistrust of established institutions to promote anti-establishment rhetoric. This dynamic undermines trust in traditional parties and political processes. At the same time, populist actors intensify conflicts between different societal groups, which further jeopardises social cohesion.

Despite these challenges, almost half of all citizens continue to trust the people's representatives. They recognise the complexity of the tasks that political actors have to deal with and understand the often difficult trade-offs.

Younger citizens tend to have a slightly higher level of trust in political actors than average. This group often shows a more optimistic or less critical attitude, which enables them to judge mistakes or deficits in politics less harshly. At the same time, they may see more opportunities for improvement. Nevertheless, even in this age group, only one in two people say they trust politicians. They are particularly disappointed by the supposed neglect of their needs, interests and fears, for example in the areas of education, pension provision, environmental policy and in the development of forward-looking visions.

Prognosis

The future of political trust in Germany could develop in two directions.

Firstly, in a 'business as usual' direction, which is tantamount to a loss of confidence with far-reaching consequences. If the current trend continues, trust in politics will continue to erode. Sceptical citizens will then withdraw from the political discourse even more than they do now and show little or no interest in democratic processes. Lower voter turnout is one consequence, as many citizens have the impression that their vote has no influence on political decisions. At the same time, the number of protest voters is increasing. Populist movements and extremist parties are becoming increasingly popular, as they promise simple solutions to complex problems and present themselves as representatives of disillusioned citizens.

The second option is to 'retreat into the private sphere'. If mistrust persists, people will focus more on their personal environment and avoid societal or political involvement. This will not only weaken democratic discourse, but also the willingness to work together on solutions to societal challenges.

Protests and resistance to measures will increase – even when they are in the public interest. Furthermore, polarisation between different societal groups will continue to increase, including conflicts between supporters and opponents of the political system.

However, it is also possible to take a path that leads to a new political trust. Positive change can be achieved through various approaches that go beyond transparent communication or citizen participation (see the corresponding texts in this book). The media can play a key role here by consistently incorporating different perspectives, successful political projects and constructive approaches to solutions into their reporting and thus reinforcing an optimistic attitude. There will also be a stronger focus on political education in the future. If citizens have a better understanding of how political processes work and the challenges involved, they will be more willing to support democratic institutions and representatives.

Can politicians communicate clearly?

Out of every 100 respondents, the following number agree with the statement:
'Political measures and decisions are hardly comprehensible to me any more. I don't think politicians can clearly communicate and justify what they are doing.'

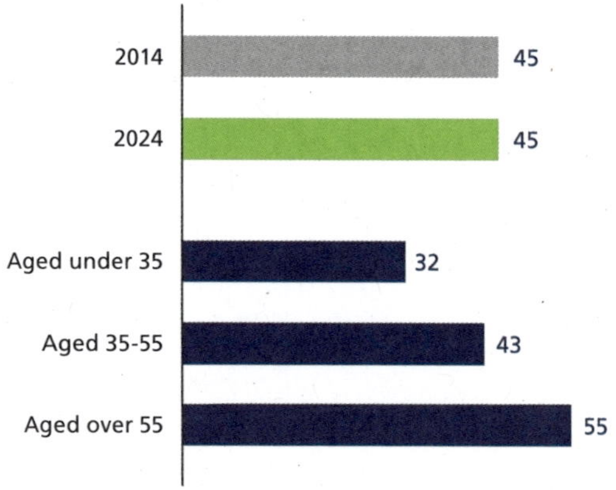

Between technical language and empty phrases

CITIZENS CRITICISE POLITICAL COMMUNICATION

Results

Just under half of citizens find political measures and decisions difficult to understand and criticise the communication skills of politicians. Differences between the generations are also observable: While around one in three of the generation under the age of 35 cannot comprehend political decisions, over half of the older generation can.

Reasons

Criticism of the mediation ability of political actors is not a new phenomenon and has not changed in the last ten years. Especially in the case of complex topics, such as climate change, digitalisation or social reforms, the difficulty of communicating political content clearly and comprehensibly is evident. The reasons for this are manifold and range from structural problems to strategic weaknesses and media distortions

One of the main reasons for this is the increasing complexity of political issues. Many decisions are closely linked to scientific, technological and international developments. Security policy, for example, does not only include national measures, but is also linked to international agreements and long-term strategies. This complexity often makes it difficult to convey the content in a comprehensible way. In addition, the speed of political processes also contributes to the perception of a lack of mediation skills. Decisions often have to be made quickly – e.g. in crisis situations – which leaves little time for detailed explanations.

Structural weaknesses within political institutions also play a role. Internal coordination between ministries or parties is often inefficient, which leads to contradictory statements. This inconsistency is perceived by citizens as a lack of professionalism. But the way in which conflicts are conducted in politics also influences the perception of the inability to mediate. Polarising debates or mutual accusations between and within parties too often dominate public discussion.

The strategic orientation of political communication also contributes to the criticism. Politicians often avoid taking up a clear position in order to be able to react flexibly to changes of opinion and keep all options open. However, this lack of commitment leads to the impression that political actors cannot convincingly justify their decisions. In addition, there is a focus on party politics, short-term successes and media productions, while long-term goals and intermediate steps are rarely communicated comprehensively.

Another aspect is the lack of empathy in political language. Citizens don't want only information about political decisions, but also an understanding of their personal concerns and life realities. However, political communication is often technocratic and distant, which reinforces the impression of a detached elite. The often 'typical' German behaviour of politicians also fits in with this: Too many political players appear matter-of-fact and serious, using political jargon with legal or technical formulations. Emotional appeal and storytelling are rarely used, although this would help to convey complex content and at the same time create sympathy. Adaptation to modern communication formats is also lacking. While companies are increasingly focusing on visual content, such as infographics or videos, political communication often remains text-heavy and not very appealing. However, citizens expect contemporary formats that make content quickly comprehensible.

In addition, today's flood of information makes the clear communication of political content more difficult. While traditional media used to serve as a filter and make complex topics comprehensible, this mechanism has changed due to the multitude of information sources. Social networks and digital platforms in particular have accelerated and fragmented the flow of information. As a result, political statements are often taken out of context or abbreviated, which promotes misunderstandings. Fake news and targeted disinformation further undermine trust in political actors (but also in the media itself).

The different expectations that younger and older citizens have regarding politicians further complicate the existing problem. Younger citizens tend to expect a digital approach and clear positions on the issues relevant to them. They have grown up with social media and are used to consuming information quickly and interactively. Older generations, on the other hand, place more value on a personalised approach and proven structures and expect seriousness instead of storytelling.

Prognosis

Communicating political decisions will remain one of the central challenges for governments in the coming years. In order to regain the trust of citizens and increase the comprehensibility of political measures, innovative approaches are required. The focus must be on an emotional appeal, a stronger link between politics and everyday realities and a reform of political culture. A key point here is the increased use of storytelling. Instead of presenting political content in an abstract or technocratic way, politicians must give concrete examples and say something about the (expected) consequences, opportunities and risks for the lives of citizens. In addition, political communication must focus more on emotions. Citizens react not only to facts, but also to values and feelings. Politicians can use empathetic language and gestures to demonstrate their understanding of the concerns and wishes of the population. This does not mean adopting populist rhetoric, but rather establishing an authentic connection with citizens.

At the same time, modern technologies should be used more intensively to involve citizens in an innovative way. One example is the use of artificial intelligence (AI), for example through chatbots or virtual assistants that provide information on political decisions around the clock and can also answer queries interactively. Digital participation platforms could enable citizens to contribute their opinions, follow discussions and track decision-making processes more transparently. Immersive technologies such as virtual reality (VR) could also be used to make the effects of political measures visually tangible. In addition, data-driven content, such as interactive infographics or short videos, could help to convey complex content in an understandable and appealing way.

In this context, the different ways of addressing target groups should also be taken into account. While older generations will continue to prefer a serious and factual approach in the future, younger citizens expect more dynamic, modern communication. A differentiated strategy is therefore required that takes both groups into account.

The political culture itself also needs to change. Polarising debates and blame-shifting between parties damage the reputation of politics as a whole. Instead, politicians must focus more on consensus-building and emphasise joint successes.

TRUST

Does trust arise through communication?

Out of every 100 respondents, the following number agree with the statement:
'I believe that mutual trust can be strengthened by communicating openly and honestly with each other.'

Trust through communication

THE POWER OF WORDS

Results

Open and honest communication is seen by the vast majority of German citizens as indispensable in order to strengthen trust within society. This trust forms the basis for stable and fair coexistence, both in interpersonal relationships and in the relationship between citizens and institutions.

TRUST

Reasons

As other charts also show, citizens see trust as the cornerstone of a stable and just society. It creates the basis for credibility, appreciation and stability. In order to promote this trust in the long term, transparent communication is necessary to ensure authenticity and minimise misunderstandings. Only through openness can citizens develop the feeling of being taken seriously and actively participate in societal life.

In everyday life, especially among family and friends, open communication plays a central role. It makes it possible to express thoughts and feelings, which facilitates a change of perspective. This ability promotes understanding of other points of view and strengthens the bond between the dialogue partners. This openness also always goes hand in hand with the courage to be vulnerable – a risk that is, however, worth it, as it creates deeper relationships and a stronger bond of trust. If this openness is missing, problems often remain unspoken, which contributes to misunderstandings and conflicts escalate. Honest communication, on the other hand, offers the opportunity to defuse tensions at an early stage and work out solutions together. This not only strengthens cohesion in the private sphere, but also trust in others in general.

An open culture of dialogue is also valued in the public sector. Citizens expect transparency and honesty from institutions such as politics, the media and science. Clearly explaining decisions is of particular importance here. Only if citizens can understand why certain measures are being taken will acceptance arise – even regarding controversial topics.

TRUST

Institutions gain credibility when they are prepared to admit mistakes and take responsibility. Concealing problems or a lack of transparency, on the other hand, quickly lead to mistrust. Open communication also helps to dispel rumours and encourage citizens to ask questions or contribute their own opinions. This then creates a culture of dialogue in which citizens feel taken seriously. The importance of open communication is particularly evident in crisis situations. Whether in times of economic uncertainty, health emergencies or other challenges, citizens look for orientation and support. When institutions communicate transparently and at the same time show empathy, citizens feel better understood and supported. The moment concerns are taken seriously and solutions are worked out together, a feeling of respect and equality is created. In the long term, this ultimately strengthens trust in public actors and strengthens the bond between citizens and institutions.

The above-average agreement rate of the older generation on this point is based on their wealth of experience and their affinity for direct dialogue as well as their lower tendency to use digital forms of communication. They have more experience with crises, often have a better understanding of human nature and know the importance of honest communication to build trust. This applies both to their own living environment and to their perception of the willingness of decision-makers to engage in dialogue. They are also more likely than others to have experienced how a lack of communication or deception (e.g. in political scandals) can lead to mistrust and often recognise the consequences of dishonest communication more quickly than others.

Prognosis

The importance of open communication will continue to gain relevance in the coming years. And the more often citizens can actively participate in decision-making processes, the stronger their trust in public actors will become. Participative approaches, such as citizens' forums or digital co-determination platforms, will help to intensify the dialogue and convey a sense of active participation. Such formats not only promote a feeling of belonging, but also make it possible to recognise and react to societal changes at an early stage.

In an increasingly individualised society, it will become more and more important for institutions to tailor their messages to the needs of different target groups. Citizens want personalised information that takes into account the realities of their lives and at the same time emphasises common values. In addition to factual information, empathetic responses to concerns and fears will also become more important. Institutions that are able to clearly present solutions and at the same time convince people emotionally will gain approval and therefore also importance. Digitalisation will both help this process and bring challenges. On the one hand, digital platforms make it possible to disseminate information quickly and directly, but on the other hand, they also increase the risk of disinformation, anonymity and manipulative content.

TRUST

Is media coverage correct?

Out of every 100 respondents, the following number agree with the statement:
'I trust the media to report objectively and truthfully.'

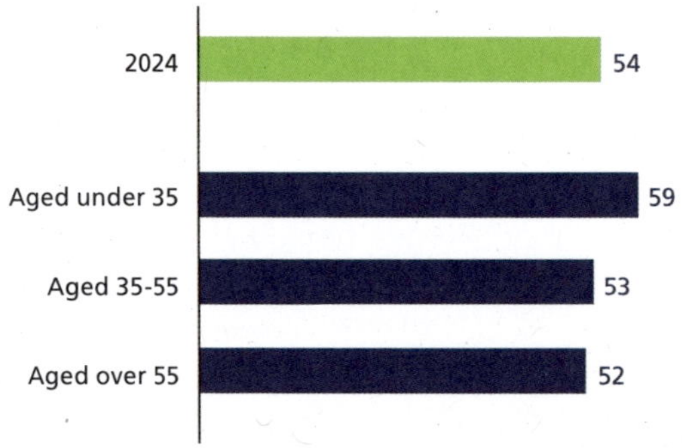

Media as a mouthpiece
BETWEEN HEADLINES AND SUBSTANCE

Results

In addition to disenchantment with politics, public debate also repeatedly addresses the growing mistrust of the media. As the fourth power in the state, the 'Fourth Estate', they influence public opinion through their reporting and – to a certain extent – also political events. The general public is divided on the question of whether the media report objectively and truthfully. A small majority express confidence and trust journalists to work objectively, impartially and seriously. At the same time, 46 percent are also sceptical and fear that they are being fed embellished, one-sided or incorrect information.

Reasons

The media have numerous means and options at their disposal to act as an independent force to form a counterpole to political influence, control and power. By means of independent reporting and distance from those in power, they are able to put relevant topics in the spotlight, uncover grievances, take challenging perspectives, present alternatives and act as a mouthpiece for the public. Thus, their representatives can be perceived as determined admonishers or courageous enlighteners. However, only just over one in two citizens recognises this role. Many criticise a lack of distance from political or economic representatives, biased reporting or even manipulation through targeted disinformation. Scepticism is particularly directed towards digital or social media. This is often accused of misinformation and simplified representations – after all, this type of media can be disseminated faster and more widely than fact-based news. It is also perceived as being susceptible to bots, trolls, non-transparent algorithms, filter bubbles and echo chambers. There are also criticisms surrounding data abuse, a lack of transparency and a lack of control, for example in the dissemination of hate speech. However, traditional media are also being increasingly criticised. The accusations here range from increasing commercialisation and a flood of information to a concentration on negative reporting.

Many people are also sceptical about the increasing use of artificial intelligence in journalism. AI-supported tools increase the efficiency and speed of news production, but at the same time, there is growing mistrust of the authenticity and quality of such content. Many citizens fear less thorough research or a higher proneness to manipulation. In addition, many people feel there is a lack of transparency about which content was created by humans and which by algorithms. The somewhat higher level of trust that young citizens place in the media can be explained by their fundamentally more trusting and optimistic attitude as well as by their specific habits of media use. The majority of them consume digital media and obtain their information from self-selected sources. They perceive these as dynamic, objective and corresponding to their point of view. The criticism of older citizens focuses both on specific content in traditional media and on the dominance of digital media. For instance, they often feel that their interests are not sufficiently represented, for example with regard to pension or healthcare policy. Also, the transition from traditional media (e.g. print and television) to digital formats is not accomplished right away by all older citizens, or some even reject it.

Prognosis

The media landscape is facing far-reaching changes. Economic pressure on editorial teams will continue to increase. Declining revenues from traditional business models, such as print advertising and subscriptions, are leading to shrinking editorial teams, reduced recruitment of qualified journalists and less time for in-depth research. At the same time, circulation pressure is forcing many media companies to focus more on high-click content and sensational news. This development will further weaken the quality of journalism and additionally impair public trust in independent reporting.

It is therefore important to think about how quality journalism can be financed in the future. On the one hand, state funding programmes or non-profit models are conceivable ways to financially secure independent journalism. On the other hand, citizens must also critically consider whether they are willing to pay for high-quality reporting. The widespread expectation of being able to compile news and information free of charge is at odds with the high demands placed on journalistic work. Investigative research, in-depth analyses and a critical examination of complex topics require time, resources and expertise – all of which come at a price. The willingness to pay for serious content would not only secure the financial basis for editorial offices, but also reduce their dependence on advertising revenue and thus reduce possible compromises. Citizens would actively contribute to ensuring journalistic quality via models such as voluntary subscriptions, crowdfunding or memberships of independent platforms. Parallel to this, however, it is also up to the media companies themselves to win back the trust of readers through transparency and quality and to clearly communicate the added value of paid content to them.

The increasing use of technology will also continue to have a strong impact on the future of the media. This will make certain journalistic processes more efficient, with automated systems taking over routine tasks such as data analysis, interview transcription, organisation and basic research. In addition, digital media will address target groups more directly and make content more interactive and personalised. At the same time, transparent communication about how and where AI is used in journalism remains a basic prerequisite for avoiding mistrust.

Niche media and independent platforms will increase. More and more citizens will make targeted use of offers that precisely reflect their interests and values. This development offers an opportunity for smaller providers to position themselves with high-quality and credible content. This applies in particular to local, on-site journalism, which will provide a counterweight to the fast pace of digital news streams.

Overall, the future of the media landscape will depend on how well a balanced equilibrium between economic constraints, technological innovations and the demand for independent reporting is maintained. If this succeeds, trust will increase again and the press will be able to continue to fulfil its role as the Fourth Estate.

Can the media build societal trust?

Out of every 100 respondents, the following number agree with the statement:
'Reputable media play a central role in maintaining public trust.'

A 'trust check' of the media

PUBLIC OPINION DIVIDED ON THE FOURTH ESTATE

Results

The media are an important component of a living democracy and stand for independence, control and opinion-forming. As the so-called 'Fourth Estate', they uncover abuses and contribute to the transparency of the state system. Consequently, eight out of ten citizens also see the media as a guarantor for preserving citizens' trust in institutions. The older generation shows an above-average rate of agreement here,, while younger people are somewhat more reserved, although still three quarters agree.

Reasons

The importance of the media for society is emphasised by their constitutional protection. Article 5 of the German Basic Law guarantees freedom of the press and broadcasting, prohibits state interference and censorship and ensures access to publicly accessible information. These protection rights emphasise the central role of the media in democracy. Their tasks include informing the public, controlling state power and promoting a free opinion-forming process. Media thus make an essential contribution to preserving basic democratic principles and ensuring an informed society. In their information function, they report to the public on societal processes and current events. They communicate political statements, explain conflicts and challenges and offer a wealth of background information. Through analyses, comments and discussions, they help us to better understand complex issues, enabling citizens to form their own differentiated opinions.

Thus, in a broader sense, they take on the task of raising political awareness, especially since, due to their independence and neutrality, in most cases they do not represent individual interests, but take all perspectives into account. The impression of independence is reinforced when media offer open platforms for discussion and debate. Through this opportunity, they promote a sense of participation, which in turn strengthens trust in the media and their role in the democratic process.

In their control function, the media uncover grievances, scrutinise the decisions of leaders and institutions and thus contribute to the transparency of the state. Citizens feel that the media's distance from politics and business is particularly important here. This integrity enables them to criticise measures and point out alternatives. Public broadcasters in particular are expected to do this, as they are more committed to balanced and diverse reporting than private media. In addition to their basic tasks and functions, the media serve as a tool for forming collective identities and promoting social cohesion. They create common points of reference that give groups a sense of unity and belonging. Examples of this are national identities, such as 'We live in a diverse society', regional affiliations, such as 'We are Bavaria', or communities of values, such as 'We are committed to protecting the planet as environmentalists'. The media therefore help to spread shared ideas, convey values and emphasise their importance for the community. At the same time, they encourage a critical examination of these values and stimulate societal dialogue, which strengthens trust between different groups.

In terms of generational differences, the lower level of agreement among younger people can be explained above all by their specific media use. They increasingly get their news from social networks, influencers or alternative platforms such as YouTube, TikTok or Reddit. Traditional media such as newspapers, television and radio play a smaller role, which is why they are also considered to be less important for building trust. In addition, they are aware of the influence of filter bubbles, echo chambers, algorithms and disinformation and are consequently also more sceptical of serious media. Older people, on the other hand, often have a longer attachment to traditional media, trust them more than social networks and above all see their potential as an instrument of control and an important pillar of democracy.

Prognosis

The media will continue to play a central role for democracy and societal cohesion in the future. Their function as the Fourth Estate remains indispensable for ensuring transparency and uncovering abuses. This control function will continue to be crucial in order to strengthen citizens' trust in institutions and ensure the integrity of democratic processes. Particularly important here is the independence of the media from political and economic interests, as this is the only way to guarantee their credibility. In order to complement their role as critical reporters in a meaningful way, the media will also increasingly emphasise positive developments in the future. Progress in science, such as new medical treatment methods, technological innovations in the field of mobility or sustainable construction projects provide inspiring examples of societal progress. Such reports strengthen trust in society's ability to master even complex challenges. Reports on civic engagement and successful societal initiatives – such as training programmes for refugees or infrastructure projects that create new jobs – also promote a sense of community, contribute to a more optimistic attitude and demonstrate concrete solutions to societal problems.

Reporting that not only highlights difficulties, but also emphasises successes and solutions, opens up new perspectives and focuses on opportunities for positive societal change.

In order to better reach the younger generation (in particular), traditional media will need to adapt their offerings even more strongly to digital formats. Their presence on social networks, video platforms or through interactive apps will help to meet their media usage habits. It remains essential to counteract disinformation, filter bubbles and echo chambers in order to secure one's own credibility in the long term.

Should fake news be penalised?

Out of every 100 respondents, the following number agree with the statement:
'The dissemination of misinformation on social networks should be made a criminal offence.'

Facts instead of fake news

WHY FALSE REPORTS SHOULD BE SANCTIONED

Results

The term 'fake news' refers to targeted false reports or misleading information that is spread primarily via social media. With the aim of manipulating the opinions, emotions or actions of the public, certain political or ideological interests are promoted. There is considerable danger that this leads to the display of prejudices, incite groups against each other and increase the polarisation of society. Accordingly, over four of every five German citizens are in favour of criminalising the dissemination of misinformation. Older citizens are particularly alarmed about this, but three out of five younger citizens are also in favour of corresponding sanctions.

TRUST

Reasons

Fake news poses a serious threat to society. Fake news finds the ideal conditions to spread in social networks in particular: algorithms reinforce its viral dynamics, while anonymity, filter bubbles and echo chambers increase its reach. Monetary incentives, such as 'click traps', and the preference for simplicity over complexity also contribute to rapid and uncontrolled dissemination.

The dangers of fake news are complex and far-reaching. It influences the formation of public opinion, promotes societal polarisation and reinforces prejudices, as well as one-sided perspectives. At the same time, general mistrust within society is increasing. Citizens increasingly doubt not only the credibility of individual news items, but also that of their fellow citizens, institutions and the media. Fake news itself often becomes a point of contention, leading to family conflicts, irreconcilable discussions in the social environment and polarised public debates. People's own opinions are often set as absolute while alternative points of view are categorically rejected. Individuals, especially in the context of bullying, and minorities are also often the target of this doubtful information, which can reinforce existing prejudices and promote discrimination and even physical violence.

An additional challenge arises from the rapid spread of fake news through the dynamics of social networks. The algorithms of these platforms prioritise content with a high interaction rate, which favours polarising or exaggerated posts. Users often share such content unchecked, which promotes the rapid spread of false information and anchors false narratives in the collective consciousness.

The differences between younger and older citizens in dealing with fake news can be traced back to their respective media use and information processing. Younger citizens use social networks intensively: 80 percent of them use them as their most common source of information, while 16 percent even use them as their only source of news. Despite this dependency, many consider their media skills to be sufficient to recognise fake news independently. Studies, however, show the opposite. In a British study, 36 percent of Generation

Z rated the veracity of at least half of the headlines in the test wrongly. Younger people also attach great importance to freedom of expression and individual freedoms in the digital space, are critical of government intervention and favour self-regulation and technical solutions, such as fact-checking tools or AI filters.

Older people, on the other hand, use social networks less intensively and are generally more sceptical about them. Their desire for state protection against fake news is more pronounced, especially as they are often the main target group for fraudulent online scams. They do not regard state measures as a restriction of legitimate opinions, but as a necessary protective measure against targeted disinformation.

Prognosis

Future developments in dealing with targeted false reports will be characterised by technological as well as societal and legal developments. Technological innovations will be able to automatically identify false reports and help to limit their spread. Platforms will implement more comprehensive monitoring mechanisms, either on a voluntary or a compulsory basis, in order to identify problematic content at an early stage. However, deepfakes and other advanced manipulation technologies will continue to make it difficult to distinguish between truth and deception.

Societally, it will be important to create greater awareness of the mechanisms behind disinformation. Accordingly, media literacy will no longer remain just an individual skill, but will become a central component of educational systems worldwide.

The increasing regulation of social networks is likely from a legal perspective. States will enforce the obligation on companies to fulfil their responsibility to disseminate truthful messages. Accordingly, penalties for the dissemination of false reports will not only affect individuals, but also the operators of digital platforms. International cooperation will be indispensable here, as disinformation knows no geographical boundaries.

However, the balance between regulation and the preservation of freedom of expression will also have to be constantly rebalanced in the future.

TRUST

Is trust (almost) everything?

Out of every 100 respondents, the following number agree with the statement:
'Trust is the basis for any successful cooperation.'

The power of trust

THE FOUNDATION OF SUCCESSFUL COOPERATION

Results

Trust is seen by the vast majority of German citizens as an indispensable basis for any successful cooperation. Agreement to this effect is particularly high among the over-55s, 93 percent of whom consider trust to be essential for collaboration. Among younger citizens, the proportion is slightly lower, at four out of five respondents, but also remains at a very high level. These values illustrate how strongly trust is perceived as the foundation for functioning relationships. Cooperation – whether in a personal environment or in larger societal structures – is hardly conceivable without a minimum level of trust for citizens.

TRUST

Reasons

As has already been made clear in this chapter on the topic of 'trust', trust reduces uncertainty and creates a basis for reliability and predictability in our dealings with one another. Without trust, however, mistrust and control mechanisms arise that make cooperation more difficult and inefficient.

In the interpersonal sphere, trust enables open communication and mutual understanding. Citizens who trust each other are more willing to share information, support each other and develop solutions together. This openness not only promotes the quality of collaboration, but also strengthens the sense of community. The importance of trust is also clearly evident in a professional context: teams with a high level of trust work more efficiently because they invest less energy in conflicts or safeguards. Leaders who create trust also promote creativity and innovation in their teams and thus increase the overall success of the company.

Trust also plays a central role in the long-term planning of cooperations. Projects that extend over longer periods of time require a high degree of reliability and certainty that commitments will be honoured. At the same time, trust makes it easier to deal with risks, as those involved are willing to share responsibility and react flexibly to unforeseen developments.

Economic crises or political upheavals have shown how important stable cooperation is in order to overcome them. These collective experiences are one reason why the older generation in particular places such a high value on trust. Another reason is the opposite experience: many collaborations failed because disharmony prevailed or individual interests took centre stage. In addition, older citizens are even more strongly influenced by a type of socialisation in which the sense of community was of greater importance. The more they hold fast to this value, the more they see it as being threatened by technological developments. In an increasingly digital world, it is becoming more difficult to build personal relationships and establish trust. At the same time, new forms of cooperation are emerging via digital platforms or global networks, in which trust mechanisms function more pragmatically than in traditional

TRUST

structures. This also explains why younger generations also place a high value on trust, but experience and evaluate it more functionally than older citizens. For them, the success and efficiency of cooperation also depend on rules, contracts, clear framework conditions and a practical cost-benefit calculation.

Prognosis

In an increasingly complex world of globalised markets and digital networks,trust will continue to play a central role in reducing uncertainty and enabling collaboration. Societies with a high level of trust are better able to overcome challenges because they can cooperate more quickly and act more effectively.

A decline in trust, on the other hand, would have considerable disadvantages. For example, without a sufficient basis of trust, additional control mechanisms and more bureaucracy would be required in the economic sector, which in turn would slow down processes and increase costs.

The promotion of trust-based relationships should therefore be seen as a central task – both at an individual level and within larger structures, such as companies or political systems.

TRUST

RESPONSIBILITY

Responsibility

Responsibility is also a concept that currently plays a central role in many societal and political debates. However, it is often only used in a negative context, when referring to the lack of a sense of responsibility or unwillingness to take responsibility. The term itself offers a multitude of positive implications and possibilities that are rarely emphasised. Responsibility means not only taking responsibility for mistakes, but also acting actively and with foresight to promote positive developments – both at a private and societal level. In order to be able to better categorise the meaning of responsibility, the various facets and historical origins of the term are briefly presented below.

Etymology

The term 'responsibility' has a long linguistic history that is closely linked to legal and ethical concepts. The German word for responsibility, 'Verantwortung', originally stems from the Middle High German verb 'verantwürten', which was equated with 'to defend oneself as a defendant in court'. This verb has been used since the 12th century, while the noun 'Verantwortung' can only be proven to have been used from the 15th century onwards. The root of the noun stems from the Old High German 'antwurti', which is related to 'Antwort' ('answer'), and originally denoted a reply or justification. The Latin equivalent 'respondere' (to answer), from Roman legal language, also strongly influenced the development of the English word 'responsibility'. In the legal context, responsibility initially meant standing up for one's actions and justifying oneself before a higher authority. This link between responsibility and accountability is also evident in modern meanings. Over time, the term underwent a semantic expansion. While it was primarily used as a legal term in the Middle Ages, from the 19th century onwards, it became a central ethical and philosophical concept. With the secularisation of society, responsibility was also increasingly related to human coexistence, for example as a moral obligation towards others or society.

Today, the term encompasses various dimensions: from personal responsibility for one's own actions to collective responsibility in social or political contexts. In all these meanings, however, the original idea of responding to and standing up for one's actions remains central, which underlines the dialogical character of the term.

Scientific classification

Like trust and cooperation, responsibility is also an interdisciplinary concept and plays a role in different scientific disciplines. In philosophy, responsibility is discussed above all in ethics: Aristotle emphasised the importance of a virtuous character, while Kant focused on moral duties. Both approaches place the individual at the centre – either through the development of virtues or through the observance of duties. The philosopher Hans Jonas expanded this understanding in the 20th century through his concept of ethics of responsibility, which is particularly focused on the long-term consequences of human action. He called for a sense of responsibility towards future generations and warned of the effects of technology on people and the environment.

In sociology, responsibility is often considered in the context of complex social structures. Max Weber emphasised the role of managers and decision-makers, whose responsibility goes far beyond individual intentions. They must not only act in a morally correct manner, but also consider the real effects of their decisions. Psychological approaches, on the other hand, often address the phenomenon of diffusion of responsibility. In groups, individuals tend to take on less responsibility than in situations they face alone. This phenomenon can be seen in everyday life in numerous situations, for example, be it in the office, in clubs, schools, parties, circles of friends or neighbourhoods – people always hope that they won't have to take responsibility themselves or that others will take responsibility for the group.

RESPONSIBILITY

In economics, the term 'responsibility' is primarily discussed in the context of corporate ethics and corporate social responsibility (CSR). Companies bear responsibility not only for their economic results, but also for the social and ecological impact of their actions. CSR describes the voluntary integration of sustainability principles into business practices, going beyond legal requirements in order to promote social justice, environmental protection and ethical standards. This responsibility encompasses both internal aspects, such as fair working conditions and diversity, and external dimensions, such as the economical use of resources or support for local communities. A central point of discussion here is the conflict between short-term profit targets and long-term responsibility. Companies are often faced with moral dilemmas, for example when economic profit collides with ethical principles. Business ethics approaches therefore demand a balance between economic rationality and moral responsibility. Studies show how responsible business practices strengthen a company's image and create long-term competitive advantages, for example through greater employee loyalty, or increased customer confidence.

Significance for the individual and society

There is no such thing as responsibility, but there are various forms of it that are of central importance to society and influence the way we live together. In general, responsibility ensures that individuals and organisations are held accountable for their actions and their consequences. As a result, reliability and trust in social interactions are strengthened. In the individual context, responsibility enables individuals to act independently, make conscious decisions and take responsibility for the consequences. Connected with this is the promotion of self-awareness and personal development. This is particularly evident among young adults. Before they can take responsibility for others, they first learn to take responsibility for themselves, for example with regard to school, education or relationships.

They practise organising themselves, making independent decisions and agreements and developing their own moral and value standards. They also learn to reflect on the consequences of their actions and to bear these consequences. This self-responsibility enables them to set personal goals, develop perseverance and achieve their plans independently and confidently. This also includes recognising one's own mistakes and taking responsibility for them, as well as resolving conflicts respectfully and seeing them as learning opportunities. In later life, self-responsibility goes beyond one's own life and also influences friends, family, neighbours and the community. In this context, individuals develop empathy, consideration, tolerance and respect, among other things. Positive experiences with reliable actions strengthen a person's confidence to accept challenges, so that responsibility subsequently grows into a key ability to both achieve private goals and support the community. In this respect, self-responsibility transforms into societal responsibility through responsibility for others. As part of a larger community, this extends to other social and political areas, for example in the form of societal engagement. Collaborations are often entered into with others in order to motivate each other on the one hand, and not have to bear sole responsibility on the other.

Diffusion of responsibility

As versatile and significant as the assumption of responsibility is for the development of the individual and the stability of a society, its negation can also have numerous destabilising effects. This is illustrated by the example of diffusion of responsibility. This concept describes a socio-psychological phenomenon in which the responsibility for actions, decisions or tasks in groups is distributed among several people. This makes each person involved feel less personally responsible than if they were alone in the situation. As a result, this leads to a lack of commitment and a reduced willingness to help, as everyone assumes that the other person will act. Other characteristics are pluralistic ignorance (the non-action of others is interpreted as a sign of unnecessary action), anonymity (the larger the group, the less everyone feels obliged to act), unclear responsibilities and fear of judgement.

RESPONSIBILITY

Strategies for increasing a sense of responsibility

As with trust and cooperation, responsibility also has great potential for overcoming societal challenges. To activate or increase this, various measures can be taken. In the area of diffusion of responsibility, it makes sense to ensure an appropriate group size in decision-making processes and to define the respective responsibilities before all else. It is also important to address individuals directly and guarantee them expertise and support (empowerment). Specific concepts such as the OAABS communication scheme (each person only has one task), the Scrum framework (self-organised and cross-functional team for agile project management) or rotation models can also be helpful.

At the same time, in the spirit of ethics of conviction, it is important to motivate citizens to take responsibility as early as possible, for example in the area of teaching values at home and at school. This can be done, for example, by thematising and exemplifying personal responsibility and creating independent projects for younger people.

With regard to future challenges in particular, it is also important to identify a clear need for action. People cannot rely solely on the state to take responsibility: instead, the importance of individual responsibility should be emphasised.

All in all, this reveals that responsibility is a core principle of a democratic society. It offers both individual and collective actors the opportunity to participate with integrity and commitment for the good of society. In doing so, responsible behaviour not only creates a more stable community, but also a feeling of fulfilment and togetherness.

RESPONSIBILITY

Best practice examples

1. Teach for all

is a global network of 61 independent and locally-led organisations working to improve educational opportunities for children and young people worldwide. They aim to take responsibility for change by redesigning the framework conditions for better access to education.

2. Patagonia

is a global network of 61 independent and locally-led organisations working to improve educational opportunities for children and young people worldwide. They aim to take responsibility for change by redesigning the framework conditions for better access to education.

3. The Bonn Institute

is dedicated to the promotion of constructive journalism. It assumes responsibility for the media landscape by developing ethical standards and supporting journalists in shedding light on societal challenges in a solution-orientated way. Its aim is to strengthen trust in the media and initiate positive societal change.

Fairtrade International is an umbrella organisation for fair trade. It takes responsibility for monitoring compliance with social, economic and ecological standards and establishing a fair and sustainable trading system.

4. The Canadian Ryan Hreljac

began collecting money for well construction in developing countries when he was six years old. He felt a sense of responsibility as a child in a rich, industrialised country to help underprivileged children. Today, Ryan's Well Foundation has implemented over 1,700 water projects in 17 countries, helping to improve access to clean water.

RESPONSIBILITY

How important is responsibility?

Out of every 100 respondents, the following number agree with the statement:
'It is important that each individual takes responsibility for the community and for a better future.'

From I to we

RESPONSIBILITY AS THE KEY TO THE FUTURE

Results

The fundamental personal willingness to take responsibility is closely related to the specific question of responsibility for the community and a better future. Almost nine out of ten people feel personally responsible for the cohesion of the community and believe it is important for each individual to focus their actions on making the future a little better.

RESPONSIBILITY

In this context, citizens understand the term 'community' to mean an association of people who live in similar environments, share common interests or pursue common goals. The scope of this community can vary depending on the perspective. While some focus primarily on their immediate social environment, others include their neighbourhood, their school community, their clubs, their professional environment or their church community.

Citizens associate a better future in particular with equal opportunities and justice, for example with regard to access to education, health and prosperity. In addition, more empathy and solidarity as well as the sustainable and careful use of the environment and natural resources are among the key aspects of a positive vision for the future.

Reasons

The willingness to take responsibility for the community and a better future is deeply rooted in the moral values of German citizens. The longing for social stability and security plays a central role here. Citizens see the community not only as a place of exchange, but also as an essential basis for a fulfilled life. The need for a sense of belonging and mutual support is particularly strong in times of societal tension and uncertainty.

Another reason lies in the realisation that personal engagement not only benefits others but also increases one's own well-being. Those who actively contribute to the improvement of their environment usually also experience an increased feeling of meaningfulness and satisfaction. This can be seen, for example, in the cultivation of neighbourhood relationships, the commitment to social projects or the promotion of initiatives.

RESPONSIBILITY

Many citizens also recognise the importance of role models and their positive influence on future generations. In this respect, responsibility does not end with the organisation of one's own life, but extends to the creation of a sustainable basis for one's family and friends, as well as for strangers.

Finally, the pursuit of justice and equal opportunities drives many citizens. They want a society in which solidarity and empathy are not just slogans, but are actively practised. These values not only strengthen cohesion, but also help to prevent social conflicts and promote an overall harmonious coexistence.

In terms of generational differences, younger people show a below-average agreement level to this end, while older people prove to be particularly responsible. They have more life experience, know the importance of individual responsibility – even in smaller areas – have a stronger need for stability and security and emphasise traditional values, such as a sense of duty and community. They also derive greater satisfaction and self-affirmation from the feeling of helping others and contributing to the community, especially as they have fewer family and work commitments, in keeping with their age.

In contrast, the younger generation has grown up in a more individualised society and often feels less responsible for societal grievances. In a time of crises and challenges, they more often seek personal fulfilment in professional and family contexts or in achieving individual goals. Nevertheless, they also show an overall high willingness to take responsibility.

RESPONSIBILITY

Prognosis

The willingness of citizens to take responsibility for the community and for the future will continue to play a central role in the coming years. The desire for a harmonious coexistence and a fairer society will continue to grow. At the same time, citizens will become more aware of how decisive their personal actions are in shaping the social environment. Gestures of helpfulness, consideration and solidarity will be integrated even more strongly into everyday life. In addition, citizens will increasingly look for concrete ways to actively contribute to societal cohesion – be it through involvement in the neighbourhood, in clubs or in other social structures.

Education will also play a key role in this context: the better citizens are informed about societal contexts, the more willing they will be to actively assume responsibility. It is therefore not only the task of schools and other educational institutions to focus more on teaching values such as solidarity and a sense of community. It is also important to promote these values within one's own area of responsibility and life – in the family, among friends or at work.

RESPONSIBILITY

Who takes personal responsibility?

Out of every 100 respondents, the following number agree with the statement:
'I take responsibility for my actions and for my mistakes.'

The majority show backbone

SHAPING THE FUTURE RESPONSIBLY

Results

An overwhelming majority of German citizens – 87 percent, to be exact – agree with the statement: 'I take responsibility for my actions and for my mistakes.' This figure illustrates the strong sense of responsibility within society. Within the age groups, agreement is particularly high among the over-55s, while there is still some upward potential among the under-35s.

RESPONSIBILITY

Reasons

In addition to reliable behaviour, the concept of responsibility encompasses the individual obligation to stand up for one's own decisions and actions and to accept their consequences. This stance is usually based on inner moral and ethical principles, which are often shaped by one's own conscience, and are closely linked to the virtues of courage and honesty. The high agreement rate of citizens with regard to the importance of responsibility indicates that this principle is deeply rooted in societal values.

In the personal sphere, taking responsibility can encompass many different aspects, depending on which priorities are set and what the individual feels responsible for. A striking example of this is the choice of a degree programme, which is often perceived as challenging. This decision implies accepting the associated challenges and consequences or, in the case of a revision of the choice, gaining the knowledge to think future decisions over more carefully. Both scenarios illustrate an adaptation to new circumstances and, at the same time, open up the opportunity for reflection. Citizens emphasise that mistakes should not be regarded as final, but rather as opportunities to learn from and to break new ground.

In professional terms, by expressing a willingness to take responsibility, citizens signal that they have personal integrity, have the well-being of the company or colleagues in mind and are reliable. In particular, a positive error culture is valued, in which mistakes can be honestly admitted and new solutions developed. In most cases, this meets with a positive reaction. People appreciate this willingness to take responsibility and admit mistakes, recognise the absence of excuses and perceive those involved as trustworthy, respectable personalities.

RESPONSIBILITY

In other societal contexts, citizens often take on tasks in social or political areas that are closely linked to their personal convictions. They attach particular importance to openly communicating their convictions and actively committing to their implementation. As these are often deeply rooted in their own personality or in emotional interests, it is sometimes difficult for them to revise decisions they have made or to admit their own mistakes. The courage required to do this, however, is valued all the more highly by others as it signals authenticity and personal integrity.

No matter in which areas citizens stand up for their actions, what they all have in common is a developed capacity for reflection and respectful interaction, as this always entails consequences for others.

Older citizens are often characterised by a particularly pronounced sense of responsibility, while younger generations tend to have slightly below-average values. Older people have a broad spectrum of experience, which includes both successes and failures. Through these reflection processes, they have not only internalised the positive effects of responsible action, but also developed greater equanimity in dealing with mistakes. They recognise mistakes as valuable learning opportunities and are aware of their potential benefits.
In contrast, many younger citizens still lack extensive experience and the assurance that comes with it, which is reflected in a more reserved approach. This uncertainty is further intensified by the dominant role of social networks in their living environment. Platforms of this kind harbour an increased risk of public criticism, bullying and social exclusion, whereby the permanent pressure to compare makes an authentic error culture more difficult. In addition, younger people often lack the opportunity to demonstrate their willingness to take responsibility, especially in a professional context, as they often have to take a back seat to more experienced colleagues.

Prognosis

The high willingness to take responsibility and admit mistakes gives reason for hope. In a world full of uncertainties, it forms a stable anchor for societal cohesion. It will be particularly important to pass this value on to the coming generations.

A rethink within companies would help here: instead of judging mistakes as failures or as poor performance, a positive error culture would promote innovation and strengthen trust between employees and managers. Leadership role models would be required to set an example of leadership not through perfection, but through the ability to take responsibility for mistakes and learn from them.

However, not only in the world of work will it be important to encourage people to take responsibility, face challenges and emerge stronger from setbacks. All citizens will be called upon to trust themselves and to deal openly with difficulties. After all, responsibility is not a burden or a constraint – it provides support and orientation in every life situation. Citizens must therefore be encouraged to support each other and work together towards a better future. If this succeeds, Germany will not only overcome challenges, but will also be a role model for other nations in the long term – a country full of people with the courage to take responsibility and the will to change.

RESPONSIBILITY

Who takes on more responsibility than others?

Out of every 100 respondents, the following number agree with the statement:
'I like to take on more responsibility than others.'

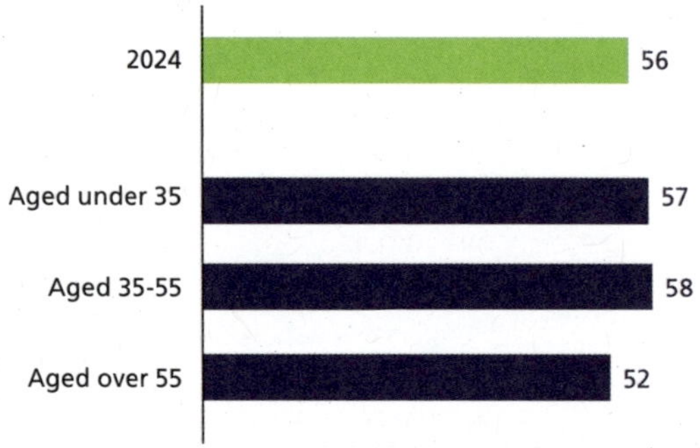

Leading the way instead of catching up

A MAJORITY WANT TO TAKE ON MORE RESPONSIBILITY THAN OTHERS

Results

Taking responsibility means using freedom to shape things, making courageous decisions and putting them into practice with confidence and determination. It means getting involved and standing up for other people, personal values, ideas or even content. A little over half of the population is willing or inclined to take on more responsibility than others. This affects almost all population groups equally.

RESPONSIBILITY

Reasons

Responsibility plays a central role in every society. It is the basis for cooperation and cohesion, influences every area of society, is supported by individuals and institutions and influences how citizens interact with each other. It is not a rigid construct, but changes in its content and meaning in line with societal developments. For example, while for many years the economy focused primarily on steady growth (without thinking about sustainability), many companies are now increasingly taking responsibility in connection with employees, customers or suppliers. And while responsibility for pension provisions, further education and healthcare was almost exclusively left to the state until the 1980s, today there is an increasing emphasis on personal responsibility. A majority of the population has recognised this and is even prepared to take on more responsibility than others.

This individual responsibility can manifest itself in a wide variety of areas, but always has the same core: The individual makes an ethical decision and takes responsibility for its consequences. This may concern the family sphere, the close social environment, the professional field or a larger social context, for example by taking on political, economic or ecological responsibility. Citizens particularly often and willingly take on responsibility in the family setting, in the neighbourhood and within their professional position.

The motives for this adoption of responsibility vary and range from an altruistic worldview to a pronounced sense of duty and to a feeling of self-realisation, satisfaction or pride. Responsibility always has a positive effect on individual development – especially for younger people. It promotes personal maturity, resilience and the ability to deal with setbacks. Those who take responsibility learn to make decisions and bear their consequences. These experiences strengthen self-confidence and help an individual to better assess their own abilities.

RESPONSIBILITY

Prognosis

In the future, the willingness of citizens to assume responsibility will play a central role, as it will make a decisive contribution to overcoming numerous societal challenges. This attitude will not only promote societal cohesion, but also strengthen personal development and open up new opportunities in professional contexts.

In the personal sphere, a willingness to take responsibility is essential in order to better manage uncertainty and develop increased resilience. The more personal responsibility an individual takes on, the stronger their sense of self-determination will be and the more they will be able to take on wider responsibilities. This development is all the more positive the more a supportive societal framework is created that recognises and promotes personal responsibility.

The importance of a willingness to take responsibility will also continue to increase in the world of work. Individuals who take on responsibility are often characterised by strong leadership qualities and contribute significantly to a stronger team spirit. They not only foster productivity, but also create a working environment that is characterised by initiative and engagement. They are also more courageous in dealing with new challenges and act as a driving force for innovation. Those who take responsibility show a willingness to develop and implement new ideas – a characteristic that will become increasingly important in the modern working world.

In this way, the willingness to take responsibility, if it is encouraged, will help to form the basis for a functioning, sustainable and fair coexistence.

RESPONSIBILITY

Who helps without expecting anything in return?

Out of every 100 respondents, the following number agree with the statement:
'I like to help others, even without receiving anything in return.'

Altruism in society

ALMOST NINE OUT OF TEN CITIZENS GIVE HELP UNCONDITIONALLY

Results

Almost nine out of ten German citizens are willing to help others without expecting anything in return. There are hardly any differences in terms of gender, income, education or place of residence. Altruistic behaviour thus proves to be a universal property that exists largely independently of external living conditions. Only among the under-35s is a somewhat more reserved attitude evident, but here too more than four out of five are prepared to give without taking. The forms of help are diverse: they range from spontaneous support in acute emergencies to long-term neighbourly help and long-term involvement in charitable projects.

Reasons

The motives for selfless behaviour are complex and can be explained biologically, psychologically and socially. In terms of evolutionary biology, altruistic behaviour strengthens cohesion within a group and promotes the survival of the community. Psychologically, intrinsic motivations play a central role, whereby values such as empathy and generosity are deeply rooted in the nature of the individual. These characteristics are further reinforced by social, cultural, moral and religious beliefs. Societies promote a collective social conscience that is internalised through education and socialisation. Altruistic behaviour is therefore often perceived as meaningful – a feeling that is often perceived as more valuable than material benefits, as it gives people the feeling of being needed and making a positive contribution. Helpers predominantly favour immaterial support and only resort to donations of money, clothing or goods in exceptional cases.

The forms of help range from spontaneous gestures in the face of everyday challenges, personal strokes of fate or natural disasters to long-term engagement. While spontaneous help often takes place in the immediate social environment, medium-term support manifests itself, for example, in neighbourhood help or local projects such as building a playground or organising a street festival. Long-term engagement can be seen, for example, in work with non-profit organisations, in mentoring or in voluntary services. Such societal engagement not only strengthens social cohesion, but also gives helpers a sense of individual effectiveness and inner satisfaction.
The differences between the generations can be explained above all by experience and the time available. Older citizens benefit from their life experience and from a strong awareness of the positive emotions that helping others triggers. Their reduced professional and family commitments also allow them to devote more time and resources to societal activities. The younger generation, on the other hand, often faces challenges such as professional qualifications, career and family obligations, which tie up more of their resources. Nevertheless, they are also very willing to help.

RESPONSIBILITY

Prognosis

The great willingness of German citizens to help will remain a pillar of societal cohesion in the future. In particular, the interpersonal aspects of this behaviour give cause for optimism. The willingness to help others without expecting anything in return not only creates individual satisfaction, but also strengthens the social fabric. Relationships and networks will play a decisive role here. People help above all where they feel emotionally connected – be it in the family, among friends or in the neighbourhood. Neighbourhood help in particular will experience a renaissance, as it offers both practical and emotional support. In an ageing society, this will become particularly relevant for older citizens, as they are often more dependent on mutual support.

Role models will play an important part. Children and young people orient themselves strongly towards the behaviour of their parents, teachers or other caregivers. If they show a high degree of helpfulness, this behaviour is often adopted and passed on. A society that makes altruistic behaviour visible and values it will be able to promote a culture of helping in the long term. Schools and educational institutions should promote social skills such as empathy and team spirit.

Another positive trend is the growing societal appreciation of altruistic behaviour. Citizens who are selflessly engaged receive recognition and gratitude – be it through personal words or public appreciation. This appreciation strengthens the feeling of meaningfulness of one's own actions and motivates others to contribute as well.

Opportunities may also arise from a stronger connection between the generations. Older people have time and experience, while younger generations often bring more energy and fresh ideas to the table. Joint projects could help to unite these strengths and build bridges between the generations. Such intergenerational initiatives would not only provide practical help, but also promote mutual understanding and social cohesion.

A society that places solidarity and compassion at the centre will not only be resilient to crises, but will also achieve a higher level of satisfaction through cohesion.

RESPONSIBILITY

What help do citizens provide privately?

Out of every 100 respondents, the following number agree with the statement:
'I have provided the following assistance in the last two to three years.'

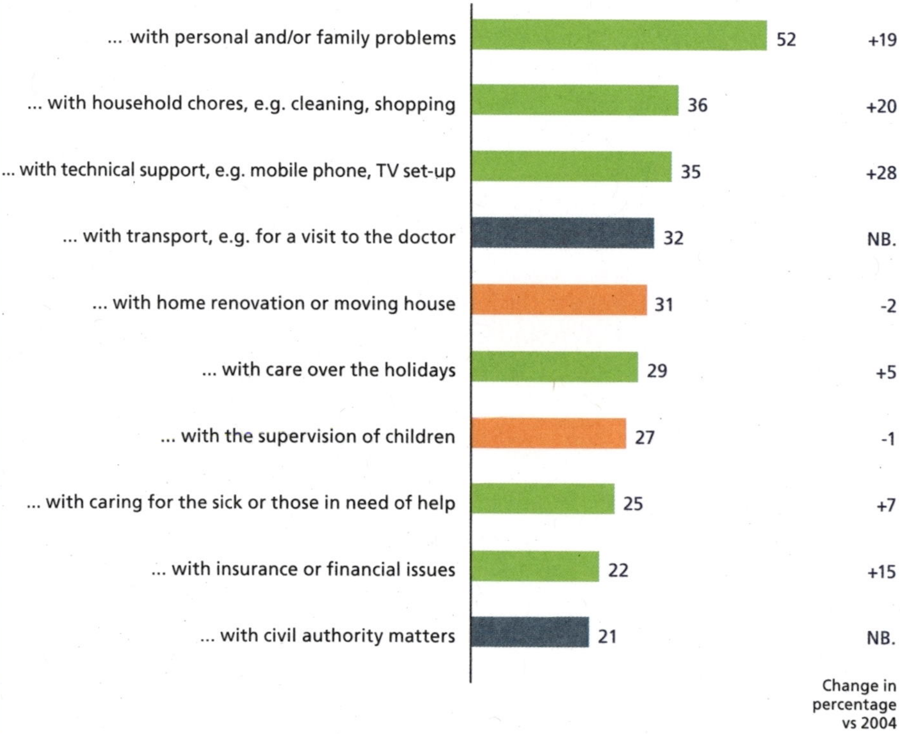

Willingness to help compared over time

MUTUAL SUPPORT HAS INCREASED

Results

Societal cohesion is often viewed critically: complaints are made about a lack of respect and increasing selfishness. However, the year-on-year comparison illustrates how strongly citizens have increased their support for each other in recent years. The willingness to help has increased, especially in family and friend relationships. More than one in two people – ten years ago, this was only one in three – support others with personal or family problems, be it through dialogue, emotional support or financial help. This type of support conveys a sense of belonging and understanding and also strengthens the self-esteem of those seeking help.

Many citizens are also much more active than in the past when it comes to household chores and technical problems. More than one in three help their parents, grandparents or friends with everyday tasks such as cleaning, shopping or setting up technical devices. Other areas, such as assistance with transport, childcare or renovations, are also taken on by many citizens, which is particularly positive, as they often require spontaneity during their own working hours.

Reasons

The increased willingness to help can be attributed to various factors. The crises of the last few years – above all, the coronavirus pandemic – have made it clear how important mutual support is and how small gestures can make a big difference. The demographics of society have also changed: more older people, more single households and more people with dual incomes have increased the need for many forms of assistance. Digitisation has also played a role: social networks and neighbourhood platforms make it easier to organise offers of help.

The younger generation in particular uses such channels to provide support or at least coordinate practical help. Older citizens, on the other hand, show an above-average willingness to help with childcare or emotional support.

In addition, a change in societal values can be seen, which places greater emphasis on the importance of solidarity and social responsibility as well as the wider effects of helpfulness, such as fulfilment and recognition.

Prognosis

The increasing willingness to help shows a pleasing development in societal interaction. In the future, it will be crucial to further promote this dynamic and extend it to broader societal circles. Initiatives such as neighbourhood help can play a central role here in reaching people outside their close social environment. It will be particularly important to sensitise broad sections of the population to societal responsibility. Education programmes can help to convey the value of community and mutual support. At the same time, (even) more older people should be encouraged to contribute more of their time, experience and skills.

Despite all the positive developments, there are still challenges: A lack of time and money as well as work commitments limit the possibilities for help. The geographical distance between family members also makes spontaneous support difficult.

Nevertheless, it is clear: societal cohesion is stronger than is often assumed. The willingness to help is growing – not only within the family, but also among friends and neighbours. This development forms the basis for more solidarity in society, in which mutual support remains a matter of course and new forms of togetherness can emerge.

RESPONSIBILITY

RESPONSIBILITY

How important is intergenerational cohesion?

Out of every 100 respondents, the following number agree with the statement:
'Generational cohesion between grandchildren, children, parents and grandparents is becoming increasingly important and helpful in many crises.'

Generational cohesion

A GUARANTEE OF STABILITY AND SECURITY

Results

Generational cohesion is a central element of societal life. In an age characterised by individualisation, isolation, childlessness and crises,family support is becoming increasingly important. The family remains the place where citizens can find emotional security and can count on reliable caregivers. A large majority of the population sees cohesion between the generations as essential. Within the age groups, nine out of ten older people emphasise the importance of the family, but three out of four young citizens also emphasise cohesion.

RESPONSIBILITY

Reasons

A sense of cohesion between the generations is perceived as a guarantee of stability, as it stands for steadiness, security and orientation precisely when external structures begin to falter. In addition to emotional support, many German citizens also appreciate the practical advantages of this. For example, parents support may their adult children in caring for grand-children or helping with household chores, while younger family members may support older relatives with health problems or mobility restrictions. This mutual care creates a sense of community and appreciation that endures throughout all phases of life.

Older people place a stronger focus on family relationships overall, as they are less involved in their careers and have more time (especially in retirement). They often play a key role by supporting both their children and their grandchildren, be it through financial support, care or practical help in everyday life. The younger generation, on the other hand, is more focused on their professional development and building an independent life. This life situation sometimes leads to a temporary greater distance from the family, but without diminishing the importance of family support.

Prognosis

Societal change will continue to alter traditional family structures. In addition to the traditional nuclear family, a variety of models have already been established, including patchwork, rainbow and single-parent families. Despite this diversity, all forms have one thing in common: they will continue to function as a community of care and responsibility in the future. The emotional bond between the generations remains a central value.

With an ageing society, the role of older citizens within the family will continue to increase. They will increasingly act as supporters for younger generations – be it through childcare or financial assistance. At the same time, the need for support for older people will increase, which will further increase the importance of intergenerational cohesion.

RESPONSIBILITY

Digital technologies will be used more frequently in the future to facilitate the exchange between generations. Video telephony and social media enable family members to stay in touch even over long distances. This offers older people in particular an opportunity to actively participate in family life, regardless of whether their own children or grandchildren live locally.

Ultimately, the family – despite all individualisation tendencies – remains an indispensable component of the social fabric. Generational cohesion will therefore continue to play a central role in the future, be it as a source of safety, stability or emotional security.

RESPONSIBILITY

RESPONSIBILITY

Who is involved locally?

Out of every 100 respondents, the following number agree with the statement:
'I am socially and politically involved in my community to make a positive difference.'

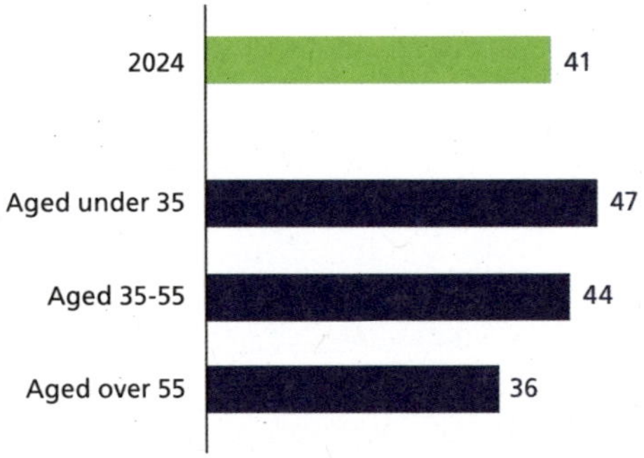

Political and social engagement

THE YOUNG GENERATION IN PARTICULAR WANTS TO MAKE A POSITIVE DIFFERENCE

Results

Social and political engagement is an important part of societal life in Germany. Around four in ten citizens are actively involved in their community to make a positive difference. Almost one in two people under the age of 35 are actively involved, while just over one in three people over the age of 55 are active.

RESPONSIBILITY

Reasons

Many citizens get involved to strengthen the community and promote social cohesion. The desire to help others, build social networks or support cultural projects also often plays a role. Young citizens in particular feel inspired by their circle of friends and want to be part of a community. They enjoy the feeling of belonging and strive for positive change in their environment. Accordingly, they are often involved in environmental protection, educational projects or social initiatives. Their motivation is based on a strong sense of justice and the desire to actively help shape the world. At the same time, they also use their commitment to develop new skills or to bridge transitional periods in a meaningful way. The flexibility of their phase of life allows them to devote time to voluntary work, while at the same time acquiring social skills and boosting their self-confidence.

In the middle age group, other motivations take centre stage. Many people feel a sense of societal responsibility at this stage of life – whether through their role as parents or through their desire to actively shape the future. Professional stability and stable family structures often provide them with the basis for involvement in their community. At the same time, many see their work as an opportunity to be a role model for their own children or to use their professional skills in a different context. Networks from the professional or private environment help individuals to find easy access.

Older citizens, on the other hand, often shift their priorities: Health restrictions, family obligations such as caring for grandchildren or parents in need of care and the transition to retirement influence their level of engagement. Many use this phase of life to focus more on personal interests such as travelling or cultural activities. However, many also recognise the potential of engagement for establishing social contacts or pursuing new goals. Older people are particularly willing to help in areas such as neighbourhood support or cultural projects.

RESPONSIBILITY

The fact that almost three out of five citizens are not currently active in their community is due to a lack of time, a lack of recognition or a lack of flexibility in ways to engage, in addition to the reasons already mentioned. Negative experiences, such as a lack of creative opportunities, little fun or a lack of integration into existing groups, also prevent many people from becoming active.

Prognosis

Social and political engagement remains an important pillar for societal cohesion. In the future, it will be crucial to further break down barriers and encourage morecitizens to volunteer – regardless of their age. It will be particularly important to make ways to engage more flexible and to create low-threshold opportunities so that working people or citizens with limited time can also get involved. Parallel initiatives will (have to) respond more strongly to the needs of different age groups – for example, through programmes for young citizens, for singles, for migrants or for senior citizens.

RESPONSIBILITY

Who is prepared to take initiative?

Out of every 100 respondents, the following number agree with the statement:
'Many citizens are quite prepared to take more initiative and don't want to simply leave all their problems to the state.'

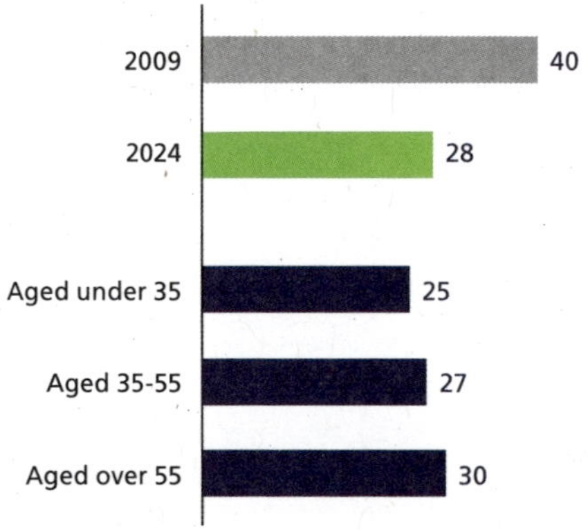

Nanny state instead of self-help

INDIVIDUAL INITIATIVE IS DECREASING

Results

A quarter of citizens are currently willing to show more initiative and not leave challenges to the state alone. The older generation shows a slightly higher willingness than the younger generation. A year-on-year comparison shows a significant decline: in 2009, two out of five citizens were still willing to take more personal initiative.

RESPONSIBILITY

Reasons

The reasons for being proactive are diverse and range from altruistic motives to personal interests. Many citizens get involved because they feel a sense of responsibility towards their community. They want to help others, show solidarity or make a positive contribution to their personal environment, the neighbourhood or society.

Initiative also offers the opportunity for personal development. It opens up opportunities to learn new skills, realise your own values or experience social recognition. Politically aware citizens in particular see this as an opportunity to actively tackle grievances and initiate change. Proactivity conveys a sense of autonomy and control, which contrasts with passivity when relying solely on government measures.

Despite these positive aspects, there are also obstacles: a lack of time and money as well as professional obligations limit the possibilities of many citizens. In addition, an increased focus on government solutions has developed in recent years. Many citizens expect the state to play an active role in overcoming crises and often feel that individual efforts are insufficient. Younger people in particular emphasise the duties of the state more strongly – especially regarding social and ecological issues – and show less trust in the effectiveness of private initiatives. The older generation, on the other hand, has a more pronounced creative drive due to their life experience and socialisation. Their higher frustration tolerance as well as their greater time and financial resources enable them to be more engaged than average.

The higher values from 2009 can be partly explained by a different societal mood, characterised by economic and political factors at the time: lower confidence in the government, the global financial and economic crisis and controversial issues, such as the deployment of the German armed forces in Afghanistan, dominated public debate. High unemployment and pension insecurity meant that many citizens felt they needed to take the initiative to improve their situation. Examples of this were the founding of start-ups and small businesses, the demand for further training and involvement in networks and associations to combat local problems, such as poverty and youth unemployment. This do-it-yourself mentality was an expression of a growing awareness of self-responsibility and independence from state structures.

In recent years, however, global crises have characterised the perception of many citizens, which often makes individual efforts seem insufficient. The complexity of these challenges makes them increasingly rely on government measures, which are seen as more promising.

Prognosis

The declining willingness to take initiative poses a challenge, but also offers opportunities for new approaches to promoting societal engagement. In the future,it will be important to combine individual and collective commitment more closely. Education programmes can help to convey the value of personal commitment and community involvement at an early stage. Young people in particular must be encouraged to contribute their ideas and take responsibility for their environment – be it through neighbourhood help, volunteering or setting up their own initiatives. At the same time, it is important to reduce bureaucratic hurdles and make government structures more flexible in order to better support private initiatives.

It will be crucial to regard personal initiative as an indispensable component of a resilient society. This will not only enable individual fulfilment, but also help to overcome challenges – whether locally or globally – together.

RESPONSIBILITY

Who wants a debt brake?

Out of every 100 respondents, the following number agree with the statement: **'At least half of every additional euro that the state earns in good economic times should be used to reduce debt, to ensure a future worth living for generationsto come.'**

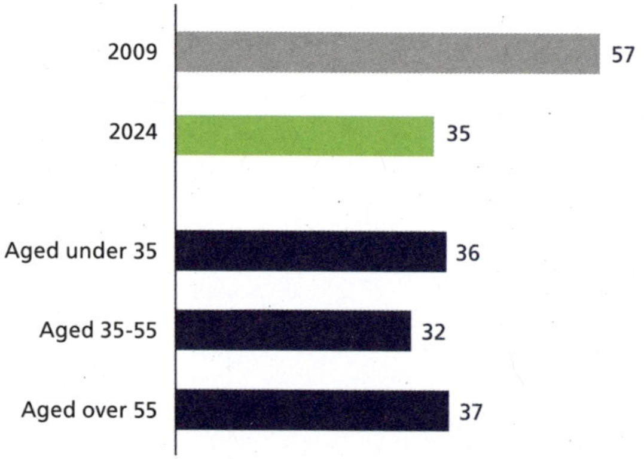

Debt brake scrapped

TWO THIRDS WANT INVESTMENTS INSTEAD OF SAVINGS

Results

The debt brake is a German fiscal policy instrument for limiting new government debt. There have been repeated public discussions about a reform of this system, not only in recent months. While some want to reform it as quickly as possible, others want to hold on to it at all costs. A recurring argument here is to secure future economic stability. In the population, there is a clear trend in this respect. Only just over a third of citizens want to use part of the state's income to reduce debt, with the middle generation having a slightly below-average rate. On the other hand, 25 years ago, more than half of citizens agreed with this statement

Reasons

In 2009, global crises such as the financial crisis and the euro debt crisis characterised public awareness and fuelled fears of the burden of high national debt. The example of Greece showed how much debt restricts the financial capacity of a state and leads to drastic austerity measures. In order to prevent such a development in Germany, the debt brake was enshrined in the Basic Law in 2009, and since then, the idea of debt reduction and budgetary discipline has become a central political issue. Politicians and the media have repeatedly emphasised its necessity and thus shaped public opinion, so that debt reduction has been seen by the majority as a prerequisite for a stable and liveable future.

Another argument is the moral obligation not to leave an excessive debt burden for future generations, especially when interest payments are higher, repayment periods are shorter and demographic challenges demand more financial contributions. With a sufficient financial buffer, the state would be considered well prepared for further crises.

The German government's debt increased by 62 billion euros, to 2.62 trillion euros, in 2023. The increase was thus similar to the previous year, but significantly less than in the years before. By contrast, the debt ratio fell for the second year in a row, to 64 percent. Many economists find this ratio more meaningful than absolute debt, as here, debt is set in relation to total economic power.

Accordingly, two thirds of the population currently take a critical view of limiting the debt budget. They see more urgent challenges that require immediate investment, such as internal and external security, the care sector, education and digitalisation, or the energy transition. Many citizens also fear that reducing debt will not solve problems, but rather delay them – with negative consequences for maintaining a socially just and economically stable society. As a result, moderate debt is accepted if it enables short and medium-term goals to be achieved.

In addition, for most citizens, the argument of concern for the quality of life of future generations is invalid, as for them, consistent saving does not automatically guarantee this. In contrast, debt is seen as a kind of investment that creates more wealth in the long term.

In politics, too, the focus on debt reduction has recently been de-emphasised (suspension of the debt brake), and issues such as crisis management, investment and green transformation have taken centre stage instead. Instead of austerity, the majority expect the state to play an active and formative role in favour of more investment and debt as a means of effectively countering current challenges and future crises.

Prognosis

The coming years will be characterised by a financial policy that is increasingly moving away from rigid savings targets. Citizens will expect the state to play an active role in tackling key challenges such as security, digitalisation and pension increases. Fiscal policy dogmas such as the debt brake will therefore continue to lose importance and be seen as counter-productive, while future-oriented investments will be seen as the key to keeping Germany competitive and liveable in the long term. At the same time, the focus on efficiency and transparency in government spending will become more important. Projects with clear objectives and measurable benefits will enjoy correspondingly broad acceptance.

The financial policy of the future will also be characterised by flexibility and pragmatism. Rigid rules will give way to dynamic strategies, as these can react much better to current developments.

> Citizens will not demand a return to the past, but a courageous shaping of the future. This is a paradigm shift that could have a lasting impact on Germany.

RESPONSIBILITY

RESPONSIBILITY

What is expected of companies?

Out of every 100 respondents, the following number agree with the statement:
'Companies should also take on social and societal responsibility.'

Profit with a conscience

COMPANIES HAVE AN OBLIGATION

Results

In the societal debates of recent years, questions of societal responsibility have increasingly taken centre stage. These concern specific topics or areas on the one hand, as well as different actors, such as politicians, initiatives, citizens and business representatives on the other. A central focus here is on weighing up the limits, opportunities and obligations of societal responsibility. For 85 percent of the population, it is part of the task of companies to assume social and societal responsibility. Older citizens demand this more often than younger citizens.

RESPONSIBILITY

Reasons

The general public increasingly views companies not just as economic players, but as an integral part of society, with responsibility for its development. In recent decades, society's perception of companies has changed fundamentally. While economic responsibility used to be at the forefront – for example, by maximising profits, producing goods or securing jobs – today, social and ecological aspects are also moving into focus. Globalisation has turned companies into global players that control supply chains worldwide and influence international standards. Cases of poor working conditions in textile factories in south-east Asia or in raw material extraction in Africa illustrate how strongly companies can shape social and ecological aspects in other countries and are increasingly being held responsible for this. They are no longer just expected to limit damage, but also to take active measures to minimise negative effects.

In addition, the general public expect companies to make a positive contribution to society, as trust in state institutions has declined. Many citizens no longer see the state as being able to overcome all societal challenges on its own. Companies are therefore seen as important partners that can make a big difference thanks to their resources and influence. They should also act as role models. In particular, large corporations with a global reach have the opportunity to set sustainable standards that smaller companies can use as a benchmark.

Another reason for these high values is the demand for more transparency and accountability in the actions of companies. Consumers want to be able to understand how products are manufactured, what conditions prevail along the supply chain and which environmental standards are met. This also offers opportunities for companies: Many are increasingly recognising that acting responsibly not only serves the common good, but also strengthens their own competitiveness.

RESPONSIBILITY

Prognosis

Corporate social responsibility will play an even more central role in the coming years. This will create both opportunities and obligations. One key aspect of future developments is the increasing importance of sustainability as a strategic leitmotif. Companies will no longer only be measured by economic success, but also by how they integrate ecological and social values into their business models. The introduction of binding standards, such as the European Union's Corporate Sustainability Reporting Directive, will make sustainability strategies more transparent and comprehensive.

Advances in areas such as artificial intelligence, blockchain and data analysis will make the monitoring of supply chains more precise, the traceability of raw materials better and the implementation of sustainability initiatives more efficient. At the same time, these developments will bring new moral challenges, for example in the handling of data or the automation of work processes. Companies will therefore not only have to utilise such technologies to increase efficiency, but also for the benefit of society.

The role of the consumer will continue to grow in importance. More and more people will be making purchasing decisions based on a company's ethical standards. Brands that take on social responsibility will be favoured in the long term. Initiatives such as Fairtrade or circular economy programmes already show how companies can not only strengthen consumer confidence through sustainable approaches, but also open up new markets. This development will be supported by media transparency – social media in particular will quickly publicise misconduct and force companies to react quickly to criticism and take action.

RESPONSIBILITY

Another development relates to cooperation. As many challenges cross borders, it will be essential for companies to enter into partnerships with governments, NGOs and other companies. These collaborations will help to develop common standards and tackle global problems more effectively.

RESPONSIBILITY

Which future skills are important?

Out of every 100 respondents under the age of 35, the following number agree with the statement:
'I consider the following qualities to be particularly important so that future generations can shape their lives in a meaningful and successful way.'

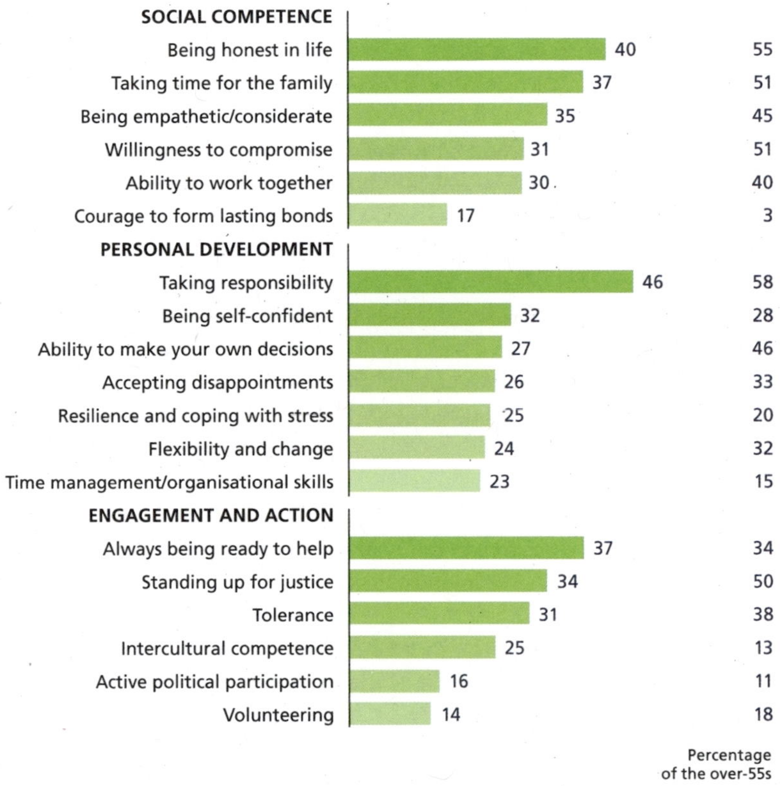

Qualities for the future

YOUNG AND OLD SET DIFFERENT PRIORITIES

Results

The priorities of younger and older German citizens with regard to important characteristics and behaviours for future generations can be divided into three categories: social skills, personal development and engagement and action. The ranking order is basically similar for both age groups: Honesty and taking responsibility are at the top of the list for both. Consideration, helpfulness, justice and the importance of family also play a similarly important role for both generations.

Nevertheless, there are differences in the weighting of individual competences. Younger citizens under the age of 35 feel that the courage to make lasting commitments is more important. Older citizens over 55, on the other hand, prioritise other values such as honesty, consideration, time for the family, willingness to compromise or the ability to work together.

Differences also arise in the area of personal development. Younger citizens rate self-confidence, resilience and stress management as well as time management and organisational skills higher, which shows an orientation towards self-optimisation. Older citizens, on the other hand, place greater value on responsibility, independence, flexibility and the acceptance of setbacks.

In the area of engagement and action, younger citizens emphasise helpfulness, intercultural competence and active political participation. Older citizens, on the other hand, prioritise values such as volunteering, justice and tolerance, which suggests a stronger orientation towards basic moral values

RESPONSIBILITY

Reasons

The differences in the assessment of social competences between the generations can be explained by different phases of life and priorities. Younger citizens emphasise the courage to form lasting bonds, as they are in a phase of network building – both professionally and privately. They see empathy as a key skill in a globalised and increasingly diversified world, as it can resolve conflicts and build bridges between different groups. For them, relationships are the basis for harmonious coexistence, as they offer emotional security and support in a complex world.

Older citizens, on the other hand, attach much greater importance to a willingness to compromise and to family ties. For them, family relationships are not only for emotional support, but also places where values are conveyed. A willingness to compromise is considered particularly relevant in a polarised society. Honesty and the ability to work together is also highly valued by older people, whether in a private, professional or societal context.

In the area of personal development, younger citizens value skills such as stress management and time management more highly, as these are essential in modern working environments. Resilience enables them to cope better with uncertainties and setbacks, while time management helps them to coordinate multiple commitments efficiently. Older citizens, on the other hand, prioritise characteristics such as responsibility, the ability to make their own decisions and the acceptance of disappointments. These competences reflect their life experience and their role as mentors, grandparents or experienced professionals. They do not perceive setbacks as failures, but as part of a continuous learning process.

In the area of engagement and action, younger citizens show a greater interest in intercultural competence and active political participation. They recognise the importance of intercultural competence for dealing with global mobility and migration. They see involvement in political parties or NGOs as an opportunity to take on societal responsibility and develop personal skills at the same time. Older citizens, on the other hand, emphasise moral values such as justice and tolerance. These values are seen as the basis for social interaction and societal cohesion.

Prognosis

Future skills will become increasingly important in a changing society. The requirements for social skills, personal development, engagement and action will affect all generations. In a globalised and digitalised world, skills such as empathy, resilience and intercultural competence will become increasingly important. At the same time, traditional values such as honesty, justice and a willingness to compromise will remain of central importance, as they form the foundation for societal cohesion.

The ability to empathise will play a decisive role in the face of growing diversity, as it not only makes it easier to deal with cultural differences, but also resolves conflicts and promotes dialogue between perspectives. The family will remain a central anchor point that offers emotional stability and social support. The willingness to compromise and the ability to work in a team will also become more important, as projects and decision-making processes will increasingly require different people to work together.

The ability to adapt will be a key competence for the future. This ability will make it possible to overcome crises and emerge stronger from them. The combination of traditional and modern competences will be able to create a society that is not only stable, but also innovative and able to successfully meet the challenges of the future.

Resilience will not only be needed in individual lives, but also at a societal level: only a resilient society will be equipped to deal with challenges and able to develop solutions quickly.

RESPONSIBILITY

The promotion of all these competences requires targeted measures in educational systems and by societal institutions. Schools and universities must teach social skills as well as technical knowledge or problem-solving skills. Interdisciplinary learning will help to develop innovative approaches to complex challenges. At the same time, further training opportunities must be expanded to give all age groups access to new skills. The development of society as a whole will also depend on how well it succeeds in combining different competences. Social intelligence will form the basis for a harmonious coexistence; personal development will create adaptability; engagement willdrive change. These three areas will complement each other and, together, represent a great opportunity for the future of Germany.

RESPONSIBILITY

COOPERATION

Cooperation

In an increasingly individualised society, the question of the relevance and necessity of cooperation arises. The plurality of lifestyles and values characterises the modern world, in which optimisation, self-responsibility and self-realisation are considered desirable goals. Competition and rivalry dominate many areas of life. One might think that cooperation is becoming less important, as the anonymity of modern societal structures often pushes the collective into the background. Nevertheless, there are many forms of cooperation that operate in less visible ways and form the foundation of social communities. In times of increasing isolation, it is particularly relevant to emphasise the potential of cooperation and highlight its benefits for both the individual and society.

Etymology

The term 'cooperation' comes from the Latin 'cooperatio'. It is made up of 'co' (together) and 'operatio' (work or collaboration) and literally means 'working together'. In ancient times, the term was closely associated with the state and the military. Cooperation was seen as a prerequisite for a functioning community. In the Middle Ages, the term was mainly used in religious contexts. Then, cooperation meant the interaction between God and the people. This concept included good deeds and the cooperation of angels and saints to fulfil divine plans. With the Enlightenment and the associated secularisation, the focus then shifted to secular cooperation, and economic, social and political areas gained in importance. The emerging sciences, especially philosophy and political science, began to deal intensively with the concept of cooperation, because they found in it the ideals of reason, common good and universal human rights. In the 19th century, the term was strongly influenced by industrialisation. The word 'cooperations' (plural) was used to describe collaborations between companies to achieve common goals such as innovation, the division of labour or profit maximisation. In addition, it was linked to themes such as solidarity and societal cohesion. It served as a model for the formation of cooperatives and was associated with collective action to overcome social inequalities and political challenges. In a global context, the first approaches to international cooperation were then developed, for example at the Congress of Vienna in 1815 or through the founding of international organisations such as the Red Cross in 1863. These tendencies intensified in the 20th century, especially in economic and political as well as ecological areas. Examples of global cooperation include the founding of the UN, the World Trade Organisation, the EU and international environmental and climate protection projects. Currently, the term 'cooperation' stands for a universal value that applies to all areas of life. Characteristics include mutual respect, voluntariness, equality and the pursuit of solutions to common challenges.

Scientific classification

Within science, there are various theories and approaches that deal with the complexity of the phenomenon of cooperation. They deal with the question of how individuals, groups or organisations work together to achieve common goalsand which prerequisites, mechanisms and consequences of cooperative behaviour can be observed. Depending on the discipline, different focal points are set, whereby interdisciplinary research work is also valued and utilised here. Within economics, cooperation is often analysed using game theory and contract theory. The former examines strategic decision-making behaviour in which the success of an individual or company depends on the decisions of others (cooperation or self-interest). Contract theory analyses how external incentive mechanisms (contracts) can be used to resolve conflicts or work together efficiently.

COOPERATION

Psychology is focused on individual and social factors, whereby here too there are different approaches. According to social exchange theory, cooperation is based on the principle of costs and benefits. People cooperate when the benefits (e.g. recognition, support) outweigh the costs (e.g. effort). In Social Identity Theory, the focus is on group cooperation, according to which people are more likely to cooperate with members of their own group (in-group) than with outsiders (out-group), as this strengthens their social identity. However, intrinsic and extrinsic motivation or cultural values and traditions can also characterise the psychological aspects of cooperation.

In sociology, cooperation is regarded as a central object of study that is considered an essential basis for the functioning of a dynamic society. It is necessary to ensure security and stability and, at the same time, acts as an instrument for the distribution of power. Cooperation arises in particular when groups pursue common interests. However, it can fail if there are significant power or resource inequalities or if there is a lack of trust and a lack of willingness to cooperate.

Political science theories often focus on the global level, in particular on successful cooperation between states through the establishment of common institutions, norms and rules. At the same time, however, these approaches also highlight the challenges and conflicts that arise when states prioritise their own individual interests.

In all approaches, cooperation is perceived as a goal-oriented process and forms an important basis for the development of individuals, organisations and societies.

COOPERATION

Importance of cooperation for the individual and forsociety

Cooperation plays a central role in many areas. In business, it enables companies to utilise resources efficiently and drive innovation. In social contexts, it promotes cohesion within communities and improves the well-being of their members. In education, cooperation between teachers, pupils and parents is crucial for learning success, as pupils develop social skills and teamwork through cooperative learning methods. Cooperation is also essential in science, as it is often only interdisciplinary research projects that lead to ground-breaking discoveries. The need for global cooperation is particularly evident in the area of environmental protection. The effects of climate change require a joint effort by all countries. International agreements such as the Paris Climate Agreement are examples of how states can work together to tackle global challenges.

The prerequisites for cooperation are complex and linked to their respective societal, historical and cultural framework conditions. Irrespective of this, trust and empathy form the basis for believing in the fairness and reliability of others and in honouring joint agreements. The more often one has had positive experiences in this regard, the more willing one will be to enter into new cooperations. Further influences for a cooperative society can be found in social norms and values – for example, solidarity, respect, public spirit – in external influences – including reward and sanction structures – and in crises and challenges that require cooperation. However, organisational and structural contexts are also responsible for how strongly a cooperative climate is anchored in certain areas of society. This includes, for example, clear communication, the distribution of responsibilities, the availability of complementary skills, familiar players and the promotion of teamwork and solidarity.

COOPERATION

Although cooperation is always related to group processes, it also has relevance for the individual, especially with regard to their personal, social and professional development. As social beings, humans have a basic need for a sense of belonging. Initially as a member of the family, later at school, with friends, in clubs, at work or in the neighbourhood. In order to feel valued and accepted there, it is necessary to build friendships, networks and social connections. Cooperation is a central element here in order to promote understanding, support and stability. It indicates the willingness and ability to support each other, to realise common goals and to overcome crises and challenges. As a result, cooperation strengthens trust in the reliability of others, increases empathy and understanding and promotes the stability of relationships. This is also where the positive characteristics with regard to personal development become apparent. Through cooperation, the individual learns to broaden their own perspective to include that of others, thus becoming more team-oriented and reducing selfish individual decisions. Successful cooperation experiences then increase their own satisfaction, self-esteem, communication skills and the certainty that they will be able to draw on their own cooperation skills in the future. In practice, these become apparent in everyday working life, among other things. Knowing that you can overcome problems together, share responsibility and rely on each other creates a climate of security, reduces stress and strain and promotes resilience.

The importance of cooperation within group processes can be well explained using the example of politics and public perception. Just as every individual shapes and forms societal coexistence through their willingness to cooperate, politics also has a decisive influence on the importance of binding cooperation in society. In principle, cooperation is a central component of political work and important for how it is perceived by the public. In positive cases, it influences the efficiency, stability and legitimacy of political decisions and presents the actors as responsible persons for whom constructive cooperation to solve societal challenges is more important than the achievement of party or individual interests. Currently, for example, issues such as Germany as a business location and migration are seen as challenges that require cross-party cooperation and a longer-term perspective. In this context, respectful interaction, transparent communication, equal exchange and the courage to make changes are expected. Different points of view should be weighed up with an open mind, compromises sought, personal perspectives broadened and decision-making processes made comprehensible. If these expectations are not met, the political work or the people involved are perceived as self-serving, inflexible, inefficient, short-term thinkers and power-focused.

Overall, it should be noted that: Cooperation arises from a combination of social, psychological and structural factors and is an essential factor for the cohesion of a society. It enables the exchange of different perspectives, the pursuit of common goals and the solving of collective challenges.

Cooperative communities are more resilient than competitive ones, as the ability to work together enables them to respond flexibly and efficiently to challenges.

COOPERATION

Best practice examples

1. The construction of the International Space Station (ISS)

Participants: NASA (USA), ESA (Europe), Roskosmos (Russia), JAXA (Japan), CSA (Canada) and many more.

Objective: Joint research in space, the promotion of technology and international cooperation.

Success: Since 1998, the ISS has symbolised international cooperation by bringing together scientists and astronauts from different countries.

2. The COVAX Initiative

Participants: WHO, GAVI, CEPI and governments worldwide.

Objective: Ensuring equitable access to COVID-19 vaccines for all countries, especially poorer countries.

Success: By 2023, around two billion vaccine doses had been delivered to countries in need to combat the pandemic worldwide.

3. The Erasmus+ exchange programme

Participants: The European Union and educational institutions in member states.

Objective: Promoting mobility and exchange between students, lecturers and interns.

Success: Since its foundation in 1987, over 15 million students have taken part in this programme and experienced cultural exchange. International mobility and networking have been promoted and European cohesion strengthened.

4. The Ocean Cleanup

Participants: NGOs, scientists, governments, companies.

Objective: Reducing plastic pollution in the world's oceans and rivers.

Success: In 2023 alone, innovative technologies such as the 'Interceptor' system removed over 8,000 tonnes of plastic from rivers and oceans. This programme also leads to technological innovations and scientific studies, sensitises people to the problem and raises awareness for greater sustainability.

5. 'Tafeln' in Germany

Participants: Volunteers, supermarkets, companies and people in need.

Objective: Distributing surplus food to people in need.

Success: The food banks in Germany support over two million people every year and, at the same time, prevent food waste. They have a strong volunteer base.

COOPERATION

What does it take to master crises?

Out of every 100 respondents, the following number agree with the statement:
'Joint efforts and cooperation are crucial to successfully overcome crises.'

Mastering crises

A LARGE MAJORITY CALLS FOR MORE COMMUNITY

Results

Engagement and cooperation are seen by almost nine out of ten German citizens as an essential response to crises and challenges. There is great unity within the population, and there are few differences in terms of income, level of education or marital status. The only differences are in age: while around three quarters of under-35s agree with this statement, 91 percent of over-55s agree.

COOPERATION

Reasons

For the majority of citizens, one thing is clear: Only joint efforts enable effective crisis management. It does not matter whether this cooperation takes place between individuals, communities, parties, institutions or nations – the decisive factor is a joint approach and a clear objective. Cooperation brings together different perspectives, skills and resources, utilises finances and infrastructure efficiently and promotes innovative approaches. This becomes all the more relevant the more complex the challenges are, such as economic crises, pandemics or climate change.

Cooperative behaviour has far-reaching effects beyond the actual goal: it strengthens mutual trust and a sense of community, conveys solidarity and distributes responsibility among different actors. This applies not only to global, national or local challenges, but also to everyday crisis situations. In addition, joint action increases resilience to future crises. Voluntary work and volunteers in civil protection are essential examples of how community structures not only offer short-term solutions, but also promote solidarity in the long term.

Another reason for cooperation lies in the efficiency of networks: collaboration creates synergies that enable innovative solutions – whether at a local level or in international cooperation between countries and organisations.

The above-average agreement rate of older citizens can be attributed to their life and crisis experiences. Economic recessions, post-war experiences, political upheavals and societal challenges have shown them that individual efforts are often not enough and that community involvement is more promising. In addition, they were socialised at a time when collective values such as solidarity and community played a central role.

COOPERATION

Younger citizens, on the other hand, have grown up in a more individualised society that emphasises personal achievement and personal responsibility. This has led to the development of an awareness that favours individual efforts and quick, independent solutions. In the political sphere in particular, cooperation is sometimes perceived as a watering down, as compromises often serve to take into account the individual interests of all parties involved. Despite these reservations, a majority of the younger generation also recognise the need for community involvement to overcome crises.

Prognosis

The importance of engagement and cooperation will continue to increase in the future. In view of increasingly complex national (e.g. shortage of skilled labour, demographic change, polarisation, loss of trust) and global challenges (e.g. climate change, geopolitical tensions), joint action remains indispensable. It will be crucial to develop new forms of cooperation – at both the local and international level.

It is particularly important to raise young citizens' awareness of cooperative action and to familiarise them with the benefits of joint efforts. At the same time, existing structures must be strengthened: volunteers should be better supported and recognised in order to maintain their motivation in the long term.

All in all, this reveals that only a balanced interplay of individual initiative and collective responsibility can keep a society resilient. The ability to co-operate not only determines success in overcoming current crises, but also forms the basis for a sustainable future.

COOPERATION

COOPERATION

How high is the willingness to compromise?

Out of every 100 respondents, the following number agree with the statement:
'I am prepared to compromise in order to resolve conflicts.'

Building bridges instead of walls

WILLINGNESS TO COMPROMISE IS HIGH

Results

Compromises are more than just a middle path between different views, needs and demands. They are a necessity in an increasingly diverse and complex society and a central component of communication, social interaction and conflict resolution. Almost nine out of ten citizens are prepared to compromise in order to resolve conflicts. Older people have the highest agreement rate, while slightly fewer younger people agree – but still four out of five.

COOPERATION

Reasons

The historical development of compromises can be described as a process of increasing complexity and institutionalised cooperation. While early societies focused on simple and pragmatic solutions, these have evolved over time into complex negotiation systems that respond to the diversity of interests and challenges. And although societal contexts and actors have changed, compromises are an indispensable tool for finding viable solutions in a pluralistic and often conflict-laden world.

Not only states, organisations or societies benefit from compromises – they also play a decisive role for individuals. The willingness to make concessions is closely linked to the expected consequences. An open attitude, empathy and the ability to listen actively significantly promote this willingness. In addition, aspects such as justice, maintaining relationships and pragmatism are important factors. The positive effects of compromise include strengthened communication skills, increased reflective competence, resilience and the prevention of serious conflicts. It also promotes inspiration and innovation and helps to build stable relationships based on understanding and trust.

The importance of compromises becomes particularly clear in societies that are strongly characterised by globalisation – such as Germany. More and more citizens with different backgrounds, values and perspectives live here. Compromises can help to unite different points of view and find solutions that are acceptable to all. Justice and fairness play a major role here. All parties to a compromise must make concessions that involve giving in. But as long as all parties keep something that is important to them, satisfaction increases (win-win situation).

COOPERATION

Even for many of the challenges in working life or in personal relationships, there is rarely a simple solution that is equally satisfactory for everyone involved. However, compromises make it possible to find pragmatic answers and ways forward. Particularly in a professional environment, they also create a basis for productive collaboration: they defuse conflicts, focus on common goals and everyone benefits from the different ideas and perspectives.

The different views of the generations can be explained by different social influences and expectations as well as technological developments. The younger generation has grown up in a time that is more strongly characterised by individualism, self-confidence, authenticity and personal development. As a result, many younger people tend to prioritise their own needs and desires and are more sceptical about making compromises – especially if these conflict with their personal values or goals. This basic attitude is reinforced by their affinity for digital communication. Polarising views and reactions often prevail on such platforms, with little room for compromise. Instead, one's own opinion is clearly represented and propagated as 'right'. Another reason can be found in the high expectations regarding justice and equal opportunities. If young citizens are of the opinion that a compromise is not fair, their willingness to compromise decreases.

In contrast, a pragmatic attitude often prevails among the older generation. Through their lives and professional experiences, they have already made many compromises and thus recognised their effective potential for conflict resolution. In addition, they attach great importance to consensus and long-term harmony and are less convinced of absolute positions.

When it comes to conflicts in particular, the willingness to compromise is a key competence for successful cooperation. It doesn't show weakness, but strength, because it requires the ability to transcend one's own ego, to change perspective and to think long-term.

COOPERATION

Prognosis

In a globalised society characterised by different interests and perspectives, the ability to make viable compromises will become increasingly important. This applies both on a collective and individual level.

At a societal level, the willingness to compromise will play a key role in overcoming global challenges. Issues such as climate change, migration and resource security require multilateral negotiations and, at the same time, the willingness of all participants to make concessions. The willingness to compromise will also play an increasingly important role in the economy. Companies are increasingly faced with the challenge of combining economic goals with societal expectations. More dialogue formats between companies, local communities and NGOs will help to develop joint projects that offer both economic and social benefits while strengthening trust in entrepreneurial action.

At an individual level, the willingness to compromise in personal relationships will continue to play a central role. Partnerships and friendships regularly require the ability to balance different needs and make joint decisions. This applies both to everyday topics, such as household management or leisure activities, and to fundamental questions, such as life goals or values. The willingness to engage with each other and find solutions together strengthens trust and the bond between those involved. Even within families, the willingness to compromise remains indispensable. Different generations often have different values and ideas. However, the ability to compromise enables family members to find a common path and resolve tensions in a way that remains acceptable to all.

The willingness to engage in personal development will also increase. The ability to rethink one's own points of view and engage with other perspectives not only promotes understanding of others, but also contributes to one's own growth. Those who harmonise their own needs with those of others develop emotional intelligence and strengthen their own resilience.

COOPERATION

Who values collaboration?

Out of every 100 respondents, the following number agree with the statement:
'I like working together with others, for example to achieve common goals.'

The power of the collective

COOPERATION AS A DRIVING FORCE FOR PROGRESS

Results

A clear majority of German citizens place value on collaboration with others in order to successfully implement joint projects or plans. There are hardly any differences between the generations: both younger and older citizens value cooperation as a central component of their actions and recognise the advantages of joint efforts.

COOPERATION

Reasons

One of the main reasons for the high approval rate is the sense of community created by working together. Joint considerations, planning and efforts create trust and strengthen interpersonal relationships. This not only leads to better results in projects, but also increases the personal well-being of those involved. Particularly in social initiatives, such as neighbourhood help or volunteer projects, many citizens experience how their contributions are valued, interesting contacts are made and mutual support motivates new collaborations.

Another important aspect is the division of labour, which makes collaboration particularly attractive. Group work makes it possible to divide up tasks in a targeted manner and utilise individual strengths effectively. The distribution of responsibilities and competences across several shoulders increases efficiency, improves the quality of results and reduces the burden on the individual.

Another reason for the popularity of collaborations is the exchange of knowledge and ideas. Working together creates space for mutual learning and insight into different perspectives. Different competences and approaches within a group promote the development of innovative solutions and contribute significantly to the success of projects. The value of such collaborations is particularly evident in the world of work: Teams from different specialist areas or with different backgrounds can combine their strengths to develop more efficient processes and creative approaches to solving complex tasks.

In addition, trust in collective solutions plays a central role. Many citizens recognise the need for joint efforts, especially in tackling local challenges, such as city beautification, maintaining community centres, shared projects, sponsorships or intergenerational initiatives. The conviction that effective solutions can be found through collaboration not only promotes the willingness to cooperate and strengthens societal interaction, but also conveys the feeling of achieving something positive together.

COOPERATION

Prognosis

The importance of collaboration will continue to grow in the future and establish itself as a central component for the successful implementation of projects and the management of societal challenges.

Educational institutions such as schools and universities will increasingly rely on cooperative learning methods to teach pupils and students the benefits of joint efforts at an early stage. Group projects, interdisciplinary approaches and collaborative platforms will not only promote the exchange of knowledge, but also the development of social skills, such as empathy, communication skills and conflict resolution. These skills are not only of great importance for later professional success, but also for a better understanding of different perspectives in the personal environment.

Cooperation will increasingly be perceived as a key competence for developing sustainable solutions in an ever more complex world.

Overcoming numerous – local and regional, but also national and global – challenges will hardly be possible in future without cooperation. Cooperation is therefore not only to be understood as a means of achieving goals, but also as a fundamental principle for a functioning society. The ability to work together on solutions and to contribute individual strengths will increasingly be an indispensable competence. Political leaders, educational institutions, companies and social organisations have the opportunity to actively promote this development and create spaces for cooperation. A society that focuses on cooperation will be better equipped for the challenges of the future – be it in dealing with global crises or maintaining a liveable local community.

COOPERATION

COOPERATION

Do citizens want fewer regulations?

Out of every 100 respondents, the following number agree with the statement:
'There are too many laws, bans, regulations and government rules: many things would run better without the state.'

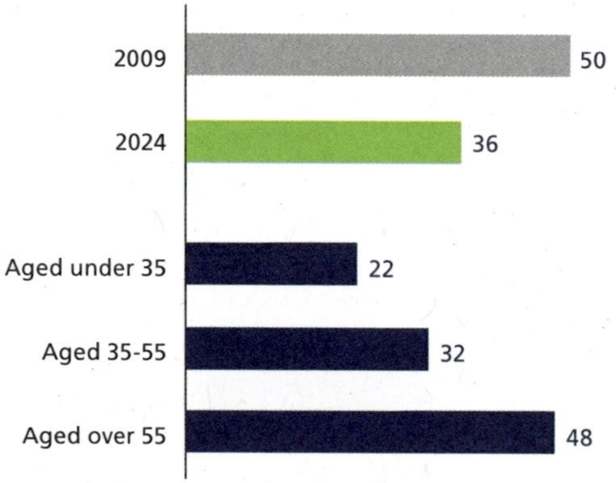

Regulation or autonomy

GENERATIONS DIVIDED

Results

The concept of the state is based on a complex relationship between state authority, individual freedoms of citizens and communal responsibility. The state is not a rigid entity, but is subject to constant change in societal contexts, whereby it strives for a balance between regulations and independence.International gilt Deutschland als ein Land mit zahlreichen Internationally, Germany is regarded as a country with numerous laws and extensive bureaucracy. Whereas in 2009, every other citizen still thought there were too many government regulations , in 2024, only one in three held that view. There are clear differences between the age groups: A good fifth of young people are in favour of less government regulation, and almost half of those aged 55 and over.

Reasons

The German state fulfils numerous tasks and duties, but also has extensive powers. As a democratic institution, it guarantees the rule of law and security, is responsible for social justice (e.g. taxes, social benefits, education, health), provides infrastructure and public goods and monitors rules and laws. The majority of citizens trust these state services, but regularly criticise excessive bureaucracy and over-regulation that restricts individual freedoms.

The high level of scepticism in 2009 can be explained by a combination of crises, political scepticism and structural weaknesses in the state apparatus. The financial crisis and the associated mistrust of the state's power to shape things intensified this criticism. Many citizens felt that rescue programmes for banks were anti-social and saw the government debt as a waste of public funds. At the same time, the bureaucracy was perceived as inefficient and detached from the people, which further weakened trust in the state. Political scandals and a media debate that favoured neoliberal ownership also contributed to this mood.

By 2024, however, the state gained greater trust again. Several crises have been overcome in recent years – including the European sovereign debt crisis, the refugee crisis, the COVID-19 pandemic and the war in Ukraine. Measures such as lockdowns, vaccination campaigns and financial relief packages were perceived by many citizens as effective crisis management. In addition, the perception of previous regulations has normalised, for example with regard to waste separation, data protection or child daycare. More transparent political communication and participatory measures have therefore strengthened trust in the state.

COOPERATION

The differences between the age groups reflect different perspectives and experiences. Younger citizens have been socialised at a time when issues such as climate change, social justice and digitalisation dominate. State interventions in these areas, such as subsidies for renewable energies or CO2 pricing, are predominantly perceived positively by them. Older citizens, on the other hand, place more value on personal autonomy and often see state regulations as a restriction of their freedoms.

Prognosis

The balance between state regulation and individual freedom will remain a key issue in the coming years. While the demands of citizens are constantly changing, the core tasks of the state, such as ensuring security, justice and stability, will remain unchanged.

Technological innovations will play a key role: Digitalisation and the use of artificial intelligence could make administrative processes more efficient and simplify administrative procedures. At the same time, the state must create clear rules for data protection and the transparency of state decisions in order to preserve the trust of citizens.

Future global challenges will increase the state's room for manoeuvre. Citizens expect proactive crisis management that combines short-term measures with long-term strategies. It will be crucial to take into account the diverging expectations of the generations: while younger citizens are usually open to state intervention, older generations value personal autonomy. Transparent communication and greater citizen participation will be needed to bridge these differences.

All in all, the state will be required to harmonise both individual needs and community goals in order to ensure a resilient and sustainable society.

In future, a state model should be established that is both lean and highly regulative: efficient through innovation and, at the same time, reliable in key areas.

Do we need more referendums?

Out of every 100 respondents, the following number agree with the statement: **'There should be more referendums and other forms of direct participation for citizens.'**

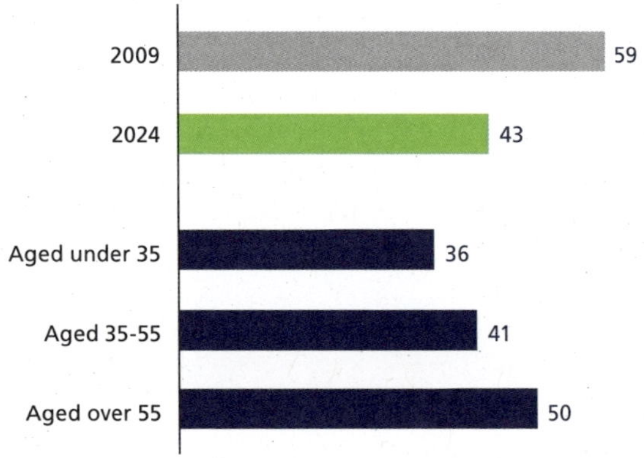

Desire for referendums is decreasing

SIMPLE SOLUTIONS ARE NO LONGER SUFFICIENT

Results

Referendums can be a central element of direct democracy. They enable citizens to actively participate in political decision-making processes. Fifteen years ago,six out of ten citizens were still in favour of extending these participatory opportunities accordingly. In 2024, this proportion fell by a quarter, to 43 percent. Considerable differences can be observed between age groups: Whereas every other member of the older generation calls for more referendums, only just over one in three younger people do so.

Reasons

The high level of agreement with this statement in 2009 can be attributed to the growing scepticism towards the political elite, which was already evident in other studies for this period. Representative democracy was often perceived as being less citizen-centred. The desire for more say in political decisions resulted from the feeling that the population had too little influence on central political decisions. Referendums were therefore considered suitable instruments to compensate for this democratic deficit. In addition, many citizens criticised the increasing shift of political decisions to the European level, for example in the area of financial policy, which reinforced the need for greater co-determination at a national level. Against this backdrop, elements of direct democracy gained widespread approval and have been increasingly introduced at municipal and state level since the 1990s.

Whereas in 2009, the demand for referendums was primarily interpreted as an expression of a democratic will to shape the future, this perception changed fundamentally by 2024. Today, the focus is particularly on the potential disadvantages. A key factor in the increasing scepticism towards referendums is the complexity of many political issues. Questions on migration, climate policy, digitalisation or international trade agreements require specialised expertise and differentiated analyses. Many citizens do not feel sufficiently empowered to make informed judgements on such decisions. This leads to uncertainty and a growing reluctance regarding direct democracy.

Brexit is a prominent negative example. The referendum in the United Kingdom illustrated how emotionally charged campaigns and simplistic messages can shape votes. Many Brits later said they had not fully grasped the implications of their decision. The resulting societal division and economic instability illustrate the risks of referendums without sufficient information.

Social media further exacerbates this problem. Platforms such as Facebook or X encourage the spread of disinformation and polarisation. Algorithms often reinforce extreme positions, making balanced discussions more difficult. This dynamic undermines trust in the ability of individuals to make their own judgements on complex political issues.

Another argument against referendums lies in the danger of a short-term interest-based orientation. Decisions are often based on momentary emotions or local needs and take insufficient account of long-term consequences or the common good. Examples from Germany show how local referendums have blocked important infrastructure projects, even though these might have brought long-term benefits.

Despite the challenges mentioned, referendums also offer numerous opportunities for democracy. They enable citizens to participate directly in political decisions and thus strengthen trust in political processes. Political measures gain greater legitimacy through direct co-determination and meet with broader societal acceptance – especially when it comes to controversial issues.

Another advantage lies in the increased accountability of politicians. Direct votes prompt politicians to formulate their positions more clearly and act more transparently. Civil participation gives their decisions and measures greater legitimacy and they can hope for broader societal approval, which is particularly important for controversial topics. In uncertain times in particular, this is an essential prerequisite for reducing the alienation between decision-makers and the population.

At the municipal level, referendums have also proven many times over that they can accelerate reform processes. Initiatives for urban development or the implementation of environmental measures have been successfully driven forward through direct coordination. There is also an opportunity for referendums to overcome political blockades. Issues that are stagnating due to party-political differences can be advanced through direct votes. This encourages citizens to identify more strongly with political processes and strengthens their sense of participation.

The different views between the generations can be explained by the greater reliance of younger people on representative structures and multilateral approaches. Correspondingly, they increasingly favour expert solutions instead of grassroots, democratic votes. In addition, they have grown up in a society in which participatory approaches (e.g. citizens' forums, petitions, online platforms) are more established and perceive these as sufficient. Older citizens, on the other hand, see referendums as an important tool for controlling political power and promoting co-determination. Having grown up at a time when these were not yet widely established, they believe in their impact on raising political awareness.

Prognosis

The future of referendums will largely depend on the extent to which they can be adapted to the requirements of modern societies. Political decisions increasingly require in-depth knowledge and differentiated analyses. It is therefore of central importance to inform citizens comprehensively about the advantages and disadvantages, opportunities and risks of the respective topic. Only on this basis can they be empowered to make decisions based on factual information and sound judgements. Under these conditions, referendums can be an effective instrument to involve citizens more closely in political decision-making processes and to strengthen trust in democratic institutions in the long term. Especially in the case of localised or clearly defined issues, direct coordination offers the potential to resolve reform backlogs and overcome political blockades.

COOPERATION

However, the introduction of binding quotas and multi-stage procedures remains an essential prerequisite for the legitimisation of referendums. These mechanisms ensure broad societal acceptance and protect against the dominance of interests of an active, well-organised minority. Only in this way can the results of referendums reflect the overall will of the population.

A promising perspective for the further development of referendums lies in the implementation of new formats, such as citizens' councils or hybrid models. Such approaches would make it possible to discuss complex topics in a structured manner in advance and create a sound basis for decision-making. In addition to increasing the quality of decision-making, these formats would also promote participants' sense of responsibility. In addition, successful practices from local governance structures – in particular from the New Public Governance approach – could be further developed. Through such integrative policy-making, responsibilities could be distributed more effectively and the cooperation of a wide range of actors, such as administrations, business, politics and non-governmental organisations, could be optimised.

In view of the increasing complexity of political issues, however, it is to be expected that referendums will be used primarily in areas that are either locally limited or have a high symbolic significance. Topics such as municipal infrastructure projects or local environmental measures are particularly suitable for direct consultation

votes, as they can promote a stronger identification of the population with decision-making processes. Global challenges, such as climate policy or international trade agreements, on the other hand, continue to require the expertise and negotiating skills of parliaments and specialist bodies. Representative democracy remains indispensable in such areas, as it enables long-term planning and the necessary multilateral cooperation.

COOPERATION

In the long term, referendums can be established as a useful addition to representative democracy. The well-founded further development of these instruments offers the opportunity to position them as an effective means of promoting co-determination and societal cohesion. Direct democracy has the potential not only to make political processes more transparent, but also to strengthen citizens' trust in these processes. It gives people the feeling of being actively involved in shaping their common future and can therefore make a significant contribution to strengthening democratic structures.

COOPERATION

Do we need to make more uncomfortable decisions?

Out of every 100 respondents, the following number agree with the statement:
'The state should also make more uncomfortable decisions than it has in the past, which demand something from citizens, for example on issues such as savings, climate protection measures or speed limits.'

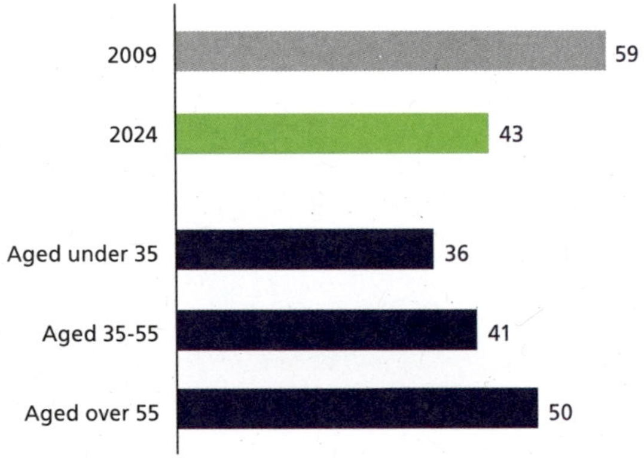

Acceptance or resistance

HOW CITIZENS REACT TO UNCOMFORTABLE DECISIONS

Results

Overcoming societal challenges not only requires the state to be able to make difficult decisions, but also entails perceptible restrictions and impositions for the individual citizen. These can be of a financial nature or require an adjustment of previous habits, for example in the form of a speed limit or climate protection measures. Whereas in 2009, one in five citizens believed that the state should increasingly take uncomfortable measures that challenged citizens, this proportion increased to 28 percent by 2024. The level of agreement among the under-35s is particularly striking, with almost one in three sharing this opinion, while among the over-55s, around one in four agree with stronger state intervention.

Reasons

The year-on-year increase in agreement can be explained by a change in societal awareness and societal values. This applies above all to the assessment of individual responsibility and the willingness to change. Geopolitical challenges in particular are making the population aware of the relevance and urgency of reforms and, in some cases, far-reaching changes. More and more citizens are recognising the need to actively contribute to change as individuals. This can be seen, for example, in the increasing awareness of climate change. Heatwaves and floods in recent years have heightened awareness of this challenge, making more people willing to accept appropriate measures. In addition, international climate targets and EU requirements, such as CO2 reductions, emphasise the need for uncomfortable measures, which is why many citizens are also voluntarily trying to reduce their ecological footprint. In a similar way, the willingness to change with regard to financial and economic challenges has increased. The consequences of inflation, the energy crisis and the uncertainties caused by global conflicts promote the view that individual savings and more personal responsibility are necessary to stabilise the state budget, which should also be demanded from the state.

The greater agreement rate of the younger generation can be explained by their greater sensitivity to ecological and social issues. They are more affected than others by the long-term consequences. Many of them doubt that the majority of the population will make voluntary efforts in this regard without pressure and, in view of the urgency of effective measures, call for greater state decision-making power. In addition, they are less attached to traditional lifestyles (more open to change) and are less affected by certain burdens than other groups due to their starting financial positions (e.g. no car or property). In contrast,older people tend to cling to old habits, are somewhat less open to change and are more afraid of financial losses. The lower level of support for this stance in 2009 is also due to the fact that the urgency of uncomfortable political decisions did not yet have such a strong influence on societal awareness. This applies in particular to climate change, the effects of which were less noticeable. Instead, other topics dominated the public debate, such as the economic uncertainties caused by the global financial crisis. The German economy shrank more than at any time since 1945 and many citizens feared for their jobs. In this tense economic situation, state intervention was seen as necessary, but was primarily associated with bank bailouts. Parts of the population viewed these measures rather critically or saw them as favouring large companies and banks. At the time, this increased scepticism towards further state intervention, which would have meant additional burdens or restrictions for the individual.

Overall, despite the increase in 2024, it should be critically noted that the vast majority of Germans do not want stronger state measures that would result in restrictions for the individual. This mainly affects sections of the population with a pronounced scepticism about the effectiveness or fairness of political decisions. Individualism also plays a role: many people prioritise personal short-term advantages or supposedly indispensable freedoms over long-term societal goals. A structural theme here is the communication deficit among political decision-makers: it is often not possible to communicate complex topics, such as more personal responsibility or necessary pension reforms and tax increases, in an understandable and convincing way.

Prognosis

The societal divide between the willingness to change and the preservation of existing lifestyles will remain for the time being. The younger generation will continue to show a greater willingness to change than older citizens. Their greater openness to ecological and social issues and their lesser attachment to traditional lifestyles make them a driving force behind the acceptance of uncomfortable decisions.

The awareness of ecological issues will continue to increase in the future. Extreme weather events will make the consequences of climate change ever more tangible and international climate targets and EU requirements will simultaneously increase the pressure on national governments to implement concrete measures. These developments will make more and more citizens realise how important it is to accept personal restrictions in order to achieve long-term goals. Economic uncertainties, such as inflation and energy crises, will also play a key role in the future. Many citizens understand how important personal responsibility is in order to stabilise both their own budget and the national budget.

A core task of politics will be to achieve broad societal acceptance for far-reaching reforms. Many citizens will remain sceptical about government intervention, especially if it is perceived as unfair or ineffective. The individualisation of society and decreasing solidarity promote the danger that short-term personal benefits will continue to take precedence over long-term societal goals. Accordingly, the necessity of measures must be communicated clearly and comprehensibly in order to increase citizens' understanding. As soon as this happens, broader societal acceptance will develop – a development that is urgently needed in view of all the challenges.

Should the state promote more private initiatives?

Out of every 100 respondents, the following number agree with the statement:
'The state could save a lot of money if it were to support and promote private initiatives from the ranks of citizens more actively.'

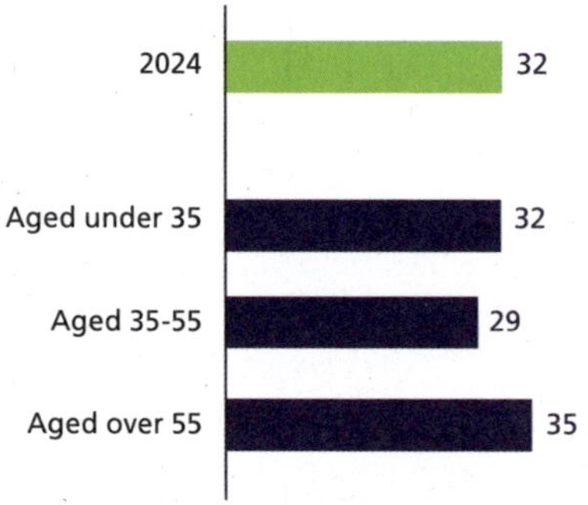

State support for private initiatives

POSSIBILITY OF FINANCIAL RELIEF

Results

In times of increasing financial challenges and limited government capacities, the question of new ways to limit government spending is becoming ever more urgent. About one in three Germans see the increased promotion of private initiatives as an opportunity to relieve the burden on public finances. The power of civil society should be used to spread responsibility more broadly across many shoulders, and open up innovative paths for the future.

COOPERATION

Reasons

Private initiatives can not only reduce costs, but also strengthen societal structures and generate new solutions. The interplay between individual initiative and government support makes a significant contribution to overcoming challenges.

A key advantage of private initiatives lies in their flexibility and adaptability. While government programmes are often tied down by lengthy planning and decision-making processes, private projects include better local knowledge and can respond more quickly to specific needs. Examples such as community buses, ride-sharing benches, car-sharing models or waste collection campaigns show how targeted measures can have a major impact with limited resources.

Another approach is the promotion of social entrepreneurship. This form of private initiative makes it possible to tackle societal problems in an entrepreneurial way and, at the same time, work in a financially sustainable way. In rural regions in particular, such projects can strengthen regional economic cycles and counteract urban migration trends. Initiatives that incorporate local products and services not only promote local economic stability, but also increase resilience to global dependencies.

In addition, private initiatives promote a sense of responsibility among citizens. Those who actively get involved take responsibility for specific projects and strengthen the sense of community. This form of engagement increases trust between citizens and helps to overcome societal divisions – an essential aspect in an increasingly polarised society.

Private projects also enable long-term prevention. Health-promoting programmes, such as sports and nutrition initiatives, can reduce medical costs, while educational projects, such as tutoring or language courses, create better labour market opportunities in the long term. Such preventive measures not only promote the independence of citizens, but are also cost-efficient. The financing of private initiatives also offers a high leverage effect. State funding can be supplemented by donations or private investment, which considerably strengthens the financial basis of such projects. This not only mobilises additional resources, but also motivates other stakeholders to participate.

COOPERATION

Prognosis

Private initiatives will play an increasingly important role in the coming years. The state's tight budget situation and the need to find innovative solutions to societal challenges will make private involvement indispensable. However, private initiatives are not a panacea. Complex and long-term challenges, such as caring for older citizens or integrating refugees, will require stable state structures and reliable resources. Without this basis, civil society approaches will quickly reach their limits.

New financing models, such as social impact bonds or public-private partnerships, could significantly extend the reach of private projects. While social impact bonds appeal to investors willing to invest in social outcomes, public-private partnerships create synergies between public resources and private expertise. Such models not only offer financial advantages, but also increase the efficiency and impact of private initiatives.

Strengthening rural areas could become a central field of action for private initiatives. Local measures would not only promote social cohesion, but also offer a concrete response to demographic changes.

Overall, the future lies in a balanced interplay between the state and society. The state must remain responsible for basic services and, at the same time, create framework conditions that promote private engagement. Private initiatives can act as a valuable addition with their own added value, but not as a substitute for state services.

COOPERATION

COOPERATION

Do party interests put the brakes on change?

Out of every 100 respondents, the following number agree with the statement:
'The lack of cooperation between politicians from different parties is slowing down or even preventing change.'

Party politics prevent progress

LARGE MAJORITY CRITICISE LACK OF COOPERATION

Results

The majority of German citizens see the lack of cooperation between politicians from different parties as an obstacle to change. Nine out of ten citizens are convinced that a lack of cooperation is slowing down or even preventing political progress. This opinion is particularly strong among the over-55s, while agreement is somewhat lower among the under-35s.

COOPERATION

Reasons

The lack of cooperation between politicians from different parties has many causes, which can be divided into different categories: structural, ideological, social, external and systemic. All these factors influence not only the patterns of interaction between political actors, but also the perception of citizens with regard to political action.

A central structural reason lies in party political interests. The primary goal of political action is often to sharpen one's own profile and differentiate oneself from competing parties. This pushes the willingness to compromise into the background and makes constructive cooperation considerably more difficult. In addition, different worldviews and political convictions represent a major barrier to agreeing on common goals. These differences are particularly evident in controversial topics such as climate policy, migration or social justice. Populist movements exacerbate this problem by deliberately relying on confrontation and demarcation in order to mobilise their voter base. This strategy not only makes an objective debate with other parties more difficult, but often also prevents the necessary consensus for sustainable political change.

Social and psychological factors also play a major role. A lack of trust between parties causes cooperations to fail or not even materialise. Politicians often see their political rivals as opponents instead of potential partners for joint solutions. Instead of building bridges, many players concentrate on defending their own position or emphasising the weaknesses of others. This creates a climate of confrontation that makes constructive cooperation almost impossible. In addition, many politicians focus on short-term successes that are quickly visible and resonate with the electorate. Long-term Change, however, requires patience and continuous cooperation across party borders – something that rarely happens in everyday politics. External influences also contribute significantly to the lack of cooperation. The role of the media in particular should not be underestimated here. Polarising statements and conflicts often receive more attention in reporting than factual debates or compromises. As a result, politicians increasingly focus on confrontation, as this increases their media presence. In addition, the complexity of many political issues poses a key challenge. Almost all problem areas – be it bureaucracy reduction, tax policy, infrastructure or housing – are highly complex and cannot be solved with simple solutions. This applies all the more to particularly controversial topics, such as migration, climate policy or security issues.

They require interdisciplinary approaches and the integration of different perspectives. Without a clear strategy for overcoming these challenges, many initiatives get stuck or fail right from the start.

Finally, systemic factors also contribute to making cooperation between political actors more difficult. Strict parliamentary group discipline reduces the flexibility of deputies in their decisions and binds them more closely to the party line, which limits the scope for compromise. In addition, short election periods often direct the political focus towards short-term successes and securing their own re-election instead of promoting long-term and sustainable solutions. These structural conditions create an environment in which consensus-building and cooperation are subject to additional challenges.

The combination of the aforementioned reasons leads to a stagnation of political processes in the perception of the population. They experience this as a standstill or blockade policy and increasingly lose confidence in the ability of their representatives to cooperate and act.

COOPERATION

Prognosis

The lack of cooperation between politicians from different parties will remain an obstacle to political progress in the future if no fundamental changes are introduced. What is needed are innovative approaches that make the political discourse more constructive and promote a willingness to cooperate.

A central starting point here is the creation of new dialogue formats. More cross-party working groups or interdepartmental committees would help to intensify dialogue and focus on joint solutions. Such formats also offer the opportunity to introduce different perspectives and develop innovative approaches. The increased integration of external expertise should also play a greater role. Many political challenges require interdisciplinary approaches and cooperation with scientists, politicians and citizens. Citizens' councils or citizens' forums offer the opportunity to incorporate opinions from the population into decision-making processes. Such formats would not only promote dialogue between politics and society, but could also serve as a bridge between different parties. Joint work on proposals from the population would direct the focus to factual issues and allow ideological differences to fade into the background.

The way in which political work is communicated should also be reconsidered. At present, the focus is often on conflicts and party-political differences. A stronger emphasis on cooperation and joint successes would positively change the public image of politics. Media could play a supporting role here by highlighting examples of successful collaboration and focusing less on polarisation.

COOPERATION

The promotion of long-term concepts is another important approach. Many political projects fail due to their focus on short-term success. However, issues such as infrastructure development or education reforms require continuous cooperation over several legislative periods. Political players should therefore work more towards defining long-term goals and driving these forward regardless of party affiliations.

The implementation of such measures requires a clear will to change and a common understanding that cooperation is the key to a sustainable policy.

COOPERATION

COOPERATION

Who helps with integration?

Out of every 100 respondents, the following number agree with the statement:
'I endeavour to actively help with the integration of refugees and newcomers.'

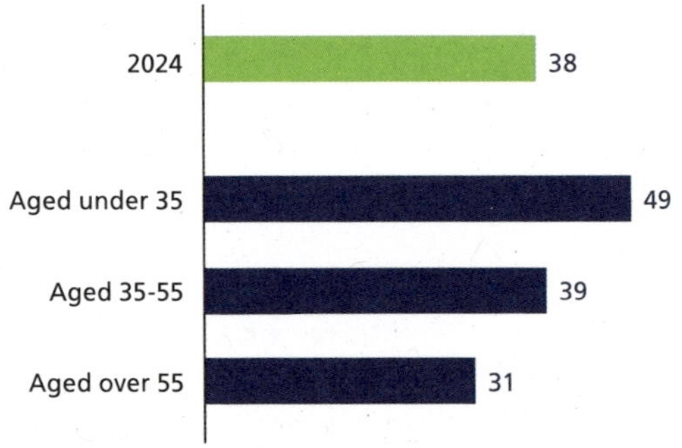

Integration through action

EVERY OTHER PERSON UNDER 35 IS ACTIVELY ENGAGED

Results

The integration of newcomers is a central societal challenge, which requires both political measures and the commitment of citizens and the initiative of migrants. At present, 38 percent of the population is actively involved in supporting refugees in their integration. In contrast, just under two thirds do not take an active role in this process. There is a significant difference between age groups: While every other citizen under the age of 35 is actively engaged, the proportion of over-55s is less than a third.

COOPERATION

Reasons

The reasons for or against engagement vary considerably and include both individual and societal aspects. Prejudices towards newcomers, uncertainty in dealing with cultural differences and critical public debates and reporting on migration and integration problems have a dampening effect on the willingness to get actively involved. In addition, a lack of points of contact with people who belong to the community, a lack of time due to work and family commitments and insufficient information about specific engagement opportunities lead to a reluctance to get involved. Language barriers, bureaucratic hurdles and the emotional strain of dealing with the complex challenges faced by refugees add to these obstacles. Many citizens regard integration measures as being primarily the task of state institutions, especially if these are perceived as inefficient. This often leads to frustration and a decline in motivation among those involved.

On the other hand, those who are actively involved in integration demonstrate a high degree of responsibility and societal engagement. In addition to altruistic motives, the joy of helping others and the meaningfulness of one's own actions play a central role. Younger citizens in particular show a strong interest in intercultural encounters. This is often due to their regular contact with newcomers in educational institutions and at work. This leads to a greater understanding of the realities of their lives and personal connections. The lower level of willingness among older citizens could be due to fewer points of contact with refugees and a stronger rootedness in existing cultural structures, which lead to scepticism towards change.

COOPERATION

Prognosis

The integration of migrants harbours considerable potential that goes beyond overcoming societal challenges. It not only promotes the political, social, cultural and economic integration of people with a migration background, but also strengthens societal cohesion and harmonious coexistence. The potential for the labour market to reduce the shortage of skilled workers should be particularly emphasised. Migrants bring specific skills and qualifications that are urgently needed in many sectors. Targeted measures, such as language courses, professional qualification programmes and the recognition of foreign qualifications, could effectively exploit this potential. This would not only strengthen Germany's economic competitiveness, but also contribute to coping with demographic change.

Successful integration also requires the creation of meeting spaces that promote intercultural exchange. Cultural events, sports initiatives or neighbourhood programmes could serve as platforms for exchange and cooperation. Another key focus could be integration through education. Access to educational institutions would open up long-term prospects for migrants and enable them to actively participate in society.

In order to successfully master integration, it will in future be crucial to remove the existing barriers and get more citizens involved. Low-threshold opportunities and success stories of successful integration will help to break down prejudices and increase motivation to provide support.

COOPERATION

How great is the tolerance for cultural freedom?

Out of every 100 respondents, the following number agree with the statement:
'Everyone should have the freedom to live out their cultural identity and religion.'

Religious freedom and cultural diversity

THE MAJORITY ARE IN FAVOUR

Results

In 2023, 25 million of Germany's 84 million inhabitants had a migrant background, which corresponds to 30 percent of the total population. Cultural diversity – 61 percent of migrants come from Europe – thus shapes everyday life in most regions. Many citizens see this international diversity as an enrichment. Three quarters of the population are in favour of every person being allowed to live out their cultural identity and religion in their individual free time. This agreement level is independent of gender, age, level of education or income.

COOPERATION

Reasons

The right to free cultural development and freedom of religion is enshrined in the German Basic Law (Article 4 GG) and is also reflected in international agreements such as the United Nations Universal Declaration of Human Rights. A significant proportion of the German population sees these democratic principles as an expression of pluralism and individual freedom and is proud of these achievements. This commitment to individual freedom is granted to all people, regardless of their cultural or religious background. This is particularly important in view of the challenges of integration and the influx of populist movements, which have been intensified by migration in recent decades. Nevertheless, the majority of citizens regard tolerance as an essential requirement for peaceful coexistence in a pluralistic society. Mutual acceptance is seen as the foundation for mutual understanding, strengthening the sense of community and broadening individual perspectives.

This attitude is strengthened by educational initiatives and societal discourses that emphasise the value of freedom and respect for other cultures. The existence of religious and cultural conflicts is not negated, but always considered in the context of dialogue and cooperation.

Beyond the individual sphere, cultural and religious tolerance is also valued in the wider societal framework, especially in business. Cultural diversity is seen as a catalyst for innovation, creativity and attracting global talent. Companies with diverse teams benefit from the different perspectives and can develop products and services that cater to international and multicultural markets.

In addition, Germany's historical experience plays a central role in emphasising religious freedom. The crimes of national socialism made the devastating consequences of cultural and religious homogeneity clear. This has since created a pronounced awareness of the importance of diversity and tolerance among the population.

COOPERATION

Prognosis

Germany's increasing cultural diversity will bring with it both potential and challenges. Prejudices and resentment could increase in parts of the population, jeopardising social cohesion and making targeted counter-measures necessary. Integration will continue to prove complex, as factors such as language barriers, the lack of recognition of foreign qualifications and discrimination on the labour and housing markets will make it difficult for many migrants to participate in society. Refugees in particular still often remain in shared accommodation for years with limited opportunities for integration. Populist movements and parties that instrumentalise fears of foreign infiltration and economic insecurity pose a threat to democratic values and awelcoming culture. Educational initiatives and political programmes will therefore have to increasingly promote intercultural exchange and dismantle prejudices.

However, the opportunities of successful integration for Germany as a business location are considerable. Companies could benefit from a diverse workforce that drives innovation thanks to different perspectives. In addition, cultural openness would facilitate the recruitment of urgently needed skilled workers from abroad and counteract demographic change and the shortage of skilled labour.

However, successful integration requires efforts on both sides. The host society must show openness and create structures that enable comprehensive participation. At the same time, it is essential that migrants take the initiative and play an active role in society. The acquisition of the German language plays a key role in promoting social and professional participation. The willingness to adapt to basic social norms and the acceptance of democratic values are further essential foundations for harmonious coexistence. The aim should be to preserve one's own cultural identity, without separating oneself or forming parallel societies.

COOPERATION

COOPERATION

How important is freedom of choice?

Out of every 100 respondents, the following number agree with the statement:
'The freedom to make my own decisions is an important asset for me.'

Individual freedom and the common good

SELF-EVIDENT FOR CITIZENS

Results

In a time characterised by global crises, economic uncertainties and profound societal challenges, individual freedom of choice remains a central concern of the population. The ability to make self-determined decisions is considered indispensable by nine out of ten citizens. Older generations in particular share this view almost unanimously. Agreement is also high among younger population groups, albeit to a somewhat lesser extent.

Reasons

The high relevance of freedom of choice can be attributed to psychological, social and historical life factors. The certainty that you have the freedom to make your own decisions gives you a sense of control and is a fundamental part of the human psyche. Autonomy promotes a sense of strength, resilience and self-efficacy by enabling the individual to actively influence personal and societal circumstances. It also constitutes an essential part of social identity and the sense of being a responsible individual.

In times of crisis or in societal discourses in which moral questions – about solidarity, security or justice – are increasingly addressed or individual restrictions are demanded, many citizens strive to preserve their autonomy. Examples of this include debates about smoking bans, video surveillance, planned speed limits on motorways or reduced meat consumption. Self-determined decisions contribute significantly to reducing feelings of heteronomy or helplessness , coping with stress and creating active room for manoeuvre. They thus symbolise not only autonomy, but also hope and resilience.

Freedom of choice by no means exclusively serves personal interests. Rather, it can promote creative thought processes and innovative solutions that have a positive impact on the challenges facing society as a whole. In today's society, it is therefore essential to be able to express uncomfortable opinions and stimulate discussion. At the same time, the right to independence strengthens trust in institutions, which is an important factor for social cohesion. Conversely, restrictions on individual freedoms can foster mistrust, resistance and societal polarisation.

The particularly high value placed on freedom of choice among the older generation can be explained, among other things, by their concern about a loss of autonomy in old age. For this population group, the ability to act independently is closely linked to quality of life. In addition, they have tried and tested strategies for overcoming crises, which they would also like to be able to draw on without restriction in the future. Their very high level of agreement reflects not only the high value placed on self-determination, but also the fear of losing it.

Younger generations, on the other hand, have a more pragmatic attitude towards restrictions. They tend to be somewhat more willing to restrict personal freedoms in favour of long-term societal goals or the common good. This willingness is reflected in the acceptance of measures that are less strongly perceived as interfering with their quality of life. For example, younger people support measures to combat climate change more strongly than other age groups and are willing to give up certain freedoms in return. In addition, many young people still live in relatively dependent structures – be it at home or during their education – and therefore associate freedom of choice less strongly with their social identity.

Prognosis

The ability to strike a balance between individual freedom and the collective common good will play a decisive role for societal cohesion in the future. Adjustments and restrictions will only be widely accepted if they are perceived as fair and balanced. The challenge is to preserve individual freedoms without losing sight of the common good – a 'both/and' instead of an 'either/or'.

Freedom of choice will remain not only a symbol of autonomy and resilience in the future, but also a basis for creative thinking and societal innovation. Especially in times of crisis, freedom means not only independence from external coercion, but also the assumption of responsibility for the common good.

COOPERATION

CONCLUSION

These analyses have highlighted the central importance of trust, responsibility and cooperation for the functioning of our society. The prerequisites, potentials and positive effects as well as the dangers and risks associated with a decline in these values or when they are no longer represented and practised by all societal actors have been discussed. The key findings can be summarised as follows:

- Citizens' trust in the relevance of state bodies is still deeply rooted in societal consciousness, but is being increasingly let down by numerous current developments.

- The population's willingness to take responsibility is pronounced, but manifests itself primarily in the immediate social environment and is only utilised to a limited extent in its potential and in connection with civil initiatives.

- All reliable forms of cooperation are regarded by citizens as indispensable for overcoming individual crises and societal challenges while preserving individual freedom.

- In all three areas, more effort and a willingness to reform are required from decision-makers, especially with regard to communication and willingness to compromise. The population is quite prepared to support even uncomfortable decisions and actively participate in shaping society.

- Strengthening community, trust, a sense of responsibility and cooperation is crucial to creating a broader societal basis for an optimistic view of the future.

Finally, the question arises as to the relationship between trust, the willingness to take responsibility and cooperation in order to be able to exert a targeted influence on their interaction and efficiency. The relationship between trust, the willingness to take responsibility

CONCLUSION

and cooperation should not be understood as a linear relationship, but as a circular one. Even if trust appears to be the basis at the beginning, they all relate to each other and can be seen as a prerequisite or effect according to the respective context.

Trust is the basis for responsibility. In order to assume responsibility or hand it over, mutual trust in the abilities of the other is a prerequisite.. This creates a feeling of reliability and security as well as the possibility of not having to constantly scrutinise the actions and decisions of the other. At the same time, trust is the basis of cooperation. It creates a feeling of security, positive expectations and enables open communication. Without a trusting relationship between citizens, they will not be prepared to work together in a binding manner.

Responsibility is the basis of trust. Those who take responsibility show their reliability. This characteristic is crucial in building long-term trust. At the same time, responsibility is the basis for cooperation. Only when citizens are willing to take responsibility for themselves and others are they able to enter into equal cooperation.

Cooperation is the basis of trust. Trust is not a static state, but develops over time through repeated positive interactions, transparent processes and shared agreements. Cooperation leads to a broadening of perspectives, a reduction in uncertainty and a strengthening of trust. At the same time, cooperation is also the basis of responsibility. Through cooperating with others or based onthe desire to achieve a common goal, citizens are willing to take responsibility.

The reciprocal relationships between the three concepts clearly reveal the following: trust, responsibility and the willingness to cooperate are mutually dependent and weaken and strengthen each other.

A society that places trust, responsibility and willingness to cooperate in the spotlight is not only more capable of overcoming the challenges of the present, but can also shape asustainable and future-oriented world.

QUESTIONS ABOUT THE FUTURE

INTERVIEW

PHILIPP AMTHOR

MdB (CDU)

What strategies or concepts could be used to strengthen trust in government and corporate structures?

In order to regain trust in our state, we need to fundamentally reform it. Credibility begins when politicians start with reforms of themselves: the working methods of the government and the federal administration must be modernised and put to the test in a self-critical manner – in terms of structure, personnel, digitisation and processes. Germany needs a more efficient, leaner administration with clearer competences. The tasks and effects as well as the personnel and financial resources for the federal administration must return to focusing on the essentials. We must stop creating new positions and structures for every new problem. On the contrary: ministries and the administration system must be restructured and, as part of a cross-departmental administrative reform, the number of staff in the ministries and the record number of over 950 federal authorities must be reduced to an appropriate level. I am convinced that our state must do a better job with better work processes and fewer staff. Then, it will also regain trust.

How do you personally see the relationship between individual freedom and 'taking responsibility for society oneself' and how do you put this into practice?

For me personally, the freedom of the individual and responsibility for the community are two sides of the same coin in the best Christian Democratic sense: the starting point of our policy is always the individual, with their inviolable dignity and individual abilities, but we also always regard their freedom as being linked to their responsibility for the community. For me, this simultaneity of freedom and responsibility is the essence of our democratic constitutional state and, at the same time, one of its distinguishing features: the concept of freedom in responsibility immunises us against an exaggerated libertarian individualism in which the individual's claim to freedom is the sole focus. But it also immunises us against left-wing identity politics that divide a community into

conflicting groups and thereby endanger the cohesion of society. And it is the right historical lesson against socialist, nationalist and populist thinking that gives an ideologically based collective priority over individual people. In this sense, to me the relationship between freedom and responsibility is not just a private matter, but a systemic issue.

Does this also require more cooperation across party and competitive boundaries and how could this lead to a 'miracle of change'?

Certainly, cross-party efforts are needed to renew the promise of the future of our Federal Republic: freedom, peace, prosperity and security for usall. However, for the sake of democracy, differences between the parties must always remain clearly recognisable – and not only at the political margins, but also in the political centre. And regarding the keyword 'miracle of change', the following applies: change is usually achieved less by waiting for miracles, but more through courageous action. The best guarantee of this is a competent federal government.

LAURA BORNMANN

Managing Director STARTUP TEENS

What strategies or concepts could be used to strengthen trust in government and corporate structures?

With honest interests, authenticity and humanity: government and company representatives must once again engage more closely with people's concerns, fears and hopes. This is the only way to create solutions that solve real problems in our society. Trust is therefore not created by abstract institutions, but rather by the people they represent. Leaders are needed who take a clear stance, communicate transparently and admit their mistakes. We all have a responsibility to ensure that such a cultural change succeeds: with politicians in particular, we should question whether the demand for immediate resignations is always justified – especially since in the past, these were often about issues that concerned neither their competence nor their actual work, because if openness always

How do you personally see the relationship between individual freedom and 'taking responsibility for society oneself' and how do you put this into practice?

Freedom and responsibility are inextricably linked: the greater our individual freedom, the greater our room for manoeuvre – and thus the greater our responsibility for society. For me personally, treating others with respect and volunteering in the areas of equality, education and economics is important. To me, responsibility means that everyone who can do so gives something back. This also includes taking a clear stand against injustice and discrimination. In a time of increasing polarisation, this requires courage. Many remain silent out of a fear of hostility, which I can understand. But right now, strong leaders must not give up. Economic players play a key role here. With their resources and influence, they can make a significant contribution to promoting a fairer society.

Does this also require more cooperation across party and competitive boundaries and how could this lead to a 'miracle of change'?

Yes, absolutely. The challenges of our time, whether climate change, economic transformation or social justice, require a fundamental rethink and joint action. A 'miracle of change' is only possible if politics and business see themselves as partners that pull together. It's time to emphasise commonalities, to understand diversity as a strength and to see differences as a valuable enrichment. Perhaps we also need to fundamentally rethink our political and economic systems: are rigid party structures still in keeping with the times or shouldn't the issues be the focus instead? How might decision-making processes be made more transparent and citizens and employees more directly involved? Should individual companies join forces more closely to develop innovative solutions together? Wouldn't it also make sense to involve more people from business and civil society in political systems? And above all: isn't more courage the key ingredient for all this?

ZARAH BRUHN

Founder & CEO Social-Bee

What strategies or concepts could be used to strengthen trust in government and corporate structures?

Trust is the basis for a functioning society, whether in a political or economic context. As the founder and managing director of socialbee, I experience almost daily how crucial it is to ensure that transparency, credibility and social responsibility take centre stage. Companies and governments can strengthen trust by pursuing the following strategies:

Transparency and communication: Open, honest communication is essential. Decisions should be comprehensible and well explained so that people feel included and integrated.

Participation and involvement: People should also be actively involved in decision-making processes. For example, through open dialogue formats or co-determination in companies.

Sustainability and social responsibility: Companies and governments should assume long-term social and ecological responsibility and not aim for short-term profits or electoral success. Social entrepreneurship proves that economic success and societal added value are not mutually exclusive, but can strengthen each other.

The role model function of managers: Leaders in business and politics must set a good example themselves in order to build trust in the long term.

How do you personally see the relationship between individual freedom and 'taking responsibility for society oneself' and how do you put this into practice?

I am firmly convinced that individual freedom and societal responsibility are not opposites, but can complement each other perfectly. Freedom doesn't mean acting selfishly, but having the opportunity to take responsibility. In my work at socialbee, I see on a daily basis how important, as well as wonderful it is to apply individual strengths for the common good. Freedom means having opportunities. People should, of course, have the freedom to realise their potential. At the same time, however, this also means that they have

a responsibility to utilise those opportunities sensibly. In this way, each person can add value to the community in their own individual way. Taking on responsibility can also be fulfilling. It should not be seen as a constraint, but as an opportunity to actively help shape our society and contribute to the greater good.

At socialbee, we manage this very well. With concrete solutions to societal challenges, by offering refugees real prospects through work and training. This shows that economic freedom and social engagement are compatible.

Does this also require more cooperation across party and competitive boundaries and how could this lead to a 'miracle of change'?

Change does not happen in isolation. If we want real change and long-term solutions, political parties, companies and civil society actors must work together.

Cross-industry and cross-party dialogue: Instead of ideological trench warfare, we need open exchange. The best solutions often result from a mix of different perspectives.

Collaborative innovation: Competitors can work together to tackle major societal challenges. Cooperations between start-ups, established companies and politics can have transformative effects.

Sharing best practices and knowledge: If successful approaches are publicised and made imitable, they can be scaled up more quickly and transferred to new areas.

Creating shared visions: For change to be sustainable, it must be supported by a shared vision. The focus should not be on short-term gains, but on long-term positive changes.

A 'miracle of change' can come about if we don't remain stuck in rigid thought patterns, but instead tread new paths together. Social entrepreneurship is an example of how creative solutions and collaboration make real transformation possible.

KIRA MARIE CREMER

Consultant, Founder QUINGS

What strategies or concepts could be used to strengthen trust in government and corporate structures?

Trust is not only created by the best arguments, but above all by consistent action. The younger generation in particular expects a clear stance, transparent communication and tangible change from companies and politicians today. My favourite topic, 'New Work', for example, is not just a question of working from home or a four-day week. It's about a new way of working that is based on personal responsibility, meaningfulness and fairness. In my opinion, there are three decisive factors here:

1. Credibility: Companies and politicians must practise what they preach. If a company celebrates diversity on LinkedIn, but still has glass ceilings internally, that's a breach of trust.

2. Participation: Decisions must no longer be made over the heads of those affected by them Companies need to involve their employees more; politicians need to seriously seek dialogue with young people.

3. Measurability: Lip service is not enough. Progress must be visible and verifiable – be it through independent audits, salary transparency or specific measures to combat skills shortages.

How do you personally see the relationship between individual freedom and 'taking responsibility for society oneself' and how do you put this into practice?

For me, freedom does not just mean having the right to do things – but also taking responsibility to exercise that right in a meaningful way. As a lecturer and author, I am committed to helping people learn how to actively shape their work instead of being forced into outdated structures. At the same time, employers need to change their thinking: it isn't enough to just complain about a shortage of skilled labour while the working conditions are not right. Freedom in a job does not mean unlimited flexibility without security – but a fair framework in which people can realise their full potential. The German labour market is currently facing

a challenge: while companies are desperately looking for skilled workers, a large number of apprentice positions remain unfilled. At the same time, many young people are unable to find a suitable apprenticeship. In order to understand exactly how young people today perceive their entry into a career, I conducted a comprehensive study together with the market research institute Appinio. We analysed the expectations and fears of the young generation at the start of their careers and derived specific recommendations for action for politicians, schools, employers and parents. The results clearly show: young people want to take on personal responsibility – but they need practical experience, fair conditions and real development opportunities to be able to do so. I also see it as my responsibility to actively lead this debate – be it through my book, my lectures, the FUNKE podcast 'New Work Now' or my newsletter, in which I regularly present best practices.

Does this also require more cooperation across party and competitive boundaries and how could this lead to a 'miracle of change'?

Yes, urgently. The future of work is not just an HR trend, but also an issue for society as a whole, not least due to the worsening shortage of skilled labour. The fact that we are discussing topics such as remote work, the four-day week and AI in the workplace today shows that we are at a turning point. But instead of genuine cooperation, we often encounter blockades – whether due to political trench warfare or short-term profit-seeking. Real change will only happen when we have the courage to dare to experiment. Businesses and politicians must work together to test new models. For example, what's stopping us from launching government-funded pilot projects for more mental health awareness in the workplace? Cross-industry dialogue is also crucial. The best ideas are often not generated in your own bubble, but through interdisciplinary collaboration. The concept of 'New Work' needs to get out of the elitist bubble: Flexible working models cannot apply not only to highly qualified office workers – but also to the skilled trades, care and production sectors also need innovative ideas. The younger generation is ready for this change. What are needed now are decisionmakers who don't just talk about the future but boldly shape it .

CATHARINA ENDERLEIN

Founder & CEO von ELSCP

What strategies or concepts could be used to strengthen trust in government and corporate structures?

The more fundamental question is: What culture and values do we need to rediscover and awaken in ourselves right now in order to meet each other as human beings? Real trust arises at this level. Strong companies, strong organisations and strong governments – in the perception of many, these are created through the experience of people who embody values, as well as goals, in a true and authentic way and who, at the same time, are able to chart a beautiful, tangible, realistic and sustainable future based on them. One that is tangible and experiential. It all starts with courage. And: humanity, empathy, the gift of listening and turning what you hear into something with which many people can identify. This conveys security. This conveys a sense of togetherness. This results in trust. Both short and long term. In uncertain times, the 'how' is more important than the 'what'. And also more important than claiming to be perfect or to present complete results. The positive feeling is the central element. Alongside team spirit, simplicity, a sense of ease and communal strength – knowingly heading towards a goal called the future. When this feeling is fuelled by a circle of diverse people who pool their interests precisely because of their differences and work together, it carries even more weight. This is about more than individual interest. Here, people sit down together, connected by neutral spaces, wanting to network – far removed from set roles – about overarching issues, as human beings. Free and unconstrained. This creates a strong circulatory system, full of optimism, that supports us.

How do you personally see the relationship between individual freedom and 'taking responsibility for society oneself' and how do you put this into practice?

Individual freedom means taking responsibility for society yourself. I have experienced this myself and have built networks for the future based on this feeling in recent years. As founder and CEO of the European Lab for Sustainable Companies & Personalities for the emergence of sustainable business solutions through new participatory

processes between business, science, public institutions, young groups and citizens, as well as in my communicative sustainability consulting activities with MOMENTUM. In particular, also as the initiator of the 'Sinnflut – Zukunft gesunde Stadt' movement that was launched in 2020 for joint change, with new media communication and citizen formats, digital and in completely new, positive forms of real-time communication on Ströer screens in all German cities. And as a partner initiative of the European Commission's 'New European Bauhaus', the European mission 'Beautiful. Sustainable. Together.' to make good and successful things visible, to bring people along in unity through unifying, comprehensible language, to create a completely natural sense of neighbourhood across borders in freedom – I am setting a lot in motion for this vision.

Does this also require more cooperation across party and competitive boundaries and how could this lead to a 'miracle of change'?

Cooperation is the core building block for this. Based on new lab structures, participatory processes, co-creations and collaborations to surprise, produce something new, make unused spaces visible and create in them together, without prejudice, for the common cause. This ultimately also creates the foundation for a socially just, modern market economy that builds on strong values and takes natural resources such as recyclable systems into consideration from the outset. We will also experience a new feeling of 'more'. To do this, we need to breathe life into a narrative that allows us to recognise in the process that these new forms of collaboration offer a much more meaningful and useful 'more'. This is based on constant building blocks in which we simply discover more possible combinations than before through creativity and utilise them flexibly and variably. The combination of apparent opposites will be the driving force. We don't have to reinvent anything to do this. We just have to combine what already exists in a meaningful way!

INTERVIEW

FABIAN LUKAS GOSLAR

NGO-Founder „Intergenerational Intelligence"

What strategies or concepts could be used to strengthen trust in government and corporate structures?

We should focus on having responsible leaders, seeking them and building them up. Public trust in structures has been harmed by human error and a lack of leadership. This includes an error culture at the highest level in which leaders admit their mistakes and face the consequences of those mistakes. This promotes authenticity and credibility. At the same time, the visions and ambitions of our companies and governments must be clearly internalised and communicated by management personnel, combined with clear short-term and long-term goals. Orientation and trust are created through long-term plans and holistic but pragmatically well-reasoned decisions. Even in challenging times, we must agree on a clear framework. An idea of where we want to go as a society, as a government and as a company, what we want to maintain and achieve. All of this must be underpinned by strong, fully present and visibly authentic leadership with backbone.

How do you personally see the relationship between individual freedom and 'taking responsibility for society oneself' and how do you put this into practice?

We young people especially have grown up with relatively great prosperity, in peace and freedom. Here, it helps to 'zoom out' a little further: there are 58 to 68 years between my grandparents' birth years and my own. Over those decades, Europe changed incredibly after the upheaval of the Second World War. From that change and the horror that my grandparents' generation experienced at the beginning of that change in Europe, grows

a natural responsibility for me to recognise and appreciate the value of my individual freedom. For me, it is self-evident that I should use my skills in such a way that they add value to society. In my case, these are in particular various social entrepreneurial projects and the commitment to political education through my NGO. Anyone born in freedom is always also responsible for preserving, maintaining and actively further developing the free society.

Does this also require more cooperation across party and competitive boundaries and how could this lead to a 'miracle of change'?

We need more cooperation in the centre of the party landscape. The collateral damage caused by conflicts within this centre causes resentment and reinforces a shift away from the centre towards the margins. We need a strong common narrative that sets free a unifying force: 80 years after the end of the Second World War there are historical lessons that we can transfer to the present in order to advance our Europe as a project for peace and freedom, and thereby ask ourselves, 'What needs to happen to avoid falling back into the patterns of societal division that once tore us to shreds?' The answer clearly lies in a united, strategic approach, a pragmatic reduction of bureaucracy that unfetters political and entrepreneurial innovation and develops Europe further in a process of change. Cooperation between parties and competitors in an agile think tank – a European mind – would be a first step.

INTERVIEW

MAX KLEMMER

Managing Partner Miss Germany Studios

What strategies or concepts could be used to strengthen trust in government and corporate structures?

To strengthen trust in our management structures, it is essential to ensure transparency and integrity in many more processes. It is crucial that organisations disclose their decision-making processes much better and make the effects of these transparent. Authenticity is not a weakness, but rather a strength in creating understanding and trust. Accountability must be promoted so that managers take responsibility for their actions and don't hide behind mistakes – and don't have to do so, because we need to establish a far more positive error culture again. It is also vital to establish an inclusive approach that takes into account diverse voices, especially those of younger generations and marginalised groups, in order to promote equity and build inclusive trust. We must not now roll backwards on the subject of diversity – especially not because of America as a role model. Diversity is a gift and not a burden.

How do you personally see the relationship between individual freedom and 'taking responsibility for society oneself' and how do you put this into practice?

Individual freedom and societal responsibility are complementary aspects of our democracy that must be in balance with each other. We have a societal responsibility to promote individual freedom in order to really develop the true potential of ambitious individuals. Miss Germany promotes this understanding by supporting womenwho are both pursuing their personal goals and actively participting in shaping a fairer society. We create platforms that enable the exchange of ideas and networking, and support initiatives that promote both individual ambitionsand the common good. This balance of freedom

and responsibility manifests itself in projects that promote real equal opportunities and enable everyone involved to work together as equals. On the other hand, individual freedom must not restrict our coexistence as a society, nor ride roughshod over our security.

Does this also require more cooperation across party and competitive boundaries and how could this lead to a 'miracle of change'?

Cross-sector collaboration is essential for sustainable change. We must break down the existing barriers between political, economic and societal sectors and promote a climate of cooperation and mutual respect. Such a 'miracle of change' requires continuous dialogue and the development of bridges in order to develop innovative solutions together. The battle of the election campaign should now be relegated to the past. A climate of opportunity and ambition must now be realised. It is particularly important to move closer together as Europe and to pursue independent, continent-specific approaches instead of imitating external models such as America. This strengthens our unique position and promotes solutions that are tailored to our specific cultural and societal needs.

INTERVIEW

JAN KÖNIG

Co-founder ODALINE

What strategies or concepts could be used to strengthen trust in government and corporate structures?

Authenticity. Everyone under 40 has been bombarded with adverts since they were babies. They recognise when someone is selling them rubbish. Or is simply lying. As our politicians have unfortunately shown in this election campaign. Credibility is not helped by 'quickly forgetting', as in the case of the CDU and the debt brake. What would have been needed then would have been a video in which Merz admitted his mistakes and why the lifting of the brake was necessary (after all). In the past, only Habeck has actually achieved this with social media content – directly addressing the people. Taking responsibility for mistakes. Honesty. The same applies to companies. Brands need faces. Faces must be honest. Mistakes must be admitted. The worst thing you can do is to stay silent or turn off comments. Without approachability, there can be no success.

How do you personally see the relationship between individual freedom and 'taking responsibility for society oneself' and how do you put this into practice?

Freedom and responsibility work together. Freedom means taking responsibility. This applies to the economy and politics, but also in society, e.g. in associations. I myself joined a party for the first time in my life this year and am trying to expand my reach (both within my circle of friends and on social media) for a better future. We all need to get louder, because the blue supporters of the AfD are constantly increasing.

Does this also require more cooperation across party and competitive boundaries and how could this lead to a 'miracle of change'?

Our biggest problem is that we are not solution-oriented, but put far too much energy into working against each other rather than into going forwards. Problems stand at the forefront:, we say 'I don't like their opinion', instead of actually tackling challenges. We are failing to discard the old ways of thinking and our biggest problem is the lack of openness to digitalisation. When I look at how many faxes are still being sent today, the system has simply remained stuck in the past. There is no point in blaming the CDU, we simply have to change now. And learn from other countries. Estonia is the digital European state – how do they manage their system with much less IT power in the country? Our companies too must work to ensure that our country gets back on track. As co-creators of the future. Our own interests must take second place if we want to preserve the prosperity of our country.

ALICIA LINDNER

Co-CEO ANNEMARIE BÖRLIND

What strategies or concepts could be used to strengthen trust in government and corporate structures?

Trust is like a good natural cosmetic formula: it takes transparency, patience and the will to deal with the 'ingredients'. For companies, this means less glossy promises, and taking more of a real stance. If you want trust, you have to make decisions comprehensible – both internally and externally.

If you don't just talk about sustainability, but practise it radically – from the supply chain to communication – then something stable is created. The same applies to politics: less spin, more substance. And once in a while daring to say: 'We don't know any better right now – but we are listening.' Trust does not grow through perfection, but through taking a stance.

How do you personally see the relationship between individual freedom and 'taking responsibility for society oneself' and how do you put this into practice?

For me, freedom is not a carte blanche, but a privilege – and from privilege comes responsibility. This starts with questions such as: 'What products do I offer?' 'Under what conditions are they produced?' And it doesn't stop at the big picture by a long chalk: 'What stance do I take in public?' We run an independent family business. This means we can say 'no' – to greenwashing, to short-term thinking. And 'yes' – to a clear stance, social commitment and ambitious sustainability goals. For me, that is the most beautiful form of freedom: being allowed to create – with a sense of responsibility.

Does this also require more cooperation across party and competitive boundaries and how could this lead to a 'miracle of change'?

Definitely. If we all only think in our silos – politically, economically, societally – change will not happen. We need alliances at eye level, even between supposed competitors. If we work together on solutions instead of only on market shares, a 'miracle of change' can actually occur.

At Börlind, we believe in collaboration: we work with research institutions, start-ups – and sometimes also with companies from the industry. Because real change is not an ego trip, but teamwork.

Closing statement:

'Responsibility is not a trend, but our duty. When business, politics and society have the courage to think outside the box together, not only change – but a real future is created.'

BRADLEY MUNDT

Founder & CEO PLAN-B NET ZERO ENERGY

Trust, responsibility, change – A new look at sustainable business

Trust in politics and business is not a given. It doesn't come from big promises, but from comprehensible decisions, reliability and taking a clear position. As an entrepreneur in the renewable energy sector, I experience time and again how sceptical many people have become about political and economic institutions, and often rightly so. Too many strategies stay on paper: too few lead to real change.

How can we change that?

For me, the key is a combination of transparency and consistency. Companies need to clearly communicate what they are doing, but also prove that they are actually doing it. Trust arises when we are reliable in the long term and don't buckle at the first difficulty. In the energy industry in particular, we often see political and economic knee-jerk reactions that hinder sustainable solutions. Instead of unsettling markets with changing subsidies and contradictory regulations, we need a stable framework that enables innovations and attracts investment.

Freedom and responsibility – no contradiction

Many see climate protection as having to make sacrifices. Less CO_2, less resource consumption, less growth. I think that's a mistake. Freedom does not mean having as much of something as possible, but making the right decisions.

At PLAN-B NET ZERO, we think in terms of abundance rather than sacrifice:

- The more clean energy, the more environmental protection
- The more renewable energies, the less CO_2
- The more usage, the more sustainability

For us, climate protection is not a restriction, but part of sustainable consumption. We believe that access to renewable energy should not be more expensive or more complicated than fossil alternatives. That is why we develop business models that are not only ecologically meaningful, but also economically attractive.

Collaboration is needed as the key to real change

The great challenges of our time cannot be solved by individual measures or individual players. Those who really want to change something must think beyond company and party boundaries. The energy transition will only succeed if politics, business and society pull together. I am convinced that we need more cooperation, not less. Competitiveness and cooperation are not mutually exclusive. We see this every day in our growth: every company that we integrate into our group brings expertise, networks and innovations with it. This creates a dynamic that could never be achieved with individual measures. Change does not come by itself. But we can actively shape it: with smart decisions, economic foresight and a stance that not only points out problems, but also enables solutions.

DR. CHRISTOPH PLOSS

MdB (CDU)

What strategies or concepts could be used to strengthen trust in government and corporate structures?

How do you personally see the relationship between individual freedom and 'taking responsibility for society oneself' and how do you put this into practice?

Does this also require more cooperation across party and competitive boundaries and how could this lead to a 'miracle of change'?

After months of constant bickering in the final phase of the so-called traffic light coalition, its failure was a great relief for most people. However, the publicly displayed behaviour of the coalition partners, taken to extremes by the undignified manner in which Olaf Scholz dismissed his finance minister, has greatly undermined confidence in the reliability and seriousness of the actors involved and in our community as a whole, – trust that had already been considerably damaged after projects such as the heating law, an unconstitutional federal budget and the attempt to enforce an obviously partisan electoral law.

The upcoming new elections offer the opportunity to win back this trust. To achieve this, we need a cross-party policy that focuses less on ideological cultural battles over annual gender changes and more on issues such as the preservation of jobs, affordable energy, personal responsibility and the principle of performance, a functioning infrastructure and the utilisation of future opportunities instead of technological scepticism and doomsday scenarios. Citizens must once again be able to trust that our state will first and foremost fulfil its most important core tasks: protecting its citizens and organising an efficient administration system.

It is crucial that our state counteracts the disastrous impression that it can no longer protect its borders. We must consistently combat illegal migration through effective border controls. This is the only way to achieve societal acceptance regarding the necessary recruitment of skilled labour. In view of the Russian attack on Ukraine, it is obvious that we must also further strengthen our military capabilities.

Social stability and security must also be better guaranteed again. The policy of the past years has mainly harmed workers and low earners. Whereas for a long time a well-paid job in industry used to be enough to support an entire family, this is often no longer possible today due to taxes, levies and inflation. The average income of an employee in Germany last year was €3,540 gross per month. Above all, the broad mass of average earners must not be crushed by taxes and levies, but must also be able to build up assets again and provide for their own future.

Last but not least, we need to revitalise our administrative structures. In an industrialised country, individual infrastructure projects such as the Köhlbrand Bridge in the Port of Hamburg cannot be allowed to take decades. Faster planning and construction, for example by restricting the options for environmental associations close to the Greens to take legal action, as well as faster digitalisation of the administration system, must be at the top of the agenda for a new federal government.

In short: to regain trust in the state and in politics, a new promise of prosperity for citizens is needed. Politics will have to be measured by its fulfilment.

INTERVIEW

VIKTORIA RENNER

Co-Founder & Content Strategist OZMOZE

What strategies or concepts could be used to strengthen trust in government and corporate structures?

Trust is created through transparency, approachability and consistent action. In a digital world, people expect straightforward communication and transparent decisions. Companies and governments therefore need to become more open – through interactive formats in which they ask themselves real questions, through a clear communication of values and through the courage to admit mistakes. Social media in particular make it possible to have dialogue at eye level and to create a sense of closeness. A brand or institution that only expresses itself in PR language will not be heard.

Another key is community-driven participation: citizens and employees should be actively involved in decision-making processes – be it through open innovation, co-creation or digital citizens' councils. Trust grows when people feel taken seriously and see that their views have an impact. This also includes using comprehensible language. Political and economic actors tend to get lost in complex formulations or technical jargon. But if you want to build trust, you have to communicate comprehensibly – in a clear and straightforward manner.

Reliability is also crucial. Trust is not created through making announcements, but through consistently fulfilling promises. It is precisely in times of crisis that it becomes clear how resilient trust in institutions really is. In difficult times, companies and governments must not only react, but proactively offer guidance. Honesty counts more than perfection: people are more likely to trust an institution that admits mistakes and learns from them than one that presents itself as infallible.

How do you personally see the relationship between individual freedom and 'taking responsibility for society oneself' and how do you put this into practice?

Freedom and responsibility are not opposites, but are mutually dependent. Real freedom does not mean acting only for one's own benefit, but also taking responsibility for the collective responsibility for the discourse that arises. We all have a voice – the question is how

we use it. Responsibility begins when we stop just watching from the sidelines. Individually, I practise this by consciously engaging in discourse, sharing knowledge and campaigning for value-orientated, progressive brand communication. Brands cannot ignore societal developments – they have long been part of them. It's not enough to just be a market leader: you also have to be a cultural leader. Companies that take responsibility set standards and inspire others to do the same.

Does this also require more cooperation across party and competitive boundaries and how could this lead to a 'miracle of change'?

Yes, absolutely. In a world that seems increasingly fragmented, we need cooperation rather than competition. Old thought patterns need to be broken, especially in politics and business: brands can shape cultural trends together instead of fighting for a market share in isolation. Parties could pull together on key future issues instead of getting lost in short-term power games.

'Miracles of change' occur when unexpected collaborations create new narratives. We are already seeing this in areas such as open source, where competitors cooperate to drive innovation. Or in cross-industry sustainability initiatives, in which companies work together on solutions instead of getting lost in individual measures.

But we also need a new narrative of change: we have to move away from the idea that progress is always the result of individual heroes. In truth, it is networks, alliances and interdisciplinary teams that make the major changes of our time possible. Collaboration does not mean giving up your own identity, but strengthening it through exchange.

When we begin to understand trust as a communal good one that must be nurtured, protected and actively strengthened – then real change can occur.

A society that sees itself as a team can achieve great things.

CATARINA DOS SANTOS

MdB (CDU)

What strategies or concepts could be used to strengthen trust in government and corporate structures?

For me, trust arises and remains when promises are made and then kept. I am experiencing more and more that people no longer really believe those promises. They have the feeling that government structures do not take their concerns and needs seriously enough. In comparison: I have had the most interesting exchanges with companies in which there is great trust between the management and the employees. They have managed to exemplify their entrepreneurial motivation and value construction, develop them and actively shape them together with the employees. These businesses, often old family businesses, are usually also very successful. Of course, both only work if institutions are given the space, or create it for themselves – also in order to ultimately critically scrutinise their own structure. It is precisely the latter that we should transfer to government structures, because strengthening trust is one of the core tasks in political operations.

How do you personally see the relationship between individual freedom and 'taking responsibility for society oneself' and how do you put this into practice?

The individual freedom of all citizens forms the foundation of our society, which is essential for our prosperity, individual growth and progress. We as humans need this freedom in order to be able to develop. However, for me, freedom is also the possibility of actively shaping communities. Human nature encompasses a need to help others, which for many is expressed through voluntary work. Every day, people in Germany engage in voluntary work and as helpers for their fellow human beings. Personal responsibility and a public spirit go together, because we all hold a compass of responsibility in our hands, whose arrow always points towards our society. Personally, as a member of the Bundestag, I am focused on political education, for example through information work in social media and dialogue.

Does this also require more cooperation across party and competitive boundaries and how could this lead to a 'miracle of change'?

The ability to compromise and the willingness to cooperate are the essence of successful action in politics. Different values between parties can make it difficult to reconcile political interests – it is therefore all the more important to seize opportunities here too and utilise the possible potential for cooperation.

Therefore, parties or political groups not only need to work together, but also to involve business and society. We can achieve change if we stick together. That sounds like a very idealistic statement, but for me it comes to life in those places where I am already seeing that it can work. It's not about getting as much of your own way as possible, but about struggling hard to find the best possible solution and then getting behind a compromise that everyone can live with. Maybe we have to learn to reach compromises again. Let's be bolder.

VALENTIN STALF

Co-Founder & CEO N26

What strategies or concepts could be used to strengthen trust in government and corporate structures?

I am convinced that Germany needs a strategy in order to keep up with the global competition for digital prosperity and technological leadership. Innovations are the key to this. Innovative digital companies are particularly dependent on the influx of skilled labour from abroad. The influx of highly qualifiedpeople must therefore be made much easier – among other things, through simpler and faster visa procedures.

At the same time, international workers have high expectations of Germany, particularly with regard to the level of digitalisation in public administration. The expertise has long been in the country. Progress through digitalisation would not only be an advantage geographically: Germany would also make massive cost savings.

In addition, the incentives for top employees must be improved, for example through employee participation. Gains from Employee Stock Ownership Plans (ESOPs) should, as in the USA or France, not be taxed as income but as capital gains and therefore at a lower rate. In addition, tax reductions should be introduced for top foreign executives in Germany.

How do you personally see the relationship between individual freedom and 'taking responsibility for society oneself' and how do you put this into practice?

For myself, as a founder and entrepreneur, individual freedom is an extremely precious asset. N26 is the result of creative freedom. Of course, as a bank, we have many regulatory requirements to fulfil. Yet in this regulatory system, there is a lot of freedom to radically rethink things and modernise the banking business. This is what motivates me every day to develop our products and make N26 a bank that our customers love. N26 is more than just a successful digital bank. N26 is designed to make it easier for people to access financial services. Banking should not prevent people from achieving their goals, but instead enable

and accelerate their achievement. In particular in the area of pension provisions, access to fair and transparent conditions for savings plans, as well as in day-to-day banking, N26 is fulfilling a huge societal responsibility. Our products enable easy digital access to banking products that were previously often opaque, expensive and only accessible to a select group of customers. In this way, we make an enormous contribution to a more efficient lifestyle that enables each individual, regardless of their wealth, to make the most of their financial situation and thereby maximise their personal impact. This makes society as a whole more productive and efficient.

Does this also require more cooperation across party and competitive boundaries and how could this lead to a 'miracle of change'?

In a time that we rightly describe as disruptive in societal, political and technological terms, we not only need better cooperation between business and politics, but above all a different attitude to new technologies. In the past, innovations were too often seen as risks that first had to be thoroughly regulated before they could unfold. We have to overcome this attitude if we want to utilise the opportunities that new technologies offer us.

In addition to this positive attitude towards innovation, there needs to be a targeted pursuit of size and speed. Tesla, Amazon and Google have become global tech giants primarily because they have been able to grow very quickly. The desire to create something as big as possible as quickly as possible is part of American culture. In Europe, this culture is not particularly pronounced. The opportunities for challenger companies would be even greater in Europe if policymakers as a whole were to commit to innovation-friendly framework conditions. In this way, the chance of a digital economic miracle in Europe could at least be preserved.

INTERVIEW

JENS TEUTRINE

MdB a. D. (FDP)

What strategies or concepts could be used to strengthen trust in government and corporate structures?

It shows great disrespect if you consistently signal to people in a paternalistic way that they have no idea how to run their own lives and that you know everything better yourself. Out of such a culture of mistrust, of bossing around, suspicious bureaucratisation and state nannying, a spiral of mistrust develops instead of trust. I am convinced that if we want to restore trust in government structures, governments must first and foremost trust people again. That the best ideas do not come from the state, politicians and authorities, but from the creative power of many individuals. If we strengthen personal responsibility instead of allowing politicians to presume to be know-it-alls, then this will also strengthen trust in institutions again. Because every time a politician presumes to know something better and subsequently to regulate, bureaucratise and subsidise it, but in reality it goes wrong, trust naturally also declines. So if we strengthen people's belief in themselves again, we will also strengthen mutual trust and confidence.

How do you personally see the relationship between individual freedom and 'taking responsibility for society oneself' and how do you put this into practice?

Trust in individual freedom strengthens individuals' willingness to take responsibility for society instead of delegating all responsibility to the state. For example, for jobs and value creation as a business owner, in care work in your own family or through social initiatives. One example here is hospice work in Germany, which is supported in particular by voluntary structures. My political involvement began with the Young Liberals, where

we not only enable young people, irrespective of their backgrounds and parental homes, to engage in political participation but also provide education and create a place where they can develop further. I am also involved in personal mentoring partnerships for young people who are struggling with hurdles and challenges. This is about exchange, responsiveness, dialogue and personal support.

Does this also require more cooperation across party and competitive boundaries and how could this lead to a 'miracle of change'?

Democracy thrives on competition between the best ideas. There is no lack of cooperation in the classic sense, but rather a lack of respect for other opinions. Our discussions are often characterised by deliberate misunderstanding, distorted images and an indignant 'shitstorm' culture that is more about perceived morality than factual debate.

A cultural change is needed here. I am concerned that in the country of the Enlightenment, more and more people no longer dare to speak their minds freely. This weakens the competition between the best ideas and is a step backwards for civilisation that must be reversed.

CAROLIN VOGT

Deputy Chairwoman VOLT – Germany

What strategies or concepts could be used to strengthen trust in government and corporate structures?

In my opinion, trust in the state and democracy is created through tangible results that improve people's everyday lives. That is why Volt is focusing on massive investments in infrastructure that concretely show what the state can achieve: green cities with clean air, safer cycle paths and places for people to meet, stable, fast internet as well as a digital, efficient citizen service system. One example is the creation of a digital administration system based on the Estonian model, which simplifies administrative procedures and saves time. Transparency is crucial in the corporate sector: I think it is important that companies that act sustainably and fairly are fiscally incentivised, while consistently combatting tax evasion. Such visible results – whether in the public sphere or in economic structures – create trust and show people that change is happening for their benefit.

How do you personally see the relationship between individual freedom and 'taking responsibility for society oneself' and how do you put this into practice?

For me, freedom and responsibility are not opposites, but are mutually dependent. Freedom gives us the opportunity to make decisions; responsibility means shaping those decisions in such a way that they benefit society. Trust in democracy arises when people see that their responsibility has a visible effect – be it climate-friendly mobility, sustainable urban planning or barrier-free digital services. I hope that responsibility will not be seen as a burden, but as an opportunity to shape a better future together. Volt is committed to creating these framework conditions: for example, by investing in tangible and visible changes such as digital citizen services or the promotion of urban green spaces and cycle paths. This way, citizens can directly experience how their commitment and trust in the state lead to real improvements.

Does this also require more cooperation across party and competitive boundaries and how could this lead to a 'miracle of change'?

Absolutely. I believe that real change happens when we work together across political and national boundaries to create visible results for people. Because only with European solutions can we overcome the challenges of our time, first and foremost the climate crisis. Volt is adapting the best concepts from all over Europe – such as Estonia's digital administration system and Denmark's sustainable urban planning – and translating them to the German context. Such tangible, positive examples like green cities, better air, safe cycle paths or a digital citizen service system create trust and show that progress is possible.

I believe that cross-party cooperation is the key to a miracle of change. A 'coalition of the willing' that tackles progressive issues such as climate protection, infrastructure and social justice together can show people that politics delivers results. By investing in a liveable infrastructure – be it through sustainable mobility or modern digital services – we are making change tangible and experiential.

EMILY VONTZ

MdB a. D. (SPD)

What strategies or concepts could be used to strengthen trust in government and corporate structures?

How do you personally see the relationship between individual freedom and 'taking responsibility for society oneself' and how do you put this into practice?

Does this also require more cooperation across party and competitive boundaries and how could this lead to a 'miracle of change'?

'How come it's always the same faces in politics, no matter what they've already done?' A visitor to the Bundestag asked me this question a few weeks ago. Only a few minutes later, another guest asked: 'Why do politicians put each other down and get so personal? Shouldn't the parties work more closely together, instead of always being against each other?'

Both questions have occupied me a great deal since then, because they reflect the impression of many citizens that politicians are divided and self-centred, and that their actions are incomprehensible. An impression that is far removed from what politics should actually be – a joint endeavour to find solutions to the challenges of our time.

During my time as a member of the Bundestag, I got to know many colleagues from different parties. People who give everything for their mandate and often give up a lot to fulfil their own aspirations and the expectations of the party and society. And yet a general impression of conflict, stagnation and self-interest often remains. How come?

Our democracy is under pressure. The major crises of our time – be it climate change, the transformation of our economy or social challenges – require solutions that are complex and take time. Populists capitalise on these uncertainties, project supposedly simple answers and ultimately provoke societal division. We as a society have a key responsibility in this situation. For a vibrant democracy, it is essential that citizens not just complain about politics, but instead get actively involved – be it in associations, initiatives or elections. Politics can only improve if we endeavour to understand each other. Politicians are people who make mistakes, are under pressure and often have to make difficult judgements. In the spirit of a new togetherness, we need more clemency and less sweeping criticism.

Yet the central question remains: How can politics regain trust? I am convinced: A new political style is needed that is characterised by honesty, courage and cooperation. That seeks dialogue with citizens at eye level and could be characterised by the following approaches, for example:

1. **Simple language and clear communication** – politics must be understandable across all platforms. Complex decisions must be explained in such a way that they are comprehensible – without technical jargon and without catchphrases. This would also help young people to better understand politics. It is therefore good that the forms of political communication are slowly changing and that politics is now also taking place on social media.

2. **Normalising weakness:** politics needs more humanity. Nobody has all the answers, and it's okay to admit that. It creates trust when you say, openly: 'I honestly don't know right now, but I'll take your concerns seriously and address them.' In this context, more honesty also means admitting mistakes publicly and possibly facing the consequences.

3. **Non-partisan action** – perhaps a 'miracle of change' The challenges of our time require solutions that transcend party and ideological boundaries. Citizens rightly complain that debates often get bogged down in party politics. Instead, solutions should be worked on constructively and collaboratively. When politicians pull together across party lines, this can lead to a real 'miracle of change'.

4. **More citizen participation** – Citizens must be encouraged to become more involved and participate more. Low-threshold participation opportunities, for example in the form of citizens' councils or local dialogue formats, can strengthen trust in political institutions and enable decisions to be made jointly rather than being imposed from above.

5. **Less staging, more real encounters** – Instead of holding the tenth typical politician's meeting with a long welcoming speech, quickly taking a photo for social media and then rushing straight to the next appointment, more time should be taken for real conversations. A political style that is committed to listening, asking questions and taking people seriously would be credible proof that politicians are acting in the service of society and not for personal gain. Trust does not develop overnight. A change is needed that is characterised by more honesty, courage and cooperation. A new understanding that politics and society bear joint responsibility and can only achieve such a 'miracle of change' together.

INTERVIEW

AMELIE M. WEBER

Freelance Journalist

What strategies or concepts could be used to strengthen trust in government and corporate structures?

Many young people do not feel sufficiently heard or taken seriously by political and economic institutions. Trust arises when participation and transparency come into focus. It is not enough just to consider young people as a target group – their perspectives must be actively included.

Authenticity is indispensable. The younger generation in particular is quick to recognise when greenwashing is being practised or promises are not being kept. Concrete, verifiable measures are required instead of symbolic gestures. Admitting mistakes and communicating clearly creates respect and shows a sense of responsibility.

At the same time, education is key to counteracting disinformation. The better political and economic processes are understood, the better a sound basis for commitment and trust is created.

How do you personally see the relationship between individual freedom and 'taking responsibility for society oneself' and how do you put this into practice?

It's about making conscious decisions that serve both your own self-realisation and the common good. This can be seen, for example, in dealing with climate protection. Many are giving up flights, eating more sustainably or getting involved in politics. Not out of compulsion, but out of the conviction that one's own actions will have an impact on the future. This attitude can be put into practice in everyday life: through conscious consumer behaviour, commitment to local initiatives or by using your own voice – for example on social media. Responsibility is thereby not experienced as a restriction, but as an opportunity to actively help shape the world.

Does this also require more cooperation across party and competitive boundaries and how could this lead to a 'miracle of change'?

The great challenges of our time require new forms of cooperation. Individual parties, companies and institutions are reaching their limits. Cooperation and exchange are therefore necessary instead of competition.

A 'miracle of change' becomes possible when different players pursue a common goal. This requires the courage to allow new approaches, to share power and to listen – particularly also to young people's views, which often offer unconventional but forward-looking solutions.

Hope plays a decisive role here. It is not naïve, but the driving force for change. Every change begins with hope – it is what connects people, generations and ideas.

WOLF CHRISTIAN WEIMER

Founder & CEO ARTICLY

What strategies or concepts could be used to strengthen trust in government and corporate structures?

Trust is created through transparency, participation and a shared vision – principles that apply both in politics and in companies. People don't just want to be informed, they also want to be involved. This means making decisions comprehensible, enabling participation and formulating a common goal.

Especially in times of growing uncertainty, we need a culture of strong leadership and open dialogue at the same time. When both governments and companies communicate with citizens and stakeholders at eye level, this not only creates trust – but also a shared responsibility for the future.

How do you personally see the relationship between individual freedom and 'taking responsibility for society oneself' and how do you put this into practice?

Freedom is a core value for me – and that's exactly why I personally decided in favour of self-employment. As an entrepreneur, one thing is certain: taking responsibility is not an option, but a basic requirement. This applies not only to large companies, but also to small structures. Even in a start-up, every decision can (positively) influence employees, partners and society as a whole.

Does this also require more cooperation across party and competitive boundaries and how could this lead to a 'miracle of change'?

Competition stimulates business. Exchange with competitors also stimulates the market. 'Coopetition' is the keyword here. In our work, we regularly experience how valuable a fair exchange with competitors is. Competition does not mean isolating oneself – on the contrary: in the start-up world in particular, we benefit from sharing knowledge and learning from each other.

HAMZA R. WÖRDEMANN

CEO Soziale Dienste und Jugendhilfe GmbH

What strategies or concepts could be used to strengthen trust in government and corporate structures?

While trust in government and corporate structures has declined among many older people, young people have a more appropriate level of trust. Less high expectations reduce potential disappointments. They are generally satisfied with the advantages of living in a democratic, law-governed community. The strategy of government structures should consist of continuing to act in a fair and citizen-centred manner on the one hand and, on the other, of fostering public understanding for the fact that government action, too, cannot be completely free from mistakes.

This is more difficult when it comes to trust in corporate structures. Because most young people have never lived in a time where there was long-term, sometimes lifelong, commitment to an employer, they are understandably less loyal and have little emotional attachment. The recommended strategy is to strengthen opportunities to shape things, employee equity participation, a great deal of transparency and longer-term securities, which are more effective than short-term, artificial personnel marketing instruments that are thrown overboard in difficult times without any significant warning. Young people are bright enough to recognise true loyalty and only then can they build a sustainable bond.

How do you personally see the relationship between individual freedom and 'taking responsibility for society oneself' and how do you put this into practice?

The pursuit of individual freedom and the willingness to take responsibility for society do not represent a contradiction. 'Individual freedom' has nothing to do with the desire to achieve self-realisation alone or outside a community. It is simply a matter of choosing your own community and being able to live out your own individuality there as freely as possible. But increasing individualisation means that young people no longer want to simply do 'something or other' for

the community and subordinate the shaping of their own involvement to the rules there. They strive for maximum freedom of choice and options to shape their involvement. This is why 'freer' engagement models such as sponsorship programmes, where time can be freely allocated, are still in high demand today. The strategy should be to make access to taking responsibility 'barrier-free' and also to promote more complex mental reward systems (a human 'thank you' instead of a social media 'like').

Does this also require more cooperation across party and competitive boundaries and how could this lead to a 'miracle of change'?

The willingness to take personal responsibility for the community depends on how positively that community is perceived. Extremists try to portray 'the state' and democracy as negative and 'doomed' and the individual as helpless. One strategy to protect democracy is to promote cooperation beyond party and competitive boundaries. However, this cooperation must be organised in such a way that diversity and contradictions can be tolerated and also remain visible. The kind of polarisation that we experienced during the coronavirus pandemic must be avoided.

ULRICH REINHARDT

SHAPING GERMANY'S FUTURE

STRENGTHENING TRUST
SHARING RESPONSIBILITY
ENGAGING IN COOPERATION

ULRICH REINHARDT

SO GELINGT DEUTSCHLANDS ZUKUNFT

VERTRAUEN STÄRKEN
VERANTWORTUNG TEILEN
KOOPERATION LEBEN

Die Deutsche Bibliothek – CIP Einheitsaufnahme:

So gelingt Deutschlands Zukunft
Vertrauen stärken
Verantwortung teilen
Kooperation leben

CH. GOETZ VERLAG, Tegernsee 2025
ISBN 978-3-947140-14-5

Prof. Dr. Ulrich Reinhardt,
Stiftung für Zukunftsfragen – Eine Initiative von BAT,
in Kooperation mit der WEIMER MEDIA GROUP GmbH

Unter Mitarbeit von Ayaan Güls und Angela Reinhardt

Gestaltung: Matthias Erhardt, WEIMER MEDIA GROUP GmbH
Druck und Bindung: Westermann Druck Zwickau GmbH

Printed in Germany

ULRICH REINHARDT

SO GELINGT DEUTSCHLANDS ZUKUNFT

VERTRAUEN STÄRKEN
VERANTWORTUNG TEILEN
KOOPERATION LEBEN

LUDWIG ERHARD GIPFEL
TEGERNSEE SUMMIT

Stiftung für Zukunftsfragen
Eine Initiative von BAT

CH. GOETZ VERLAG

INHALT

INHALT

VORWORT

USMAN ZAHUR

Sprecher der Geschäftsführung, BAT Germany

In einer Zeit, in der Deutschland vor vielfältigen Herausforderungen steht – sei es der demografische Wandel, die digitale Transformation oder die Notwendigkeit nachhaltigen Wirtschaftens –, wird deutlich, dass die Gestaltung unserer Zukunft eine gemeinsame Aufgabe ist. Es bedarf eines kollektiven Ansatzes, bei dem Verantwortung geteilt, Vertrauen gestärkt und Kooperation gelebt wird.

Die BAT Stiftung für Zukunftsfragen hat es sich zur Aufgabe gemacht, einen Beitrag zur Zukunftsfähigkeit unserer Gesellschaft zu leisten. Durch die Initiierung wissenschaftlicher Auseinandersetzungen mit Zukunftsfragen und die Entwicklung nachhaltiger Lösungsansätze widmet sie sich verantwortungsbewusst den kommenden Herausforderungen. Ihr Leitgedanke: „Die Welt im Wandel – der Mensch im Mittelpunkt".

Für BAT Germany ist gesellschaftliches Engagement seit jeher ein integraler Bestandteil unserer Unternehmensphilosophie. Die BAT Stiftung für Zukunftsfragen und Meilensteine wie dieses Buch untermauern unser Bestreben, Verantwortung zu übernehmen und positive Impulse für die Gesellschaft zu setzen. Es ist unser Ziel, eine bessere Zukunft, A Better Tomorrow™, aufzubauen.

Das vorliegende Buch ist in diesem Kontext ein bedeutender Beitrag. Es bietet eine umfassende Analyse der aktuellen gesellschaftlichen Strömungen und zeigt auf, wie durch gemeinschaftliches Handeln positive Veränderungen herbeigeführt werden können. Die in diesem Werk präsentierten Perspektiven und Lösungsansätze laden dazu ein, in den Dialog zu treten, über den eigenen Tellerrand hinauszublicken und aktiv an der Gestaltung unserer gemeinsamen Zukunft mitzuwirken.

Der Wissenschaftliche Leiter der Stiftung, Professor Dr. Ulrich Reinhardt, formuliert es wie folgt: „Mit Zuversicht blicken wir nach vorn und erkennen die vielen Chancen, die vor uns liegen. Lassen Sie uns gemeinsam an einer Zukunft arbeiten, in der Vertrauen, Verantwortung und Zusammenarbeit nicht nur Schlagworte sind, sondern gelebte Realität. Die Grundlagen dafür sind gelegt – nun liegt es an uns allen, sie mit Leben zu füllen und weiterzuentwickeln." Möge dieses Buch als Inspirationsquelle dienen und dazu beitragen, den Dialog über Deutschlands Zukunft konstruktiv voranzutreiben. Es lädt uns alle ein, Verantwortung zu teilen, Vertrauen zu stärken und Kooperation zu leben – für ein zukunftsfähiges Deutschland.

Usman Zahur

VORWORT

CHRISTIANE GOETZ-WEIMER, DR. WOLFRAM WEIMER

Verleger der WEIMER MEDIA GROUP

„The time is out of joint" ist ein Literaturzitat aus Shakespeares weltberühmtem Theaterstück „Hamlet" (1623), das uns in deutscher Sprache und in leicht abgewandelter Form als **„Die Welt ist aus den Fugen geraten"** überliefert ist.

Nicht nur Frank-Walter Steinmeier, als er noch Außenminister war, sondern auch Angela Merkel, als sie Bundeskanzlerin war, griffen in ihren Reden gerne auf dieses geflügelte Wort zurück, um die Dringlichkeit der Weltlage dramatisch, um nicht zu sagen theatralisch zu unterstreichen.

Und auch der amtierende Bundeskanzler Friedrich Merz könnte diesen Satz ohne Weiteres in seine Reden einbauen. Er würde es genau auf den Punkt bringen, denn die globalen Krisenherde sind auch 2025 noch zahlreich – von der Ukraine über den Nahen Osten bis nach China sind die Erschütterungen, die von ihnen ausgehen, weltweit zu spüren, nicht zuletzt auch in Deutschland, das mühsam versucht, seine Flanken zu sichern.

Doch wenn, wie William Butler Yeats in **„The Second Coming"** schreibt, **„alles fällt, entgleitet"** und **„keine Mitte hält"** („Things fall apart; the centre cannot hold"), scheint alles Bemühen vergeblich. Selbst auf vermeintlich alte Verbündete jenseits des Atlantiks scheint kein Verlass mehr zu sein, wenn sie Deutschland vor wirtschaftliche Hürden und politische Herausforderungen stellen, die ihresgleichen suchen. Bedenkt man dann noch die bedrohliche Zunahme von Extremen auf beiden Seiten des politischen Spektrums und den immer erdrückender werdenden Klimawandel, scheint der Blick in die Zukunft unseres Landes wenig ermutigend. Die Diagnose ist erschreckend ernüchternd, die Symptome sind unübersehbar: Deutschland ist von einer gefährlichen Malaise befallen, wie man sie sonst nur als Fin-de-siècle-Stimmung kennt.

Es sind schwierige Zeiten, und die Frage, wo Deutschland in diesen turbulenten Tagen steht, ist ebenso berechtigt wie wichtig. Wie kann sich Deutschland in dieser sich schnell verändernden Welt neu positionieren, um seine Zukunft zu sichern? Vor allem aber: Mit welchen Instrumenten kann Deutschland verhindern, vom Strom der Zeit und der Geschichte mitgerissen zu werden und Opfer statt Gestalter der eigenen Zukunft zu sein? Das sind keine einfachen Fragen, aber sie verlangen danach, beantwortet zu werden, und zwar mit mutigen Lösungen. Spätestens das Erscheinen des ersten viel beachteten Bandes dieser Buchreihe, „German Mut statt German Angst" (2023), zeigte auf, dass die Kehrseite der Angst der Mut ist. Und die größte Form des Mutes ist die überwundene Verzweiflung. Das ist der Mut wahrer Helden. Diesen Mut braucht man zum Handeln, aber auch zum Denken.

So haben wir uns auch in diesem Jahr wieder auf Spurensuche begeben, zusammen mit 20 Autoren aus verschiedenen gesellschaftlich relevanten Bereichen. Über alle Unterschiede hinweg verbindet sie ihr junges Alter und vor allem die Bereitschaft, uns mutige Antworten auf unsere Fragen zu liefern. Wer könnte schließlich besser als die Jugend, der Hoffnungsträger der Zukunft, den notwendigen Mut aufbringen, Antworten auf die Fragen zu geben, die uns bewegen?

Drei zentrale Stichworte, welche auch im Titel der hiesigen dritten Edition enthalten sind, dienten unseren Autoren als Orientierungshilfe, um angesichts der aktuellen Situation die Voraussetzungen für einen nachhaltigen, positiven Wandel zu erörtern. Auch wenn das Verhältnis zwischen unseren Begriffen eher als ein zirkuläres und wechselseitiges denn als ein lineares zu verstehen ist, wie Professor Ulrich Reinhardt zu Recht anführt, so scheint doch der Begriff des Vertrauens am Anfang zu stehen. Also Vertrauen als Grundlage, denn ohne Vertrauen kann eine Gesellschaft nicht funktionieren, ohne Vertrauen verliert sie ihren

VORWORT

Zusammenhalt. Vertrauen hat, wie Francis Fukuyama in seinem Werk „Trust: The Social Virtues and the Creation of Prosperity" (1995) feststellt, einen maßgeblichen Einfluss auf den wirtschaftlichen und sozialen Erfolg eines Landes. Es stellt sich daher die Frage, wie Vertrauen als das Fundament unserer Gesellschaft gestärkt werden kann. Aber Vertrauen allein reicht nicht aus, um etwas zu bewegen. Es braucht auch den Mut, Verantwortung zu übernehmen: Ein weises Volk vertraut und verlässt sich auf seine Eliten, womit nicht eine spezielle Gesellschaftsklasse gemeint ist, sondern all jene, die bereit sind, Verantwortung für andere zu übernehmen und etwas zu riskieren, denn Denken und Handeln sind nie ohne Risiko. Hier zeigt sich einmal mehr die von Professor Reinhardt hervorgehobene Wechselseitigkeit der von uns verwendeten Begriffe. Es geht also darum, das Verhältnis zwischen der Freiheit des Einzelnen und der Bereitschaft, Verantwortung für die Gesellschaft zu übernehmen, zu eruieren. Nicht zuletzt muss der Begriff der Kooperation zwischen zivilgesellschaftlichen Akteuren und Politik in den Mittelpunkt gestellt werden, denn Denken ohne Handeln führt zu nichts und Handeln ohne Denken ist nur Lärm. Hier ergänzen sich also Gesellschaft und Politik in ihren natürlichen Funktionen zu einer gemeinsamen und starken Zugkraft, die in der Lage ist, positive Veränderungen herbeizuführen.

Anders als die Vergangenheit ist die Zukunft noch nicht geschrieben. Die Zukunft wird in diesem Augenblick gestaltet. Mit Vertrauen, Verantwortung und Kooperation als Basis unseres Handelns und Denkens wird diese Zukunft, wie sie unsere jungen Autoren beschreiben, gelingen.

Wir wünschen Ihnen eine spannende, ermutigende und zukunftsweisende Lektüre.

Ihre Christiane Goetz-Weimer und Dr. Wolfram Weimer

VORWORT

ULRICH REINHARDT

Wissenschaftlicher Leiter der "Stiftung für Zukunftsfragen – Eine Initiative von BAT"

In einer Welt, die sich immer schneller verändert und mit Herausforderungen wie sozialer und politischer Spaltung, demografischem Wandel, Klimakrise, Migration und globalen Konflikten konfrontiert ist, suchen viele Bürger zunehmend nach Orientierung. Sie wollen Wege finden, um diese Probleme nachhaltig zu bewältigen. Dabei geht es nicht immer nur um individuelle Werte oder persönliche Lebensentwürfe. Viele sehnen sich vielmehr danach, gemeinsame Grundlagen zu entdecken, Vertrauen aufzubauen und gemeinsam mit anderen die Zukunft aktiv zu gestalten.

Notwendig ist hierfür eine Anpassung an neue Bedingungen und das Überdenken von alten Gewohnheiten. Jeder Bürger ist gefordert für sich selbst Antworten auf grundlegende Fragen zu finden: Welche Werte sind mir wichtig? Wie viel Verantwortung bin ich bereit zu übernehmen? Und wie sehe ich meine eigene Zukunft? Solche Fragen können inspirierend wirken und Innovation sowie persönliches Wachstum fördern. Doch sie können auch Ängste auslösen – etwa das Gefühl, überfordert oder isoliert zu sein. Notwendig sind daher Rahmenbedingungen, in denen sowohl individuelle Bedürfnisse als auch gemeinschaftliche Anforderungen in Einklang sind.

Dabei ist die Gesellschaft nicht nur wegweisender Akteur, sondern selbst in vielfältiger Weise von den sich wandelnden Strukturen und Entwicklungen betroffen. Seien es finanzielle und personelle Belastungen des Gesundheitssystems, Fachkräftemangel, Energiewende, Nachholbedarf in der Digitalisierung, Infrastrukturproblem, soziale und politische Polarisierung, Wohnungsnot oder Sicherheitsbedrohungen – in den unterschiedlichsten Bereichen zeigen sich Problematiken. Entsprechend müssen bisherige Konzepte überdacht und Finanzen umverteilt werden. Umso vielschichtiger die Herausforderungen sich dabei erweisen, desto mehr sind die staatlichen und privaten Institutionen auf den Zusammenhalt innerhalb der Gesellschaft angewiesen.

Damit die Neugestaltung der Gesellschaft gelingt, braucht es das Vertrauen der Bürger in die notwendigen Maßnahmen und sich ändernden Strukturen. Zudem ist auch ihre Bereitschaft gefragt, Verantwortung zu übernehmen und alle gesellschaftlichen Akteure als gleichberechtigte Partner in einer kooperierenden Zusammenarbeit zu betrachten – anstatt sie als Gegner oder Konkurrenten wahrzunehmen.

Die gute Nachricht: Die Voraussetzungen dafür sind bei der großen Mehrheit der Bürger bereits vorhanden. Denn trotz der Vielzahl an Krisen und Unsicherheiten, blickt die große Mehrheit der Bundesbürger (überraschend) optimistisch in die Zukunft – eine Haltung, die Mut macht und als Grundlage für gemeinsames Handeln dienen kann.

Überwiegt die Zuversicht?

Von je 100 Befragten stimmen der Aussage zu:
„Bei mir überwiegt die positive Einstellung zum Leben und ich blicke optimistisch in die Zukunft."

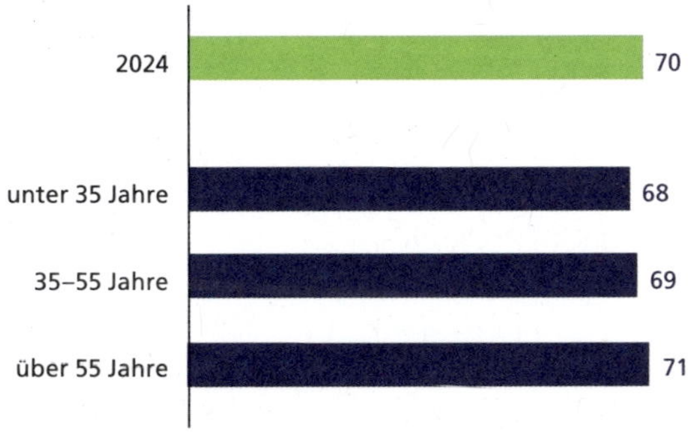

EINLEITUNG

So geben mehr als zwei Drittel der Bürger an, eine positive Einstellung zum Leben zu haben und zuversichtlich in die kommenden Jahre zu schauen. Dieser Wert zeigt, wie sehr die Bundesbürger – entgegen vielen Klischees – nicht ausschließlich das Negative sehen. Vielmehr erkennen sie zwar die Herausforderungen, konzentrieren sich jedoch auf die zuversichtlichen Entwicklungen und mutmachende Trends. Zwischen den Generationen lassen sich dabei kaum Unterschiede feststellen: Sowohl jüngere als auch ältere Bürger zeigen ähnliche Werte.

Optimismus kann als eine positive Lebenseinstellung charakterisiert werden, die durch die Überzeugung geprägt ist, dass sich die allgemeine Entwicklung langfristig zum Besseren wendet – unabhängig von den spezifischen Umständen oder Inhalten. Diese grundlegende Haltung wird maßgeblich durch eine Vielzahl von Faktoren beeinflusst, darunter familiäre und schulische Prägungen, finanzielle Ressourcen, stabile zwischenmenschliche Beziehungen, die öffentliche Stimmung sowie mediale Einflüsse. Eine zentrale Rolle spielt darüber hinaus eine hohe innere Vertrauensbereitschaft, die es Individuen ermöglicht, in unsicheren oder schwierigen Zeiten auf eine positive Zukunft zu hoffen.

Zahlreiche erfolgreiche und inspirierende Projekte tragen ebenfalls zur Förderung dieser optimistischen Perspektive bei. Fortschritte in Wissenschaft und Technologie, lokal umgesetzte Nachhaltigkeitsinitiativen oder innovative soziale Konzepte sind Beispiele für Entwicklungen, die Mut machen und eine aktive Beteiligung fördern. Diese Erfolge fungieren nicht nur als Motivation, sondern laden dazu ein, selbst Teil einer positiven Dynamik zu werden und zur Gestaltung einer besseren Zukunft beizutragen.

Im privaten Kontext trägt Optimismus maßgeblich zur Stärkung der psychischen und emotionalen Gesundheit bei, indem er ein Gefühl von Hoffnung und Zuversicht fördert. Diese positive Grundhaltung führt dazu, dass das Augenmerk stärker auf Chancen und Möglichkeiten gerichtet wird, während Hindernisse und Ablehnungen an Bedeutung verlieren.

EINLEITUNG

Insbesondere in alltäglichen Herausforderungen sowie in außergewöhnlichen Ereignissen oder Krisensituationen – wie etwa bei Krankheit, Konflikten, Verlusten oder Misserfolgen – erweist sich ein positives Denken als hilfreich. Es unterstützt nicht nur die Reduktion von Stress, sondern auch die Bewältigung von Rückschlägen, indem es die Konzentration auf Lösungsansätze und potenzielle Chancen lenkt.

Im gesellschaftlichen Kontext lassen sich vergleichbare Effekte feststellen. Optimismus trägt dazu bei, Widerstände zu überwinden, Herausforderungen anzunehmen und den Fokus weniger auf Ärgernisse, Missstände und Probleme zu richten. Stattdessen fördert er die aktive Mitgestaltung des gesellschaftlichen Lebens sowie ein zuversichtliches und unterstützendes Handeln. Dies umfasst eine Reduktion von Kritik, ein toleranteres Verhalten sowie eine stärkere Anerkennung und Förderung positiver Entwicklungen. Im zwischenmenschlichen Bereich erwarten sich die Bürger durch diese Haltung eine stärkere Gemeinschaft, einen intensiveren Zusammenhalt und eine Verringerung von egoistischem Verhalten. Optimismus überschreitet dabei die individuelle Ebene und entfaltet seine gesellschaftliche Bedeutung. Er wird nicht als Verleugnung von Problemen interpretiert, sondern als bewusste Entscheidung, den Blick auf Chancen und Möglichkeiten zu lenken. Durch diese Haltung werden soziale Bindungen und Interaktionen gestärkt, Motivation und Inspiration gefördert. Kurz gesagt: Optimismus wirkt ansteckend.

Im zweiten Teil der Publikation werden Interviews vorgestellt, die in Form dreier Fragestellungen mit 20 Persönlichkeiten aus Politik und Wirtschaft geführt wurden. Aus unterschiedlicher Perspektive und mit variabler Schwerpunktlegung äußern sie sich zu den Möglichkeiten der Vertrauensbildung in politische und ökonomische Strukturen, zum Verhältnis von individueller Freiheit und gesellschaftlicher Verantwortung sowie zur Notwenigkeit von Kooperation über Partikularinteressen hinaus. Sichtbar wir hierbei ein Kaleidoskop inspirierender Sichtweisen.

VERTRAUEN

In fast jeder gesellschaftlichen Debatte ist aktuell vom Vertrauen die Rede. Dabei werden jedoch selten die positiven Erwartungen ausgedrückt, die diesem Begriff innewohnen. Vielmehr geht es meistens um einen überall registrierten Vertrauensverlust, sei es nun gegenüber Parteien, Medien, Konzernen sowie allgemein gegenüber anderen Bürgern oder auch der Demokratie. Um dieser Entwicklung begegnen zu können, ist es zuerst einmal notwendig, Merkmale, Voraussetzungen und Formen des Vertrauens näher zu betrachten. So stellt sich die Frage, was es bedeutet zu vertrauen, was erforderlich ist, damit man jemandem Glauben schenkt, oder wann Vertrauen besonders wichtig ist. In der Folge können so Gründe für ein schwindendes Vertrauen ausgemacht werden.

Wortherkunft

Vertrauen ist ein Begriff weltanschaulichen und ethischen Denkens und drückt ein Verhältnis der Wechselseitigkeit aus. Das Wort leitet sich aus dem althochdeutschen Verb „gitrouwen" (auch „trauwen") ab. Der Ursprung liegt im indogermanischen Wortstamm „dreu-" und bedeutet in seiner historischen Auslegung „fest" oder „treu" in seinem Glauben und Hoffen. Im Griechischen steht dafür „pistis" (Glaube), im Lateinischen „fiducia" (Selbstvertrauen) oder „fides" (Treue). Im antiken und mittelalterlichen Gebrauch steht der Begriff im Spannungsfeld von Treue und Glauben (z. B. bei Demokrit, der fordert, nicht allen, sondern nur dem Bewährten zu vertrauen). Seit dem 13. Jahrhundert steht trauen auch für „ehelich verbinden." Aus dem geläufigen „hoffen", „glauben" des Althochdeutschen entwickelte sich dann im 16. Jahrhundert „vertrauen" in der Bedeutung des Zutrauens in Fähigkeiten von anderen, der Treue und Zuverlässigkeit. Dies spiegelt die Entwicklung vom Ausdruck des allgemeinen Hoffens zu einem spezifischeren zwischenmenschlichen Vertrauensbegriff wider. Seit Beginn der Neuzeit wird Vertrauen immer stärker zu einem Zutrauen in die eigenen

Fähigkeiten (Selbstvertrauen). Heute ist Vertrauen ein alltagssprachlicher Begriff, der alle Lebensbereiche durchdringt und in unterschiedlichen Handlungskonzepten und Beziehungskonstellationen zum Tragen kommt. Dies betrifft zum Beispiel die Familie, Gruppenprozesse, Schule, Medien, Arbeitswelt, Politik oder Wirtschafts- und Finanzsysteme.

Wissenschaftliche Einordnung

Vertrauen ist keiner einzelnen Disziplin zuzuordnen, sondern ein interdisziplinäres Phänomen, dessen Erforschung lange Zeit der Theologie und Philosophie überlassen wurde. Doch spätestens seit Beginn der 1990er-Jahre ist das Thema Vertrauen auch in Disziplinen wie der Soziologie, Psychologie, Wirtschaft oder Politologie, ein wichtiges Forschungsfeld. Durch eine Vielzahl von Theorien ist es schwer, eine allgemeingültige Definition aufzustellen. So gehen etwa dispositionale Theorien davon aus, dass durch frühkindliche Bindungen und Sozialisationsprozesse eine Vertrauensaneignung stattfindet, während identitätsbasierte Ansätze Vertrautheit durch bedeutende Gemeinsamkeiten und Ähnlichkeiten in den Mittelpunkt stellen. Der Reputationsansatz wiederum nennt bestimmte Eigenschaften als Voraussetzung für Vertrauenswürdigkeit und der interaktionistische Ansatz gründet sich auf der Annahme, Vertrauen könne erst durch wiederholte positive Erfahrungen und Kontakte entstehen. Der Institutionalismus schließlich geht von den weitreichenden Effekten politischer Strukturen aus, die eine gewisse Stabilität, Routine und Vorhersagbarkeit garantieren und damit ein soziales Klima des Vertrauens schaffen. Trotz aller Unterschiede sehen die meisten Ansätze Vertrauen als eine soziale Einstellung, die eine gedankliche (Vernunft, Reflexion), gefühlsmäßige und handlungsanleitende (Routine, Regelmäßigkeit) Komponente aufweist. Ein weiteres Merkmal ist die Erklärung von positiven Erwartungen und das Aufheben der Ungewissheit. Jeder Vertrauenshandlung wohnt auch das Moment der Unsicherheit bei. Ohne Unsicherheit wäre Vertrauen unnötig, da man das Verhalten der anderen Seite immer exakt vorhersehen könnte. Entsprechend kann der Vertrauensgebende nie ganz sicher

sein, nicht doch enttäuscht zu werden, sind ihm doch weder mögliche Verhaltensweisen noch deren Wahrscheinlichkeit wirklich bekannt. Um dennoch vertrauen zu können, muss er sich der Unsicherheit gewiss sein, diese aber zurückstellen.

Menschen bauen somit Vertrauen auf, indem sie die positiven Erwartungen an das Verhalten anderer stärker gewichten als die Unsicherheit über deren tatsächliche Absichten.

Bedeutung für den Einzelnen und die Gesellschaft

Für jeden Bürger ist Vertrauen die Basis für seine Beziehungs- und Handlungsfähigkeit. Dies betrifft anfangs vor allem seine familiären Bindungen, später seine Interaktionen mit seinem sozialen Umfeld, seiner Arbeitswelt, seinem Wohnumfeld und seiner Beziehung zu Institutionen. Das stärkste Vertrauen wird in der Regel Personen geschenkt, die ähnliche Erfahrungen haben und Halt spenden (Bonding-Beziehungen). Bei diesem identifikationsbasierten Vertrauen besteht eine starke emotionale Bindung zwischen den Beteiligten. Merkmale sind zum Beispiel eine enge Zusammenarbeit, regelmäßige Kommunikation und Interaktion, Identifikation mit den Werten und Zielen des anderen sowie gegenseitige Sympathie. Zu finden sind diese Vertrauensbeziehungen vor allem im Familien- und Freundeskreis.
Eher lose Beziehungen (Bridging-Beziehungen) geht der Einzelne mit Gruppen ein, mit denen er sich austauschen und spezifische Gruppeninteressen verfolgen kann. Hier wird Vertrauen situativ oder eigenschaftsbasiert geschenkt und beruht auf bestimmten Merkmalen oder Eigenschaften einer Person oder Organisation. Diese äußern sich vor allem in Kompetenz, Integrität und Wohlwollen. Die Kompetenz kann sich hierbei auf Fachwissen, Fähigkeiten oder Erfahrungen beziehen, die Integrität auf moralische Werte und ethische Standards wie Ehrlichkeit und Verlässlichkeit und das Wohlwollen auf eine optimistische, gewogene und offene Grundhaltung. Häufig ist diese Art des Vertrauens im Arbeitsumfeld, bei Vereinen, aber auch in Kundenbeziehungen zu finden.

VERTRAUEN

Durch Linking-Beziehungen wird eine Verbindung mit Institutionen eingegangen. Stärker als bei familiären oder freundschaftlichen Bindungen ist der Grad des Nichtwissens über das Verhalten des anderen beziehungsweise der Institutionen hier höher. Der Einzelne wägt bei seinem Verhalten ab, ob es sich lohnt, dem anderen zu vertrauen. Linking-Beziehungen basieren häufig auf situationsbasiertem oder eigenschaftsbasiertem Vertrauen. Ersteres entsteht oft spontan und ist stark von äußeren Faktoren geprägt. Es wird für die Dauer einer besonderen Situation aufgebaut beziehungsweise ist nur vorrübergehend. Das Vertrauen basiert weniger auf einer tiefen zwischenmenschlichen Beziehung als auf der Erwartungshaltung oder Notwendigkeit einer Situation heraus. Dies betrifft zum Beispiel Krisensituationen oder spontane politische Kooperationen. Da ein situationsbedingtes Vertrauen kein „echtes" Vertrauen ist, müssen die Akteure vom Mehrwert der Kooperation überzeugt sein. Längerfristig kann diese Art des Vertrauens die Grundlage für tiefere Formen von Vertrauen sein. Eigenschaftsbasiertes Vertrauen ruht auf bestimmten Merkmalen einer Person, eines Systems oder einer Organisation anstatt auf einer persönlichen Beziehung oder bisherigen Interaktionen. Diese Merkmale müssen nicht zwangsläufig menschlicher Natur sein, sondern umfassen auch technische oder organisatorische Attribute wie bestimmte Sicherheitszertifikate (Software), Berechtigungen (Juristen oder Ärzte) oder vorgegebene Standards (Organisationen).

Welche Folgen ergeben sich durch die verschiedenen Arten eines vertrauensvollen Vorgehens nun für den Einzelnen? Er kann eine optimistische Grundhaltung entwickeln, neue Erfahrungen sammeln, aus denen er lernen und neue Beziehungen aufbauen kann. Er ist in der Lage, zuversichtlich Kooperationen einzugehen und gemeinsame Ziele zu verwirklichen. Durch Kontakte mit Personen unterschiedlicher Hintergründe lernt er, Vertrauen über Gruppen hinweg zu entwickeln und Vorurteile zu reduzieren. Hinsichtlich der Linking-Beziehungen kann der Vertrauensaufbau in den Staat gefördert werden, wenn dieser die Partizipation an gesellschaftlichen und politischen Findungs- und Entscheidungsprozessen ermöglicht. Gleichzeitig kann Vertrauen gerade in komplexen Gemeinschaften Funktionen

der Entlastung bieten. Die Bürger können Prioritäten setzen, ohne ständig alles hinterfragen zu müssen, und stattdessen bestimmten Prozessen, Menschen oder Institutionen „blind" vertrauen. Dadurch werden sie in ihrer Handlungsfähigkeit gestärkt.

> Gesamtgesellschaftlich gesehen bilden die vertrauensvollen Verbindungen der Bürger ein unerlässliches Sozialkapital für die Stabilität, den Wohlstand und den Zusammenhalt einer Gesellschaft.

Sie sind die Grundlage für ziviles Engagement, fördern die Identifikation mit dem Gemeinwesen und unterstützen solidarisches Verhalten. Hiervon profitieren die unterschiedlichsten Bereiche. Im wirtschaftlichen Sektor oder innerhalb der Finanzsysteme etwa bildet Vertrauen eine zentrale Grundlage für einen funktionierenden Markt und Handel. Im politischen System gewährleistet sie die Legitimität für ihre Vertreter, während sie innerhalb der Justiz, Verwaltung oder Polizei Gerechtigkeit und Sicherheit garantiert. Vertrauen in einer Gesellschaft ist somit ein Zeichen dafür, wie stabil und offen die zwischenmenschlichen Beziehungen sind, wie stark diese den Institutionen vertrauen und wie gefestigt demokratische Strukturen sind.

Vertrauensverlust

Trotz der vielschichtigen Potenziale und Möglichkeiten, die einem vertrauensvollen Bewusstsein und Verhalten innewohnen, wird die öffentliche Diskussion eher von seinem Gegenteil, dem Vertrauensverlust bestimmt. Dabei ist Misstrauen nicht einfach als das Gegenteil von Vertrauen zu verstehen, sondern bildet einen eigenen Zustand ab. Zweifel und Unsicherheiten werden hierbei bewusst betont. Und auch wenn sich der gegenwärtige Vertrauensverlust vordergründig vor allem auf den politischen Bereich fokussiert, sind auch andere Institutionen hiervon betroffen – von Unternehmen, über Kirchen oder die Medien bis hin zur Polizei und Gerichten. Auch gegenüber anderen Ländern, Minderheiten oder Religionsgruppen ist ein zunehmendes Misstrauen nachzuweisen.

VERTRAUEN

Überall dort, wo Vertrauen schwindet, werden Unterschiede nicht mehr als Bereicherung gesehen, die man mit Respekt akzeptiert, sondern als unüberbrückbare Gegensätze, die sich der Mehrheitsmeinung unterzuordnen haben.

In der Folge ist eine verständnisvolle Koexistenz kaum noch möglich und die Spaltung innerhalb der Gesellschaft verfestigt sich. Besonders weitreichende Folgen kann ein Vertrauensverlust bei der jüngeren Generation nach sich ziehen. Wenn junge Bürger nur wenige vertrauensvolle Erfahrungen machen, wenn sie öfter enttäuscht oder zurückgewiesen werden, obwohl sie Vertrauen geschenkt haben, wenn sie das Gefühl haben, von Entscheidungsträgern nicht ernst genommen zu werden, entwickeln sie ein zunehmendes Misstrauen und werden anfällig für populistische Positionen. Verstärkt werden diese Prozesse durch eine Zunahme – nicht immer seriöser – (Online-) Informationsquellen und einer Erosion traditioneller Medien, sodass das Ungewisse und das Temporäre noch verstärkt werden. Die Sehnsucht nach Vertrauen bleibt dabei bestehen und findet ihre Erfüllung dann oftmals in Gemeinschaften oder Vereinigungen, die einfache, aber identitätsstiftende Erklärungen und scheinbare Sicherheiten bieten.

Beim viel zitierten Vertrauensverlust in die politischen Parteien handelt es sich um ein Zusammenspiel verschiedener Aspekte. So verspüren viele Bürger gerade in Zeiten wirtschaftlicher Unsicherheiten, politischen Spannungen und einem rasanten technologischen Wandel Verunsicherung. Sie fragen sich zunehmend, ob das demokratische System ihre Anliegen noch wahrnimmt und angemessen auf die Herausforderungen unserer Zeit – sei es global oder national – reagiert. Hinzu kommt ein Gefühl von Intransparenz, einer schwachen Profilierung der Volksparteien, einer Kluft beziehungsweise Entfremdung zwischen Politikern und Bevölkerung. Verbunden mit Misstrauen in andere staatliche Organe, wie Polizei, Justiz oder auch unabhängige Medien, kann es zu einem schwindenden Gefühl der Sicherheit und Stabilität kommen. In der Folge nimmt die politische Polarisierung zu, verknüpft mit einer

wachsenden Feindseligkeit zwischen verschiedenen politischen Lagern, einem Rückgang des gesellschaftlichen Konsenses und des Vertrauens in den Kompromiss und den demokratischen Diskurs. Der Aufstieg populistischer Bewegungen ist dabei sowohl eine Folge als auch ein Verstärker des Vertrauensverlusts.

Maßnahmen für Vertrauensaufbau

Grundlage für eine vertrauensvollere Beziehung im zwischenmenschlichen Bereich ist der Aufbau von einem stabilen empathischen und respektvollen Umgang. Von familiären Strukturen ausgehend, stehen später vor allem schulische Institutionen, Vereinsstrukturen oder andere soziale Netzwerke in der Verantwortung, diesen zu fördern und somit das soziale Kapital zu stärken. Hierfür ist eine lokale Infrastruktur mit Begegnungsorten notwendig, die breite gesellschaftliche Gruppierungen anspricht, sowie eine gezielte Förderung von interkulturellen Initiativen und Programmen. Wichtig ist der regelmäßige Austausch, auch und gerade mit andersdenkenden Gruppen, um Respekt, Toleranz und Reflexion zu fördern und eine längerfristige Basis für ein verständnisvolles Miteinander zu schaffen. Weitere vertrauensfördernde Maßnahmen können unter anderem der Aufbau von Bridging-Projekten, Diversitätsprogramme, Austauschprogramme sowie eine Kultur des Vereinslebens und des zivilen Engagements sein.

Für eine Überwindung des Misstrauens zwischen Bürgern und Institutionen sind eine höhere Transparenz, klare Kommunikation, Zugang zu verlässlichen Informationen und offene Prozesse der Entscheidungsfindung eine Art Grundvoraussetzung. Dann werden auch unpopuläre staatliche Maßnahmen eher von den Bürgern mitgetragen werden, da diese dann nicht nur Einzelinteressen, sondern dem Gemeinwohl dienen.

VERTRAUEN

Für eine stärkere zivile Beteiligung an politischen Prozessen kommt partizipativen Strukturen eine hohe Bedeutung zu. Diese beinhalten zum Beispiel kommunale Beteiligungsformate, Bürgerforen, Runde Tische und Volksbefragungen. Daneben fördern Maßnahmen für mehr zivilgesellschaftliches Engagement das Vertrauen in Institutionen und das Gemeinwesen.

Als besonders nachhaltig erweist sich ein Konglomerat von Einstellungen, Verhaltensweisen, Entscheidungen und Interaktionen, die der Unsicherheit mit pragmatischen Lösungen begegnen, materielle Sicherheit mit dem Gefühl von Gerechtigkeit verbinden und trotz des Wissens über die Notwendigkeit von Veränderungen angesichts der zahlreichen Herausforderungen eine positive Zukunftssichtweise bereithalten.

Best-Practice-Beispiele

1. Transparenz in der Regierung

In skandinavischen Ländern haben Bürger Zugang zu staatlichen Regierungsdokumenten. So ermöglicht zum Beispiel das seit 1766 in der Verfassung verankerte Recht „Offentlighetsprincipen" Bürgern, nahezu alle Dokumente und Informationen von Behörden und Ämtern einzusehen, einschließlich E-Mails, Gesprächsnotizen und sogar Ermittlungsakten. Das Prinzip der Transparenz ist in Schweden die Regel, während Geheimhaltung die Ausnahme darstellt und nur unter strengen gesetzlichen Voraussetzungen angewendet werden darf.

Vorteile: Regelmäßige Berichterstattung, offene Datenplattformen und Bürgerbeteiligung an politischen Entscheidungen. Verringertes Risiko von Korruption und Missmanagement. Entscheidungsprozesse können einfacher nachvollzogen werden.

VERTRAUEN

2. Integrität und ethisches Verhalten in Unternehmen

Unternehmen, die nach dem B-Corporation-Standard zertifiziert sind, verpflichten sich zu sozialen und ökologischen Zielen, einem gesellschaftlichen Mehrwert und ökologischer Nachhaltigkeit. Diese Transparenz und Verantwortung gegenüber der Gesellschaft stärken das Vertrauen der Kunden und Bürger in das Unternehmen. Ein Beispiel ist das niederländische Schokoladenunternehmen Tony's Chocolonely. Es verfolgt nicht nur soziale sowie ökologische Standards, sondern setzt sich aktiv für eine faire und nachhaltige Kakaoproduktion ein, um moderne Sklaverei und Ausbeutung in der Lieferkette zu beenden.

Vorteile: Unternehmen gewinnen durch ethische Geschäftspraktiken, Nachhaltigkeitsinitiativen und transparente Kommunikation das Vertrauen der Gesellschaft und steigern ihre langfristige Reputation und ihre Gewinne.

3. Soziale Inklusion und Integration

Kanada hat eines der inklusivsten Einwanderungssysteme der Welt. Die Einwanderer werden als Gewinn betrachtet und ihre Integration durch Bildungs- und Arbeitsprogramme aktiv gefördert. Durch diese Maßnahmen hat das Land ein hohes Maß an sozialem Vertrauen und Integration erreicht sowie das zwischenmenschliche Miteinander und Verständnis füreinander gestärkt.

Vorteile: Maßnahmen, die Minderheiten und benachteiligte Gruppen einbeziehen, sowie Initiativen zur Förderung der sozialen Kohäsion, wie Sprach- und Integrationskurse, tragen sowohl dazu bei, Vertrauen innerhalb der Gesellschaft zu stärken, als auch wirtschaftliche Herausforderungen (zum Beispiel Fachkräftemangel) konstruktiv anzugehen.

4. Stärkung von Gemeinschaft und Zivilgesellschaft im Bereich der Sicherheit

In zahlreichen Städten der USA, unter anderem in New York, hat die Polizei die Praxis des „Community Policing" eingeführt, bei der Polizisten eng mit den lokalen Behörden und der Öffentlichkeit zusammenarbeiten. Dabei sollen Probleme besser und präventiv identifiziert und gemeinsam Lösungen entwickelt werden. Diese Maßnahme hat das gesunkene Vertrauen der Bürger in die Polizei gestärkt und die Kriminalitätsrate nachweislich gesenkt.

Vorteile: Der Aufbau von Gemeinschaftsorganisationen, die auf Vertrauen und Kooperation zwischen Institutionen und Bürgern setzen, kann das Sicherheitsgefühl ebenso wie Gemeinschaftsgefühl verstärken.

5. Digitale Bildung und Teilhabe

Estland gilt als Vorreiter im Bereich der digitalen Bildung und Teilhabe. Bereits in den 1990er-Jahren begann das Land mit dem Aufbau eines umfassenden E-Government-Systems und einer digitalen Infrastruktur, die es allen Bürgern ermöglichen, online auf staatliche Dienstleistungen zuzugreifen. Schulen sind flächendeckend digitalisiert, und Schüler lernen früh, mit digitalen Technologien umzugehen. Durch das Programm „ProgeTiiger" wird die digitale Kompetenz von Kindern und Jugendlichen bereits früh gefördert, indem sie Programmieren und andere IT-Fähigkeiten erlernen.

Vorteile: Das Vertrauen in digitale Systeme wird gestärkt, da die Bürger frühzeitig lernen, wie sie sicher und kompetent mit Technologie umgehen können. Zudem fördert der Zugang zu digitalen Ressourcen Chancengleichheit und soziale Teilhabe, wodurch das Vertrauen in das Bildungssystem und die Regierung erhöht wird.

VERTRAUEN

Wie entwickelt sich das Vertrauen?

Von je 100 Befragten stimmen der Aussage zu:
„Den meisten Mitbürgern kann man vertrauen."

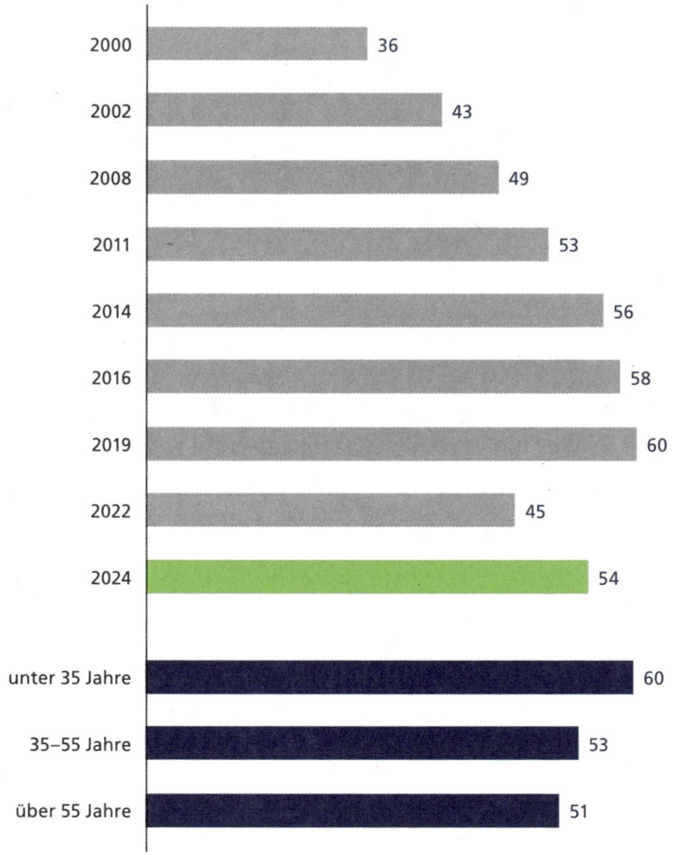

Renaissance des Vertrauens

MEHRHEIT GLAUBT WIEDER AN DIE VERLÄSSLICHKEIT ANDERER

Ergebnis

Vertrauen bildet eine essenzielle Grundlage für das gesellschaftliche Zusammenleben. Aktuell vertraut eine knappe Mehrheit der Bevölkerung den meisten Mitbürgern. Bei den unter 35-Jährigen liegt der Anteil mit 60 Prozent über dem Wert der älteren Generationen, von denen nur etwa jeder Zweite Vertrauen in seine Mitmenschen äußert.

Ein Blick auf die Entwicklung über die Jahre zeigt eine wechselhafte Dynamik. Im Jahr 2000 lag der Anteil bei lediglich 36 Prozent und stieg bis 2019 kontinuierlich auf einen Höchststand von 60 Prozent an. Anschließend folgte ein Rückgang im Jahr 2022 auf 45 Prozent, bevor sich der Wert auf aktuell 54 Prozent erholte.

Gründe

Für das Individuum bildet Vertrauen die Grundlage seiner Beziehungs- und Handlungsfähigkeit. Zunächst betrifft dies vor allem seine familiären Bindungen, später auch die Interaktionen mit seinem sozialen Umfeld, seiner Arbeitswelt und seinen Mitbürgern. Das stärkste Vertrauen wird allgemein Personen entgegengebracht, die ähnliche Erfahrungen teilen, Identität und Halt vermitteln oder sich in einer vergleichbaren sozialen Lebenswelt befinden.

Das steigende Vertrauen zwischen 2000 und 2019 ist vor allem im Kontext gesellschaftlicher und wirtschaftlicher Entwicklungen zu betrachten. Hierzu zählen beispielsweise eine relativ stabile wirtschaftliche Lage mit niedriger Arbeitslosigkeit über den gesamten Zeitraum sowie die nachhaltige Zuversicht, die sich auch nach der Finanzkrise 2008/2009 einstellte. Die Erfahrung, diese Krisenzeiten unbeschadet zu überstehen, hatte einen tiefgreifenden Einfluss auf das soziale Vertrauen der Menschen zueinander. Sie förderte das Gefühl von Sicherheit und Stabilität und stärkte damit das Vertrauen in die Gesellschaft allgemein sowie in den Mitmenschen.

Darüber hinaus konnten weitere gesellschaftliche Herausforderungen bewältigt werden, etwa die Förderung von Gleichberechtigung und Diversität, die Verbesserung der

VERTRAUEN

Kriminalitätsbekämpfung sowie Maßnahmen gegen den Klimawandel. All diese Aspekte trugen zu einem wachsenden Gemeinschaftsgefühl bei, das sich unter anderem in einem verstärkten freiwilligen Engagement der Bevölkerung zeigte – sei es in Form von Nachbarschaftshilfe, der Mitarbeit in Sportvereinen oder in Hilfsorganisationen.

Die intensive Wechselwirkung zwischen der Wahrnehmung gesellschaftlicher Stabilität und persönlicher Vertrauensbereitschaft zeigte sich deutlich im Jahr 2022, als das Vertrauen der Bundesbürger nicht nur in Institutionen und politische Akteure, sondern auch gegenüber Mitbürgern um insgesamt 15 Prozent zurückging. Dieser Rückgang lässt sich unter anderem durch die Auswirkungen der Coronapandemie erklären und ebenso durch den Frust über teils nicht transparente politische Maßnahmen und Widersprüche. Hinzu kamen der Ukrainekrieg mit seinen wirtschaftlichen und sozialen Unsicherheiten, die Energiekrise, steigende Inflation und höhere Lebenshaltungskosten, zunehmende Unzufriedenheit mit politischen Entscheidungen (z. B. Energiepolitik, Waffenlieferungen), wachsende soziale Ungleichheit (z. B. Energiepreisdeckel oder Gasumlage), gesellschaftliche Spaltungen, die Erstarkung populistischer Kräfte sowie die Verbreitung von Fake News und Desinformationen.

Im Vergleich dazu ist seit 2024 das Vertrauen der Bundesbürger zueinander wieder um fast 10 Prozentpunkte auf 54 Prozent gestiegen. Dies lässt sich unter anderem durch ein stärkeres Zusammenrücken der Bürger in gefühlt unsicheren Zeiten erklären. Beobachtbar ist dies beispielsweise an der zunehmenden Nachbarschaftshilfe, Gemeinschaftsaktionen, Hilfsangeboten für Ukraine-Flüchtlinge oder der Nutzung von Tauschbörsen. Besonders die Erfahrungen der Coronapandemie mit Isolation, fehlenden sozialen Kontakten und gesellschaftlicher Polarisierung haben viele Bürger dazu bewogen, sich wieder intensiver persönlich zu vernetzen, aktiv gegen soziale Spaltung vorzugehen und soziale Interaktionen bewusster zu suchen. In ähnlicher Weise hat der Krieg in der Ukraine die Bereitschaft der Bürger gestärkt, sich auf gemeinsame Werte zu besinnen, die gesellschaftliche Stabilität zu schätzen und sich verstärkt zu engagieren. Dadurch haben zwischenmenschliche Beziehungen insgesamt eine neue Wertschätzung erfahren, was letztlich auch zu einem Anstieg des gegenseitigen Vertrauens geführt hat.

VERTRAUEN

Die Unterschiede zwischen jüngeren und älteren Bürgern offenbaren verschiedene Lebensrealitäten. Jüngere zeigen ein höheres Vertrauen in ihre Mitmenschen, was durch stärkere Vernetzung und Offenheit gegenüber sozialen Kontakten gefördert wird. Digitale Plattformen ermöglichen dieser Altersgruppe, vielfältige Beziehungen aufzubauen und positive Erfahrungen zu sammeln. Auch die Lebensphase spielt eine entscheidende Rolle: Jüngere befinden sich in einem Umfeld, das stärker auf Kooperation und Austausch ausgerichtet ist, etwa in Schule, Studium oder beim Berufseinstieg. Zudem neigen sie zu einer optimistischeren und idealisierten Haltung, sind offener für Neues, häufig in sozialen Gemeinschaften integriert und im ständigen Austausch mit anderen. Diese Faktoren führen zu einer erhöhten Vertrauensbereitschaft. Da jüngere Bürger weniger stark in wirtschaftlicher Verantwortung stehen und seltener mit schwierigen Entscheidungen konfrontiert werden, ist ihr Misstrauen gegenüber anderen geringer.

Die mittlere und ältere Generation hingegen sieht sich häufiger beruflichen, finanziellen oder persönlichen Herausforderungen ausgesetzt und erfährt entsprechend mehr zwischenmenschliche Enttäuschungen. Diese Erfahrungen fördern Zurückhaltung und größere Vorsicht im Umgang mit anderen. Negative gesellschaftliche Entwicklungen wie Polarisierung und Unsicherheiten verstärken diese Haltung zusätzlich.

Auch die Gründe der Bürger, die aktuell kein Vertrauen in ihre Mitmenschen haben, sind von Bedeutung. Die Ursachen hierfür liegen häufig in persönlichen Enttäuschungen oder negativen Erfahrungen wie mangelnder Hilfsbereitschaft oder Konflikten im Alltag. Gesellschaftliche Faktoren wie soziale Spaltung, wirtschaftliche Unsicherheiten oder der Einfluss von Desinformation verstärken dieses Misstrauen zusätzlich. Ein solches Klima erschwert es vielen Bürgern, auf andere zuzugehen, und fördert Isolation sowie Vorbehalte. Auch die Wahrnehmung von Ungleichheit spielt eine Rolle: Bürger, die sich benachteiligt fühlen oder den Eindruck haben, unfair behandelt zu werden, entwickeln häufiger Misstrauen gegenüber anderen. Der Rückgang gemeinschaftlicher Aktivitäten wie Vereinsarbeit oder Nachbarschaftsprojekte sowie die zunehmende Anonymität in urbanen Räumen tragen ebenfalls dazu bei, da persönliche Kontakte seltener werden und das Gefühl von Gemeinschaft schwindet.

VERTRAUEN

Prognose

Ein hohes Maß an Vertrauen in die Mitmenschen stellt eine zentrale Ressource für das Zusammenleben dar. Vertrauen erleichtert Kooperationen, reduziert Konflikte und stärkt den sozialen Zusammenhalt. Gesellschaften mit einem hohen Vertrauensniveau zeichnen sich durch eine größere Stabilität und Resilienz aus, da die Bürger bereit sind, Verantwortung zu übernehmen und sich aktiv in Gemeinschaftsprojekte einzubringen. Auch die Bereitschaft, auf andere zuzugehen und gemeinsame Lösungen für Probleme zu entwickeln, steigt mit wachsendem Vertrauen.

Wichtig ist, dieses vielfältige Potenzial von Vertrauen zukünftig zu nutzen.

Besonders jüngere Generationen bieten durch ihr höheres Vertrauensniveau Potenziale für den Aufbau einer vertrauensvollen Gesellschaft. Ihre stärkere Vernetzung und Offenheit gegenüber neuen Kontakten können dazu beitragen, Brücken zwischen verschiedenen sozialen Gruppen zu schlagen. Digitale Plattformen ermöglichen es ihnen, Beziehungen über geografische und kulturelle Grenzen hinweg aufzubauen. Diese Vernetzung sollte gezielt genutzt werden, um Dialoge zu fördern und Vorurteile abzubauen. Jüngere befinden sich zudem häufig in Lebensphasen, die von Kooperation geprägt sind, etwa in Ausbildung, Berufseinstieg oder Familiengründung. Diese Umfelder bieten ideale Voraussetzungen, um Vertrauen als Grundlage für langfristige soziale Bindungen zu etablieren.

Ein Rückgang des Vertrauens birgt hingegen erhebliche Risiken für das gesellschaftliche Gefüge. Misstrauen erschwert den Aufbau sozialer Beziehungen und fördert Isolation sowie Polarisierung. In einer Gesellschaft mit geringem Vertrauen sinkt die Bereitschaft zur Zusammenarbeit, was sowohl das soziale als auch das wirtschaftliche Leben negativ beeinflusst. Zudem würde ein Klima des Misstrauens soziale Spaltungen verstärken und die Engagementbereitschaft der Bürger verringern.

VERTRAUEN

Die Förderung von Vertrauen erfordert gezielte Maßnahmen auf individueller und gesellschaftlicher Ebene. Begegnungen zwischen unterschiedlichen sozialen Gruppen schaffen Möglichkeiten, Vorurteile abzubauen und gegenseitiges Verständnis zu fördern. Gemeinschaftsprojekte oder Nachbarschaftsinitiativen bieten Räume für positive Interaktionen und stärken das Gefühl von Zugehörigkeit. Bildungseinrichtungen können durch Programme zur Förderung sozialer Kompetenzen und interkultureller Sensibilität frühzeitig Grundlagen für vertrauensvolle Beziehungen legen. Auch die Politik könnte durch mehr Transparenz in Entscheidungsprozessen und eine verbesserte Kommunikation das Vertrauen in Institutionen stärken, was sich wiederum positiv auf das zwischenmenschliche Vertrauen auswirken würde.

Es gilt daher, Strukturen zu schaffen, die Begegnungen ermöglichen und soziale Sicherheit gewährleisten. Eine Zukunftsgesellschaft mit einem hohen Maß an Vertrauen ist nicht nur stabiler, sondern auch besser gerüstet, zukünftige Herausforderungen gemeinsam zu bewältigen. Die Förderung von Vertrauen sollte als ein kontinuierlicher Prozess verstanden werden, der sowohl individuelle Bemühungen als auch institutionelle Unterstützung erfordert.

Wie hoch ist das Vertrauen in Familie und Freunde?

Von je 100 Befragten stimmen der Aussage zu:
„Ich vertraue darauf, dass meine Freunde und meine Familie in schwierigen Zeiten für mich da sind.“

Familie und Freunde als Anker

ZUSAMMENHALT IN KRISENZEITEN

Ergebnis

Von allen sozialen Netzwerken ist die eigene Familie das stabilste. Sie hat nicht nur für den Einzelnen eine wichtige Bedeutung, prägt und schützt ihn, sondern spielt auch für den Zusammenhalt in der Gesellschaft eine zentrale Rolle.

Innerhalb der Bevölkerung vertrauen acht von zehn Bürgern auch in Krisenzeiten auf die eigene Familie, wobei die über 55-Jährigen eine deutlich überdurchschnittliche Zustimmung äußern.

VERTRAUEN

Gründe

Während der gesamten kindlichen Entwicklung spielen die familiären Beziehungen eine zentrale Rolle, schaffen ein Gefühl der Sicherheit und des Vertrauens. Eine liebevolle Umgebung hilft dabei, emotionale Sicherheit und Selbstbewusstsein zu erlangen und seine Persönlichkeit zu entwickeln. Darrüber hinaus ist die Familie die erste Instanz, in der Kinder moralische Werte, Normen, Verhaltensweisen und soziale Kompetenzen erlernen. In späteren Jahren erweitert sich der enge Kernbereich und Freunde nehmen eine bedeutende Rolle ein. Ihre enge Bindung beruht dabei vor allem auf gemeinsam gemachten Erfahrungen und gleichaltrigen Gesprächspartnern. Auch im Erwachsenenalter verlässt sich die große Mehrheit der Bürger auf die langjährigen Beziehungen beziehungsweise das nächste soziale Umfeld und greift vertrauensvoll darauf zurück.

Besonders deutlich zeigt sich die Bedeutung der engen sozialen Verhältnisse in Krisenzeiten. Beispielsweise bei Problemen während der Jobsuche, in Ausbildung oder Studium, bei wegweisenden Entscheidungsfindungen, bei Beziehungsproblemen, Mobbing oder Ausgrenzung, bei finanziellen Sorgen, Identitätskrisen oder Orientierungslosigkeit. Hier bieten Familie, aber auch Freunde einen sicheren Rückzugsort, wo man sich der emotionalen Unterstützung, des Trostes, der Ermutigung, der Wertschätzung, der Orientierungs- und der Entscheidungshilfe gewiss sein kann. Im Laufe des Lebens zeigen sich Krisen dann vor allem in den Bereichen von Übergängen – Auszug der Kinder, Trennungen, Einstieg in den Ruhestand – ,aber auch bei Gesundheitsfragen, Todesfällen und im Zusammenhang von Isolation und Vereinsamung. Daneben können mitunter auch äußere Krisen zu einem inneren Konflikt führen. Hierunter fallen zum Beispiel politische und soziale Spannungen, Erlebnisse von Gewalt, Naturkatastrophen und Pandemien, Auswirkungen von Flucht und Migration oder Wirtschaftskrisen mit hoher Inflation und Rezession.

Durch stabile persönliche Verbindungen und positive Erfahrungen entwickeln Bürger zudem auch ein stärkeres Vertrauen zu Mitbürgern sowie Institutionen und stärken damit das soziale Kapital der Gesellschaft. In der Folge werden Solidarität, Verantwortungsgefühl,

die Kooperationsfähigkeit und Resilienz der Gemeinschaft insgesamt gefördert, da sich gerade in Krisenzeiten Bürger mit stabilen sozialen Verbindungen schneller von persönlichen Rückschlägen erholen. Daneben leistet die Familie auch praktische Hilfe, indem sie durch ihre Unterstützung die Belastungen für gesellschaftliche Institutionen oder soziale Dienste reduziert, zum Beispiel bei der Bildung, im Beruf, bei der Kinderbetreuung, im Krankheitsfall oder auch bei temporären finanziellen Schwierigkeiten.

Als weitere Gründe für die hohe Zustimmung sind unter anderem zu nennen: die Vertrautheit durch die oftmals langfristigen Verbindungen, das Gefühl von bedingungsloser Unterstützung und Loyalität (dies existiert in anderen sozialen Netzwerken seltener), ähnliche Werte und Normen oder auch das Gefühl der Familie als sicherem Rückzugsort, an dem man vor äußeren Belastungen geschützt ist und gleichzeitig Unterstützung erfährt.

Die Generation über 55 Jahre zeigt höhere Werte im Vertrauen in die Familie, da mit zunehmendem Alter das soziale Umfeld oft kleiner wird und enge Freundschaften seltener werden. Gleichzeitig wächst das Bedürfnis nach emotionaler und praktischer Sicherheit, die vor allem durch die Familie gewährleistet wird. Gesundheitliche Einschränkungen machen familiäre Unterstützung mitunter unverzichtbar, sei es bei der Pflege, im Alltag oder bei emotionalem Beistand. Zudem ziehen sich viele Ältere schrittweise aus beruflichen und gesellschaftlichen Verpflichtungen zurück und fokussieren sich verstärkt auf ihr privates Umfeld. Die Familie wird dadurch zum zentralen Ort für Stabilität, Unterstützung und Geborgenheit.

Prognose

Die Zukunft des Vertrauens in Familie, aber auch Freunde zeigt ein hoffnungsvolles Bild. In einer von sozialen, wirtschaftlichen und politischen Umbrüchen geprägten Welt wird die Bedeutung persönlicher Beziehungen weiter zunehmen. Die Familie bleibt dabei eine Art unverzichtbarer Anker, der den Bürger in allen Lebenslagen Stabilität und Geborgenheit bietet. Noch mehr als gegenwärtig bietet die Familie in Zukunft emotionale Unterstützung ebenso wie Orientierung und auch konkrete Hilfe.

VERTRAUEN

Die Gewissheit, jederzeit Rückhalt im engsten sozialen Umfeld zu finden, bleibt ein entscheidender Faktor für das persönliche Wohlbefinden und den Zusammenhalt in der Gesellschaft.

Die Familie wird sich in ihrer Struktur dabei weiter diversifizieren, ohne ihre zentrale Funktion zu verlieren. Patchworkfamilien, Mehrgenerationenhaushalte oder Wahlfamilien werden zunehmend (wieder) akzeptiert und geschätzt. Diese Vielfalt ermöglicht es Menschen, sich in unterschiedlichen Konstellationen aufgehoben zu fühlen und soziale Bindungen flexibel zu gestalten.

Die Bedeutung persönlicher Beziehungen wird auch in der Gesellschaft insgesamt zunehmen. Denn je mehr Flexibilität, Individualität oder Unzuverlässlichkeit in einer Multioptionsgesellschaft zunehmen, desto stärker wird das Bedürfnis nach Verlässlichkeit, Solidarität und Gemeinschaftsgefühl – Qualitäten, die zunehmende Wertschätzung erfahren. Langfristig wird das Vertrauen in Familie eine Schlüsselrolle bei der Resilienz moderner Gesellschaften spielen. Persönliche Bindungen schaffen nicht nur individuelle Sicherheit, sondern tragen dazu bei, gesellschaftliche Herausforderungen gemeinsam zu bewältigen. Wichtig wird es daher, die hohe Vertrautheit innerhalb von Familienstrukturen kontinuierlich zu erweitern.

Wie hoch ist das Vertrauen in Institutionen?

Von je 100 Befragten stimmen der Aussage zu:
„Vertrauen in Institutionen (zum Beispiel Parlamente, Gerichte, Medien) ist eine wichtige Basis für eine stabile Gesellschaft.“

Rückhalt für die Demokratie

VERTRAUEN IN INSTITUTIONEN BLEIBT UNVERZICHTBAR

Ergebnis

Vertrauen in Institutionen bildet das Fundament einer stabilen Gesellschaft. Es ermöglicht zentralen Einrichtungen wie Parlamenten, Gerichten oder Medien, ihre Aufgaben effektiv zu erfüllen. Mehr als drei Viertel der Bürger teilen diese Überzeugung. Unterschiede zwischen den Altersgruppen sind dabei nur gering ausgeprägt. Ältere Bürger messen dem Vertrauen eine etwas größere Bedeutung bei, während die jüngere Generation eine etwas zurückhaltendere Haltung zeigt. Insgesamt herrscht jedoch ein breiter Konsens, der die essenzielle Rolle von Vertrauen für gesellschaftliche Stabilität und ein friedliches Zusammenleben verdeutlicht.

VERTRAUEN

Gründe

In den letzten Jahren war die öffentliche Diskussion oftmals von einem Vertrauensverlust gegenüber Institutionen wie Parteien, Wissenschaft und Medien geprägt. Verschiedene Ursachen und Entwicklungen haben zu dieser Situation beigetragen, zum Beispiel politische Polarisierung, populistische Bewegungen, mangelnde Transparenz, schlechtes Krisenmanagement, missverständliche Kommunikation oder auch Desinformation. Trotz all dieser Fehler und Kritik bleibt für den Großteil der Bürger Vertrauen in Institutionen essenziell, um ein sicheres Zusammenleben zu ermöglichen.

Vertrauen bildet somit die Grundlage für die Legitimation von Entscheidungen und deren Akzeptanz, selbst wenn diese nicht den eigenen Vorstellungen entsprechen. Es schafft die Gewissheit, Konflikte friedlich lösen zu können und grundlegende Bedürfnisse wie Bildung, Gesundheitsversorgung oder Rentensicherheit zu gewährleisten. Ohne Vertrauen droht nicht nur eine Erosion der Demokratie und des sozialen Zusammenhalts, sondern auch wirtschaftliche Stagnation und eine geringere Innovationskraft.

Ältere Bürger messen dem Vertrauen in Institutionen eine etwas größere Bedeutung bei als jüngere Generationen. Ihre Erfahrungen mit Krisenzeiten haben sie gelehrt, stabile Strukturen zu schätzen. Für sie stehen Institutionen für Sicherheit, Stabilität und besonnenes Handeln. Mit zunehmendem Alter steigt zudem die direkte Abhängigkeit von funktionierenden Systemen, etwa im Bereich der Gesundheits- oder Rentenversorgung. Die Sozialisation dieser Generation erfolgte in einer Zeit, in der Institutionen mit Autorität gleichgesetzt wurden und Respekt genossen. Dieses hat dazu geführt, dass ältere Bürger weniger misstrauisch gegenüber staatlichen Strukturen eingestellt sind. Ihre geringere Affinität zu digitalen Medien schützt sie zudem vor der Skepsis und Kritik, die dort oft verbreitet werden.

Im Gegensatz dazu ist die jüngere Generation in einer Welt der Digitalisierung aufgewachsen und sieht sich eher als Teil einer globalisierten Welt, in der lokale oder nationale Institutionen weniger wichtig für ihre Lebensgestaltung sind. Zudem spielen Autoritäten und traditionelle

Bindungen zu staatlichen Einrichtungen eine geringere Rolle in ihrer Lebenswelt. Dies zeigt sich auch in ihrer Betonung von Selbstbestimmung und Selbstverwirklichung sowie ihrer stärkeren Ablehnung von institutionellen Regelungen oder Vorgaben, von denen sie sich öfter eingeschränkt fühlen.

Prognose

Das Vertrauen in Institutionen wird in den kommenden Jahren eine zentrale Rolle für die Stabilität der Demokratie und Gesellschaft spielen. Die Entwicklung dieses Vertrauens hängt maßgeblich davon ab, wie die politischen Vertreter auf Herausforderungen wie Migration und wirtschaftliche Unsicherheiten reagieren. Parteien, die durch effektives Krisenmanagement überzeugen, werden an Ansehen gewinnen. Gleichzeitig besteht die Gefahr, dass ineffizientes Handeln oder mangelnde Transparenz bestehendes Vertrauen weiter untergraben. Erfahrungen aus der Vergangenheit zeigen, wie schnell Vertrauen verloren gehen kann, wenn Entscheidungen als unzureichend oder widersprüchlich wahrgenommen werden.

Auch werden technologische Entwicklungen wie der Einsatz von künstlicher Intelligenz das Vertrauensverhältnis zwischen Bürgern und Institutionen prägen. Fehlende oder unklare Regulierungen werden Misstrauen fördern, insbesondere wenn Technologien Fehler machen oder zur Verbreitung von Desinformationen beitragen. Institutionen, die ethische Standards setzen und Innovation transparent gestalten, werden hingegen als vertrauenswürdiger wahrgenommen werden.

Ein weiterer entscheidender Faktor wird die Fähigkeit von Institutionen sein, ihre Arbeit nachvollziehbar und transparent zu gestalten. Soziale Medien spielen hierbei eine doppelte Rolle: Einerseits können sie Misstrauen verstärken, andererseits eröffnen sie neue

Möglichkeiten für den Dialog zwischen Bürgern und Entscheidungsträgern. Langfristig wird sich zeigen, ob Institutionen nicht nur kurzfristige Erfolge erzielen möchten („Denken in Legislaturperioden", „Denken an die Schlagzeile/Auflage/Klickzahlen"), sondern auch komplexe Herausforderungen glaubwürdig bewältigen wollen.

Vertrauen bleibt somit auch in Zukunft eine Schlüsselressource für die Legitimität staatlicher Maßnahmen und die Stabilität demokratischer Strukturen.

Wie hoch ist das Politikervertrauen?

Von je 100 Befragten stimmen der Aussage zu:
„Vertrauen in Politiker ist entscheidend für das Funktionieren einer Gesellschaft."

Glaubwürdigkeit von Politikern

VERTRAUEN IST UNVERZICHTBAR

Ergebnis

Eine Gesellschaft kann nur dann funktionieren, wenn die Bürger den staatlichen Entscheidungsträgern des Landes vertrauen. Dieser Ansicht stimmen sieben von zehn Bürgern zu.

Gründe

Die Bedeutung des Vertrauens in Politiker für das Funktionieren einer Gesellschaft wird von den meisten Bürgern so hoch eingeschätzt, weil Vertrauen für sie eine zentrale Grundlage

für den gesellschaftlichen Zusammenhalt ist. Durch sie erhalten die gewählten Vertreter des Volkes die Legitimation ihrer Entscheidungs- und Handlungsfähigkeit. Dies ist besonders in Bereichen wichtig, die den Alltag der Bürger betreffen (Bildung, Gesundheit, Sicherheit), beim Krisenmanagement (Naturkatastrophen, Wirtschaftskrisen, Pandemien) oder bei globalen Herausforderungen (Sicherheit, Diplomatie, Klimaschutz). Hier erwarten die Bürger von politischen Führungskräften ein Zurückstellen aller Parteiinteressen und eine verantwortungsvolle, sozial gerechte, effektive und nachhaltige Fokussierung auf Lösungen.

Weitere Merkmale beziehungsweise Voraussetzungen für ein offenes Verhältnis der Zuverlässigkeit sehen sie in der verständlichen, ehrlichen und transparenten Kommunikation, in bürgernahen Gestaltungs- und Steuerungsprozessen (vor allem auf kommunaler Ebene), Authentizität sowie realistischen Wahlversprechen (statt kurzfristigem Populismus), Sach- und Fachkompetenz, Bereitschaft zu mutigen (und auch unbeliebten) Entscheidungen sowie der Fähigkeit, positive Zukunftsvisionen zu entwickeln.

Ein wichtiges Merkmal des Vertrauens zeigt sich dabei auch in dem Wunsch nach politischen Vorbildern. Als Mandatsträger auf unterschiedlichen Ebenen vertreten Politiker nicht nur die Interessen der eigenen Partei, sondern sind der allgemeinen politischen Willensbildung und Gestaltung zum Wohle der Gesellschaft verpflichtet. Als Person der Öffentlichkeit stehen sie im besonderen Fokus der Bürger, die an ihr Verhalten oft hohe Ansprüche stellen. Im Idealfall sind sie integre Persönlichkeiten, die sich durch Authentizität, Umsicht, Zielorientierung und Vertrauenswürdigkeit auszeichnen. Ihr Vorbildcharakter wird vor allem im Zusammenhang mit den oben erwähnten gesellschaftlichen Herausforderungen und unsicheren Krisensituationen genannt. Die Bürger wünschen sich Vorbilder, die mit Weitsicht, Überzeugung, Zuversicht und Tatkraft die Bevölkerung durch ihr Verhalten inspirieren und mögliche Lösungswege aufzeigen. Im Hinblick auf ihre öffentliche Wirkung sollen die politischen Vorbilder dabei nicht nur nachahmenswert für die eigene Lebenswelt sein, sondern eine Signalwirkung für die gesamte Gesellschaft haben.

VERTRAUEN

Besteht ein grundlegendes Vertrauen in sozial gerechte, effiziente und nachhaltige Maßnahmen und Konzepte, wird die Umsetzung deutlich eher unterstützt. In der Folge betonen die Bürger auch die weiterreichenden positiven Effekte eines vertrauensvollen Umgangs, zum Beispiel hinsichtlich des zwischenmenschlichen Zusammenlebens, des Gefühls des gemeinschaftlichen Zusammenhaltes und der Bereitschaft sich aktiv an der gesellschaftlichen Gestaltung zu beteiligen. Hierzu gehört zudem die Befürchtung, schwindendes Politikvertrauen steigere den Zulauf zu populistischen Bewegungen, die einfache Lösungen für komplexe Probleme versprechen.

Trotz aller Argumente für Politikervertrauen und trotz der hohen Zustimmung innerhalb der Bevölkerung dürfen nicht diejenigen vergessen werden, die das anders sehen. Fast jeder dritte Bürger sieht andere Mechanismen für die Stabilität einer Gesellschaft verantwortlich (zum Beispiel Medien, Governance-Strukturen, ziviles Engagement), hat eine pragmatische Sichtweise (Vertrauen ist nicht so wichtig wie Kontrollmechanismen) oder hegt grundsätzliches Misstrauen oder sogar Ablehnung gegenüber politischen Vertretern.

Prognose

Die zukünftige Entwicklung des politischen Vertrauens wird stark von gesellschaftlichen und globalen Veränderungen geprägt sein. Angesichts wachsender Herausforderungen wird die Fähigkeit von Regierungen, langfristige Stabilität und Gerechtigkeit zu gewährleisten, entscheidend sein. Bürger erwarten zunehmend eine Politik, die nicht einfach nur auf Krisen reagiert, sondern viel öfter proaktiv Lösungen für grundlegende Probleme bietet.

Ein zentraler Schwerpunkt wird dabei auf der Stärkung des Dialogs zwischen Bürgern und politischen Entscheidungsträgern liegen. Transparente Kommunikation und echte Mitgestaltungsmöglichkeiten werden das Gefühl der Zugehörigkeit und Verantwortung innerhalb der Gesellschaft fördern. Politischen Führungskräften, die sich durch Authentizität, Integrität, Orientierung und eine klare Vision auszeichnen, wird vertraut werden.

VERTRAUEN

In Zukunft werden Regierungen nicht nur verwalten, sondern auch gestalten – mit Weitsicht, Zuversicht und einem klaren Fokus auf die Bedürfnisse der Bürger. Nur durch diese Haltung wird ein stabiles Fundament für den gesellschaftlichen Zusammenhalt entstehen und bestehen.

Handeln Politiker im Interesse der Bürger?

Von je 100 Befragten stimmen der Aussage zu:
„Ich vertraue darauf, dass gewählte Politiker im besten Interesse der Bürger handeln."

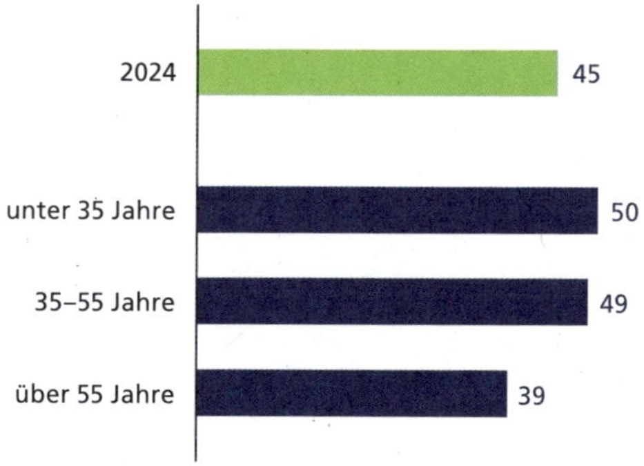

Politik ohne Bürgerinteresse

MEHRHEIT MISSTRAUT DEN VOLKSVERTRETERN

Ergebnis

Bei den gesellschaftlichen Diskussionen über das Vertrauen der Bürger in die Politiker stand in den letzten Jahren vorwiegend der Vertrauensverlust im Mittelpunkt. Thematisiert wurden fehlende Vorbildfunktion, Enthüllungen über Korruption oder moralisches Fehlverhalten, Unverbindlichkeiten, fehlende Bürgernähe oder intransparente Entscheidungsprozesse. Entsprechend gespalten äußert sich die Bevölkerung. Eine knappe Mehrheit traut den Volksvertretern nicht zu, im besten Interesse der Bürger zu handeln. Das größte Vertrauen genießen die gewählten Abgeordneten dabei noch bei der jungen Generation, während bei den Älteren nur noch zwei von fünf das Gefühl haben, sich auf deren Handlungen verlassen zu können.

VERTRAUEN

Gründe

Ein zentraler Grund für das Misstrauen vieler Bürger liegt in der Wahrnehmung, politische Akteure verfolgten häufig Eigeninteressen und stellten parteipolitische Ziele oder die Interessen spezifischer Gruppen über das Gemeinwohl. Diese Sichtweise wird durch eine unzureichende Transparenz bei Entscheidungsprozessen zusätzlich verstärkt. Infolgedessen zweifeln viele Bürger an der Neutralität und Unabhängigkeit politischer Entscheidungen.

Ein weiterer Faktor für das Misstrauen ist die Wahrnehmung eines ineffizienten Krisenmanagements. Insbesondere in herausfordernden Situationen erwarten Bürger entschlossenes Handeln und klare Strategien. Verzögerungen, widersprüchliche Maßnahmen oder offensichtliche Fehlentscheidungen erwecken hingegen den Eindruck mangelnder Kompetenz und Entscheidungsfähigkeit.

Auch die Rolle der Medien trägt maßgeblich zur Vertrauensbildung oder zum Vertrauensverlust bei. Eine Berichterstattung, die sich stark auf Fehlverhalten und Probleme konzentriert, verstärkt negative Wahrnehmungen. Während kritische Auseinandersetzungen mit politischen Prozessen notwendig sind, führt eine einseitige Darstellung dazu, positive Entwicklungen weniger wahrzunehmen und bestehende Vorurteile weiter zu zementieren.

Die zunehmende Polarisierung innerhalb der Gesellschaft stellt einen weiteren wesentlichen Grund für den Vertrauensverlust dar. Populistische Bewegungen nutzen gezielt das bestehende Misstrauen gegenüber etablierten Institutionen, um eine Anti-Establishment-Rhetorik zu fördern. Diese Dynamik untergräbt das Vertrauen in traditionelle Parteien und politische Prozesse. Gleichzeitig intensivieren populistische Akteure Konflikte zwischen verschiedenen gesellschaftlichen Gruppen, was den sozialen Zusammenhalt zusätzlich gefährdet.

Trotz dieser Herausforderungen vertrauen fast die Hälfte der Bürger weiterhin den Volksvertretern. Sie erkennen die Komplexität der Aufgaben, die politische Akteure bewältigen müssen, und verstehen die oft schwierigen Abwägungen.

VERTRAUEN

Bei jüngeren Bürgern ist das Vertrauen in politische Akteure tendenziell etwas höher als im Durchschnitt. Diese Gruppe zeigt oftmals eine optimistischere oder weniger kritische Haltung, die es ihr ermöglicht, Fehler oder Defizite in der Politik weniger stark zu bewerten. Gleichzeitig sehen sie möglicherweise mehr Chancen zur Verbesserung. Dennoch spricht auch in dieser Altersgruppe lediglich jeder Zweite den Politikern sein Vertrauen aus. Besonders enttäuscht sind sie über die vermeintliche Vernachlässigung ihrer Bedürfnisse, Interessen und Ängste, beispielsweise in den Bereichen Bildung, Altersvorsorge, Umweltpolitik oder bei der Entwicklung zukunftsweisender Visionen.

Prognose

Die Zukunft des politischen Vertrauens in Deutschland kann sich in zwei Richtungen entwickeln.

Erstens in ein „weiter wie bisher", was einem Vertrauensverlust mit weitreichenden Folgen gleichkommt. Setzt sich die derzeitige Entwicklung fort, wird das Vertrauen in die Politik weiter erodieren. Skeptische Bürger ziehen sich dann noch stärker als schon gegenwärtig aus dem politischen Diskurs zurück und zeigen kaum beziehungsweise kein Interesse mehr an demokratischen Prozessen. Eine geringere Wahlbeteiligung ist eine Konsequenz, da viele Bürger den Eindruck haben, ihre Stimme habe keinen Einfluss auf politische Entscheidungen. Gleichzeitig nimmt die Anzahl an Protestwählern zu. Populistische Bewegungen und extreme Parteien erhalten verstärkt Zuspruch, versprechen sie doch einfache Lösungen für komplexe Probleme und inszenieren sich als Vertreter der enttäuschten Bürger.

Zweitens in den „Rückzug ins Private." Bei einem anhaltenden Misstrauen wird sich stärker auf das persönliche Umfeld konzentriert und gesellschaftliche oder politische Engagements werden vermieden. Diese schwächt dann nicht nur den demokratischen Diskurs, sondern auch die Bereitschaft, gemeinsam an Lösungen für gesellschaftliche Herausforderungen zu

arbeiten. Proteste und Widerstand gegen Maßnahmen werden zunehmen – selbst dann, wenn diese im öffentlichen Interesse liegen. Ebenso nimmt auch die Polarisierung zwischen verschiedenen gesellschaftlichen Gruppen weiter zu, inklusive Konflikte zwischen Befürwortern und Gegnern des politischen Systems.

Es kann aber auch ein Weg zu einem neuen politischen Vertrauen eingeschlagen werden. Ein positiver Wandel kann durch verschiedene Ansätze erreicht werden, die über transparente Kommunikation oder Bürgerbeteiligung hinausgehen (siehe hierzu die entsprechenden Texte in diesem Buch). Die Medien spielen hierbei eine Schlüsselrolle, indem sie konsequent verschiedene Perspektiven, erfolgreiche politische Projekte und konstruktive Lösungsansätze in ihre Berichterstattung einfließen lassen und somit eine optimistische Grundhaltung stärken. Zudem wird zukünftig ein stärkerer Fokus auf politische Bildung gelegt werden. Verstehen Bürger besser, wie politische Prozesse funktionieren und welche Herausforderungen damit verbunden sind, wächst die Bereitschaft zur Unterstützung demokratischer Institutionen und Volksvertreter.

Können Politiker klar vermitteln?

Von je 100 Befragten stimmen der Aussage zu:
„Politische Maßnahmen und Entscheidungen sind für mich kaum mehr nachvollziehbar. Ich finde, Politiker können nicht klar vermitteln und begründen, was sie tun."

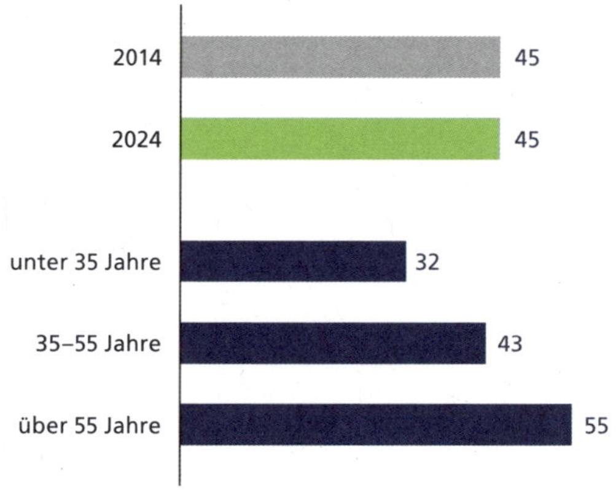

Zwischen Fachsprache und Floskeln

BÜRGER BEMÄNGELN POLITISCHE KOMMUNIKATION

Ergebnis

Knapp die Hälfte der Bürger empfindet politische Maßnahmen und Entscheidungen als schwer nachvollziehbar und bemängelt dabei die Vermittlungskompetenz von Politikern. Unterschiede zwischen den Generationen sind ebenfalls erkennbar: Während bei der Generation unter 35 Jahre etwa jeder Dritte politische Entscheidungen nicht nachvollziehen kann, ist es bei der älteren Generation mehr als jeder Zweite.

Gründe

Die Kritik an der Vermittlungsfähigkeit politischer Akteure ist kein neues Phänomen und hat sich in den letzten zehn Jahren nicht verändert. Besonders bei komplexen Themen wie

Klimawandel, Digitalisierung oder soziale Reformen zeigt sich die Schwierigkeit, politische Inhalte klar und verständlich zu kommunizieren. Die Ursachen hierfür sind vielfältig und reichen von strukturellen Problemen über strategische Schwächen bis hin zu medialen Verzerrungen.

Ein wesentlicher Grund liegt in der zunehmenden Komplexität politischer Themen. Viele Entscheidungen sind eng mit wissenschaftlichen, technologischen und internationalen Entwicklungen verbunden. Sicherheitspolitik bedeutet beispielsweise nicht nur nationale Maßnahmen, sondern steht auch im Zusammenhang mit internationalen Abkommen und langfristigen Strategien. Diese Vielschichtigkeit erschwert es oftmals, die Inhalte auf verständliche Weise zu vermitteln. Daneben trägt die Geschwindigkeit politischer Prozesse ebenfalls zur Wahrnehmung mangelnder Vermittlungsfähigkeit bei. Entscheidungen müssen oft schnell getroffen werden – etwa in Krisensituationen –, was wenig Zeit für ausführliche Erklärungen lässt.

Auch strukturelle Schwächen innerhalb der politischen Institutionen spielen eine Rolle. Die interne Abstimmung zwischen Ministerien oder Parteien ist häufig ineffizient, was zu widersprüchlichen Aussagen führt. Diese Inkonsistenz wird von Bürgern als fehlende Professionalität wahrgenommen. Ebenso beeinflusst aber auch die Art und Weise, wie Konflikte in der Politik ausgetragen werden, die Wahrnehmung der Vermittlungsunfähigkeit. Gerade polarisierende Debatten oder gegenseitige Schuldzuweisungen zwischen und innerhalb von Parteien dominieren zu oft die öffentliche Diskussion.

Die strategische Ausrichtung der politischen Kommunikation trägt ebenfalls zur Kritik bei. Politiker vermeiden oft klare Positionierungen, um flexibel auf Meinungsänderungen reagieren zu können und sich alle Möglichkeiten offenzuhalten. Diese Unverbindlichkeit führt jedoch zu dem Eindruck, politische Akteure könnten ihre Entscheidungen nicht überzeugend begründen. Hinzu kommt ein Fokus auf Parteipolitik, kurzfristige Erfolge und mediale Inszenierungen, während langfristige Ziele und Zwischenschritte selten umfassend kommuniziert werden.

Ein weiterer Aspekt ist die mangelnde Empathie in der politischen Sprache. Bürger wünschen sich nicht nur Informationen über politische Entscheidungen, sondern auch ein Verständnis für ihre persönlichen Sorgen und Lebensrealitäten. Politische Kommunikation wirkt jedoch oft technokratisch und distanziert, was den Eindruck einer abgehobenen Elite verstärkt. Hierzu passt auch das oftmals „typisch" deutsche Verhalten von Politikern: Zu viele politische Akteure treten sachlich und nüchtern auf, verwenden eine politische Fachsprache mit juristischen

oder technischen Formulierungen. Emotionale Ansprache oder Storytelling werden selten eingesetzt, obwohl diese bei der Vermittlung komplexer Inhalte helfen und gleichzeitig Sympathie erzeugen würden. Auch fehlt die Anpassung an moderne Kommunikationsformate. Während Unternehmen zunehmend auf visuelle Inhalte wie Infografiken oder Videos setzen, bleibt politische Kommunikation oft textlastig und wenig ansprechend gestaltet. Bürger erwarten jedoch zeitgemäße Formate, die Inhalte schnell erfassbar machen.

Zusätzlich erschwert die heutige Informationsflut eine klare Kommunikation politischer Inhalte. Während früher traditionelle Medien als Filter dienten und komplexe Themen verständlich aufbereiteten, hat sich dieser Mechanismus durch die Vielzahl an Informationsquellen verändert. Gerade durch soziale Netzwerke und digitale Plattformen hat sich der Informationsfluss beschleunigt und gleichzeitig fragmentiert. In der Konsequenz werden politische Aussagen häufig aus dem Kontext gerissen oder verkürzt dargestellt, was Missverständnisse fördert. Fake News und gezielte Desinformation untergraben zusätzlich das Vertrauen in politische Akteure (aber auch in die Medien selbst).

Die unterschiedlichen Erwartungen an Politiker vonseiten der jüngeren und älteren Bürger verkomplizieren zusätzlich die vorhandene Problematik. Jüngere Bürger erwarten eher eine digitale Ansprache sowie klare Positionen zu den für sie relevanten Themen. Sie sind mit sozialen Medien aufgewachsen und es gewohnt, Informationen schnell und interaktiv zu konsumieren. Ältere Generationen hingegen legen mehr Wert auf persönliche Ansprache und bewährte Strukturen und erwarten Seriosität statt Storytelling.

Prognose

Die Vermittlung politischer Entscheidungen wird in den kommenden Jahren eine der zentralen Herausforderungen für Regierungen bleiben. Um das Vertrauen der Bürger zurückzugewinnen und die Nachvollziehbarkeit politischer Maßnahmen zu erhöhen, sind innovative Ansätze erforderlich. Der Fokus muss auf einer emotionalen Ansprache, einer stärkeren Verknüpfung von Politik mit Alltagsrealitäten und einer Reform der politischen Kultur liegen.

VERTRAUEN

Ein zentraler Punkt dabei ist die stärkere Nutzung von Storytelling. Anstatt politische Inhalte abstrakt oder technokratisch zu präsentieren, müssen Politiker konkrete Beispiele anführen sowie etwas zu den (erwartbaren) Folgen, Chancen und Risiken für das Leben der Bürger sagen. Darüber hinaus muss die politische Kommunikation stärker auf Emotionen setzen. Bürger reagieren nicht nur auf Fakten, sondern auch auf Werte und Gefühle. Politiker können durch empathische Sprache und Gestik ihr Verständnis für die Sorgen und Wünsche der Bevölkerung darlegen. Dies bedeutet nicht, populistische Rhetorik zu übernehmen, sondern vielmehr eine authentische Verbindung zu den Bürgern herzustellen.

Gleichzeitig sollten moderne Technologien verstärkt eingesetzt werden, um Bürger auf innovative Weise einzubinden. Ein Beispiel ist der Einsatz von künstlicher Intelligenz (KI), etwa durch Chatbots oder virtuelle Assistenten, die rund um die Uhr Informationen zu politischen Entscheidungen liefern und auch Rückfragen interaktiv beantworten können. Digitale Partizipationsplattformen könnten es Bürgern ermöglichen, ihre Meinungen einzubringen, Diskussionen zu verfolgen und Entscheidungsprozesse transparenter nachzuvollziehen. Auch immersive Technologien wie Virtual Reality (VR) könnten verwendet werden, um die Auswirkungen politischer Maßnahmen visuell greifbar zu machen. Ergänzend könnten datengetriebene Inhalte wie interaktive Infografiken oder kurze Videos dazu beitragen, komplexe Inhalte verständlich und ansprechend zu vermitteln.

Berücksichtigt werden sollte in diesem Zusammenhang auch die unterschiedliche Ansprache von Zielgruppen. Während ältere Generationen auch zukünftig eher eine nüchterne und sachliche Ansprache bevorzugen, erwarten jüngere Bürger eine dynamischere und modernere Kommunikation. Erforderlich ist daher eine differenzierte Strategie, die beide Gruppen berücksichtigt.

Auch die politische Kultur selbst benötigt Veränderungen. Polarisierende Debatten und Schuldzuweisungen zwischen Parteien schaden dem Ansehen der Politik insgesamt. Stattdessen müssen Politiker verstärkt auf Konsensfindung setzen und gemeinsame Erfolge betonen.

Entsteht Vertrauen durch Kommunikation?

Von je 100 Befragten stimmen der Aussage zu:
„Ich glaube daran, dass gegenseitiges Vertrauen gestärkt werden kann, indem wir offen und ehrlich miteinander kommunizieren."

Vertrauen durch Kommunikation

DIE MACHT DER WORTE

Ergebnis

Eine offene und ehrliche Kommunikation wird von der großen Mehrheit der Bundesbürger als unverzichtbar angesehen, um das Vertrauen innerhalb der Gesellschaft zu stärken. Dieses Vertrauen bildet die Grundlage für ein stabiles und gerechtes Miteinander, sowohl im zwischenmenschlichen Bereich als auch im Verhältnis zwischen Bürgern und Institutionen.

VERTRAUEN

Gründe

Wie auch andere Grafiken zeigen, sehen die Bürger Vertrauen als einen Grundpfeiler einer stabilen und gerechten Gesellschaft an. Es schafft die Basis für Glaubwürdigkeit, Wertschätzung und Stabilität. Um dieses Vertrauen nachhaltig zu fördern, ist eine transparente Kommunikation notwendig, die Authentizität gewährleistet und Missverständnisse minimiert. Nur durch Offenheit können Bürger das Gefühl entwickeln, ernst genommen zu werden und aktiv am gesellschaftlichen Leben teilzuhaben.

Im Alltag, besonders im Familien- und Freundeskreis, spielt eine offene Kommunikation grundsätzlich eine zentrale Rolle. Sie ermöglicht es, Gedanken und Gefühle auszudrücken, wodurch ein Perspektivwechsel erleichtert wird. Diese Fähigkeit fördert das Verständnis für andere Standpunkte und stärkt die Bindung zwischen den Gesprächspartnern. Diese Offenheit geht auch immer mit dem Mut zur Verletzlichkeit einher – ein Risiko, das sich jedoch lohnt, da es tiefere Beziehungen und ein stärkeres Vertrauensverhältnis schafft. Fehlt diese Offenheit, bleiben Probleme oft unausgesprochen, was Missverständnisse begünstigt und Konflikte eskalieren lässt. Eine ehrliche Kommunikation dagegen bietet die Möglichkeit, Spannungen frühzeitig zu entschärfen und Lösungen gemeinsam zu erarbeiten. Dies stärkt nicht nur den Zusammenhalt im privaten Umfeld, sondern auch das allgemeine Vertrauen in die Mitmenschen.

Auch im öffentlichen Bereich wird eine offene Gesprächskultur geschätzt. Bürger erwarten von Institutionen wie Politik, Medien oder Wissenschaft Transparenz und Ehrlichkeit. Die verständliche Erläuterung von Entscheidungen ist hierbei von besonderer Bedeutung. Nur wenn Bürger nachvollziehen können, warum bestimmte Maßnahmen ergriffen werden, entsteht Akzeptanz – selbst bei kontroversen Themen.

VERTRAUEN

Institutionen gewinnen in dem Moment an Glaubwürdigkeit, wenn sie bereit sind, Fehler einzugestehen und Verantwortung zu übernehmen. Das Verschweigen von Problemen oder mangelnde Transparenz hingegen führt schnell zu Misstrauen. Eine offene Kommunikation hilft zudem dabei, Gerüchte zu entkräften und Bürger zu ermutigen, Fragen zu stellen oder eigene Meinungen einzubringen. Dies schafft dann eine Kultur des Dialogs, in der sich Bürger ernst genommen fühlen. In Krisensituationen zeigt sich die Bedeutung einer offenen Kommunikation besonders deutlich. Ob bei wirtschaftlichen Unsicherheiten, gesundheitlichen Notlagen oder anderen Herausforderungen – Bürger suchen in solchen Zeiten nach Orientierung und Halt. Wenn Institutionen transparent kommunizieren und gleichzeitig Empathie zeigen, fühlen sich Bürger besser verstanden und unterstützt. In dem Moment, in dem Sorgen ernst genommen und Lösungen gemeinsam erarbeitet werden, entsteht ein Gefühl von Respekt und Gleichberechtigung. Langfristig stärkt dies schließlich das Vertrauen in öffentliche Akteure und festigt die Bindung zwischen Bürgern und Institutionen.

Die überdurchschnittliche Zustimmungsquote der älteren Generation gründet auf deren Erfahrungsschatz und ihrer Affinität zum direkten Austausch sowie die geringere Neigung zu digitalen Kommunikationsformen. Sie verfügen über vermehrte Erfahrungen mit Krisen, haben oftmals eine bessere Menschenkenntnis und wissen um die Bedeutung ehrlicher Kommunikation zur Vertrauensbildung. Dies betrifft sowohl die eigene Lebenswelt als auch die Wahrnehmung der Dialogbereitschaft von Entscheidungsträgern. Ebenso haben sie häufiger als andere erlebt, wie mangelnde Kommunikation oder Täuschung (z. B. bei politischen Skandalen) zu Misstrauen führen kann, und erkennen oft schneller als andere die Konsequenzen unehrlicher Kommunikation.

Prognose

Die Bedeutung offener Kommunikation wird in den kommenden Jahren weiter an Relevanz gewinnen. Und je häufiger Bürger aktiv an Entscheidungsprozessen teilhaben können, desto stärker wird ihr Vertrauen in öffentliche Akteure sein. Partizipative Ansätze wie Bürgerforen oder digitale Mitbestimmungsplattformen werden dabei helfen, den Dialog zu intensivieren und den Eindruck von Mitgestaltung zu vermitteln. Solche Formate fördern nicht nur das Gefühl von Zugehörigkeit, sondern ermöglichen es auch, gesellschaftliche Veränderungen frühzeitig zu erkennen und darauf zu reagieren.

In einer zunehmend individualisierten Gesellschaft wird es für Institutionen immer wichtiger werden, ihre Botschaften auf die Bedürfnisse verschiedener Zielgruppen zuzuschneiden. Bürger wünschen sich personalisierte Informationen, die ihre Lebensrealitäten berücksichtigen und gleichzeitig gemeinsame Werte betonen. Neben den sachlichen Informationen werden auch empathische Reaktionen auf Sorgen und Ängste wichtiger werden. Institutionen, die in der Lage sind, Lösungswege klar darzulegen und gleichzeitig emotional zu überzeugen, werden an Zustimmung und damit auch an Bedeutung gewinnen. Die Digitalisierung wird hierbei sowohl helfen als auch Herausforderungen mit sich bringen. So ermöglichen digitale Plattformen es einerseits, Informationen schnell und direkt zu verbreiten, erhöhen andererseits aber auch das Risiko von Desinformation, Anonymität und manipulativen Inhalten.

VERTRAUEN

Ist die mediale Berichterstattung korrekt?

Von je 100 Befragten stimmen folgender Aussage zu:
„Ich vertraue darauf, dass die Medien objektiv und wahrheitsgemäß berichten."

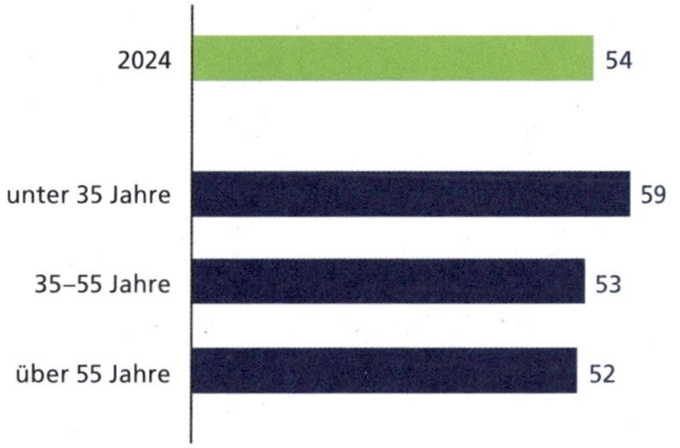

Medien als Sprachrohr

ZWISCHEN SCHLAGZEILEN UND SUBSTANZ

Ergebnis

Neben der Politikverdrossenheit ist in der öffentlichen Diskussion auch immer wieder vom wachsenden Misstrauen gegenüber den Medien die Rede. Als vierte Macht im Staat beeinflussen sie durch ihre Berichterstattung die öffentliche Meinung und – zu gewissen Teilen – auch das politische Geschehen. Bei der Frage, ob die Medien objektiv und wahrheitsgemäß berichten, zeigt sich die Bevölkerung uneinig. Eine knappe Mehrheit äußert sich zuversichtlich und vertraut auf eine sachliche, unparteiliche und seriöse Arbeit von Journalisten. Gleichzeitig sind aber auch 46 Prozent skeptisch und fürchten, eher geschönte, einseitige oder falsche Informationen zu erhalten.

Gründe

Medien verfügen über zahlreiche Mittel und Optionen, um als unabhängige Kraft einen Gegenpol zu politischer Einflussnahme, Kontrolle und Macht zu bilden. Mittels einer unabhängigen Berichterstattung und Distanz zu den Regierenden sind sie in der Lage, relevante Themen in den Mittelpunkt zu stellen, Missstände aufzudecken, unbequeme Perspektiven einzunehmen, Alternativen zu präsentieren und als Sprachrohr der Bevölkerung zu agieren. Damit können ihre Vertreter als entschlossene Mahner oder mutige Aufklärer wahrgenommen werden. Diese Rolle gesteht ihnen jedoch nur gut jeder zweite Bürger zu. Viele bemängeln eine fehlende Distanz zu den politischen oder wirtschaftlichen Vertretern, voreingenommene Berichterstattung oder sogar Manipulation durch gezielte Desinformation. In besonderer Weise richtet sich die Skepsis gegen digitale beziehungsweise soziale Medien. Ihnen werden oftmals Falschinformationen und vereinfachte Darstellungen vorgeworfen – lassen sich diese doch schneller und breiter als faktenbasierte Nachrichten verbreiten. Auch werden sie als anfällig für Bots, Trolle, intransparente Algorithmen, Filterblasen und Echokammern wahrgenommen. Bemängelt werden zudem Datenmissbrauch, mangelnde Transparenz und fehlende Kontrolle zum Beispiel bei der Verbreitung von Hassreden. Aber auch traditionelle Medien stehen immer häufiger in der Kritik. Hier reichen die Vorwürfe von einer zunehmenden Kommerzialisierung, über eine Informationsflut bis hin zur Konzentration auf eine negative Berichterstattung.

Auch der zunehmende Einsatz von künstlicher Intelligenz im Journalismus stimmt viele skeptisch. KI-gestützte Tools steigern zwar die Effizienz und Geschwindigkeit in der Nachrichtenproduktion, gleichzeitig wächst jedoch das Misstrauen gegenüber der Authentizität und Qualität solcher Inhalte. Viele Bürger befürchten eine geringere Gründlichkeit bei der Recherche oder eine höhere Anfälligkeit für Manipulation. Zudem vermissen viele die Transparenz, welche Inhalte von Menschen und welche durch Algorithmen erstellt wurden.

Das etwas höhere Vertrauen der jungen Bürger in die Medien lässt sich durch ihre grundsätzlich vertrauensvollere und optimistischere Haltung sowie durch ihre spezifischen Gewohnheiten der

Mediennutzung erklären. So konsumieren sie mehrheitlich digitale Medien und erhalten dabei ihre Informationen aus selbst gewählten Quellen. Diese nehmen sie als dynamisch, objektiv und ihrer Sichtweise entsprechend wahr.

Die Kritik der älteren Bürger konzentriert sich sowohl auf spezifische Inhalte in den traditionellen Medien als auch auf die Dominanz von digitalen Medien. So fühlen sie sich mit ihren Interessen oftmals nicht genügend vertreten, etwa hinsichtlich der Themen Renten- oder Gesundheitspolitik. Auch wird der Übergang von traditionellen Medien (z. B. Print und Fernsehen) zu digitalen Formaten nicht von allen älteren Bürgern gleich mitvollzogen beziehungsweise wird dieser von ihnen abgelehnt.

Prognose

Die Medienlandschaft steht vor tiefgreifenden Veränderungen. Der wirtschaftliche Druck auf Redaktionen wird weiter zunehmen. Sinkende Einnahmen aus traditionellen Geschäftsmodellen wie Printwerbung und Abonnements führen zu schrumpfenden Redaktionen, weniger Einstellungen von qualifizierten Journalisten und weniger Zeit für gründliche Recherche. Gleichzeitig zwingt der Auflagendruck viele Medienhäuser, sich stärker auf klickstarke Inhalte und Sensationsmeldungen zu konzentrieren. Diese Entwicklung wird die journalistische Qualität weiter schwächen und das Vertrauen der Bevölkerung in unabhängige Berichterstattung zusätzlich beeinträchtigen.

Entsprechend gilt es darüber nachzudenken, wie guter Journalismus in Zukunft finanziert werden kann. Denkbar sind einerseits staatliche Förderprogramme oder gemeinnützige Modelle, um unabhängigen Journalismus finanziell abzusichern. Andererseits muss auch der Bürger sich selbst kritisch hinterfragen, ob er bereit ist, für qualitativ hochwertige Berichterstattung zu bezahlen. Die weitverbreitete Erwartung, Nachrichten und Informationen kostenlos konsumieren zu können, steht im Widerspruch zu den hohen.Anforderungen an journalistische

Arbeit. Investigative Recherchen, fundierte Analysen und eine kritische Auseinandersetzung mit komplexen Themen erfordern Zeit, Ressourcen und Expertise – all das hat seinen Preis. Die Bereitschaft für seriöse Inhalte zu bezahlen, würde nicht nur die finanzielle Grundlage für Redaktionen sichern, sondern auch die Abhängigkeit von Werbeeinnahmen und damit einhergehenden möglichen Kompromissen reduzieren. Über Modelle wie freiwillige Abonnements, Crowdfunding oder Mitgliedschaften bei unabhängigen Plattformen würden Bürger aktiv zur Sicherung journalistischer Qualität beitragen. Parallel dazu liegt es aber auch an den Medienhäusern, durch Transparenz und Qualität das Vertrauen der Leser zurückzugewinnen und ihnen den Mehrwert bezahlter Inhalte klar zu vermitteln.

Auch der zunehmende Einsatz von Technologien wird die Zukunft der Medien weiterhin stark prägen. So werden bestimmte journalistische Prozesse effizienter gestaltet werden, indem automatisierte Systeme Routineaufgaben wie Datenanalyse, Transkription von Interviews, Organisation und Grundrecherchen übernehmen. Zudem werden digitale Medien Zielgruppen direkter ansprechen und Inhalte interaktiver sowie personalisierter gestalten. Gleichzeitig bleibt eine transparente Kommunikation darüber, wie und wo KI im Journalismus eingesetzt wird, eine Grundvoraussetzung, um Misstrauen zu vermeiden.

Zunehmen werden Nischenmedien und unabhängigen Plattformen. Immer mehr Bürger werden gezielt Angebote nutzen, die genau ihre Interessen und Werte widerspiegeln. Diese Entwicklung bietet eine Chance für kleinere Anbieter, sich mit hochwertigen und glaubwürdigen Inhalten zu positionieren. Das gilt insbesondere für den lokalen Vor-Ort-Journalismus, der ein Gegengewicht zur Schnelllebigkeit digitaler Nachrichtenströme bilden wird.

Insgesamt wird die Zukunft der Medienlandschaft davon abhängen, wie eine ausgewogene Balance zwischen wirtschaftlichen Zwängen, technologischen Innovationen und dem Anspruch auf unabhängige Berichterstattung erhalten bleibt. Gelingt dies, wird das Vertrauen wieder steigen und die Presse wird ihre Rolle als vierte Macht im Staat weiterhin erfüllen können.

Können Medien gesellschaftliches Vertrauen schaffen?

Von je 100 Befragten stimmen der Aussage zu:
„Seriöse Medien spielen eine zentrale Rolle dabei, das Vertrauen der Öffentlichkeit zu erhalten."

Medien im Vertrauenscheck

BEVÖLKERUNG BLICKT GESPALTEN AUF DIE VIERTE GEWALT

Ergebnis

Medien sind ein wichtiger Bestandteil einer lebendigen Demokratie und stehen für Unabhängigkeit, Kontrolle und Meinungsbildung. Als sogenannte vierte Macht im Staat decken sie Missstände auf und tragen zur Transparenz des Staatswesens bei. Folglich sehen auch acht von zehn Bürgern Medien als Garant, um das Vertrauen der Bürger in Institutionen zu erhalten. Die ältere Generation zeigt hierbei eine überdurchschnittliche Zustimmungsrate, während sich die Jüngeren etwas zurückhaltender äußern, aber immer noch zu drei Vierteln zustimmen.

VERTRAUEN

Gründe

Die Bedeutung der Medien für die Gesellschaft wird durch ihre verfassungsrechtliche Absicherung hervorgehoben. Artikel 5 des Grundgesetzes garantiert die Presse- und Rundfunkfreiheit, verbietet staatliche Eingriffe und Zensur und sichert den Zugang zu öffentlich zugänglichen Informationen. Diese Schutzrechte unterstreichen die zentrale Rolle der Medien in der Demokratie. Ihre Aufgaben umfassen die Information der Öffentlichkeit, die Kontrolle staatlicher Macht und die Förderung eines freien Meinungsbildungsprozesses. Medien tragen somit wesentlich dazu bei, demokratische Grundprinzipien zu bewahren und eine informierte Gesellschaft zu gewährleisten. In ihrer Informationsfunktion berichten sie der Öffentlichkeit über gesellschaftliche Vorgänge und aktuelle Ereignisse. Sie übermitteln politische Stellungnahmen, erläutern Konflikte und Herausforderungen und bieten zahlreiche Hintergrundinformationen. Durch Analysen, Kommentare und Diskussionen helfen sie, komplexe Sachverhalte besser zu verstehen, wodurch sich die Bürger eine eigene differenzierte Meinung bilden können.

Damit übernehmen sie im weiteren Sinne die Aufgabe der politischen Bewusstseinsbildung, insbesondere da sie durch ihre Unabhängigkeit und Neutralität in den meisten Fällen keine Einzelinteressen vertreten, sondern alle Perspektiven berücksichtigen. Verstärkt wird der Eindruck der Unabhängigkeit noch, wenn Medien offene Plattformen für Diskussionen und Debatten bieten. Durch diese Möglichkeit fördern sie das Gefühl der Partizipation, was wiederum das Vertrauen in die Medien und ihre Rolle im demokratischen Prozess stärkt.

In ihrer Kontrollfunktion decken Medien Missstände auf, hinterfragen Entscheidungen von Führungspersönlichkeiten und Institutionen und tragen so zur Transparenz des Staatswesens bei. Als besonders wichtig empfinden die Bürger hierbei die Distanz der Medien zu Politik und Wirtschaft. Diese Integrität ermöglicht es ihnen, Maßnahmen zu kritisieren und Alternativen aufzuzeigen. Besonders von den öffentlich-rechtlichen Sendern wird dies erwartet, da sie der ausgewogenen und vielfältigen Berichterstattung stärker verpflichtet sind als private Medien. Neben ihren grundlegenden Aufgaben und Funktionen dienen Medien als Werkzeug zur Bildung kollektiver Identitäten und zur Förderung des sozialen Zusammenhalts. Sie schaffen

gemeinsame Bezugspunkte, die Gruppen ein Gefühl von Einheit und Zugehörigkeit vermitteln. Beispiele hierfür sind nationale Identitäten wie „Wir leben in einer vielfältigen Gesellschaft", regionale Zugehörigkeiten wie „Wir sind Bayern" oder Wertegemeinschaften wie „Wir setzen uns als Umweltschützer für den Planeten ein." Medien tragen demnach dazu bei, gemeinsame Vorstellungen zu verbreiten, Werte zu vermitteln und deren Bedeutung für die Gemeinschaft hervorzuheben. Gleichzeitig fördern sie die kritische Auseinandersetzung mit diesen Werten und regen den gesellschaftlichen Dialog an, wodurch das Vertrauen zwischen unterschiedlichen Gruppen gestärkt wird.

Hinsichtlich der Generationsunterschiede lässt sich die geringere Zustimmung der Jüngeren vor alle durch deren spezifische Mediennutzung erklären. Sie beziehen ihre Nachrichten zunehmend aus sozialen Netzwerken, von Influencern oder alternativen Plattformen wie YouTube, TikTok oder Reddit. Traditionelle Medien wie Zeitungen, Fernsehen und Radio spielen eine kleinere Rolle, weshalb diesen auch eine geringere Bedeutung zur Vertrauensbildung zugesprochen wird. Zudem wissen sie um den Einfluss von Filterblasen, Echokammern, Algorithmen und Desinformationen und sind in der Folge auch gegenüber seriösen Medien skeptischer. Ältere Menschen haben dagegen oft eine längere Bindung an traditionelle Medien, vertrauen ihnen mehr als den nozialen Netzwerken und sehen vor allem ihr Potential als Kontrollinstrument und wichtige Stütze der Demokratie.

Prognose

Medien werden auch in Zukunft eine zentrale Rolle für die Demokratie und den gesellschaftlichen Zusammenhalt spielen. Ihre Funktion als vierte Macht bleibt unverzichtbar, um Transparenz zu gewährleisten und Missstände aufzudecken. Diese Kontrollfunktion wird weiterhin entscheidend sein, um das Vertrauen der Bürger in Institutionen zu stärken und die Integrität demokratischer Prozesse zu sichern. Besonders wichtig bleibt dabei die Unabhängigkeit der Medien von politischen und wirtschaftlichen Interessen, da sie nur

so ihre Glaubwürdigkeit gewährleisten können. Um ihre Rolle als kritische Berichterstatter sinnvoll zu ergänzen, werden Medien in Zukunft verstärkt auch positive Entwicklungen hervorheben. Fortschritte in der Wissenschaft, wie neue medizinische Behandlungsmethoden, technologische Innovationen im Bereich der Mobilität oder nachhaltige Bauprojekte bieten inspirierende Beispiele für gesellschaftlichen Fortschritt. Solche Berichte stärken das Vertrauen in die Fähigkeit der Gesellschaft, auch komplexe Herausforderungen zu meistern. Ebenso fördern Berichte über ziviles Engagement und erfolgreiche soziale Initiativen – wie Ausbildungsprogramme für Geflüchtete oder Infrastrukturprojekte, die neue Arbeitsplätze schaffen – das Gemeinschaftsgefühl, tragen zu einer optimistischeren Grundhaltung bei und zeigen gleichzeitig konkrete Lösungsansätze für gesellschaftliche Probleme auf.

Eine Berichterstattung, die nicht nur Schwierigkeiten beleuchtet, sondern auch Erfolge und Lösungen in den Vordergrund rückt, eröffnet neue Perspektiven und lenkt den Fokus auf die Chancen eines positiven gesellschaftlichen Wandels.

Um (gerade) die jüngere Generation besser zu erreichen, werden traditionelle Medien ihre Angebote noch deutlich stärker an digitale Formate anpassen. Die Präsenz in sozialen Netzwerken, Videoplattformen oder durch interaktive Apps wird helfen, um deren Mediennutzungsgewohnheiten zu entsprechen. Dabei bleibt es essenziell, auch dort Desinformationen, Filterblasen und Echokammern entgegenzuwirken, um die eigene Glaubwürdigkeit langfristig zu sichern.

Sollten Fake News bestraft werden?

Von je 100 Befragten stimmen folgender Aussage zu:
„Die Verbreitung von Fehlinformationen in sozialen Netzwerken sollte strafbar gemacht werden."

Fakten statt Fake News

WESHALB FALSCHMELDUNGEN SANKTIONIERT WERDEN SOLLTEN

Ergebnis

Der Begriff „Fake News" bezeichnet gezielte Falschmeldungen oder irreführende Informationen, die vor allem über soziale Medien verbreitet werden. Mit dem Ziel, die Meinungen, Emotionen oder Handlungen der Öffentlichkeit zu manipulieren, sollen bestimmte politische oder ideologische Interessen gefördert werden. Die Gefahr ist groß, hierdurch Vorurteile zu manifestieren, Gruppen gegeneinander aufzuwiegeln und eine Polarisierung der Gesellschaft zu verstärken. Entsprechend plädieren mehr als vier von fünf Bundesbürgern dafür,

die Verbreitung von Fehlinformationen unter Strafe zu stellen. Ältere Bürger zeigen sich hierbei besonders alarmiert, aber auch bei den Jüngeren sind drei von fünf für eine entsprechende Sanktionierung.

Gründe

Fake News stellen eine ernsthafte Gefahr für die Gesellschaft dar. Gerade in sozialen Netzwerken finden Fake News ideale Bedingungen zur Verbreitung: Algorithmen verstärken ihre virale Dynamik, während Anonymität, Filterblasen und Echokammern ihre Reichweite erhöhen. Monetäre Anreize wie „Klickfallen" und die Präferenz für Einfachheit statt Komplexität tragen ebenfalls zur schnellen und unkontrollierten Verbreitung bei.

Die Gefahren durch Fake News sind vielschichtig und weitreichend. Sie beeinflussen die öffentliche Meinungsbildung, fördern gesellschaftliche Polarisierung und verfestigen Vorurteile sowie einseitige Perspektiven. Gleichzeitig steigt das allgemeine Misstrauen innerhalb der Gesellschaft. Bürger zweifeln zunehmend nicht nur an der Glaubwürdigkeit einzelner Nachrichten, sondern auch an Mitbürgern, Institutionen und Medien. Häufig werden Fake News selbst zum Streitpunkt, was zu familiären Konflikten, unversöhnlichen Diskussionen im sozialen Umfeld oder polarisierten öffentlichen Debatten führt. Dabei wird die eigene Meinung oftmals absolut gesetzt, während alternative Sichtweisen kategorisch abgelehnt werden. Einzelpersonen, insbesondere im Kontext von Mobbing, sowie Minderheiten werden ebenfalls häufig Ziel solcher zweifelhaften Informationen, die bestehende Vorurteile verstärken und Diskriminierung bis hin zu physischer Gewalt fördern können.

Eine zusätzliche Herausforderung ergibt sich aus der schnellen Verbreitung von Fake News durch die Dynamik sozialer Netzwerke. Die Algorithmen dieser Plattformen priorisieren Inhalte mit hoher Interaktionsrate, wodurch polarisierende oder überzogene Beiträge begünstigt werden. Nutzer teilen solche Inhalte oft ungeprüft weiter, was die rasche Verbreitung von Falschinformationen begünstigt und falsche Narrative im kollektiven Bewusstsein verankert.

VERTRAUEN

Die Unterschiede zwischen jüngeren und älteren Bürgern im Umgang mit Fake News lassen sich auf ihre jeweilige Mediennutzung und Informationsverarbeitung zurückführen. Jüngere Bürger nutzen soziale Netzwerke intensiv: 80 Prozent von ihnen verwenden diese als häufigste Informationsquelle, während 16 Prozent sie sogar als einzige Nachrichtenquelle nutzen. Trotz dieser Abhängigkeit bewerten viele ihre Medienkompetenz als ausreichend, um Fake News eigenständig zu erkennen. Studien zeigen jedoch das Gegenteil. So bewerteten bei einer britischen Untersuchung 36 Prozent der Generation Z den Wahrheitsgehalt von mindestens der Hälfte der getesteten Schlagzeilen falsch. Zudem legen jüngere Menschen großen Wert auf Meinungsfreiheit und individuelle Freiheiten im digitalen Raum, stehen staatlichen Eingriffen kritisch gegenüber und bevorzugen Eigenregulation sowie technische Lösungen wie Fact-Checking-Tools oder KI-Filter.

Ältere Menschen hingegen nutzen soziale Netzwerke weniger intensiv und begegnen ihnen generell mit größerer Skepsis. Ihr Wunsch nach staatlichem Schutz vor Fake News ist ausgeprägter, insbesondere da sie oft Hauptzielgruppe für betrügerische Online-Maschen sind. Sie betrachten staatliche Maßnahmen nicht als Einschränkung legitimer Meinungen, sondern als notwendige Schutzmaßnahme gegen gezielte Desinformation.

Prognose

Die zukünftige Entwicklung im Umgang mit gezielten Falschmeldungen wird sowohl von technologischen als auch gesellschaftlichen und rechtlichen Entwicklungen geprägt sein. Technologische Innovationen werden Falschmeldungen automatisiert identifizieren können und mithelfen, ihre Verbreitung einzuschränken. Plattformen werden dabei wahlweise freiwillig oder gezwungenermaßen umfassendere Überwachungsmechanismen implementieren, um problematische Inhalte frühzeitig zu erkennen. Deepfakes und andere fortgeschrittene Manipulationstechnologien werden es jedoch auch weiterhin erschweren, zwischen Wahrheit und Täuschung zu unterscheiden.

Gesellschaftlich wird es darauf ankommen, ein stärkeres Bewusstsein für die Mechanismen hinter Desinformationen zu schaffen. Entsprechend wird Medienkompetenz nicht mehr nur eine individuelle Fähigkeit bleiben, sondern zu einem zentralen Bestandteil von Bildungssystemen weltweit werden.

Rechtlich ist eine zunehmende Regulierung sozialer Netzwerke wahrscheinlich. Staaten werden Unternehmen stärker in die Pflicht nehmen, ihrer Verantwortung zur Verbreitung seriöser Meldungen nachzukommen. Entsprechend werden Strafen für die Verbreitung von Falschmeldungen nicht nur Einzelpersonen betreffen, sondern auch Betreiber digitaler Plattformen. Eine internationale Zusammenarbeit wird hierbei unverzichtbar sein, da Desinformationen keine geografischen Grenzen kennen.

Aber auch in Zukunft wird die Balance zwischen Regulierung und der Wahrung der Meinungsfreiheit stets neu austariert werden müssen.

Ist Vertrauen (fast) alles?

Von je 100 Befragten stimmen folgender Aussage zu:
„Vertrauen ist die Grundlage für jede erfolgreiche Kooperation."

Die Macht des Vertrauens

DAS FUNDAMENT ERFOLGREICHER ZUSAMMENARBEIT

Ergebnis

Vertrauen wird von der großen Mehrheit der Bundesbürger als unverzichtbare Grundlage für jede erfolgreiche Kooperation angesehen. Besonders hoch ist die Zustimmung bei den über 55-Jährigen, von denen 93 Prozent Vertrauen als essenziell für Zusammenarbeit betrachten. Bei den jüngeren Bürgern liegt der Anteil mit vier von fünf Befragten etwas niedriger, bleibt jedoch ebenfalls auf einem sehr hohen Niveau. Die Werte verdeutlichen, wie stark Vertrauen als Fundament für funktionierende Beziehungen wahrgenommen wird. Kooperationen – egal ob im persönlichen Umfeld oder in größeren gesellschaftlichen Strukturen – sind ohne ein Mindestmaß an Vertrauen für die Bürger kaum vorstellbar.

VERTRAUEN

Gründe

Wie in diesem Kapitel zum Themenkomplex „Vertrauen“ bereits deutlich wurde, reduziert Vertrauen Unsicherheiten und schafft eine Grundlage für Verlässlichkeit und Berechenbarkeit im Umgang miteinander. Ohne Vertrauen entstehen dagegen Misstrauen und Kontrollmechanismen, die Kooperationen erschweren und ineffizient machen.

Im zwischenmenschlichen Bereich ermöglicht Vertrauen offene Kommunikation und gegenseitiges Verständnis. Sich einander vertrauende Bürger sind eher bereit, Informationen zu teilen, einander zu unterstützen und gemeinsam Lösungen zu entwickeln. Diese Offenheit fördert nicht nur die Qualität der Zusammenarbeit, sondern stärkt auch das Gemeinschaftsgefühl. Auch im beruflichen Zusammenhang zeigt sich die Bedeutung von Vertrauen deutlich: Teams mit einer hohen Vertrauensbasis arbeiten effizienter, da sie weniger Energie in Konflikte oder Absicherungen investieren. Führungskräfte, die Vertrauen schaffen, fördern zudem Kreativität und Innovation in ihren Teams und steigern so den Gesamterfolg des Unternehmens.

Vertrauen spielt auch eine zentrale Rolle bei der langfristigen Planung von Kooperationen. Projekte, die sich über längere Zeiträume erstrecken, erfordern ein hohes Maß an Verlässlichkeit und die Gewissheit, dass Zusagen eingehalten werden. Gleichzeitig erleichtert Vertrauen den Umgang mit Risiken, da Beteiligte bereit sind, Verantwortung zu teilen und flexibel auf unvorhergesehene Entwicklungen zu reagieren.

Wirtschaftliche Krisen oder politische Umbrüche haben gezeigt, wie wichtig eine stabile Zusammenarbeit ist, um diese zu bewältigen. Diese kollektiven Erfahrungen sind ein Grund, weshalb gerade die ältere Generation einen so hohen Wert auf Vertrauen legt. Ein anderer ist die gegenteilige Erfahrung: Viele Kooperationen scheiterten, weil Disharmonie vorherrschte oder Einzelinteressen im Vordergrund standen. Zudem sind die älteren Bürger noch stärker von Sozialisationseinflüssen geprägt, in denen dem Gemeinschaftsgefühl eine höhere Bedeutung zukam. An diesem Wert halten sie umso stärker fest, je mehr sie ihn

durch technologische Entwicklungen bedroht sehen. So wird es in einer zunehmend digitalen Welt schwieriger, persönliche Bindungen aufzubauen und Vertrauen zu etablieren. Gleichzeitig entstehen neue Formen von Kooperationen über digitale Plattformen oder globale Netzwerke, bei denen Vertrauensmechanismen pragmatischer funktionieren als in traditionellen Strukturen. Dies erklärt auch, weshalb jüngere Generationen zwar ebenfalls einen hohen Wert auf Vertrauen legen, diesen jedoch funktionaler erleben und bewerten als ältere Bürger. Für sie hängen Erfolg und Effizienz von Kooperation auch von Regeln, Verträgen, klaren Rahmenbedingungen und einer nüchternen Kosten-Nutzen-Rechnung ab.

Prognose

In einer zunehmend komplexen Welt mit globalisierten Märkten und digitalen Netzwerken wird Vertrauen weiterhin eine zentrale Rolle spielen, um Unsicherheiten zu reduzieren und Zusammenarbeit zu ermöglichen. Gesellschaften mit einem hohen Maß an Vertrauen sind besser in der Lage, Herausforderungen zu bewältigen, da sie schneller kooperieren und effektiver handeln können.

Ein Rückgang des Vertrauens hätte hingegen erhebliche Nachteile. Beispielsweise wären im Wirtschaftsbereich ohne eine ausreichende Vertrauensbasis zusätzliche Kontrollmechanismen und mehr Bürokratie erforderlich, was wiederum Prozesse verlangsamen und Kosten erhöhen würde.

Die Förderung von vertrauensbasierten Beziehungen sollte daher als zentrale Aufgabe verstanden werden – sowohl auf individueller Ebene als auch innerhalb größerer Strukturen wie Unternehmen oder politischen Systemen.

VERTRAUEN

VERANTWORTUNG

Verantwortung

Auch Verantwortung ist ein Begriff, der gegenwärtig in vielen gesellschaftlichen und politischen Debatten eine zentrale Rolle spielt. Häufig wird er jedoch nur in einem negativen Zusammenhang verwendet, wenn es um das Fehlen von Verantwortungsbewusstsein oder -bereitschaft geht. Dabei bietet der Begriff selbst eine Vielzahl positiver Implikationen und Möglichkeiten, die selten hervorgehoben werden. Verantwortung bedeutet nicht nur, für Fehler einzustehen, sondern auch aktiv und vorausschauend zu handeln, um positive Entwicklungen zu fördern – sowohl auf privater als auch gesellschaftlicher Ebene. Um die Bedeutung der Verantwortung besser einordnen zu können, werden die verschiedene Facetten und historischen Ursprünge kurz dargestellt.

Wortherkunft

Der Begriff Verantwortung hat eine lange sprachgeschichtliche Entwicklung, die eng mit rechtlichen und ethischen Konzepten verbunden ist. Ursprünglich stammt das Wort aus dem mittelhochdeutschen „verantwürten", was mit „sich als Angeklagter vor Gericht verteidigen" gleichgesetzt wurde. Dieses Verb ist seit dem 12. Jahrhundert belegt, während das Substantiv Verantwortung erst im 15. Jahrhundert nachweisbar ist. Die Wurzel des Begriffs liegt im althochdeutschen „antwurti", das mit „Antwort" verwandt ist und ursprünglich eine Erwiderung oder Rechtfertigung bezeichnete. Die lateinische Entsprechung „respondere" (antworten) aus der römischen Rechtssprache beeinflusste die Entwicklung des Begriffs ebenfalls stark. Im juristischen Zusammenhang bedeutete Verantwortung zunächst, für Handlungen einzustehen und sich vor einer höheren Instanz zu rechtfertigen. Diese Verbindung zwischen Verantwortung und Rechenschaftspflicht zeigt sich auch in modernen Bedeutungen. Im Laufe der Zeit erlebte der Begriff eine semantische Erweiterung. Während er im Mittelalter primär juristisch geprägt war, entwickelte er sich ab dem 19. Jahrhundert zu einem zentralen ethischen und philosophischen Konzept. Mit der Säkularisierung der Gesellschaft wurde Verantwortung zunehmend auch auf das menschliche Zusammenleben bezogen, etwa als moralische Verpflichtung gegenüber anderen oder der Gesellschaft.

Heute umfasst der Begriff verschiedene Dimensionen: von der persönlichen Verantwortung für eigenes Handeln bis hin zur kollektiven Verantwortung in sozialen oder politischen Zusammenhängen. In all diesen Bedeutungen bleibt jedoch die ursprüngliche Idee des Antwortens und Einstehens für Handlungen zentral, was den dialogischen Charakter des Begriffs unterstreicht.

Wissenschaftliche Einordnung

Wie Vertrauen und Kooperation ist auch Verantwortung ein interdisziplinäres Konzept und spielt in unterschiedlichen wissenschaftlichen Disziplinen eine Rolle. In der Philosophie wird Verantwortung vor allem in der Ethik diskutiert: Aristoteles betonte die Bedeutung eines tugendhaften Charakters, während Kant den Fokus auf moralische Pflichten legte. Beide Ansätze stellen den Einzelnen in den Mittelpunkt – entweder durch die Entwicklung von Tugenden oder durch die Einhaltung von Pflichten. Der Philosoph Hans Jonas erweiterte dieses Verständnis im 20. Jahrhundert durch seine Verantwortungsethik, die besonders auf die langfristigen Folgen menschlichen Handelns abzielt. Er forderte eine Verantwortung gegenüber zukünftigen Generationen und warnte vor den Auswirkungen der Technik auf Menschen und Umwelt.

In der Soziologie wird Verantwortung oft im Zusammenhang komplexer sozialer Strukturen betrachtet. Max Weber betonte die Rolle von Führungskräften und Entscheidungsträgern, deren Verantwortung weit über individuelle Absichten hinausgeht. Sie müssen nicht nur moralisch korrekt handeln, sondern auch die realen Auswirkungen ihrer Entscheidungen berücksichtigen. Psychologische Ansätze hingegen beschäftigen sich häufig mit dem Phänomen der Verantwortungsdiffusion. In Gruppen neigt der Einzelne dazu, weniger Verantwortung zu übernehmen als in Einzelsituationen. Dieses Phänomen zeigt sich zum Beispiel im Alltag in zahlreichen Situationen, sei es im Büro, in Vereinen, Schulen, Parteien, Freundeskreis oder Nachbarschaft – stets wird darauf gehofft, nicht selbst Verantwortung übernehmen zu müssen beziehungsweise dass andere diese für die Gruppe übernehmen.

VERANTWORTUNG

In der Wirtschaftswissenschaft wird der Begriff Verantwortung vor allem im Kontext von Unternehmensethik und Corporate Social Responsibility (CSR) diskutiert. Unternehmen tragen Verantwortung nicht nur für ihre ökonomischen Ergebnisse, sondern auch für die sozialen und ökologischen Auswirkungen ihres Handelns. CSR beschreibt hierbei die freiwillige Integration von Nachhaltigkeitsprinzipien in die Geschäftspraktiken, wobei diese über gesetzliche Anforderungen hinausgehen, um soziale Gerechtigkeit, Umweltschutz und ethische Standards zu fördern. Diese Verantwortung umfasst sowohl interne Aspekte, wie faire Arbeitsbedingungen und Diversität, als auch externe Dimensionen, etwa den sparsamen Umgang mit Ressourcen oder die Unterstützung lokaler Gemeinschaften. Ein zentraler Diskussionspunkt ist hierbei der Konflikt zwischen kurzfristigen Gewinnzielen und langfristiger Verantwortung. Unternehmen stehen oft vor moralischen Dilemmata, beispielsweise wenn wirtschaftlicher Gewinn mit ethischen Prinzipien kollidiert. Wirtschaftsethische Ansätze fordern daher eine Balance zwischen ökonomischer Rationalität und moralischer Verantwortung. Studien zeigen dabei, wie verantwortungsbewusstes Wirtschaften das Unternehmensimage stärkt und langfristig Wettbewerbsvorteile schafft, etwa durch höhere Mitarbeiterbindung oder gesteigertes Kundenvertrauen.

Bedeutung für Individuum und Gesellschaft

Die Verantwortung gibt es nicht, sondern verschiedene Ausprägungen, die eine zentrale Bedeutung für die Gesellschaft haben und das Zusammenleben beeinflussen. Allgemein gewährleistet Verantwortung, Individuen und Organisationen für ihr Handeln und dessen Folgen in die Pflicht zu nehmen. In der Folge werden dadurch Verlässlichkeit und das Vertrauen in sozialen Interaktionen gestärkt. Im individuellen Zusammenhang befähigt Verantwortung den Einzelnen, dazu selbstständig zu handeln, bewusste Entscheidungen zu treffen und für die Konsequenzen einzustehen. Verbunden hiermit ist eine Förderung des Selbstbewusstseins und der persönlichen Entwicklung. Besonders deutlich wird dies bei jungen Erwachsenen. Bevor sie Verantwortung für andere übernehmen können, erlernen sie zunächst Selbstverantwortung, etwa in Bezug auf Schule, Ausbildung oder auch Beziehungen.

Sie üben, sich selbst zu organisieren, unabhängige Entscheidungen und Vereinbarungen zu treffen und eigene Moral- und Wertmaßstäbe zu entwickeln. Auch lernen sie die Folgen ihres Handelns zu reflektieren und die entsprechenden Konsequenzen zu tragen. Diese Selbstverantwortung befähigt sie dazu, persönliche Ziele zu setzen, Durchhaltevermögen zu entwickeln und ihre Vorhaben eigenständig und selbstbewusst in die Tat umzusetzen. Dazu gehört auch, eigene Fehler zu erkennen und für diese einzustehen sowie Konflikte respektvoll zu lösen und diese als Lernchancen zu begreifen. Im späteren Leben geht die Selbstverantwortung über das eigene Leben hinaus und beeinflusst auch Freunde, Familie, Nachbarn und die Gemeinschaft. Hierbei werden unter anderem Empathie, Rücksichtnahme, Toleranz und Respekt weiterentwickelt. Positive Erfahrungen mit zuverlässigem Handeln stärken dabei die Zuversicht, Herausforderungen anzunehmen, sodass in der Folge die Verantwortung zu einer zentralen Fähigkeit heranwächst, um sowohl private Ziele zu erreichen als auch die Gemeinschaft zu unterstützen. Insofern wandelt sich die Selbstverantwortung über die Verantwortung für andere in eine gesellschaftliche Verantwortung. Als Teil einer größeren Gemeinschaft weitet sich diese auf weitere soziale und politische Bereiche aus, etwa in Form eines gesellschaftlichen Engagements. Häufig werden hierbei Kooperationen mit anderen eingegangen, um sich einerseits gegenseitig zu motivieren und andererseits die Verantwortung nicht allein tragen zu müssen.

Verantwortungsdiffusion

So vielseitig und bedeutsam die Übernahme von Verantwortung für die Entwicklung des Einzelnen und die Stabilität einer Gesellschaft auch sind, so kann sie in ihrer Negation auch zahlreiche destabilisierende Auswirkungen nach sich ziehen. Dies wird am Beispiel der Verantwortungsdiffusion deutlich. Dieses Konzept beschreibt ein sozialpsychologisches Phänomen, bei dem sich die Verantwortung für Handlungen, Entscheidungen oder Aufgaben in Gruppen auf mehrere Personen verteilt. Hierdurch fühlt sich jede beteiligte Person persönlich weniger verantwortlich, als wenn sie allein in der Situation wäre. In der Folge führt dies zu mangelndem Engagement und reduzierter Hilfsbereitschaft, da jeder davon ausgeht,

dass der andere schon aktiv werden wird. Weitere Merkmale sind pluralistische Ignoranz (das Nichthandeln der anderen wird als Zeichen einer nicht erforderlichen Aktion gedeutet), Anonymität (je größer die Gruppe dabei ist, umso weniger fühlt sich jeder in der Verpflichtung), unklare Zuständigkeiten und Bewertungsangst.

Strategien zur Stärkung von Verantwortung

Genau wie beim Vertrauen und Kooperieren besitzt auch Verantwortung ein hohes Potenzial, um gesellschaftliche Herausforderungen zu bewältigen. Um dieses zu aktivieren beziehungsweise zu erhöhen, bieten sich verschiedene Maßnahmen an. So ist es im Bereich der Verantwortungsdiffusion sinnvoll, bei Entscheidungsprozessen auf eine angemessene Gruppengröße zu achten und vor allen die jeweiligen Zuständigkeiten festzulegen. Zudem ist es wichtig, Einzelne direkt anzusprechen und ihnen Kompetenz und Unterstützung zu garantieren (Empowerment). Hilfreich sind darüber hinaus spezifische Konzepte wie das OAABS-Kommunikationsschema (jede Person nur eine Aufgabe), das Scrum-Framework (selbstorganisiertes und funktionsübergreifendes Team für ein agiles Projektmanagement) oder Rotationsmodelle.

Gleichzeitig ist es im Sinne der Gesinnungsethik wichtig, Bürger möglichst frühzeitig zur Verantwortung zu motivieren, etwa im Bereich der familiären und schulischen Wertevermittlung. Dies geschieht zum Beispiel durch die Thematisierung und das Vorleben eigener Verantwortung sowie der Schaffung von eigenverantwortlichen Projekten für Jüngere.

Gerade hinsichtlich zukünftiger Herausforderungen ist es zudem wichtig, einen klaren Handlungsbedarf aufzuzeigen. Es kann nicht nur auf staatliche Verantwortlichkeiten vertraut werden, sondern es gilt, die Bedeutung von individueller Verantwortlichkeit zu betonen.

Insgesamt zeigt sich: Verantwortung ist ein Kernprinzip einer demokratischen Gesellschaft. Diese bietet sowohl individuell als auch kollektiv Handelnden die Chance, sich integer und engagiert zum Wohle der Gesellschaft zu beteiligen. Dabei schafft ein verantwortungsbewusstes Handeln nicht nur eine stabilere Gemeinschaft, sondern auch ein Gefühl der Erfüllung und Zusammengehörigkeit.

VERANTWORTUNG

Best-Practise Beispiele

1. Teach for all

ist ein globales Netzwerk aus 61 unabhängigen und lokal geführten Organisationen, die die Bildungsmöglichkeiten von Kindern und Jugendlichen weltweit verbessern wollen. Man möchte Verantwortung für Veränderungen übernehmen, indem man die Rahmenbedingungen für einen besseren Bildungszugang neu gestaltet.

2. Patagonia

ist ein Unternehmen, das sich durch nachhaltige Geschäftspraktiken auszeichnet. Es übernimmt Verantwortung für die Umwelt, indem es recycelte Materialien verwendet, umweltfreundliche Produktionsmethoden fördert und 1 Prozent seines Umsatzes an Umweltprojekte spendet. Zudem setzt sich Patagonia aktiv für den Klimaschutz und den Erhalt natürlicher Ressourcen ein.

3. Das Bonn Institute

widmet sich der Förderung von konstruktivem Journalismus. Es übernimmt Verantwortung für die Medienlandschaft, indem es ethische Standards entwickelt und Journalisten unterstützt, gesellschaftliche Herausforderungen lösungsorientiert zu beleuchten. Ziel ist es, Vertrauen in die Medien zu stärken und einen positiven gesellschaftlichen Wandel anzustoßen.

Fairtrade International ist eine Dachorganisation für fairen Handel. Sie fühlt sich dafür verantwortlich, die Einhaltung von sozialen, ökonomischen und ökologischen Standards zu kontrollieren und ein faires und nachhaltiges Handelssystem zu etablieren.

4. Der Kanadier Ryan Hreljac

begann als Sechsähriger Gelder für den Brunnenbau in Entwicklungsländern zu sammeln. Er fühlte sich mitverantwortlich, als Kind in einem reichen Industrieland, anderen unterprivilegierten Kindern zu helfen. Heute hat die Ryan's Well Foundation über 1.700 Wasserprojekte in 17 Ländern realisiert und hilft so, den Zugang zu sauberem Wasser zu verbessern.

Wie wichtig ist Verantwortungsbereitschaft?

Von je 100 Befragten stimmen folgender Aussage zu:
„Es ist wichtig, dass jeder Einzelne Verantwortung für die Gemeinschaft und eine bessere Zukunft übernimmt."

Von ich zu wir

VERANTWORTUNG ALS SCHLÜSSEL FÜR DIE ZUKUNFT

Ergebnis

Die grundsätzliche persönliche Verantwortungsbereitschaft steht in engem Zusammenhang mit der spezifischen Fragestellung nach der Verantwortung für die Gemeinschaft und eine bessere Zukunft. Fast neun von zehn Personen fühlen sich persönlich für den Zusammenhalt der Gemeinschaft verantwortlich und halten es für wichtig, dass jeder Einzelne sein Handeln darauf ausrichtet, die Zukunft ein wenig besser zu gestalten.

VERANTWORTUNG

Unter dem Begriff Gemeinschaft verstehen die Bürger in diesem Zusammenhang einen Zusammenschluss von Menschen, die in ähnlichen Lebenswelten leben, gemeinsame Interessen teilen oder gemeinschaftliche Ziele verfolgen. Je nach Perspektive kann die Reichweite dieser Gemeinschaft variieren. Während einige vor allem ihr unmittelbares soziales Umfeld im Blick haben, beziehen andere die Nachbarschaft, die Schulgemeinschaft, den Verein, das berufliche Umfeld oder die Kirchengemeinde ein.

Eine bessere Zukunft wird von den Bürgern insbesondere mit Chancengleichheit und Gerechtigkeit assoziiert, beispielsweise im Hinblick auf den Zugang zu Bildung, Gesundheit und Wohlstand. Darüber hinaus zählen mehr Empathie und Solidarität sowie ein nachhaltiger und schonender Umgang mit der Umwelt und den natürlichen Ressourcen zu den zentralen Aspekten einer positiven Zukunftsvision.

Gründe

Die Bereitschaft, Verantwortung für die Gemeinschaft und eine bessere Zukunft zu übernehmen, ist tief in den moralischen Werten der Bundesbürger verwurzelt. Dabei spielt die Sehnsucht nach sozialer Stabilität und Sicherheit eine zentrale Rolle. Bürger sehen in der Gemeinschaft nicht nur einen Ort des Austauschs, sondern auch eine wesentliche Grundlage für ein erfülltes Leben. Das Bedürfnis nach Zugehörigkeit und gegenseitiger Unterstützung wird besonders in Zeiten von gesellschaftlichen Spannungen und Unsicherheiten verstärkt wahrgenommen.

Ein weiterer Grund liegt in der Erkenntnis, dass persönliches Engagement nicht nur anderen zugutekommt, sondern auch das eigene Wohlbefinden steigert. Wer aktiv zur Verbesserung seiner Umgebung beiträgt, empfindet in der Regel auch ein gesteigertes Gefühl von Sinnhaftigkeit und Zufriedenheit. Dies zeigt sich beispielsweise in der Pflege von Nachbarschaftsbeziehungen, dem Einsatz für soziale Projekte oder bei der Förderung von Initiativen.

VERANTWORTUNG

Viele Bürger erkennen zudem die Bedeutung von Vorbildern und deren positiven Einfluss auf die kommenden Generationen. Die Verantwortung endet insofern nicht bei der eigenen Lebensgestaltung, sondern reicht bis hin zur Schaffung einer nachhaltigen Basis für die eigene Familie und Freunde, aber auch für Fremde.

Und schließlich ist es das Streben nach Gerechtigkeit und Chancengleichheit, was viele Bürger antreibt. Sie wünschen sich eine Gesellschaft, in der Solidarität und Empathie nicht nur Schlagworte sind, sondern aktiv gelebt werden. Diese Werte stärken nicht nur den Zusammenhalt, sondern wirken auch präventiv gegen soziale Konflikte und fördern ein insgesamt harmonisches Zusammenleben.

Hinsichtlich der Generationsunterschiede zeigen die Jüngeren ein unterdurchschnittliches Zustimmungsniveau, während sich die Älteren als besonders verantwortungsbewusst erweisen. Sie verfügen über mehr Lebenserfahrung, kennen die Bedeutung individueller Verantwortung – auch in kleineren Bereichen –, haben ein stärkeres Bedürfnis nach Stabilität und Sicherheit und betonen traditionelle Werte wie Pflichtbewusstsein und Gemeinschaft. Zudem ziehen sie verstärkt Zufriedenheit und Selbstbestätigung aus dem Gefühl, anderen zu helfen und sich für die Gemeinschaft einzusetzen, insbesondere da sie ihrem Alter entsprechend weniger familiäre und berufliche Verpflichtungen haben.

Im Gegensatz dazu ist die jüngere Generation in einer stärker individualisierten Gesellschaft aufgewachsen und fühlt sich für gesellschaftliche Missstände oft weniger verantwortlich. In einer Zeit der Krisen und Herausforderungen suchen sie ihre persönliche Erfüllung häufiger in beruflichen und familiären Zusammenhängen oder im Erreichen individueller Ziele. Dennoch zeigt sich auch bei ihnen eine insgesamt hohe Verantwortungsbereitschaft.

Prognose

Die Bereitschaft der Bürger, Verantwortung für Gemeinschaft und Zukunft zu übernehmen, wird auch in den kommenden Jahren eine zentrale Rolle spielen. Der Wunsch nach einem harmonischen Zusammenleben und einer gerechteren Gesellschaft wird dabei weiter wachsen. Gleichzeitig wird das Bewusstsein der Bürger dafür steigen, wie entscheidend ihr persönliches Handeln für die Gestaltung des sozialen Umfelds ist. Gesten der Hilfsbereitschaft, Rücksichtnahme und Solidarität werden entsprechend noch stärker in den Alltag integriert. Zudem werden die Bürger zunehmend nach konkreten Wegen suchen, aktiv zum gesellschaftlichen Zusammenhalt beizutragen – sei es durch Engagement in der Nachbarschaft, in Vereinen oder in anderen sozialen Strukturen.

In diesem Zusammenhang wird auch der Bildung eine Schlüsselrolle zukommen: Je besser Bürger über gesellschaftliche Zusammenhänge informiert sind, desto eher werden sie bereit sein, aktiv Verantwortung zu übernehmen. Es ist daher nicht nur Aufgabe von Schulen und anderen Bildungseinrichtungen, verstärkt auf die Vermittlung von Werten wie Solidarität und Gemeinsinn einzugehen. Auch innerhalb des eigenen Verantwortungs- und Lebensbereichs – in der Familie, im Freundeskreis oder am Arbeitsplatz – gilt es, diese Werte zu fördern.

Wer übernimmt Eigenverantwortung?

Von je 100 Befragten stimmen folgender Aussage zu:
„Ich übernehme Verantwortung für mein Handeln und stehe auch für meine Fehler ein."

Die Mehrheit zeigt Rückgrat

EIGENVERANTWORTLICH ZUKUNFT GESTALTEN

Ergebnis

Eine überwältigende Mehrheit der Bundesbürger – genau 87 Prozent – stimmen der Aussage zu: „Ich übernehme Verantwortung für mein Handeln und stehe auch für meine Fehler ein." Diese Zahl verdeutlicht das starke Verantwortungsbewusstsein innerhalb der Gesellschaft. Innerhalb der Altersgruppen ist die Zustimmung bei den über 55-Jährigen besonders hoch, wohingegen bei den unter 35-Jährigen noch etwas Potenzial nach oben vorhanden ist.

VERANTWORTUNG

Gründe

Der Begriff der Verantwortung umfasst neben einem zuverlässigen Handeln die individuelle Verpflichtung, für die eigenen Entscheidungen und Handlungen einzustehen sowie deren Konsequenzen zu übernehmen. Diese Haltung basiert in der Regel auf inneren moralischen und ethischen Grundsätzen, die häufig durch das eigene Gewissen geprägt werden, und steht in enger Verbindung mit den Tugenden des Mutes und der Ehrlichkeit. Die hohe Zustimmungsrate der Bürger hinsichtlich der Bedeutung von Verantwortung deutet auf eine tiefgreifende Verankerung dieses Prinzips in den gesellschaftlichen Werten.

Im persönlichen Bereich kann die Übernahme von Verantwortung vielfältige Aspekte umfassen, abhängig davon, welche Prioritäten gesetzt werden und wofür sich der Einzelne verantwortlich fühlt. Ein prägnantes Beispiel hierfür ist die Wahl eines Studienfachs, die oft als herausfordernd wahrgenommen wird. Diese Entscheidung impliziert, die damit verbundenen Herausforderungen und Konsequenzen anzunehmen oder, im Falle einer Revision der Wahl, die Erkenntnis zu gewinnen, künftige Entscheidungen sorgfältiger zu überdenken. Beide Szenarien verdeutlichen eine Anpassung an neue Gegebenheiten und eröffnen zugleich die Möglichkeit zur Reflexion. Die Bürger heben hierbei hervor, dass Fehler nicht als endgültig betrachtet werden sollten, sondern vielmehr als Chancen, aus ihnen zu lernen und neue Wege zu beschreiten.

In beruflicher Hinsicht signalisieren die Bürger mit ihrer Verantwortungsbereitschaft, über persönliche Integrität zu verfügen, das Wohl des Unternehmens oder der Kollegen im Blick zu haben und verlässlich zu sein. Dabei wird insbesondere eine positive Fehlerkultur geschätzt, in der man Fehler ehrlich zugeben und neue Lösungen entwickeln kann. In den meisten Fällen erfolgt danach eine positive Reaktion. Die Mitmenschen schätzen die Verantwortungsbereitschaft und das Eingestehen von Fehlern, erkennen das Fehlen von Ausreden an und nehmen die Handelnden als vertrauenswürdige, respektable Persönlichkeiten wahr.

VERANTWORTUNG

In weiteren gesellschaftlichen Zusammenhängen übernehmen Bürger häufig Aufgaben in sozialen oder politischen Bereichen, die eng mit ihren persönlichen Überzeugungen verknüpft sind. Dabei legen sie besonderen Wert darauf, ihre Überzeugungen offen zu kommunizieren und sich aktiv für deren Umsetzung zu engagieren. Da diese häufig tief in der eigenen Persönlichkeit oder in emotionalen Belangen verwurzelt sind, fällt es ihnen mitunter schwer, getroffene Entscheidungen zu revidieren oder eigene Fehler einzugestehen. Der Mut, der hierfür erforderlich ist, wird jedoch von anderen umso höher geschätzt, da er Authentizität und persönliche Integrität signalisiert.

Egal in welchen Bereichen die Bürger für ihre Handlungen einstehen, allen gemeinsam ist ein ausgeprägtes Reflexionsvermögen und ein respektvolles Interagieren, da dies auch immer Folgen für andere nach sich zieht.

Ältere Bürger zeichnen sich häufig durch ein besonders ausgeprägtes Verantwortungsbewusstsein aus, während bei jüngeren Generationen tendenziell leicht unterdurchschnittliche Werte zu verzeichnen sind. Ältere Personen verfügen über ein breites Spektrum an Erfahrungen, das sowohl Erfolge als auch Misserfolge umfasst. Durch diese Reflexionsprozesse haben sie nicht nur die positiven Effekte verantwortungsvollen Handelns verinnerlicht, sondern auch eine größere Gelassenheit im Umgang mit Fehlern entwickelt. Sie erkennen Fehler als wertvolle Lerngelegenheiten und wissen um deren potenzielle Vorteile.

Im Gegensatz dazu fehlt es vielen jüngeren Bürgern noch an umfassender Erfahrung und der damit einhergehenden Sicherheit, was sich in einer eher reservierten Haltung widerspiegelt. Diese Unsicherheit wird zusätzlich durch die dominante Rolle sozialer Netzwerke in ihrem Lebensumfeld verstärkt. Plattformen dieser Art bergen ein erhöhtes Risiko öffentlicher Kritik, Mobbing und sozialer Ausgrenzung, wodurch der permanente Vergleichsdruck eine authentische Fehlerkultur erschwert. Zudem fehlt jüngeren Menschen, insbesondere im beruflichen Kontext, häufig die Gelegenheit, ihre Verantwortungsbereitschaft unter Beweis zu stellen, da sie oft hinter erfahreneren Kollegen zurücktreten müssen.

Prognose

Die hohe Bereitschaft zur Verantwortungsübernahme und zum Fehlereingeständnis gibt Anlass zur Hoffnung. In einer Welt voller Unsicherheiten bildet sie einen stabilen Anker für den gesellschaftlichen Zusammenhalt. Besonders wichtig wird es sein, diesen Wert an die kommenden Generationen weiterzugeben.

Helfen wird hierbei ein Umdenken in Unternehmen: Statt Fehler als Versagen oder schlechte Leistung zu bewerten, fördert eine positive Fehlerkultur Innovationen und stärkt das Vertrauen zwischen Mitarbeitern und Führungskräften. Vorbilder in leitenden Positionen sind entsprechend gefordert, Führung nicht durch Perfektion vorzuleben, sondern durch die Fähigkeit, die Verantwortung für Fehler zu übernehmen und aus diesen zu lernen.

Aber nicht nur in der Arbeitswelt wird es darum gehen, Mut zu machen, Verantwortung zu übernehmen, sich Herausforderungen zu stellen und aus Rückschlägen gestärkt hervorzugehen. Alle Bürger sind aufgefordert, sich selbst zu vertrauen und offen mit Schwierigkeiten umzugehen. Schließlich bedeutet Verantwortung nicht Last oder Zwang – sondern sie gibt Halt und Orientierung in jeder Lebenssituation. Die Bürger müssen daher ermutigt werden, sich gegenseitig zu unterstützen und gemeinsam an einer besseren Zukunft zu arbeiten. Wenn dies gelingt, wird Deutschland nicht nur Herausforderungen meistern, sondern langfristig ein Vorbild für andere Nationen sein – ein Land voller Menschen mit Mut zur Verantwortung und dem Willen zur Veränderung.

Wer übernimmt mehr Verantwortung als andere?

Von je 100 Befragten stimmen folgender Aussage zu:
„Ich übernehme gerne mehr Verantwortung als andere"

Vorangehen statt mitlaufen

MEHRHEIT WILL MEHR VERANTWORTUNG ALS ANDERE ÜBERNEHMEN

Ergebnis

Verantwortung zu übernehmen bedeutet, Freiräume zur Gestaltung zu nutzen, mutige Entscheidungen zu treffen und mit Zuversicht und Entschlossenheit praktisch umzusetzen. Es bedeutet, sich zu engagieren und sich für andere Menschen, persönliche Werte, Ideen oder auch Inhalte einzusetzen. Etwas über die Hälfte der Bevölkerung ist bereit beziehungsweise davon angetan, mehr Verantwortung als andere zu übernehmen. Dies betrifft fast alle Bevölkerungsgruppen gleichermaßen.

VERANTWORTUNG

Gründe

Verantwortung spielt eine zentrale Rolle in jeder Gesellschaft. Sie ist die Grundlage für Zusammenarbeit und Zusammenhalt, beeinflusst jeden gesellschaftlichen Bereich, wird von Individuen und Institutionen getragen und beeinflusst, wie die Bürger miteinander interagieren. Dabei ist sie kein starres Konstrukt, sondern wandelt sich in ihren Inhalten und ihrer Bedeutung den gesellschaftlichen Entwicklungen entsprechend. Legte die Wirtschaft zum Beispiel viele Jahre lang ihren Fokus primär auf stetiges Wachstum (ohne Gedanken an Nachhaltigkeit), übernehmen viele Unternehmen heute zunehmend Verantwortung im Zusammenhang mit Mitarbeitenden, Kunden oder Zulieferern. Und während bis in die 1980er-Jahre die Verantwortung für Altersvorsorge, Weiterbildung oder Gesundheit fast ausschließlich dem Staat überlassen wurde, gibt es heute eine zunehmende Betonung der Eigenverantwortung. Dies hat eine Mehrheit innerhalb der Bevölkerung erkannt und ist dabei sogar bereit mehr Verantwortung als andere zu übernehmen.

Diese individuelle Verantwortung kann sich dabei in den unterschiedlichsten Bereichen zeigen, hat aber stets den gleichen Kern: Der Einzelne trifft eine ethische Entscheidung und übernimmt für deren Folgen Rechenschaft. Dies kann den familiären Bereich betreffen, das nahe soziale Umfeld, das berufliche Feld oder auch in einem größeren gesellschaftlichen Zusammenhang stehen, indem man etwa politische, wirtschaftliche oder ökologische Verantwortung übernimmt. Besonders häufig und gern übernehmen die Bürger Verantwortung in der Familie, der Nachbarschaft und innerhalb der beruflichen Position.

Die Motive für diese Übernahme variieren und reichen von einem altruistischen Weltbild über ein ausgeprägtes Pflichtverständnis bis hin zum Gefühl der Selbstverwirklichung, der Zufriedenheit oder des Stolzes. Verantwortung wirkt sich dabei immer positiv auf die individuelle Entwicklung aus – gerade bei Jüngeren. Sie fördert die persönliche Reife, Resilienz und die Fähigkeit, mit Rückschlägen umzugehen. Wer Verantwortung übernimmt, lernt, Entscheidungen zu treffen und deren Konsequenzen zu tragen. Diese Erfahrungen stärken das Selbstbewusstsein und helfen dabei, die eigenen Fähigkeiten besser einzuschätzen.

VERANTWORTUNG

Prognose

Für die Zukunft wird die Bereitschaft der Bürger, Verantwortung zu übernehmen, eine zentrale Rolle spielen, da sie entscheidend zur Bewältigung zahlreicher gesellschaftlicher Herausforderungen beiträgt. Diese Haltung fördert nicht nur den sozialen Zusammenhalt, sondern stärkt auch die persönliche Weiterentwicklung und eröffnet neue Möglichkeiten in beruflichen Kontexten.

Im persönlichen Bereich ist Verantwortungsbereitschaft essenziell, um Unsicherheiten besser bewältigen zu können und eine gesteigerte Resilienz zu entwickeln. Je mehr Eigenverantwortung ein Individuum übernimmt, desto stärker wird es das Gefühl der Selbstbestimmung empfinden und in der Lage sein, weiterreichende Verantwortlichkeiten wahrzunehmen. Diese Entwicklung verläuft umso positiver, je stärker ein unterstützender gesellschaftlicher Rahmen geschaffen wird, der Eigenverantwortung anerkennt und fördert.

Auch in der Arbeitswelt wird die Bedeutung von Verantwortungsbereitschaft weiter zunehmen. Individuen, die Verantwortung übernehmen, zeichnen sich häufig durch ausgeprägte Führungsqualitäten aus und tragen maßgeblich zu einem stärkeren Teamgeist bei. Sie fördern nicht nur die Produktivität, sondern schaffen ein Arbeitsumfeld, das von Eigeninitiative und Engagement geprägt ist. Darüber hinaus sind sie mutiger im Umgang mit neuen Herausforderungen und fungieren als treibende Kraft für Innovationen. Wer Verantwortung übernimmt, zeigt Bereitschaft, neue Ideen zu entwickeln und umzusetzen – eine Eigenschaft, die in der modernen Arbeitswelt immer wichtiger werden wird.

So wird die Verantwortungsbereitschaft, wenn sie denn gefördert wird, dazu beitragen, die Grundlage für ein funktionierendes, nachhaltiges und gerechtes Miteinander zu bilden.

VERANTWORTUNG

Wer hilft, ohne Gegenleistung zu erwarten?

Von je 100 Befragten stimmen folgender Aussage zu:
„Ich helfe anderen gerne, auch ohne Gegenleistung."

Altruismus in der Gesellschaft

FAST NEUN VON ZEHN BÜRGERN HELFEN OHNE WENN UND ABER

Ergebnis

Fast neun von zehn Bundesbürgern sind bereit, anderen ohne Erwartung einer Gegenleistung zu helfen. Dabei zeigen sich kaum Unterschiede hinsichtlich des Geschlechts, Einkommens, der Bildung oder des Wohnorts. Altruistisches Verhalten erweist sich somit als universelle Eigenschaft, die weitgehend unabhängig von äußeren Lebensbedingungen besteht. Lediglich bei den unter 35-Jährigen zeigt sich eine etwas zurückhaltendere Haltung, jedoch sind auch hier mehr als vier von fünf bereit zu geben, ohne zu nehmen. Die Formen der Hilfe sind dabei vielfältig: Sie reichen von spontaner Unterstützung in akuten Notlagen über dauerhafte Nachbarschaftshilfe bis hin zu langfristigem Engagement in gemeinnützigen Projekten.

VERANTWORTUNG

Gründe

Die Beweggründe für selbstloses Handeln sind komplex und lassen sich biologisch, psychologisch und sozial erklären. Evolutionsbiologisch betrachtet, stärkt altruistisches Verhalten den Zusammenhalt innerhalb einer Gruppe und fördert das Überleben der Gemeinschaft. Psychologisch spielen intrinsische Motivationen eine zentrale Rolle, wobei Werte wie, Empathie und Großzügigkeit tief im Wesen des Einzelnen verankert sind. Diese Eigenschaften werden durch soziale, kulturelle, moralische und religiöse Prägungen weiter verstärkt. Gesellschaften fördern ein kollektives soziales Gewissen, das durch Erziehung und Sozialisation verinnerlicht wird. Altruistisches Verhalten wird daher oft als sinnerfüllend empfunden – eine Empfindung, die häufig als wertvoller wahrgenommen wird als materielle Vorteile, da sie dem Menschen das Gefühl vermittelt, gebraucht zu werden und einen positiven Beitrag zu leisten. Helfende bevorzugen dabei überwiegend immaterielle Unterstützung und greifen nur in Ausnahmefällen auf Geld-, Kleider- oder Sachspenden zurück.

Die Formen der Hilfe reichen von spontanen Gesten bei alltäglichen Herausforderungen, persönlichen Schicksalsschlägen oder Naturkatastrophen bis hin zu langfristigem Engagement. Während spontane Hilfe oft im näheren sozialen Umfeld stattfindet, äußert sich mittelfristige Unterstützung beispielsweise in der Nachbarschaftshilfe oder bei lokalen Projekten, wie dem Bau eines Spielplatzes oder der Organisation eines Straßenfestes. Langfristiges Engagement zeigt sich etwa in der Arbeit bei gemeinnützigen Organisationen, beim Mentoring oder in Freiwilligendiensten. Solches Engagement stärkt nicht nur den sozialen Zusammenhalt, sondern vermittelt den Helfenden auch ein Gefühl der individuellen Wirksamkeit und inneren Zufriedenheit.

Die Unterschiede zwischen den Generationen lassen sich vor allem durch Erfahrung und verfügbare Zeit erklären. Ältere Bürger profitieren von ihrer Lebenserfahrung und einem ausgeprägten Bewusstsein für die positiven Emotionen, die Helfen auslöst. Ihre geringeren beruflichen und familiären Verpflichtungen ermöglichen es ihnen zudem, mehr Zeit und Ressourcen für soziale Aktivitäten aufzuwenden. Die jüngere Generation steht hingegen oft vor Herausforderungen wie beruflicher Qualifikation, Karriere und familiären Verpflichtungen, die ihre Ressourcen stärker binden. Dennoch zeigt sich auch bei ihnen eine hohe Bereitschaft zu helfen.

VERANTWORTUNG

Prognose

Die hohe Hilfsbereitschaft der Bundesbürger wird auch in Zukunft eine tragende Säule des gesellschaftlichen Zusammenhalts bleiben. Besonders die zwischenmenschlichen Aspekte dieses Verhaltens geben Anlass zu Optimismus. Die Bereitschaft, anderen ohne Erwartung einer Gegenleistung zu helfen, schafft nicht nur individuelle Zufriedenheit, sondern stärkt auch das soziale Gefüge. Beziehungen und Netzwerke werden hierbei eine entscheidende Rolle spielen. Menschen helfen vor allem dort, wo sie sich emotional verbunden fühlen – sei es in der Familie, im Freundeskreis oder in der Nachbarschaft. Insbesondere die Nachbarschaftshilfe wird eine Renaissance erleben, da sie sowohl praktische als auch emotionale Unterstützung bietet. Angesichts einer alternden Gesellschaft wird dies für ältere Bürger besonders relevant, da sie häufiger auf gegenseitige Unterstützung angewiesen sind.

Eine wichtige Rolle werden Vorbilder einnehmen. Kinder und Jugendliche orientieren sich stark an den Verhaltensweisen ihrer Eltern, Lehrer oder anderer Bezugspersonen. Wenn diese ein hohes Maß an Hilfsbereitschaft zeigen, wird dieses Verhalten oft übernommen und weitergegeben. Eine Gesellschaft, die altruistisches Handeln sichtbar macht und wertschätzt, wird langfristig eine Kultur des Helfens fördern können. Schulen und Bildungseinrichtungen sollten dabei verstärkt soziale Kompetenzen wie Empathie und Teamgeist fördern.

Ein weiterer positiver Trend ergibt sich aus der wachsenden gesellschaftlichen Wertschätzung für altruistisches Verhalten. Bürger, die sich uneigennützig engagieren, erfahren Anerkennung und Dankbarkeit – sei es durch persönliche Worte oder öffentliche Würdigung. Diese Wertschätzung stärkt das Gefühl der Sinnhaftigkeit des eigenen Handelns und motiviert andere, sich ebenfalls einzubringen.

Chancen ergeben sich auch durch eine stärkere Verbindung zwischen den Generationen. Ältere verfügen über Zeit und Erfahrung, während jüngere Generationen oft mehr Energie und frische Ideen einbringen. Gemeinsame Projekte können dazu beitragen, diese Stärken zu vereinen und Brücken zwischen den Generationen zu schlagen. Solche intergenerationellen Initiativen leisten nicht nur praktische Hilfe, sondern fördern auch das gegenseitige Verständnis und den sozialen Zusammenhalt.

Eine Gesellschaft, die Solidarität und Mitgefühl in den Mittelpunkt stellt, wird nicht nur resilienter gegenüber Krisen sein, sondern auch ein höheres Maß an Zufriedenheit durch Zusammenhalt erreichen.

Welche Hilfe leisten die Bürger privat?

Von je 100 Befragten sagen:
„Ich habe in den letzten zwei bis drei Jahren folgende Hilfeleistungen erbracht bei/beim."

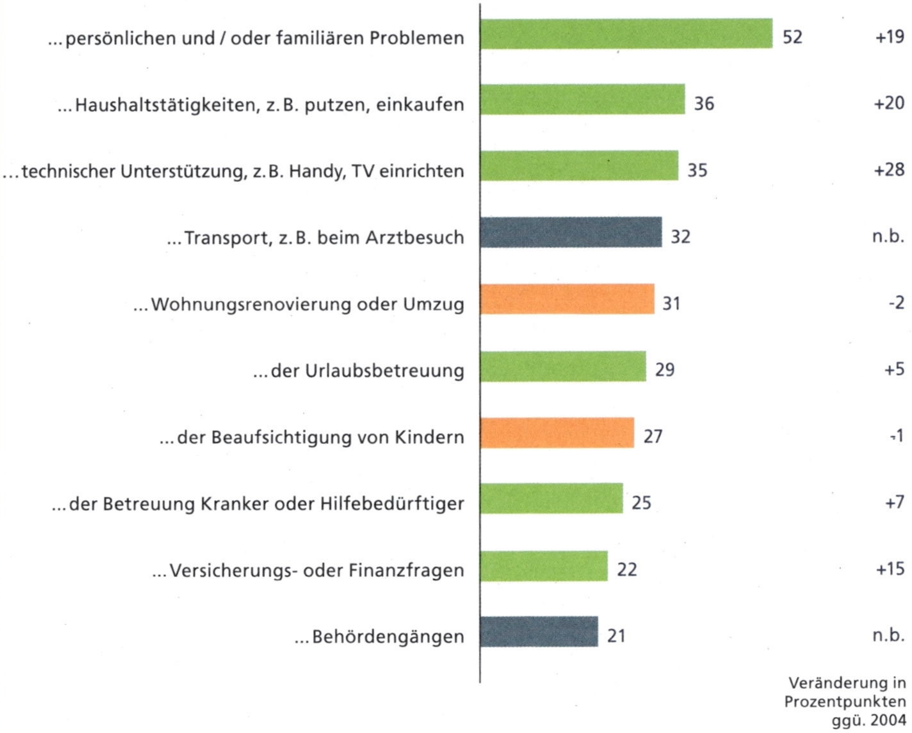

Hilfsbereitschaft im Zeitvergleich

GEGENSEITIGE UNTERSTÜTZUNG NIMMT ZU

Ergebnis

Der gesellschaftliche Zusammenhalt wird oft kritisch betrachtet: Es wird über mangelnden Respekt und zunehmenden Egoismus geklagt. Der Jahresvergleich verdeutlicht jedoch, wie stark Bürger in den letzten Jahren ihre Unterstützung füreinander ausgeweitet haben. Besonders im familiären und freundschaftlichen Bereich ist die Hilfsbereitschaft gestiegen. Mehr als jeder Zweite – vor zehn Jahren war es lediglich jeder Dritte – unterstützt andere bei persönlichen oder familiären Problemen, sei es durch Gespräche, emotionale Begleitung oder finanzielle Hilfe. Diese Art der Unterstützung vermittelt Zugehörigkeit, Verständnis und stärkt zudem das Selbstwertgefühl der Hilfesuchenden.

Auch bei Haushaltstätigkeiten und technischen Problemen waren viele Bürger deutlich aktiver als in der Vergangenheit. Mehr als jeder Dritte half Eltern, Großeltern oder Freunden bei alltäglichen Aufgaben wie Putzen, Einkaufen oder der Einrichtung technischer Geräte. Weitere Bereiche wie Transporthilfe, Kinderbetreuung oder Renovierungsarbeiten wurden ebenfalls von vielen Bürgern übernommen, was besonders positiv zu bewerten ist, erfordern sie doch oft Spontaneität während der eigenen Arbeitszeit.

Gründe

Die gestiegene Hilfsbereitschaft lässt sich auf verschiedene Faktoren zurückführen. So haben die Krisen der letzten Jahre – allen voran Corona – verdeutlicht, wie wichtig gegenseitige Unterstützung ist und wie sehr kleine Gesten einen großen Unterschied machen können. Auch hat sich die Demografie der Gesellschaft verändert: Mehr ältere Bürger, mehr Singlehaushalte und mehr Doppeltverdienende haben die Notwendigkeiten vieler Hilfeleistungen gesteigert. Einen Anteil hatte zudem die Digitalisierung: Über soziale Netzwerke und Nachbarschaftsplattformen lassen sich Hilfsangebote leichter organisieren. Besonders die

jüngere Generation nutzt die entsprechenden Kanäle, um Unterstützung zu gewähren oder zumindest praktische Hilfe zu koordinieren. Ältere Bürger zeigen sich dagegen überdurchschnittlich hilfsbereit bei der Kinderbetreuung oder emotionalen Unterstützung.

Zudem lässt sich ein gesellschaftlicher Wertewandel erkennen, der die Bedeutung von Solidarität und sozialer Verantwortung sowie die weiterreichenden Effekte von Hilfsbereitschaft, wie Erfüllung und Anerkennung, stärker betont.

Prognose

Die steigende Hilfsbereitschaft zeigt eine erfreuliche Entwicklung im sozialen Miteinander. In Zukunft wird es entscheidend sein, diese Dynamik weiter zu fördern und auf breitere gesellschaftliche Kreise auszudehnen. Initiativen wie Nachbarschaftshilfen können hierbei eine zentrale Rolle spielen, um auch Menschen außerhalb des engen sozialen Umfelds zu erreichen. Besonders wichtig wird es sein, breite Bevölkerungsgruppen für soziale Verantwortung zu sensibilisieren. Bildungsprogramme können dazu beitragen, den Wert von Gemeinschaft und gegenseitiger Unterstützung zu vermitteln. Gleichzeitig sollten (noch) mehr ältere Menschen ermutigt werden, ihre Zeit, Erfahrungen und Fähigkeiten verstärkt einzubringen.

Trotz aller positiven Entwicklungen bestehen Herausforderungen: Zeit- und Geldmangel sowie berufliche Verpflichtungen schränken die Möglichkeiten zur Hilfe ein. Auch die geografische Distanz zwischen Familienmitgliedern erschwert spontane Unterstützung.

Dennoch wird deutlich: Der gesellschaftliche Zusammenhalt ist stärker als oft angenommen. Die Bereitschaft zur Hilfe wächst – nicht nur innerhalb der Familie, sondern auch in Freundeskreisen und Nachbarschaften. Diese Entwicklung bildet eine Grundlage für eine solidarischere Gesellschaft, in der gegenseitige Unterstützung selbstverständlich bleibt und neue Formen des Miteinanders entstehen können.

VERANTWORTUNG

Wie wichtig ist der Generationenzusammenhalt?

Von je 100 Befragten stimmen folgender Aussage zu:
„Der Generationenzusammenhalt von Enkeln, Kindern, Eltern und Großeltern wird immer wichtiger und hilft bei vielen Krisen."

Generationenzusammenhalt

EIN GARANT FÜR STABILITÄT UND SICHERHEIT

Ergebnis

Der Generationenzusammenhalt ist ein zentrales Element des gesellschaftlichen Lebens. In einer Zeit, die von Individualisierung, Versingelung, Kinderlosigkeit und Krisen geprägt ist, gewinnt der familiäre Rückhalt zunehmend an Bedeutung. Die Familie bleibt der Ort, an dem Bürger emotionale Sicherheit finden und auf verlässliche Bezugspersonen zählen können. Dabei sieht eine große Mehrheit der Bevölkerung den Zusammenhalt zwischen den Generationen als essenziell an. Innerhalb der Altersgruppen sind es neun von zehn Älteren, die die Bedeutung der Familie betonen, aber auch drei von vier jungen Bürgern betonen den Zusammenhalt.

VERANTWORTUNG

Gründe

Ein Zusammengehörigkeitsgefühl zwischen den Generationen wird als Garant für Stabilität wahrgenommen, steht es doch gerade dann für Halt, Sicherheit und Orientierung, wenn äußere Strukturen ins Wanken geraten. Neben emotionaler Unterstützung schätzen viele Bundesbürger dabei aber auch die praktischen Vorteile. So unterstützen Eltern ihre erwachsenen Kinder bei der Betreuung von Enkeln oder helfen im Haushalt, während jüngere Familienmitglieder älteren Angehörigen bei gesundheitlichen Problemen oder Mobilitätseinschränkungen zur Seite stehen. Diese gegenseitige Fürsorge schafft ein Gefühl von Gemeinschaft und Wertschätzung, das über alle Lebensphasen hinweg Bestand hat.

Ältere Bürger legen insgesamt einen stärkeren Fokus auf familiäre Beziehungen, da sie insgesamt beruflich weniger stark eingebunden sind und mehr zeitliche Ressourcen haben (gerade im Ruhestand). Sie übernehmen dabei oft eine Schlüsselrolle, indem sie sowohl ihre Kinder als auch ihre Enkelkinder unterstützen, sei es durch finanzielle Unterstützung, Betreuung oder praktische Hilfe im Alltag. Die jüngere Generation hingegen konzentriert sich stärker auf ihre berufliche Entwicklung und den Aufbau eines eigenständigen Lebens. Diese Lebenssituation führt manchmal zu einer vorübergehenden größeren Distanz zur Familie, ohne jedoch die Bedeutung des familiären Rückhalts zu mindern.

Prognose

Der gesellschaftliche Wandel wird die traditionellen Familienstrukturen weiter verändern. Neben der klassischen Kernfamilie haben sich bereits gegenwärtig vielfältige Modelle etabliert, darunter Patchwork-, Regenbogen- oder Ein-Eltern-Familien. Trotz dieser Vielfalt ist allen Formen gemein, sie fungieren auch zukünftig als Versorgungs- und Verantwortungsgemeinschaft. Die emotionale Bindung zwischen den Generationen bleibt dabei ein zentraler Wert.

Mit einer alternden Gesellschaft wird die Rolle älterer Bürger dabei innerhalb der Familie weiter zunehmen. Sie werden verstärkt als Unterstützer für jüngere Generationen fungieren – sei es durch Kinderbetreuung oder finanzielle Hilfeleistungen. Gleichzeitig wird der Bedarf an

VERANTWORTUNG

Unterstützung für ältere Menschen steigen, was die Bedeutung des Generationenzusammenhalts zusätzlich erhöht.

Digitale Technologien werden in Zukunft häufiger genutzt werden, um den Austausch zwischen den Generationen zu erleichtern. Videotelefonie oder auch soziale Medien ermöglichen es Familienmitgliedern, auch über große Entfernungen hinweg in Kontakt zu bleiben. Besonders für ältere Bürger bietet dies eine Chance, aktiv am Familienleben teilzuhaben, unabhängig davon, ob die eigenen Kinder oder Enkel vor Ort leben.

Letztendlich bleibt die Familie – trotz aller Individualisierungstendenzen – ein unverzichtbarer Bestandteil des sozialen Gefüges. Der Generationenzusammenhalt wird daher auch in Zukunft eine zentrale Rolle spielen, sei es als Quelle von Sicherheit, Stabilität oder emotionaler Geborgenheit.

VERANTWORTUNG

Wer engagiert sich vor Ort?

Von je 100 Befragten stimmen folgender Aussage zu:
„Ich engagiere mich sozial und politisch in meiner Gemeinde, um Positives zu bewirken."

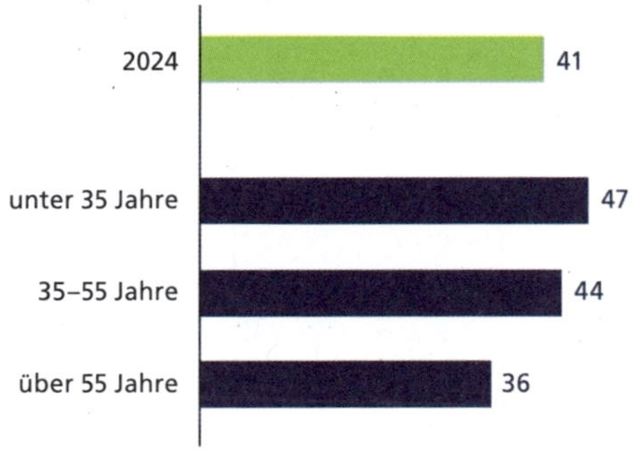

Politisches und soziales Engagement

BESONDERS DIE JUNGE GENERATION WILL POSITIVES BEWIRKEN

Ergebnis

Soziales und politisches Engagement ist ein wichtiger Bestandteil des gesellschaftlichen Lebens in Deutschland. Etwa vier von zehn Bürgern engagieren sich aktiv in ihrer Gemeinde, um Positives zu bewirken. Bei den unter 35-Jährigen zeigt sich sogar fast jeder Zweite engagiert, während bei den über 55-Jährigen etwas mehr als jeder Dritte aktiv ist.

VERANTWORTUNG

Gründe

Viele Bürger engagieren sich, um die Gemeinschaft zu stärken und den sozialen Zusammenhalt zu fördern. Auch spielt der Wunsch, anderen zu helfen, soziale Netzwerke aufzubauen oder kulturelle Projekte zu unterstützen, oftmals eine Rolle. Besonders junge Bürger fühlen sich durch ihren Freundeskreis inspiriert und möchten Teil einer Gemeinschaft sein. Sie genießen das Gefühl der Zugehörigkeit und streben nach positiven Veränderungen in ihrer Umgebung. Entsprechend engagieren sie sich häufig in Umweltschutz, Bildungsprojekten oder sozialen Initiativen. Ihre Motivation beruht auf einem ausgeprägten Gerechtigkeitssinn und dem Wunsch, die Welt aktiv mitzugestalten. Gleichzeitig nutzen sie ihr Engagement aber auch, um neue Fähigkeiten zu entwickeln oder Übergangszeiten sinnvoll zu überbrücken. Die Flexibilität ihrer Lebensphase ermöglicht es ihnen, Zeit für ehrenamtliche Tätigkeiten aufzubringen, während sie gleichzeitig soziale Kompetenzen erwerben und ihr Selbstvertrauen stärken.

In der mittleren Altersgruppe stehen andere Beweggründe im Vordergrund. Viele Mitbürger fühlen sich in dieser Lebensphase gesellschaftlich verantwortlich – sei es durch ihre Rolle als Eltern oder durch den Wunsch, die Zukunft aktiv mitzugestalten. Berufliche Stabilität und gefestigte familiäre Strukturen bieten ihnen oftmals die Grundlage für ein Engagement in ihrer Gemeinde. Gleichzeitig sehen viele in ihrem Einsatz eine Möglichkeit, Vorbild für die eigenen Kinder zu sein oder die beruflichen Fähigkeiten in einem anderen Zusammenhang einzusetzen. Netzwerke aus dem beruflichen oder privaten Umfeld helfen, einen einfachen Zugang zu finden.

Bei älteren Bürgern verschieben sich dagegen häufig die Prioritäten: Gesundheitliche Einschränkungen, familiäre Verpflichtungen wie die Betreuung von Enkelkindern oder pflegebedürftigen Eltern sowie der Übergang in den Ruhestand beeinflussen das Engagement. Viele nutzen diese Phase des Lebens, um sich eher auf persönliche Interessen wie Reisen oder kulturelle Aktivitäten zu konzentrieren. Dennoch erkennen auch viele das Potenzial des

Engagements, um soziale Kontakte aufzubauen oder neue Ziele zu verfolgen. Besonders in Bereichen wie der Nachbarschaftshilfe oder kulturellen Projekten zeigen Ältere eine hohe Bereitschaft zur Mitarbeit.

Die Tatsache, dass sich fast drei von fünf Bürgern derzeit nicht in ihrem Umfeld betätigen, basiert neben den bereits genannten Gründen unter anderem auf Zeitmangel, fehlender Anerkennung oder auf mangelnder Flexibilität seitens der Angebote. Auch negative Erfahrungen wie fehlende Gestaltungsmöglichkeiten, wenig Spaß oder hapernde Integration in bestehende Gruppen halten viele davon ab, aktiv zu werden.

Prognose

Das soziale und politische Engagement bleibt eine wichtige Säule für den gesellschaftlichen Zusammenhalt. In Zukunft wird es entscheidend sein, Hindernisse weiter abzubauen und mehr Bürger für ehrenamtliche Tätigkeiten zu gewinnen – unabhängig vom Alter. Besonders wichtig wird es sein, Angebote flexibler zu gestalten und niedrigschwellige Möglichkeiten zu schaffen, damit auch Berufstätige oder Bürger mit begrenzter Zeit sich einbringen können. Parallel werden Initiativen stärker auf die Bedürfnisse verschiedener Altersgruppen eingehen (müssen) – etwa durch Programme für junge Bürger, für Singles, für Migranten oder Senioren.

VERANTWORTUNG

Wer ist bereit zu Eigeninitiative?

Von je 100 Befragten stimmen folgender Aussage zu:
„Viele Bürger sind durchaus bereit für mehr Eigeninitiative und wollen nicht alle Probleme einfach dem Staat überlassen."

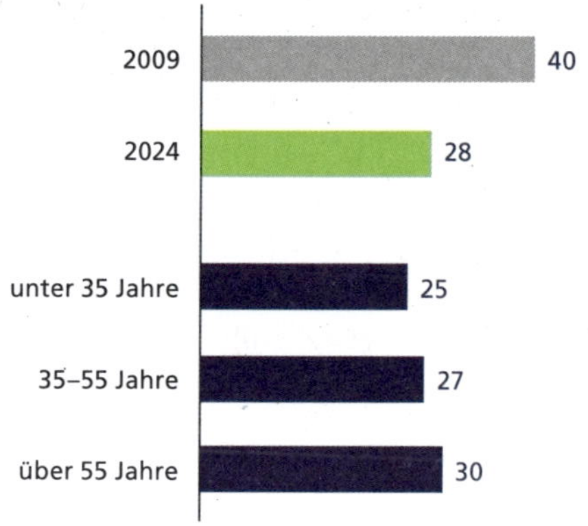

Vater Staat statt Selbsthilfe

EIGENINITIATIVE GEHT ZURÜCK

Ergebnis

Die Bereitschaft, mehr Eigeninitiative zu zeigen und Herausforderungen nicht allein dem Staat zu überlassen, ist aktuell bei etwa einem Viertel der Bürger vorhanden. Die ältere Generation zeigt dabei eine etwas höhere Bereitschaft als die jüngere. Im Jahresvergleich zeigt sich ein deutlicher Rückgang: Im Jahr 2009 waren noch zwei von fünf Bürgern bereit, mehr Eigeninitiative zu übernehmen.

Gründe

Die Beweggründe, proaktiv zu sein, sind vielfältig und reichen von altruistischen Motiven bis hin zu persönlichen Interessen. Viele Bürger engagieren sich aufgrund eines Verantwortungsgefühls gegenüber ihrer Gemeinschaft. Sie möchten anderen helfen, Solidarität zeigen oder einen positiven Beitrag für ihr persönliches Umfeld, die Nachbarschaft oder die Gesellschaft leisten.

Eigeninitiative bietet zudem die Möglichkeit zur persönlichen Weiterentwicklung. Sie eröffnet Chancen, neue Fähigkeiten zu erlernen, eigene Werte umzusetzen oder soziale Anerkennung zu erfahren. Besonders politisch bewusste Bürger sehen darin eine Gelegenheit, Missstände aktiv anzugehen und Veränderungen anzustoßen. Die Proaktivität vermittelt dabei ein Gefühl von Autonomie und Kontrolle, das im Gegensatz zur Passivität steht, wenn ausschließlich auf staatliche Maßnahmen vertraut wird.

Trotz dieser positiven Aspekte gibt es auch Hindernisse: Zeit- und Geldmangel sowie berufliche Verpflichtungen schränken die Möglichkeiten vieler Bürger ein. Zudem hat sich in den letzten Jahren ein verstärkter Fokus auf staatliche Lösungen entwickelt. Viele Bürger erwarten vom Staat eine aktive Rolle bei der Bewältigung von Krisen und empfinden individuelle Bemühungen oft als unzureichend. Besonders jüngere Menschen betonen stärker die Pflichten des Staates – gerade in sozialen und ökologischen Fragen – und zeigen weniger Vertrauen in die Wirksamkeit privater Initiativen. Die ältere Generation hingegen bringt durch ihre Lebenserfahrung und Sozialisation einen ausgeprägteren Gestaltungswillen mit. Ihre höhere Frustrationstoleranz sowie ihre besseren zeitlichen und finanziellen Ressourcen ermöglichen es ihnen, sich überdurchschnittlich stark zu engagieren.

Die höheren Werte aus dem Jahr 2009 können teilweise mit einer anderen gesellschaftlichen Stimmung erklärt werden, die von wirtschaftlichen und politischen Faktoren geprägt war: Geringes Vertrauen in die Regierung, die globale Finanz- und Wirtschaftskrise sowie kontroverse Themen wie der Auslandseinsatz der Bundeswehr in Afghanistan dominierten die öffentliche Debatte. Hohe Arbeitslosigkeit und Rentenunsicherheit führten dazu, dass viele Bürger Eigeninitiative als notwendig erachteten, um ihre Situation zu verbessern. Beispiele hierfür

waren die Gründung von Start-ups und Kleinunternehmen, die Nachfrage nach Fortbildungen oder das Engagement in Netzwerken und Vereinen zur Bekämpfung lokaler Probleme wie Armut und Jugendarbeitslosigkeit. Diese Do-it-yourself-Mentalität war Ausdruck eines wachsenden Bewusstseins für Selbstverantwortung und Unabhängigkeit von staatlichen Strukturen.

In den letzten Jahren haben jedoch globale Krisen die Wahrnehmung vieler Bürger geprägt, wodurch individuelle Anstrengungen oft als unzureichend erscheinen. Die Komplexität dieser Herausforderungen lässt sie verstärkt auf staatliche Maßnahmen vertrauen, die als erfolgversprechender angesehen werden.

Prognose

Die abnehmende Bereitschaft zur Eigeninitiative stellt eine Herausforderung dar, bietet aber auch Chancen für neue Ansätze zur Förderung gesellschaftlichen Engagements. Zukünftig wird es darauf ankommen, individuelles und kollektives Engagement stärker miteinander zu verbinden. Bildungsprogramme können helfen, den Wert von persönlichem Einsatz und Gemeinschaftsengagement frühzeitig zu vermitteln. Besonders junge Menschen müssen ermutigt werden, ihre Ideen einzubringen und Verantwortung für ihr Umfeld zu übernehmen – sei es durch Nachbarschaftshilfe, freiwilliges Engagement oder die Gründung eigener Initiativen. Parallel dazu ist es wichtig, bürokratische Hürden abzubauen und staatliche Strukturen flexibler zu gestalten, um private Initiativen besser zu unterstützen.

Entscheidend wird sein, Eigeninitiative als unverzichtbaren Bestandteil einer resilienten Gesellschaft zu betrachten. Sie ermöglicht nicht nur individuelle Entfaltung, sondern trägt auch dazu bei, Herausforderungen – ob lokal oder global – gemeinsam zu bewältigen.

VERANTWORTUNG

Wer will die Schuldenbremse?

Von je 100 Befragten stimmen folgender Aussage zu:
„Jeder Euro, den der Staat in wirtschaftlich guten Zeiten zusätzlich einnimmt, sollte mindestens zur Hälfte zum Schuldenabbau verwendet werden, um kommenden Generationen eine lebenswerte Zukunft zu sichern."

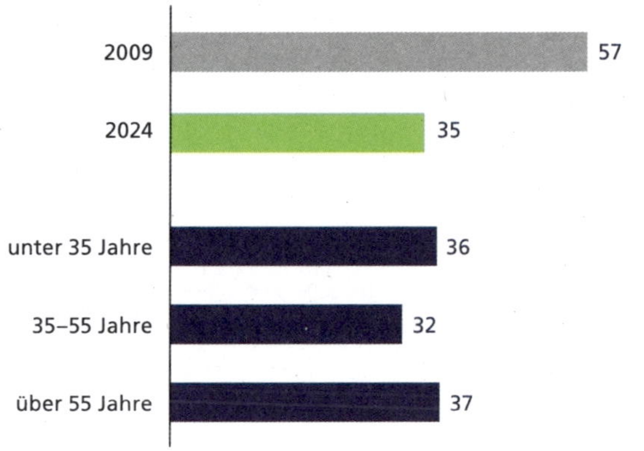

Schuldenbremse a.D.

ZWEI DRITTEL WOLLEN INVESTITIONEN STATT SPAREN

Ergebnis

Die Schuldenbremse ist ein finanzpolitisches Instrument zur Begrenzung der staatlichen Neuverschuldung. Nicht erst in den letzten Monaten wurde in der Öffentlichkeit immer wieder über eine Reform derselben diskutiert. Während die einen sie schnellstmöglich reformieren wollen, wollen die anderen unbedingt an ihr festhalten. Ein immer wiederkehrendes Argument ist hierbei die Sicherung der zukünftigen wirtschaftlichen Stabilität. In der Bevölkerung

ist diesbezüglich eine eindeutige Tendenz festzustellen. Nur etwas mehr als ein Drittel der Bürger will einen Teil der Staatseinnahmen zum Schuldenabbau verwenden, wobei die mittlere Generation eine leicht unterdurchschnittliche Quote aufweist. Vor 25 Jahren stimmte dagegen noch mehr als die Hälfte der Bürger dieser Aussage zu.

Gründe

2009 prägten globale Krisen, wie die Finanzkrise oder die Euro-Schuldenkrise, das Bewusstsein der Bevölkerung und schürten die Angst vor Belastungen durch hohe Staatsschulden. Das Beispiel von Griechenland zeigte, wie sehr Schulden die finanzielle Handlungsfähigkeit eines Staates einschränken und zu drastischen Sparmaßnahmen führen. Um solch einer Entwicklung in Deutschland vorzubeugen, wurde im Jahr 2009 die Schuldenbremse im Grundgesetz verankert, und seitdem ist die Idee des Schuldenabbaus und der Haushaltsdisziplin zu einem zentralen politischen Thema geworden. Politiker und Medien haben die Notwendigkeit immer wieder betont und damit die öffentliche Meinung geprägt, sodass der Schuldenabbau von der Mehrheit als Voraussetzung für eine stabile und lebenswerte Zukunft gesehen wurde.

Ein weiteres Argument ist die moralische Verpflichtung, den nachfolgenden Generationen keine übermäßige Schuldenlast zu hinterlassen, insbesondere wenn Zinszahlungen höher und Tilgungsräume kürzer werden und demografische Herausforderungen mehr finanzielle Zuwendungen verlangen. Mit einem ausreichenden finanziellen Puffer sah man den Staat für weitere Krisen gut vorbereitet.

Die deutschen Staatsschulden sind im Jahr 2023 um 62 Milliarden Euro auf 2,62 Billionen Euro gestiegen. Die Zunahme war damit ähnlich wie im Vorjahr, aber deutlich schwächer als in den Jahren zuvor. Die Schuldenquote ist dagegen das zweite Jahr in Folge auf 64 Prozent gesunken. Eine Quote, die für viele Ökonomen aussagekräftiger ist als die absolute Verschuldung, da hier die Schulden ins Verhältnis zur gesamten Wirtschaftskraft gesetzt werden.

Entsprechend bewerten aktuell zwei Drittel der Bevölkerung eine Begrenzung des Schuldenhaushaltes kritisch. Sie sehen dringendere Herausforderungen, die sofortige Investitionen

erfordern, wie zum Beispiel die innere und äußere Sicherheit, den Pflegebereich, die Bildung und Digitalisierung oder die Energiewende. Auch fürchten viele Bürger, mit einem Schuldenabbau Probleme nicht zu lösen, sondern eher zu verschleppen – mit negativen Folgen für den Erhalt einer sozial gerechten und wirtschaftlich stabilen Gesellschaft. In der Folge werden moderate Schulden akzeptiert, wenn dadurch kurz- und mittelfristige Ziele umgesetzt werden können.

Zudem ist für die meisten Bürger das Argument der Sorge um die Lebensqualität der nachfolgenden Generationen hinfällig, da für sie konsequentes Sparen das nicht automatisch garantiert. Dagegen werden Schulden als eine Art Investition angesehen, die langfristig mehr Wohlstand schafft.

Auch in der Politik wurde zuletzt dem Fokus auf Schuldenabbau weniger Gewicht gegeben (Aussetzen der Schuldenbremse), und Themen wie Krisenmanagement, Investitionen und grüne Transformation rückten dafür stärker in den Vordergrund. Statt Sparsamkeit erwartet die Mehrheit entsprechend eine aktive und gestaltende Aufgabe des Staates für mehr Investitionen und Schulden als Mittel, um aktuellen Herausforderungen und zukünftigen Krisen effektiv begegnen zu können.

Prognose

Die kommenden Jahre werden von einer Finanzpolitik geprägt sein, die sich zunehmend von starren Sparvorgaben löst. Bürger erwarten vom Staat eine aktive Rolle, um zentrale Herausforderungen wie Sicherheit, Digitalisierung oder Rentenerhöhungen anzugehen. Finanzpolitische Dogmen wie die Schuldenbremse werden daher weiter an Bedeutung verlieren und als kontraproduktiv eingeschätzt werden, zukunftsorientierte Investitionen dagegen als Schlüssel, um Deutschland langfristig wettbewerbsfähig und lebenswert zu halten. Gleichzeitig wird der Fokus

auf Effizienz und Transparenz bei staatlichen Ausgaben wichtiger werden. Projekte mit klaren Zielsetzungen und messbarem Nutzen werden eine entsprechend breite Akzeptanz erfahren. Die Finanzpolitik der Zukunft wird sich auch durch Flexibilität und Pragmatismus auszeichnen. Starre Regeln werden dynamischen Strategien weichen, können diese doch viel besser auf aktuelle Entwicklungen reagieren.

Die Bürger fordern keine Rückkehr zur Vergangenheit, sondern eine mutige Gestaltung der Zukunft. Ein Paradigmenwechsel, der Deutschland nachhaltig prägen könnte.

VERANTWORTUNG

Was wird von Unternehmen erwartet?

Von je 100 Befragten stimmen folgender Aussage zu:
„Unternehmen sollten auch soziale und gesellschaftliche Verantwortung übernehmen."

Gewinn mit Gewissen

UNTERNEHMEN IN DER PFLICHT

Ergebnis

In den gesellschaftlichen Debatten der letzten Jahre stehen Fragen der gesellschaftlichen Verantwortung immer stärker im Fokus. Diese betreffen zum einen spezifische Themen oder Bereiche, zum anderen aber auch verschiedene Akteure, wie Politiker, Initiativen, Bürger oder wirtschaftliche Vertreter. Ein zentraler Schwerpunkt liegt dabei auf der Abwägung von Grenzen, Chancen und Verbindlichkeiten gesellschaftlicher Verantwortung. Für 85 Prozent der Bevölkerung gehört es zur Aufgabe von Unternehmen, soziale und gesellschaftliche Verantwortung zu übernehmen. Ältere Bürger fordern dies häufiger als jüngere.

VERANTWORTUNG

Gründe

Die Bevölkerung betrachtet Unternehmen zunehmend nicht nur als wirtschaftliche Akteure, sondern als integralen Bestandteil der Gesellschaft mit Verantwortung für deren Entwicklung. In den letzten Jahrzehnten hat sich die gesellschaftliche Wahrnehmung von Unternehmen grundlegend gewandelt. Während früher wirtschaftliche Verantwortung – etwa durch Profitmaximierung, Güterproduktion oder die Sicherung von Arbeitsplätzen – im Vordergrund stand, rücken heute auch soziale und ökologische Aspekte in den Fokus. Die Globalisierung hat Unternehmen zu global agierenden Akteuren gemacht, die Lieferketten weltweit steuern und internationale Standards beeinflussen. Fälle von schlechten Arbeitsbedingungen in Textilfabriken in Südostasien oder beim Rohstoffabbau in Afrika verdeutlichen, wie stark Unternehmen soziale und ökologische Aspekte in anderen Ländern prägen können und dafür zunehmend zur Verantwortung gezogen werden. Von ihnen wird nicht mehr nur Schadensbegrenzung erwartet, sondern auch aktive Maßnahmen zur Minimierung negativer Auswirkungen.

Darüber hinaus erwartet die Bevölkerung von Unternehmen einen positiven Beitrag zur Gesellschaft, da das Vertrauen in staatliche Institutionen gesunken ist. Viele Bürger sehen den Staat nicht mehr in der Lage, alle gesellschaftlichen Herausforderungen allein zu bewältigen. Unternehmen gelten daher als wichtige Partner, die aufgrund ihrer Ressourcen und ihres Einflusses viel bewirken können. Sie sollten zudem eine Vorbildfunktion einnehmen. Insbesondere große Konzerne mit globaler Reichweite haben die Möglichkeit, nachhaltige Standards zu setzen, an denen sich kleinere Firmen orientieren können.

Ein weiterer Grund für die hohen Werte ist die Forderung nach mehr Transparenz und Verantwortlichkeit im Handeln von Unternehmen. Verbraucher möchten nachvollziehen können, wie Produkte hergestellt werden, welche Bedingungen entlang der Lieferkette herrschen und welche Umweltstandards eingehalten werden. Für Unternehmen bietet dies auch Chancen: Viele erkennen zunehmend, dass verantwortungsbewusstes Handeln nicht nur dem Gemeinwohl dient, sondern auch die eigene Wettbewerbsfähigkeit stärkt.

VERANTWORTUNG

Prognose

Die gesellschaftliche Verantwortung von Unternehmen wird in den kommenden Jahren eine noch zentralere Rolle spielen. Damit entstehen sowohl Chancen als auch Verpflichtungen. Ein wesentlicher Aspekt zukünftiger Entwicklungen ist die zunehmende Bedeutung von Nachhaltigkeit als strategisches Leitmotiv. Unternehmen werden nicht mehr nur an wirtschaftlichen Erfolgen gemessen, sondern auch daran, wie sie ökologische und soziale Werte in ihre Geschäftsmodelle integrieren. Die Einführung verbindlicher Standards, wie beispielsweise die Corporate Sustainability Reporting Directive der Europäischen Union, wird Nachhaltigkeitsstrategien transparenter und umfassender machen.

Fortschritte in Bereichen wie künstlicher Intelligenz, Blockchain und Datenanalyse werden die Überwachung von Lieferketten präzisieren, die Nachverfolgbarkeit von Rohstoffen verbessern und die Umsetzung von Nachhaltigkeitsinitiativen effizienter gestalten. Gleichzeitig bringen diese Entwicklungen neue moralische Herausforderungen mit sich, etwa im Umgang mit Daten oder der Automatisierung von Arbeitsprozessen. Unternehmen werden solche Technologien daher nicht nur zur Effizienzsteigerung nutzen, sondern auch zum Wohle der Gesellschaft einsetzen müssen.

Die Rolle der Verbraucher wird weiter an Bedeutung gewinnen. Immer mehr Menschen treffen Kaufentscheidungen auf Basis der ethischen Standards eines Unternehmens. Marken, die soziale Verantwortung übernehmen, werden langfristig bevorzugt. Initiativen wie Fairtrade oder Programme zur Kreislaufwirtschaft zeigen bereits heute, wie Unternehmen durch nachhaltige Ansätze nicht nur das Vertrauen der Verbraucher stärken, sondern auch neue Märkte erschließen können. Unterstützt wird diese Entwicklung durch die mediale Transparenz – insbesondere soziale Medien machen Fehlverhalten schnell öffentlich und zwingen Unternehmen dazu, rasch auf Kritik zu reagieren und zu handeln.

VERANTWORTUNG

Eine weitere Entwicklung betrifft die Zusammenarbeit. Da viele Herausforderungen grenzüberschreitend sind, wird es für Unternehmen unerlässlich sein, Partnerschaften mit Regierungen, NGOs und anderen Firmen einzugehen. Diese Kooperationen werden dazu beitragen, gemeinsame Standards zu entwickeln und globale Probleme effektiver anzugehen.

VERANTWORTUNG

Welche Zukunftskompetenzen sind wichtig?

Von je 100 Befragten unter 35 Jahren sagen:
„Folgende Eigenschaften erachte ich als besonders wichtig, damit die nachkommenden Generationen in Zukunft ihr Leben sinnerfüllt und erfolgreich gestalten können."

Werte der über 55-Jährigen

Eigenschaften für die Zukunft

JUNG UND ALT SETZEN UNTERSCHIEDLICHE PRIORITÄTEN

Ergebnis

Die Prioritäten jüngerer und älterer Bundesbürger in Bezug auf wichtige Eigenschaften und Verhaltensweisen für zukünftige Generationen lassen sich in die drei Kategorien soziale Kompetenzen, persönliche Entwicklung sowie Engagement und Handeln einteilen. Die Rangfolge ist bei beiden Altersgruppen grundsätzlich ähnlich: Ehrlichkeit und die Übernahme von Verantwortung stehen bei beiden auf den ersten Plätzen. Auch Rücksichtnahme, Hilfsbereitschaft, Gerechtigkeit und die Bedeutung der Familie spielen für beide Generationen eine ähnlich große Rolle.

Dennoch zeigen sich Unterschiede in der Gewichtung einzelner Kompetenzen. Jüngere Bürger unter 35 Jahren empfinden Mut zu dauerhaften Bindungen wichtiger. Ältere Bürger über 55 Jahre hingegen priorisieren andere Werte wie Ehrlichkeit, Rücksichtnahme, Zeit für die Familie, Kompromissbereitschaft und die Fähigkeit zur Zusammenarbeit.

Im Bereich der persönlichen Entwicklung treten ebenfalls Differenzen auf. Jüngere Bürger bewerten Selbstbewusstsein und Resilienz, Stressbewältigung sowie Zeitmanagement und Organisationsfähigkeit höher, was eine Orientierung an Selbstoptimierung zeigt. Ältere Bürger legen dagegen größeren Wert auf Verantwortung, Eigenständigkeit, Flexibilität und die Akzeptanz von Rückschlägen.

Im Bereich Engagement und Handeln heben jüngere Bürger Hilfsbereitschaft, interkulturelle Kompetenz und aktive politische Teilhabe hervor. Ältere Bürger hingegen priorisieren Werte wie Ehrenamt, Gerechtigkeit und Toleranz, was auf eine stärkere Orientierung an moralischen Grundwerten schließen lässt.

VERANTWORTUNG

Gründe

Die Unterschiede in der Bewertung sozialer Kompetenzen zwischen den Generationen lassen sich durch unterschiedliche Lebensphasen und Prioritäten erklären. Jüngere Bürger betonen Mut zu dauerhaften Bindungen, da sie sich in einer Phase des Netzwerkaufbaus befinden – beruflich wie privat. Empathie gilt ihnen als Schlüsselkompetenz in einer globalisierten und zunehmend diversifizierten Welt, da sie Konflikte lösen und Brücken zwischen unterschiedlichen Gruppen bauen kann. Beziehungen sind für sie Grundlage eines harmonischen Miteinanders, bieten sie doch emotionale Sicherheit und Unterstützung in einer komplexen Welt.

Ältere Bürger hingegen legen deutlich größeren Wert auf Kompromissbereitschaft und familiäre Bindungen. Für sie sind familiäre Beziehungen nicht nur emotionaler Rückhalt, sondern auch Orte der Wertevermittlung. Kompromissbereitschaft wird angesichts einer polarisierten Gesellschaft als besonders relevant erachtet. Ehrlichkeit und die Fähigkeit zur Zusammenarbeit wird von Älteren ebenfalls hochgeschätzt, sei es im privaten, beruflichen oder gesellschaftlichen Kontext.

Im Bereich der persönlichen Entwicklung bewerten jüngere Bürger Fähigkeiten wie Stressbewältigung und Zeitmanagement höher, da diese in modernen Arbeitsumfeldern essenziell sind. Resilienz ermöglicht es ihnen, mit Unsicherheiten und Rückschlägen besser umzugehen, während Zeitmanagement dabei hilft, vielfältige Verpflichtungen effizient zu koordinieren. Ältere Bürger hingegen priorisieren Eigenschaften wie Verantwortung, die Fähigkeit, eigene Entscheidungen zu treffen, und die Akzeptanz von Enttäuschungen. Diese Kompetenzen spiegeln ihre Lebenserfahrung und ihre Rolle als Mentoren, Großeltern oder erfahrene Fachkräfte wider. Rückschläge nehmen sie nicht als Scheitern wahr, sondern als Teil eines kontinuierlichen Lernprozesses.

Im Bereich Engagement und Handeln zeigen jüngere Bürger ein stärkeres Interesse an interkultureller Kompetenz und aktiver politischer Teilhabe. Sie erkennen die Bedeutung interkultureller Kompetenz für den Umgang mit globaler Mobilität und Migration. Engagement in Parteien oder NGOs wird von ihnen als Möglichkeit gesehen, gesellschaftliche Verantwortung zu übernehmen und gleichzeitig persönliche Kompetenzen zu entwickeln. Ältere Bürger betonen dagegen stärker moralische Werte wie Gerechtigkeit und Toleranz. Diese Werte werden als Grundlage für soziale Interaktion und gesellschaftlichen Zusammenhalt betrachtet.

Prognose

Zukunftskompetenzen werden in einer sich wandelnden Gesellschaft immer wichtiger. Die Anforderungen an soziale Kompetenzen, persönliche Entwicklung sowie Engagement und Handeln betreffen alle Generationen. In einer globalisierten und digitalisierten Welt werden Fähigkeiten wie Empathie, Resilienz und interkulturelle Kompetenz zunehmend an Bedeutung gewinnen. Gleichzeitig bleiben traditionelle Werte wie Ehrlichkeit, Gerechtigkeit und Kompromissbereitschaft von zentraler Bedeutung, da sie das Fundament für gesellschaftlichen Zusammenhalt bilden.

Die Fähigkeit zur Empathie wird angesichts wachsender Diversität eine entscheidende Rolle spielen, da sie nicht nur den Umgang mit kulturellen Unterschieden erleichtert, sondern auch Konflikte löst und den Dialog zwischen Perspektiven fördert. Die Familie bleibt dabei ein zentraler Ankerpunkt, der emotionale Stabilität und soziale Unterstützung bietet. Kompromissbereitschaft und Teamfähigkeit werden ebenfalls an Bedeutung gewinnen, da Projekte und Entscheidungsprozesse immer häufiger die Zusammenarbeit von unterschiedlichen Menschen erfordern.

Die Fähigkeit zur Anpassung wird eine Schlüsselkompetenz für die Zukunft sein. Sie ermöglicht es, Krisen zu bewältigen und gestärkt daraus hervorzugehen. Durch die Kombination aus traditionellen und modernen Kompetenzen kann eine Gesellschaft entstehen, die nicht nur stabil, sondern auch innovativ ist und die Herausforderungen der Zukunft erfolgreich bewältigt.

Resilienz wird nicht nur im individuellen Leben gebraucht werden, sondern auch auf gesellschaftlicher Ebene: Nur eine resiliente Gesellschaft ist für Herausforderungen gerüstet und kann schnell Lösungen entwickeln.

Die Förderung all dieser Kompetenzen erfordert gezielte Maßnahmen in Bildungssystemen sowie durch gesellschaftliche Institutionen. Schulen und Universitäten werden soziale Kompetenzen ebenso vermitteln wie technisches Wissen oder Problemlösungsfähigkeiten. Interdisziplinäres Lernen wird helfen, innovative Ansätze für komplexe Herausforderungen zu entwickeln. Gleichzeitig müssen Weiterbildungsmöglichkeiten ausgebaut werden, um allen

Altersgruppen den Zugang zu neuen Fähigkeiten zu ermöglichen. Abhängen wird die gesamtgesellschaftliche Entwicklung auch davon, wie gut es gelingt, unterschiedliche Kompetenzen miteinander zu verbinden. Soziale Intelligenz bildet die Grundlage für ein harmonisches Miteinander; persönliche Entwicklung schafft Anpassungsfähigkeit; Engagement treibt den Wandel voran. Diese drei Bereiche ergänzen sich gegenseitig und bilden zusammen eine große Zukunftschance für Deutschland.

VERANTWORTUNG

KOOPERATION

Kooperation

In einer zunehmend individualisierten Gesellschaft stellt sich die Frage nach der Relevanz und Notwendigkeit von Kooperationen. Die Pluralität von Lebensformen und Werten prägt die moderne Welt, in der Optimierung, Selbstverantwortung und Selbstverwirklichung als erstrebenswerte Ziele gelten. Wettbewerb und Konkurrenz dominieren zahlreiche Lebensbereiche. Man könnte meinen, dass Kooperationen an Bedeutung verlieren, da die Anonymität moderner Gesellschaftsstrukturen das Kollektiv häufig in den Hintergrund treten lässt. Dennoch existieren vielfältige Kooperationsformen, die im Verborgenen wirken und das Fundament sozialer Gemeinschaften bilden. Gerade in Zeiten zunehmender Vereinzelung ist es von besonderer Relevanz, das Potenzial von Kooperationen hervorzuheben und ihre Vorteile sowohl für das Individuum als auch für die Gesellschaft deutlich zu machen.

Wortherkunft

Der Begriff „Kooperation" stammt vom lateinischen „cooperatio." Er setzt sich aus „co" (gemeinsam) und „operatio" (Arbeit oder Zusammenwirken) zusammen und bedeutet wörtlich übersetzt „gemeinsames Arbeiten." In der Antike war der Begriff eng mit dem Staat und dem Militär verknüpft. Kooperationen galten als Voraussetzung für ein funktionierendes Gemeinwesen. Im Mittelalter fand der Begriff vor allem in religiösen Zusammenhängen Anwendung. Hier bedeutete Kooperation das Zusammenwirken von Gott und Menschen. Dieses Konzept umfasste gute Werke sowie die Zusammenarbeit von Engeln und Heiligen zur Erfüllung göttlicher Pläne. Mit der Aufklärung und der damit verbundenen Säkularisierung verlagerte sich der Fokus dann auf weltliche Zusammenarbeit, und wirtschaftliche, soziale und politische Bereiche gewannen an Bedeutung. Die aufstrebenden Wissenschaften, insbesondere Philosophie und Politikwissenschaft, begannen sich intensiv mit dem Konzept der Kooperation zu befassen, da sie in ihnen die Ideale der Vernunft, des Gemeinwohls und der universellen Menschenrechte wiederfanden. Im 19. Jahrhundert wurde der Begriff durch die Industrialisierung stark geprägt. Kooperationen beschrieben die Zusammenarbeit von Unternehmen zur Erreichung gemeinsamer Ziele wie Innovation,

Arbeitsteilung oder Gewinnmaximierung. Zudem wurde er mit Themen wie Solidarität und gesellschaftlichem Zusammenhalt verknüpft. Er diente als Vorbild zur Bildung von Genossenschaften und wurde mit gemeinschaftlichem Handeln zur Bewältigung sozialer Ungleichheiten und politischer Herausforderungen assoziiert. Im globalen Zusammenhang entwickelten sich erste Ansätze internationaler Zusammenarbeit, etwa beim Wiener Kongress 1815 oder durch die Gründung internationaler Organisationen wie dem Roten Kreuz 1863. Diese Tendenzen verstärkten sich im 20. Jahrhundert, insbesondere in ökonomischen und politischen, aber auch in ökologischen Bereichen. Beispiele für globale Kooperation sind die Gründung der UNO, der Welthandelsorganisation, der EU oder internationale Umwelt- und Klimaschutzprojekte. Gegenwärtig steht der Begriff Kooperation für einen universellen Wert, der in allen Lebensbereichen Anwendung findet. Merkmale sind unter anderem gegenseitiger Respekt, Freiwilligkeit, Gleichberechtigung sowie das Streben nach Lösungen gemeinsame Herausforderungen.

Wissenschaftliche Einordnung

Innerhalb der Wissenschaft gibt es verschiedene Theorien und Ansätze, die sich mit der Komplexität des Kooperationsphänomens beschäftigen. Sie befassen sich mit der Frage, wie Individuen, Gruppen oder Organisationen zusammenarbeiten, um gemeinsame Ziele zu erreichen, und welche Voraussetzungen, Mechanismen und Folgen von kooperativem Verhalten zu beobachten sind. Je nach Disziplin werden dabei unterschiedliche Schwerpunkte gesetzt, wobei auch hier die interdisziplinäre Forschungsarbeit geschätzt und genutzt wird. Innerhalb der Ökonomie wird Kooperation oft durch die Spieltheorie und Vertragstheorie analysiert. Bei Ersterer wird ein strategisches Entscheidungsverhalten untersucht, bei dem der Erfolg eines Individuums oder Unternehmens von den Entscheidungen anderer abhängt (Kooperation oder Eigeninteresse). Bei der Vertragstheorie wird analysiert, wie äußere Anreizmechanismen (Verträge) genutzt werden können, um Konflikte zu lösen oder effizient zusammenzuarbeiten.

KOOPERATION

Die Psychologie widmet sich den individuellen und sozialen Faktoren, wobei es auch hier verschiedene Ansätze gibt. Nach der Social Exchange Theory basiert Kooperation auf dem Prinzip von Kosten und Nutzen. Menschen kooperieren, wenn der Nutzen (zum Beispiel Anerkennung, Unterstützung) die Kosten (z. B. Aufwand) überwiegt. Nach der Theorie der sozialen Identität liegt der Fokus auf der Gruppenkooperation, nach der Menschen eher mit Mitgliedern ihrer eigenen Gruppe (In-Group) als mit Außenstehenden (Out-Group) zusammenarbeiten, da dies ihre soziale Identität stärkt. Daneben können aber auch intrinsische und extrinsische Motivation oder kulturelle Werte und Traditionen die psychologischen Aspekte der Kooperation prägen.

In der Soziologie wird Kooperation als zentraler Untersuchungsgegenstand betrachtet, der als essenzielle Grundlage für das Funktionieren einer dynamischen Gesellschaft gilt. Sie ist notwendig, um Sicherheit und Stabilität zu gewährleisten, und fungiert zugleich als Instrument der Machtverteilung. Kooperation entsteht insbesondere dann, wenn Gruppen gemeinsame Interessen verfolgen. Sie kann jedoch scheitern, wenn erhebliche Macht- oder Ressourcenungleichheiten bestehen oder wenn mangelndes Vertrauen und fehlende Kooperationsbereitschaft vorherrschen.

Politikwissenschaftliche Theorien richten ihren Fokus häufig auf die globale Ebene, insbesondere auf die erfolgreiche Zusammenarbeit zwischen Staaten durch die Etablierung gemeinsamer Institutionen, Normen und Regeln. Zugleich machen diese Ansätze jedoch auch die Herausforderungen und Konflikte sichtbar, die entstehen, wenn Staaten vorrangig eigene Einzelinteressen verfolgen.

Bei allen Ansätzen wird Kooperation als zielgerichteter Prozess wahrgenommen und bildet eine bedeutsame Grundlage für die Entwicklung von Individuen, Organisationen und Gesellschaften.

KOOPERATION

Bedeutung von Kooperation für Individuum und Gesellschaft

In zahlreichen Bereichen spielt Kooperation eine zentrale Rolle. In der Wirtschaft ermöglicht sie Unternehmen, Ressourcen effizient zu nutzen und Innovationen voranzutreiben. In sozialen Zusammenhägen fördert sie den Zusammenhalt innerhalb von Gemeinschaften und verbessert das Wohlbefinden ihrer Mitglieder. Im Bildungsbereich ist Zusammenarbeit zwischen Lehrern, Schülern und Eltern mitentscheidend für den Lernerfolg, denn Schüler entwickeln durch kooperative Lernmethoden soziale Kompetenzen und Teamfähigkeit. Auch in der Wissenschaft ist Kooperation unerlässlich, denn oftmals führen erst interdisziplinäre Forschungsprojekte zu bahnbrechenden Entdeckungen. Im Bereich des Umweltschutzes zeigt sich die Notwendigkeit globaler Kooperation besonders deutlich. Die Auswirkungen des Klimawandels erfordern gemeinsame Anstrengungen aller Länder. Internationale Abkommen wie das Pariser Klimaabkommen sind Beispiele dafür, wie Staaten zusammenarbeiten können, um globale Herausforderungen zu bewältigen.

Die Voraussetzungen für Kooperationen sind vielschichtig und an ihre jeweiligen gesellschaftlichen, historischen und kulturellen Rahmenbedingungen gebunden. Unabhängig davon bilden Vertrauen und Empathie die Grundbasis dafür, an die Fairness und Verlässlichkeit anderer sowie an die Einhaltung gemeinsamer Absprachen zu glauben. Je öfter man diesbezüglich positive Erfahrungen gemacht hat, desto eher ist man bereit, neue Kooperationen einzugehen. Weitere Einflüsse für eine kooperative Gesellschaft finden sich in sozialen Normen und Werten – zum Beispiel Solidarität, Respekt, Gemeinsinn –, in äußeren Einflüssen – unter anderem Belohnungs- und Sanktionsstrukturen – und in Krisen und Herausforderungen, die einer Zusammenarbeit bedürfen. Daneben sind aber auch organisatorische und strukturelle Zusammenhänge dafür verantwortlich, wie stark kooperatives Klima in bestimmten Bereichen der Gesellschaft verankert ist. Hierzu gehören zum Beispiel eine klare Kommunikation, die Verteilung von Verantwortlichkeiten, das Vorhandensein von sich ergänzenden Fähigkeiten, vertraute Akteure und die Förderung von Teamarbeit und Solidarität.

KOOPERATION

Auch wenn Kooperation immer im Zusammenhang von Gruppenprozessen steht, hat es auch eine Relevanz für den Einzelnen, insbesondere bezüglich seiner persönlichen, sozialen und beruflichen Entwicklung. Als soziales Wesen haben Menschen ein Grundbedürfnis nach Zugehörigkeit. Anfangs als Mitglied in der Familie, später in der Schule, im Freundeskreis, im Verein, im Unternehmen oder der Nachbarschaft. Um sich dort geschätzt und akzeptiert zu fühlen, ist es notwendig, Freundschaften, Netzwerke und soziale Verbindungen aufzubauen. Kooperation ist hier ein zentrales Element, um Verständnis, Unterstützung und Stabilität zu fördern. Es zeigt die Bereitschaft und Fähigkeit an, sich gegenseitig zu unterstützen, gemeinsame Ziele zu verwirklichen sowie Krisen und Herausforderungen zu bestehen. In der Folge stärkt Kooperation das Vertrauen in die Verlässlichkeit des anderen, steigert die Empathie und das Verständnis und fördert die Stabilität der Beziehungen. Hier zeigen sich auch die positiven Merkmale hinsichtlich der persönlichen Entwicklung. Durch die Kooperation erlernt der Einzelne, die eigene Perspektive um die des anderen zu erweitern, wird also teamfähiger und reduziert egoistische Einzelentscheidungen. Durch erfolgreiche Kooperationserfahrungen steigern sich dann die eigene Zufriedenheit, das Selbstwertgefühl, die Kommunikationsfähigkeit sowie die Gewissheit, zukünftig auf die eigenen Kooperationskompetenzen zurückgreifen zu können. In der Praxis zeigen sich diese unter anderem im beruflichen Alltag. Das Wissen, Probleme gemeinsam zu bewältigen, die Verantwortung zu teilen und sich aufeinander verlassen zu können, schafft ein Klima der Sicherheit, reduziert Stress sowie Belastung und fördert die Resilienz.

Die Bedeutung von Kooperation innerhalb von Gruppenprozessen lässt sich am Beispiel der Politik und der öffentlichen Wahrnehmung gut erläutern. So wie jeder Einzelne durch seine Kooperationsbereitschaft das gesellschaftliche Miteinander prägt und gestaltet, hat auch die Politik einen entscheidenden Einfluss darauf, welchen Stellenwert eine verbindliche Zusammenarbeit in der Gesellschaft hat. Grundsätzlich ist Kooperation ein zentraler Bestandteil der politischen Arbeit und wichtig dafür, wie diese in der Öffentlichkeit wahrgenommen wird. Im positiven Fall beeinflusst sie die Effizienz, Stabilität und Legitimität

politischer Entscheidungen und lässt die Akteure als verantwortungsvolle Personen erscheinen, denen eine konstruktive Zusammenarbeit zur Lösung gesellschaftlicher Herausforderungen wichtiger ist als die Verwirklichung von Partei- oder Einzelinteressen. Aktuell werden zum Beispiel Themen wie der Wirtschaftsstandort Deutschland oder die Migration als Herausforderungen angesehen, die eine parteiübergreifende Kooperation und eine längerfristige Perspektive benötigen. Erwartet werden in diesem Zusammenhang ein respektvoller Umgang miteinander, eine transparente Kommunikation, ein gleichberechtigter Austausch und der Mut zu Veränderungen. Unterschiedliche Standpunkte sollen ergebnisoffen abgewogen, Kompromisse gesucht, eigene Perspektiven erweitert und Entscheidungsprozesse nachvollziehbar gestaltet werden. Erfüllen sich diese Erwartungen nicht, werden die politische Arbeit beziehungsweise die handelnden Personen als eigennützig, unflexibel, ineffizient, kurzfristig denkend und machtfokussiert wahrgenommen.

Insgesamt ist festzuhalten: Kooperationen entstehen durch eine Kombination aus sozialen, psychologischen und strukturellen Faktoren und sind ein wesentlicher Faktor für den Zusammenhalt einer Gesellschaft. Sie ermöglichen den Austausch unterschiedlicher Perspektiven, das Verfolgen gemeinsamer Ziele und das Lösen kollektiver Herausforderungen.

> Kooperative Gemeinschaften sind resilienter als konkurrenzbasierte, da die Fähigkeit zur Zusammenarbeit es ihnen ermöglicht, flexibel und effizient auf Herausforderungen zu reagieren.

KOOPERATION

Best-Practice-Beispiele

1. Der Aufbau der Internationalen Raumstation ISS

Beteiligte: NASA (USA), ESA (Europa), Roskosmos (Russland), JAXA (Japan), CSA (Kanada) und viele weitere.

Ziel: Gemeinsame Forschung im Weltraum, Förderung von Technologie und internationaler Zusammenarbeit.

Erfolg: Seit 1998 symbolisiert die ISS internationale Kooperation, indem sie Wissenschaftler und Astronauten aus verschiedenen Ländern zusammenbringt.

2. Die COVAX-Initiative

Beteiligte: WHO, GAVI, CEPI und Regierungen weltweit.

Ziel: Sicherstellung eines gerechten Zugangs zu COVID-19-Impfstoffen für alle Länder, insbesondere für ärmere Staaten.

Erfolg: Bis 2023 wurden circa zwei Milliarden Impfdosen an bedürftige Länder geliefert, um die Pandemie weltweit zu bekämpfen.

3. Der Erasmus+-Austausch

Beteiligte: Europäische Union und Bildungseinrichtungen in Mitgliedsländern.

Ziel: Förderung von Mobilität und Austausch zwischen Studierenden, Lehrenden und Praktikanten.

Erfolg: Seit der Gründung 1987 haben über 15 Millionen Studierende an diesem Programm teilgenommen und kulturellen Austausch erlebt. Es wurden internationale Mobilität und Netzwerkbildung gefördert und der europäische Zusammenhalt gestärkt.

4. The Ocean Cleanup

Beteiligte: NGOs, Wissenschaftler, Regierungen, Unternehmen.

Ziel: Reduzierung der Plastikverschmutzung in den Weltmeeren und in Flüssen.

Erfolg: Innovative Technologien wie das „Interceptor"-System haben allein 2023 über 8.000 Tonnen Plastik aus Flüssen und Ozeanen entfernt. Zudem führt es zu technologischen Innovationen und wissenschaftlichen Studien, es sensibilisiert für das Problem und bildet ein Bewusstsein für mehr Nachhaltigkeit.

5. „Tafeln" in Deutschland

Beteiligte: Ehrenamtliche, Supermärkte, Unternehmen und Bedürftige.

Ziel: Verteilung überschüssiger Lebensmittel an Menschen in Not.

Erfolg: Die Tafeln in Deutschland unterstützen über zwei Millionen Menschen jährlich und vermeiden gleichzeitig Lebensmittelverschwendung. Sie haben eine starke Basis an Freiwilligen.

KOOPERATION

Was braucht es, um Krisen zu meistern?

Von je 100 Befragten stimmen folgender Aussage zu:
„Gemeinsame Anstrengungen und Kooperation sind entscheidend, um Krisen erfolgreich zu meistern."

Krisen meistern

GROSSE MEHRHEIT FORDERT MEHR GEMEINSCHAFT

Ergebnis

Engagement und Kooperation gelten für fast neun von zehn Bundesbürgern als wesentliche Antwort auf Krisen und Herausforderungen. Dabei herrscht eine große Einigkeit innerhalb der Bevölkerung, und Unterschiede in Bezug auf Einkommen, Bildungsgrad oder Familienstand sind gering. Lediglich beim Alter zeigen sich Unterschiede: Während rund drei Viertel der unter 35-Jährigen zustimmen, sind es bei den über 55-Jährigen 91 Prozent.

KOOPERATION

Gründe

Für die Mehrheit der Bürger ist klar: Nur gemeinsame Anstrengungen ermöglichen eine effektive Bewältigung von Krisen. Dabei spielt es keine Rolle, ob die Kooperation zwischen Einzelpersonen, Gemeinschaften, Parteien, Institutionen oder Nationen stattfindet – entscheidend ist ein gemeinsames Vorgehen und eine klare Zielsetzung. Kooperation bündelt unterschiedliche Perspektiven, Fähigkeiten und Ressourcen, nutzt Finanzen und Infrastruktur effizient und fördert innovative Ansätze. Dies wird umso relevanter, je komplexer die Herausforderungen sind, wie etwa Wirtschaftskrisen, Pandemien oder der Klimawandel.

Kooperatives Verhalten hat über das eigentliche Ziel hinaus weitreichende Auswirkungen: Es stärkt das gegenseitige Vertrauen und das Gemeinschaftsgefühl, vermittelt Solidarität und verteilt Verantwortung auf verschiedene Akteure. Dies gilt nicht nur für globale, nationale oder lokale Herausforderungen, sondern auch für alltägliche Krisensituationen. Darüber hinaus erhöht gemeinsames Handeln die Widerstandsfähigkeit gegenüber zukünftigen Krisen. Ehrenamtliches Engagement und freiwillige Helfer im Bevölkerungsschutz sind essenzielle Beispiele dafür, wie gemeinschaftliche Strukturen nicht nur kurzfristige Lösungen bieten, sondern langfristig ein solidarisches Miteinander fördern.

Ein weiterer Grund für Kooperation liegt in der Effizienz von Netzwerken: Durch Zusammenarbeit entstehen Synergien, die innovative Lösungsansätze ermöglichen – sei es auf lokaler Ebene oder in internationalen Kooperationen zwischen Staaten und Organisationen.

Die überdurchschnittliche Zustimmung älterer Bürger lässt sich auf ihre Lebens- und Krisenerfahrungen zurückführen. Wirtschaftliche Rezessionen, Nachkriegserfahrungen, politische Umbrüche oder gesellschaftliche Herausforderungen haben ihnen gezeigt, dass individuelle Bemühungen oft nicht ausreichen und gemeinschaftliches Engagement erfolgversprechender ist. Zudem wurden sie in einer Zeit sozialisiert, in der kollektive Werte wie Solidarität und Gemeinschaft eine zentrale Rolle spielten.

Jüngere Bürger hingegen sind in einer stärker individualisierten Gesellschaft aufgewachsen, die persönliche Leistung und Eigenverantwortung betont. Dadurch hat sich ein Bewusstsein entwickelt, das auf individuelle Anstrengungen und schnelle, eigenständige Lösungen setzt. Besonders im politischen Bereich wird Kooperation manchmal als verwässernd wahrgenommen, da Kompromisse oft dazu dienen, Einzelinteressen aller Beteiligten zu berücksichtigen. Trotz dieser Vorbehalte erkennt auch die jüngere Generation mehrheitlich die Notwendigkeit gemeinschaftlichen Engagements zur Bewältigung von Krisen.

Prognose

Die Bedeutung von Engagement und Kooperation wird in Zukunft weiter zunehmen. Angesichts immer komplexerer nationaler (z. B. Fachkräftemangel, demografischer Wandel, Polarisierung, Vertrauensverlust) und globaler Herausforderungen (z. B. Klimawandel, geopolitische Spannungen) bleibt gemeinschaftliches Handeln unverzichtbar. Es wird entscheidend sein, neue Formen der Zusammenarbeit zu entwickeln – sowohl auf lokaler als auch auf internationaler Ebene.

Besonders wichtig ist es, junge Bürger stärker für kooperatives Handeln zu sensibilisieren und ihnen die Vorteile gemeinsamer Anstrengungen näherzubringen. Gleichzeitig müssen bestehende Strukturen gestärkt werden: Ehrenamtliche Helfer sollten besser unterstützt und gewürdigt werden, um ihre Motivation langfristig zu erhalten.

Insgesamt zeigt sich: Nur ein ausgewogenes Zusammenspiel von individueller Initiative und kollektiver Verantwortung kann eine Gesellschaft resilient halten. Die Fähigkeit zur Kooperation entscheidet nicht nur über den Erfolg bei der Bewältigung aktueller Krisen, sondern bildet auch die Grundlage für eine nachhaltige Zukunft.

KOOPERATION

KOOPERATION

Wie hoch ist die Kompromissbereitschaft?

Von je 100 Befragten stimmen folgender Aussage zu:
„Ich bin bereit, Kompromisse einzugehen, um Konflikte zu lösen."

Brücken bauen statt Mauern errichten

KOMPROMISSBEREITSCHAFT IST HOCH

Ergebnis

Kompromisse sind mehr als nur ein Mittelweg verschiedener Ansichten, Bedürfnisse und Anforderungen. Sie sind eine Notwendigkeit in einer zunehmend vielfältigen und komplexen Gesellschaft und ein zentraler Bestandteil von Kommunikation, sozialer Interaktion und Konfliktlösung. Fast neun von zehn Bürgern sind bereit, Kompromisse einzugehen, um Konflikte zu lösen. Dabei weisen die Älteren die höchste Zustimmungsrate auf, während bei den Jüngeren etwas weniger zustimmen – jedoch immer noch vier von fünf.

KOOPERATION

Gründe

Die historische Entwicklung von Kompromissen lässt sich als ein Prozess von zunehmender Komplexität und institutionalisierter Zusammenarbeit beschreiben. Während in frühen Gesellschaften einfache und pragmatische Lösungen im Vordergrund standen, haben sich diese im Laufe der Zeit zu komplexen Verhandlungssystemen entwickelt, die auf die Vielfalt von Interessen und Herausforderungen reagieren. Und obwohl sich die gesellschaftlichen Zusammenhänge und Akteure verändert haben, sind Kompromisse gerade heute ein unverzichtbares Werkzeug, um in einer pluralistischen und oft konfliktbeladenen Welt tragfähige Lösungen zu finden.

Nicht nur Staaten, Organisationen oder Gesellschaften profitieren von Kompromissen – auch für den Einzelnen spielen sie eine entscheidende Rolle. Die Bereitschaft, Zugeständnisse zu machen, ist dabei eng mit den erwarteten Konsequenzen verbunden. Eine offene Haltung, Empathie sowie die Fähigkeit zum aktiven Zuhören fördern diese Bereitschaft erheblich. Zusätzlich wirken Aspekte wie Gerechtigkeit, Beziehungserhalt oder auch Pragmatismus als wichtige Faktoren. Zu den positiven Effekten von Kompromissen gehören eine gestärkte Kommunikationsfähigkeit, eine erhöhte Reflexionskompetenz, Resilienz sowie die Prävention schwerwiegender Konflikte. Darüber hinaus fördern sie Inspiration und Innovation und tragen dazu bei, stabile Beziehungen aufzubauen, die auf Verständnis und Vertrauen basieren.

Besonders deutlich wird die Bedeutung von Kompromissen in Gesellschaften, die stark durch die Globalisierung geprägt sind – wie zum Beispiel Deutschland. Hier leben immer mehr Bürger mit unterschiedlichen Hintergründen, Werten und Perspektiven. Kompromisse können helfen, verschiedene Standpunkte zu vereinen und Lösungen zu finden, die für alle akzeptabel sind. Hierbei spielen Gerechtigkeit und Fairness eine große Rolle. Alle Beteiligten eines Kompromisses müssen Zugeständnisse machen, die mit einem Nachgeben verbunden sind. Solange aber alle Parteien etwas behalten, was ihnen wichtig ist, steigert sich die Zufriedenheit (Win-win-Situation).

KOOPERATION

Auch für viele der Herausforderungen im Arbeitsleben oder in persönlichen Beziehungen, gibt es selten eine einfache Lösung, die für alle Beteiligten gleichermaßen zufriedenstellend ist. Kompromisse ermöglichen es jedoch pragmatische Antworten und Wege zu finden. Besonders im beruflichen Umfeld schaffen sie zudem eine Grundlage für eine produktive Zusammenarbeit: Sie entschärfen Konflikte, legen den Fokus auf gemeinsame Ziele und alle profitieren von den unterschiedlichen Ideen und Sichtweisen.

Die verschiedenen Sichtweisen der Generationen lassen sich durch unterschiedliche Sozialisationseinflüsse und Erwartungen sowie technologische Entwicklungen erklären. Die junge Generation ist in einer Zeit aufgewachsen, die stärker von Individualismus, Selbstbewusstsein, Authentizität und persönlicher Entfaltung geprägt ist. In der Folge tendieren viele Jüngere eher dazu, ihre eigenen Bedürfnisse und Wünsche zu priorisieren und skeptischer gegenüber Kompromissen zu sein – vor allem dann, wenn diese ihren persönlichen Werten oder Zielen entgegenstehen. Verstärkt wird diese Grundhaltung durch ihre Affinität zur digitalen Kommunikation. In den entsprechenden Plattformen herrschen oft polarisierende Ansichten und Reaktionen vor, mit wenig Raum für Kompromisse. Stattdessen wird die eigene Meinung klar vertreten und als „richtig" propagiert. Ein weiterer Grund findet sich in den hohen Erwartungen an Gerechtigkeit und Chancengleichheit. Wenn junge Bürger der Meinung sind ein Kompromiss ist nicht gerecht, verringert sich ihre Bereitschaft zur Kompromissfindung.

Im Gegensatz dazu herrscht bei der älteren Generation oftmals eine pragmatische Einstellung vor. Durch ihre Lebens- und Berufserfahrung haben sie bereits viele Kompromisse geschlossen und so deren effektives Potential zur Konfliktlösung erkannt. Zudem messen sie dem Konsens und einer langfristigen Harmonie eine hohe Bedeutung zu und sind weniger von absoluten Positionen überzeugt.

Gerade bei Konflikten erweist sich Kompromissbereitschaft als Schlüsselkompetenz für ein erfolgreiches Miteinander. Sie zeigt nicht Schwäche, sondern Stärke, weil sie die Fähigkeit erfordert, über den eigenen Schatten zu springen, die Perspektive zu wechseln und langfristig zu denken.

KOOPERATION

Prognose

In einer globalisierten Gesellschaft, die von unterschiedlichen Interessen und Perspektiven geprägt ist, wird die Fähigkeit, tragfähige Kompromisse einzugehen, zunehmend an Bedeutung gewinnen. Dies gilt sowohl auf kollektiver als auch auf individueller Ebene.

Auf gesellschaftlicher Ebene wird Kompromissbereitschaft eine Schlüsselrolle bei der Bewältigung globaler Herausforderungen spielen. Themen wie Klimawandel, Migration oder Ressourcensicherung erfordern multilaterale Verhandlungen und gleichzeitig die Bereitschaft aller Beteiligten zu Zugeständnissen. Auch in der Wirtschaft wird Kompromissbereitschaft eine zunehmend wichtig Rolle einnehmen. Unternehmen stehen immer häufiger vor der Herausforderung, wirtschaftliche Ziele mit gesellschaftlichen Erwartungen zu verbinden. Mehr Dialogformate zwischen Unternehmen, lokalen Gemeinschaften und NGOs werden dazu beitragen, gemeinsame Projekte zu entwickeln, die sowohl wirtschaftliche als auch soziale Vorteile bieten und gleichzeitig das Vertrauen in unternehmerisches Handeln stärken.

Auf individueller Ebene wird Kompromissbereitschaft in persönlichen Beziehungen weiterhin eine zentrale Rolle spielen. Partnerschaften und Freundschaften erfordern regelmäßig die Fähigkeit, unterschiedliche Bedürfnisse auszugleichen und gemeinsame Entscheidungen zu treffen. Dies gilt sowohl für alltägliche Themen wie Haushaltsführung oder Freizeitgestaltung als auch für grundlegende Fragen wie Lebensziele oder Werte. Die Bereitschaft, aufeinander einzugehen und zusammen Lösungen zu finden, stärkt das Vertrauen und die Verbundenheit zwischen den Beteiligten. Auch innerhalb von Familien bleibt Kompromissbereitschaft unverzichtbar. Unterschiedliche Generationen haben oft abweichende Werte und Vorstellungen. Die Fähigkeit zum Kompromiss ermöglicht es Familienmitgliedern jedoch, einen gemeinsamen Weg zu finden und Spannungen auf eine Weise zu lösen, die für alle akzeptabel bleibt.

Verstärken wird sich auch die Bereitschaft zur persönlichen Weiterentwicklung. Die Fähigkeit, eigene Standpunkte zu überdenken und sich auf andere Perspektiven einzulassen, fördert nicht nur das Verständnis für andere, sondern trägt auch zum eigenen Wachstum bei. Wer seine eigenen Bedürfnisse mit denen anderer in Einklang bringt, entwickelt emotionale Intelligenz und stärkt die eigene Resilienz.

KOOPERATION

Wer schätzt Zusammenarbeit?

Von je 100 Befragten stimmen folgender Aussage zu:
„Ich arbeite gerne mit anderen zusammen, um so zum Beispiel gemeinsame Ziele zu erreichen."

Die Kraft des Kollektivs

ZUSAMMENARBEIT ALS MOTOR FÜR FORTSCHRITT

Ergebnis

Eine deutliche Mehrheit der Bundesbürger schätzt die Zusammenarbeit mit anderen, um gemeinsame Projekte oder Vorhaben erfolgreich umzusetzen. Dabei zeigen sich kaum Unterschiede zwischen den Generationen: Sowohl jüngere als auch ältere Bürger bewerten Kooperation als zentralen Bestandteil ihres Handelns und erkennen die Vorteile gemeinschaftlicher Anstrengungen.

KOOPERATION

Gründe

Ein wesentlicher Grund für die hohe Zustimmungsrate ist das Gemeinschaftsgefühl, das durch Zusammenarbeit entsteht. Gemeinsame Überlegungen, Planungen und Anstrengungen schaffen Vertrauen und stärken zwischenmenschliche Beziehungen. Dies führt nicht nur zu besseren Ergebnissen in Projekten, sondern steigert auch das persönliche Wohlbefinden der Beteiligten. Besonders in sozialen Initiativen wie Nachbarschaftshilfen oder ehrenamtlichen Projekten erfahren viele Bürger, wie ihre Beiträge geschätzt werden, interessante Kontakte entstehen und gegenseitige Unterstützung zu neuen Kooperationen motiviert.

Ein weiterer wichtiger Aspekt ist die Arbeitsteilung, die Zusammenarbeit besonders attraktiv macht. Gruppenarbeit ermöglicht es, Aufgaben gezielt aufzuteilen und individuelle Stärken effektiv einzusetzen. Die Verteilung von Verantwortung und Zuständigkeiten auf mehrere Schultern steigert die Effizienz, verbessert die Qualität der Ergebnisse und reduziert die Belastung des Einzelnen.

Ein anderes Motiv für die Beliebtheit von Kooperationen ist der Austausch von Wissen und Ideen. Gemeinsames Arbeiten schafft Raum für gegenseitiges Lernen und den Einblick in unterschiedliche Perspektiven. Verschiedene Kompetenzen und Ansätze innerhalb einer Gruppe fördern die Entwicklung innovativer Lösungen und tragen maßgeblich zum Erfolg von Projekten bei. Besonders in der Arbeitswelt zeigt sich der Wert solcher Kooperationen: Teams aus verschiedenen Fachbereichen oder mit unterschiedlichen Hintergründen können ihre Stärken bündeln, um effizientere Prozesse und kreative Ansätze zur Lösung komplexer Aufgaben zu entwickeln.

Zudem spielt das Vertrauen in kollektive Lösungen eine zentrale Rolle. Viele Bürger erkennen die Notwendigkeit gemeinsamer Anstrengungen, insbesondere bei der Bewältigung lokaler Herausforderungen wie Stadtverschönerung, dem Erhalt von Gemeinschaftszentren, Share-Projekten, Patenschaften oder generationsübergreifenden Initiativen. Die Überzeugung, durch Zusammenarbeit effektive Lösungen zu finden, fördert nicht nur die Bereitschaft zur Kooperation und stärkt das gesellschaftliche Miteinander, sondern vermittelt auch das Gefühl, gemeinsam etwas Positives zu erreichen.

Prognose

Die Bedeutung der Zusammenarbeit wird in Zukunft weiter wachsen und sich als zentraler Bestandteil für die erfolgreiche Umsetzung von Projekten sowie die Bewältigung gesellschaftlicher Herausforderungen etablieren.

Bildungseinrichtungen wie Schulen und Universitäten werden verstärkt auf kooperative Lernmethoden setzen, um Schülern und Studierenden frühzeitig die Vorteile gemeinsamer Anstrengungen zu vermitteln. Gruppenprojekte, interdisziplinäre Ansätze und kollaborative Plattformen werden nicht nur den Austausch von Wissen fördern, sondern auch die Entwicklung sozialer Kompetenzen wie Empathie, Kommunikationsfähigkeit und Konfliktlösung. Diese Fähigkeiten sind nicht nur für den späteren Berufserfolg von großer Bedeutung, sondern auch für ein besseres Verständnis unterschiedlicher Perspektiven im persönlichen Umfeld.

> Kooperation wird zunehmend als Schlüsselkompetenz wahrgenommen, um in einer immer komplexer werdenden Welt nachhaltige Lösungen zu entwickeln.

Die Bewältigung zahlreicher – lokaler und regionaler, aber auch nationaler und globaler– Herausforderungen wird ohne Zusammenarbeit zukünftig kaum möglich sein. Zusammenarbeit ist daher nicht nur als Mittel zur Zielerreichung zu verstehen, sondern auch als grundlegendes Prinzip für eine funktionierende Gesellschaft. Die Fähigkeit, gemeinsam an Lösungen zu arbeiten und dabei individuelle Stärken einzubringen, wird zunehmend eine unverzichtbare Kompetenz sein. Politische Verantwortliche, Bildungseinrichtungen, Unternehmen und soziale Organisationen haben die Möglichkeit, diese Entwicklung aktiv zu fördern und Räume für Kooperation zu schaffen. Eine Gesellschaft, die auf Zusammenarbeit setzt, ist besser gerüstet für die Herausforderungen der Zukunft – sei es im Umgang mit globalen Krisen oder dem Erhalt einer lebenswerten Gemeinschaft vor Ort.

KOOPERATION

Wollen die Bürger weniger Reglementierungen?

Von je 100 Befragten stimmen folgender Aussage zu:
„Es gibt zu viele Gesetze, Verbote, Vorschriften und staatliche Reglementierungen: Vieles würde ohne den Staat besser laufen."

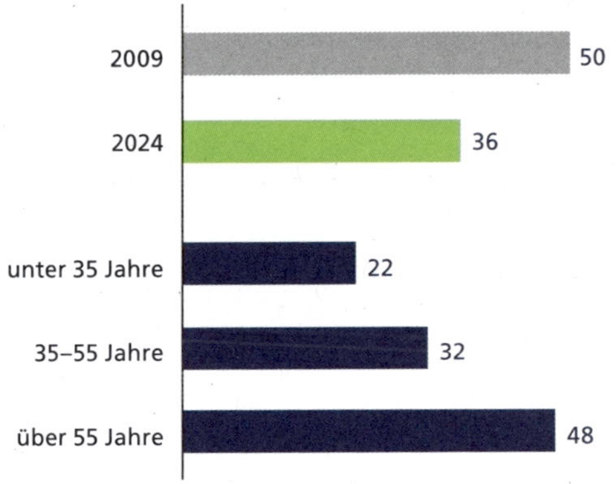

Regulierung oder Autonomie

GENERATIONEN IM ZWIESPALT

Ergebnis

Das Verständnis vom Staat basiert auf einem komplexen Verhältnis zwischen staatlicher Autorität, individuellen Freiheiten der Bürger und gemeinschaftlicher Verantwortung. Der Staat ist kein starres Gebilde, sondern unterliegt einem stetigen Wandel gesellschaftlicher Zusammenhänge, wobei er eine Balance zwischen Regularien und Unabhängigkeit anstrebt.

International gilt Deutschland als ein Land mit zahlreichen Gesetzen und umfangreicher Bürokratie. Während 2009 noch jeder zweite Bürger zu viele staatliche Reglementierungen sah, ist es 2024 nur noch jeder Dritte. Dabei zeigen sich deutliche Unterschiede zwischen den Altersgruppen: Gut ein Fünftel der jungen Bürger befürwortet weniger staatliche Reglementierungen, bei den über 55-Jährigen ist es fast die Hälfte.

Gründe

Der deutsche Staat erfüllt zahlreiche Aufgaben und Pflichten, verfügt jedoch auch über weitreichende Machtbefugnisse. Als demokratische Institution ist er Garant für Rechtsstaatlichkeit und Sicherheit, verantwortlicher Akteur für soziale Gerechtigkeit (zum Beispiel Steuern, Sozialleistungen, Bildung, Gesundheit), Dienstleister für Infrastruktur und öffentliche Güter sowie Kontrolleur von Regeln und Gesetzen. Die Mehrheit der Bürger vertraut diesen staatlichen Leistungen, kritisiert jedoch regelmäßig eine überbordende Bürokratie und Überregulierung, die die individuellen Freiheiten einschränken.

Die hohe Skepsis im Jahr 2009 lässt sich durch eine Kombination aus Krisen, politischer Skepsis und strukturellen Schwächen des Staatsapparats erklären. Die Finanzkrise und das damit einhergehende Misstrauen gegenüber staatlicher Gestaltungskraft verstärkten die Kritik. Viele Bürger empfanden Rettungsprogramme für Banken als unsozial und sahen die Staatsverschuldung als Verschwendung öffentlicher Mittel. Gleichzeitig wurde die Bürokratie als ineffizient und nicht bürgernah wahrgenommen, was das Vertrauen in den Staat weiter schwächte. Politische Skandale und eine mediale Debatte, die stärker auf neoliberale Eigenverantwortung setzte, trugen ebenfalls zu dieser Stimmung bei.

2024 hingegen genießt der Staat wieder größeres Vertrauen. In den letzten Jahren wurden mehrere Krisen bewältigt – darunter die Europäische Staatsschuldenkrise, die Flüchtlingskrise,

die COVID-19-Pandemie und der Ukrainekrieg. Maßnahmen wie Lockdowns, Impfkampagnen oder finanzielle Entlastungspakete wurden von vielen Bürgern als effektives Krisenmanagement wahrgenommen. Zudem hat sich die Wahrnehmung früherer Reglementierungen normalisiert, beispielsweise bei Mülltrennung, Datenschutz oder Kindertagesbetreuung. Eine transparentere politische Kommunikation und partizipative Maßnahmen haben das Vertrauen in den Staat daher gestärkt.

Die Unterschiede zwischen den Altersgruppen spiegeln verschiedene Perspektiven und Erfahrungen wider. Jüngere Bürger sind in einer Zeit sozialisiert worden, in der Themen wie Klimawandel, soziale Gerechtigkeit und Digitalisierung dominieren. Staatliche Eingriffe in diesen Bereichen, etwa Subventionen für erneuerbare Energien oder CO_2-Bepreisung, werden von ihnen überwiegend positiv wahrgenommen. Ältere Bürger hingegen legen mehr Wert auf persönliche Autonomie und sehen staatliche Regulierungen oft als Einschränkung ihrer Freiheiten.

Prognose

Die Balance zwischen staatlicher Regulierung und individueller Freiheit wird auch in den kommenden Jahren ein zentrales Thema bleiben. Während sich die Anforderungen der Bürger stetig wandeln, bleiben Kernaufgaben des Staates wie die Gewährleistung von Sicherheit, Gerechtigkeit und Stabilität unverändert.

Technologische Innovationen werden eine Schlüsselrolle spielen: Die Digitalisierung und der Einsatz von künstlicher Intelligenz könnten Verwaltungsprozesse effizienter gestalten und Behördengänge erleichtern. Gleichzeitig muss der Staat klare Regeln für den Datenschutz und die Transparenz staatlicher Entscheidungen schaffen, um das Vertrauen der Bürger zu bewahren.

KOOPERATION

Zukünftige globale Herausforderungen werden den Handlungsspielraum des Staates erweitern. Die Bürger erwarten ein proaktives Krisenmanagement, das kurzfristige Maßnahmen mit langfristigen Strategien kombiniert. Dabei wird es entscheidend sein, die divergierenden Erwartungen der Generationen zu berücksichtigen: Während jüngere Bürger staatlichen Eingriffen meist offen gegenüberstehen, legen ältere Generationen Wert auf persönliche Autonomie. Um diese Gegensätze zu überbrücken, wird eine transparente Kommunikation und eine stärkere Partizipation der Bürger erforderlich sein.

Insgesamt bleibt der Staat gefordert, sowohl individuelle Bedürfnisse als auch gemeinschaftliche Ziele in Einklang zu bringen, um eine resiliente und zukunftsfähige Gesellschaft zu gewährleisten.

Zukünftig wird sich ein Staatsmodell etablieren, das sowohl schlank als auch stark regulierend agiert: effizient durch Innovationen und gleichzeitig verlässlich in zentralen Bereichen.

Braucht es mehr Volksentscheide?

Von je 100 Befragten stimmen folgender Aussage zu:
„Es sollte mehr Volksentscheide und andere Formen der direkten Teilhabe für die Bürger geben."

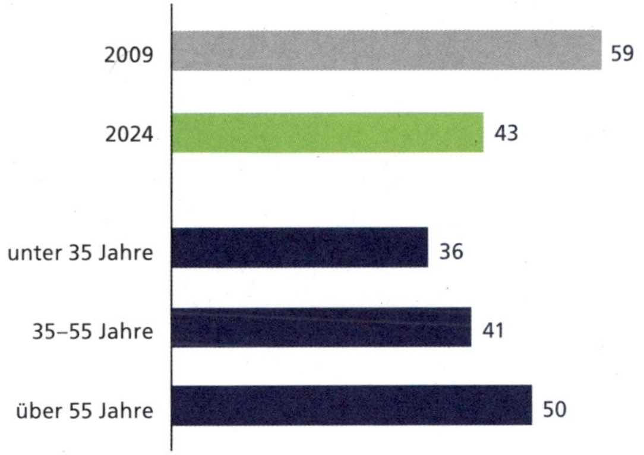

Wunsch nach Volksentscheiden nimmt ab

EINFACHE LÖSUNGEN REICHEN NICHT MEHR AUS

Ergebnis

Volksentscheide können ein zentrales Element der direkten Demokratie sein. Sie ermöglichen es den Bürgern, aktiv an den politischen Entscheidungsprozessen teilzunehmen. Vor 15 Jahren plädierten noch sechs von zehn Bürgern für eine entsprechende Ausweitung dieser partizipativen Möglichkeiten. 2024 sank dieser Anteil um ein Viertel auf 43 Prozent. Innerhalb der

Altersgruppen lassen sich hierbei erhebliche Differenzen feststellen: Während bei der älteren Generation jeder zweite mehr Volksentscheide einfordert, ist es bei den Jüngeren nur gut jeder Dritte.

Gründe

Die hohe Zustimmung im Jahr 2009 lässt sich auf die wachsende Skepsis gegenüber der politischen Elite zurückführen, die bereits in anderen Studien für diesen Zeitraum deutlich wurde. Die repräsentative Demokratie wurde vielfach als wenig bürgernah wahrgenommen. Der Wunsch nach mehr Mitspracherechten resultierte aus dem Gefühl eines zu geringen Einflusses der Bevölkerung auf zentrale politische Entscheidungen. Volksentscheide galten daher als geeignete Instrumente, dieses Demokratiedefizit auszugleichen. Zudem kritisierten viele Bürger die zunehmende Verlagerung politischer Entscheidungen auf die europäische Ebene, etwa im Bereich der Finanzpolitik, was das Bedürfnis nach stärkerer Mitbestimmung auf nationaler Ebene verstärkte. Vor diesem Hintergrund erlangten Elemente der direkten Demokratie breite Zustimmung, die seit den 1990er-Jahren verstärkt auf kommunaler und Landesebene eingeführt wurden.

Während im Jahr 2009 die Forderung auf Volksentscheide vor allem als Ausdruck eines demokratischen Gestaltungswillens interpretiert wurde, hat sich diese Wahrnehmung bis 2024 grundlegend gewandelt. Heute rücken insbesondere die potenziellen Nachteile in den Fokus. Ein zentraler Faktor für die zunehmende Skepsis gegenüber Volksentscheiden ist die Komplexität vieler politischer Themen. Fragestellungen zu Migration, Klimapolitik, Digitalisierung oder internationalen Handelsabkommen erfordern spezialisiertes Fachwissen und differenzierte Analysen. Viele Bürger fühlen sich nicht ausreichend befähigt, solche Entscheidungen fundiert zu beurteilen. Dies führt zu Unsicherheiten und einer wachsenden Zurückhaltung gegenüber direkter Demokratie.

Ein prominentes Negativbeispiel stellt der Brexit dar. Die Volksabstimmung im Vereinigten Königreich verdeutlichte, wie emotional aufgeladene Kampagnen und simplifizierte Botschaften Abstimmungen prägen können. Viele Briten gaben später an, die Tragweite ihrer Entscheidung nicht vollständig erfasst zu haben. Die daraus resultierende gesellschaftliche Spaltung und wirtschaftliche Instabilität illustrieren die Risiken von Volksentscheiden ohne hinreichende Informationsbasis.

Soziale Medien verschärfen diese Problematik zusätzlich. Plattformen wie Facebook oder X fördern die Verbreitung von Desinformationen und Polarisierung. Algorithmen verstärken oft extreme Positionen, wodurch ausgewogene Diskussionen erschwert werden. Diese Dynamik untergräbt das Vertrauen in die Fähigkeit des Einzelnen, komplexe politische Fragen eigenständig zu beurteilen.

Ein weiteres Argument gegen Volksentscheide liegt in der Gefahr kurzfristiger Interessenorientierung. Entscheidungen basieren häufig auf momentanen Emotionen oder lokalen Bedürfnissen und berücksichtigen langfristige Konsequenzen oder das Gemeinwohl nur unzureichend. Beispiele aus Deutschland zeigen, wie kommunale Volksentscheide wichtige Infrastrukturprojekte blockierten, obwohl diese möglicherweise langfristige Vorteile gebracht hätten.

Trotz der genannten Herausforderungen bieten Volksentscheide auch zahlreiche Chancen für die Demokratie. Sie ermöglichen Bürgern eine direkte Beteiligung an politischen Entscheidungen und stärken dadurch das Vertrauen in politische Prozesse. Politische Maßnahmen erhalten durch direkte Mitbestimmung eine höhere Legitimation und stoßen auf breitere gesellschaftliche Akzeptanz – insbesondere bei kontroversen Themen.
Ein weiterer Vorteil liegt in der erhöhten Rechenschaftspflicht der Politik. Direkte Abstimmungen veranlassen Politiker dazu, ihre Positionen klarer zu formulieren und transparenter zu agieren. Durch die zivile Teilhabe erhalten ihre Entscheidungen und Maßnahmen eine höhere Legitimation und können auf eine breitere gesellschaftliche Zustimmung hoffen, was

insbesondere bei umstrittenen Themen von Bedeutung ist. Gerade in unsicheren Zeiten ist dies eine unerlässliche Voraussetzung, um die Entfremdung zwischen Entscheidungsträgern und Bevölkerung zu verringern.

Auf kommunaler Ebene haben Volksentscheide zudem vielfach bewiesen, Reformprozesse beschleunigen zu können. Initiativen zur Stadtentwicklung oder zur Umsetzung von Umweltmaßnahmen wurden durch direkte Abstimmungen erfolgreich vorangetrieben. Darüber hinaus bieten Volksentscheide eine Möglichkeit, politische Blockaden zu überwinden. Themen, die aufgrund parteipolitischer Differenzen stagnieren, können durch direkte Abstimmungen vorangebracht werden. Dies fördert eine stärkere Identifikation der Bürger mit politischen Prozessen und stärkt ihr Gefühl der Teilhabe.

Die unterschiedliche Sichtweise zwischen den Generationen erklärt sich durch das stärkere Vertrauen von Jüngeren auf repräsentative Strukturen und multilaterale Ansätze. Entsprechend bevorzugen sie vermehrt Expertenlösungen statt basisdemokratischer Abstimmungen. Zudem sind sie in einer Gesellschaft aufgewachsen, in der partizipative Ansätze (z. B. Bürgerforen, Petitionen, Online-Plattformen) stärker etabliert sind, und nehmen diese als ausreichend wahr. Ältere Bürger hingegen betrachten Volksentscheide als wichtiges Werkzeug zur Kontrolle politischer Macht und zur Förderung von Mitbestimmung. Aufgewachsen in einer Zeit, in der diese noch nicht weit verankert waren, glauben sie an deren Wirkung bei der politischen Bewusstseinsbildung.

Prognose

Die Zukunft von Volksentscheiden wird maßgeblich davon abhängen, inwieweit sie an die Anforderungen moderner Gesellschaften angepasst werden können. Politische Entscheidungen erfordern zunehmend fundierte Kenntnisse und differenzierte Analysen. Daher ist es von zentraler Bedeutung, die Bürger umfassend über die Vor- und Nachteile, Chancen

und Risiken des jeweiligen Themas zu informieren. Nur auf dieser Grundlage können sie befähigt werden, Entscheidungen zu treffen, die auf sachlichen Informationen und einer fundierten Abwägung basieren. Unter diesen Voraussetzungen können Volksentscheide ein wirkungsvolles Instrument sein, um die Bürger verstärkt in politische Entscheidungsprozesse einzubinden und das Vertrauen in demokratische Institutionen nachhaltig zu stärken. Besonders bei lokal begrenzten oder klar definierten Fragestellungen bieten direkte Abstimmungen das Potenzial, Reformstaus zu lösen und politische Blockaden zu überwinden.

Eine essenzielle Voraussetzung für die Legitimation von Volksentscheiden bleibt jedoch die Einführung verbindlicher Quoten und mehrstufiger Verfahren. Diese Mechanismen gewährleisten eine breite gesellschaftliche Akzeptanz und schützen vor einer Interessendominanz einer aktiven, gut organisierten Minderheit. Nur so können die Ergebnisse von Volksentscheiden den Gesamtwillen der Bevölkerung abbilden.

Eine vielversprechende Perspektive zur Weiterentwicklung von Volksentscheiden liegt in der Implementierung neuer Formate wie Bürgerräten oder hybriden Modellen. Solche Ansätze ermöglichen es, komplexe Themen im Vorfeld strukturiert zu erörtern und fundierte Entscheidungsgrundlagen zu schaffen. Neben der Steigerung der Entscheidungsqualität fördern diese Formate auch das Verantwortungsbewusstsein der Teilnehmenden. Darüber hinaus können erfolgreiche Praktiken aus lokalen Governance-Strukturen – insbesondere aus dem Ansatz der New Public Governance – weiterentwickelt werden. Durch eine solche integrative Politikgestaltung können Verantwortlichkeiten effektiver verteilt und die Kooperation unterschiedlichster Akteure, wie Verwaltungen, Wirtschaft, Politik und Nichtregierungsorganisationen, optimiert werden.

Angesichts der zunehmenden Komplexität politischer Fragestellungen ist jedoch zu erwarten, dass Volksentscheide vorrangig in Bereichen Anwendung finden, die entweder lokal begrenzt sind oder eine hohe symbolische Bedeutung besitzen. Themen wie kommunale

Infrastrukturprojekte oder lokale Umweltmaßnahmen eignen sich besonders für direkte Abstimmungen, da sie eine stärkere Identifikation der Bevölkerung mit den Entscheidungsprozessen fördern können. Globale Herausforderungen wie die Klimapolitik oder internationale Handelsabkommen hingegen erfordern weiterhin die Expertise und die Verhandlungsfähigkeit von Parlamenten und Fachgremien. Die repräsentative Demokratie bleibt in solchen Bereichen unverzichtbar, da sie eine langfristige Planung und die notwendige multilaterale Kooperation ermöglicht.

Langfristig können Volksentscheide als sinnvolle Ergänzung zur repräsentativen Demokratie etabliert werden. Eine fundierte Weiterentwicklung dieser Instrumente bietet die Chance, sie als effektives Mittel zur Förderung von Mitbestimmung und gesellschaftlichem Zusammenhalt zu positionieren. Die direkte Demokratie birgt das Potenzial, politische Prozesse nicht nur transparenter zu gestalten, sondern auch das Vertrauen der Bürger in diese Prozesse zu stärken. Sie vermittelt den Menschen das Gefühl, aktiv an der Gestaltung ihrer gemeinsamen Zukunft beteiligt zu sein, und kann somit einen wesentlichen Beitrag zur Stärkung demokratischer Strukturen leisten.

Braucht es mehr unbequeme Entscheidungen?

Von je 100 Befragten stimmen folgender Aussage zu:
„Der Staat sollte stärker als bisher auch unbequeme Entscheidungen treffen, die den Bürgern etwas abverlangen, zum Beispiel bei Themen wie Einsparungen, Klimaschutzmaßnahmen oder Tempolimit."

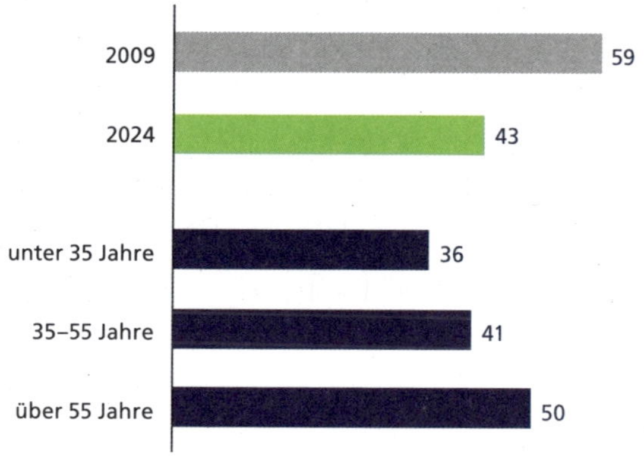

Akzeptanz oder Widerstand

WIE BÜRGER AUF UNBEQUEME ENTSCHEIDUNGEN REAGIEREN

Ergebnis

Die Bewältigung gesellschaftlicher Herausforderungen erfordert nicht nur vom Staat die Fähigkeit, schwierige Entscheidungen zu treffen, sondern bringt auch für den einzelnen Bürger spürbare Einschränkungen und Zumutungen mit sich. Diese können sowohl finanzieller Natur sein als auch eine Anpassung bisheriger Gewohnheiten erfordern, etwa in Form eines Tempolimits oder durch Maßnahmen zum Klimaschutz. Während im Jahr 2009 jeder fünfte Bürger

der Auffassung war, der Staat solle verstärkt unbequeme, den Bürger fordernde Maßnahmen ergreifen, stieg dieser Anteil bis 2024 auf 28 Prozent an. Besonders auffällig ist die Zustimmung bei den unter 35-Jährigen, von denen nahezu jeder Dritte diese Meinung teilt, während bei den über 55-Jährigen etwa jeder Vierte einer solchen stärkeren staatlichen Intervention zustimmt.

Gründe

Die Zunahme der Zustimmung im Jahresvergleich lässt sich durch einen Wandel des gesellschaftlichen Bewusstseins beziehungsweise der gesellschaftlichen Werte erklären. Dies betrifft vor allem die Einschätzung der individuellen Verantwortung und Veränderungsbereitschaft. Gerade die geopolitischen Herausforderungen führen der Bevölkerung die Relevanz und Dringlichkeit von Reformen sowie zum Teil tiefgreifenden Veränderungen vor Augen. Immer mehr Bürger erkennen die Notwendigkeit, auch als Einzelne aktiv Veränderungen mitzutragen. Dies zeigt sich zum Beispiel im zunehmenden Bewusstsein für den Klimawandel. Hitzewellen und Überschwemmungen in den letzten Jahren haben die Sensibilität für diese Herausforderung erhöht, wodurch mehr Menschen bereit sind, entsprechende Maßnahmen zu akzeptieren. Daneben verdeutlichen internationale Klimaziele und EU-Vorgaben, etwa zu CO_2-Reduktionen, die Notwendigkeit unbequemer Maßnahmen, weshalb viele Bürger auch freiwillig versuchen, ihren ökologischen Fußabdruck zu verkleinern. In ähnlicher Weise hat sich die Veränderungsbereitschaft hinsichtlich finanzieller und wirtschaftlicher Herausforderungen erhöht. Die Folgen der Inflation, der Energiekrise und die Unsicherheiten durch globale Auseinandersetzungen fördern die Zustimmung zur Ansicht, individuelle Einsparungen und mehr Eigenverantwortung seien notwendig, um den Staatshaushalt zu stabilisieren, was eben auch vom Staat eingefordert werden sollte.

Die stärkere Akzeptanz der jungen Generation erklärt sich aus deren höheren Sensibilität gegenüber ökologischen und sozialen Fragestellungen. Stärker als andere sind sie von den langfristigen Folgen betroffen. Viele von ihnen zweifeln daran, dass die Mehrheit der Bevölkerung ohne Druck freiwillige Anstrengungen diesbezüglich unternimmt, und fordern angesichts der

Dringlichkeit effektiver Maßnahmen eine stärkere staatliche Entscheidungsgewalt. Zudem haben sie eine geringere Bindung an traditionelle Lebensstile (offener für Veränderungen) und sind aufgrund ihrer monetären Ausgangssituation (zum Beispiel kein Auto oder Eigentum) von bestimmten Belastungen weniger betroffen als andere Gruppierungen. Im Gegensatz dazu tendieren ältere Menschen eher dazu, an alten Gewohnheiten festzuhalten, sind etwas weniger aufgeschlossen gegenüber Veränderungen und fürchten stärker finanzielle Einbußen.

Die geringere Zustimmung im Jahr 2009 zu dieser Haltung ist auch darauf zurückzuführen, dass die Dringlichkeit unbequemer politischer Entscheidungen noch nicht so stark das gesellschaftliche Bewusstsein beeinflusste. Dies trifft insbesondere auf den Klimawandel zu, dessen Auswirkungen weniger deutlich spürbar waren. Dafür beherrschten andere Themen die öffentliche Debatte, wie etwa die wirtschaftlichen Unsicherheiten durch die globale Finanzkrise. Die deutsche Wirtschaft schrumpfte so stark wie noch nie seit 1945 und entsprechend viele Bürger fürchteten um ihren Arbeitsplatz. In dieser angespannten wirtschaftlichen Situation wurde staatliches Eingreifen zwar als erforderlich angesehen, aber vor allem mit Bankenrettungen assoziiert. Teile der Bevölkerung betrachteten diese Maßnahmen eher kritisch beziehungsweise sahen darin eine Bevorzugung großer Unternehmen und Banken. Dies verstärkte seinerzeit die Skepsis gegenüber weiteren staatlichen Eingriffen, die noch eine zusätzliche Belastung oder Einschränkung für den Einzelnen bedeutet hätten.

Insgesamt ist trotz des Anstiegs im Jahr 2024 kritisch festzuhalten: Die große Mehrheit der Deutschen möchte keine stärkeren Maßnahmen des Staates, welche Einschränkungen für den Einzelnen nach sich ziehen würden. Dies betrifft vor allem Bevölkerungsschichten mit einer ausgeprägten Skepsis gegenüber der Effektivität oder Gerechtigkeit politischer Entscheidungen. Auch der Individualismus spielt eine Rolle: So stellen viele Menschen persönliche kurzfristige Vorteile oder vermeintlich unverzichtbare Freiheiten über langfristige gesellschaftliche Ziele. Ein strukturelles Motiv stellt hierbei das Kommunikationsdefizit bei politischen Entscheidungsträgern dar: Oft gelingt es nicht, komplexe Themen wie mehr Eigenverantwortung oder notwendige Rentenreformen sowie Steuererhöhungen verständlich zu kommunizieren und deren Notwendigkeit überzeugend darzulegen.

Prognose

Die gesellschaftliche Spaltung zwischen Veränderungsbereitschaft und Bewahrung bestehender Lebensweisen wird vorerst bestehen bleiben. Die jüngere Generation wird weiterhin eine stärkere Veränderungsbereitschaft zeigen als ältere Bürger. Ihre größere Offenheit gegenüber ökologischen und sozialen Fragestellungen sowie ihre geringere Bindung an traditionelle Lebensstile machen sie zu einer treibenden Kraft hinter der Akzeptanz unbequemer Entscheidungen.

Die Sensibilität für ökologische Themen wird in Zukunft weiter zunehmen. Extremwetterereignisse machen die Folgen des Klimawandels immer deutlicher spürbar und internationale Klimaziele und EU-Vorgaben erhöhen gleichzeitig den Druck auf nationale Regierungen, konkrete Maßnahmen umzusetzen. Diese Entwicklungen lassen immer mehr Bürger erkennen, wie wichtig es ist, persönliche Einschränkungen hinzunehmen, um langfristige Ziele zu erreichen. Auch wirtschaftliche Unsicherheiten wie Inflation und Energiekrisen spielen zukünftig eine zentrale Rolle. Viele Bürger verstehen, wie wichtig Eigenverantwortung ist, um sowohl den eigenen Haushalt als auch den Staatshaushalt zu stabilisieren.

Eine Kernaufgabe der Politik wird es sein, eine breite gesellschaftliche Akzeptanz für tiefgreifende Reformen zu erreichen. Viele Bürger stehen weiterhin staatlichen Eingriffen skeptisch gegenüber, insbesondere wenn diese als ungerecht oder ineffektiv wahrgenommen werden. Die Individualisierung der Gesellschaft sowie eine abnehmende Solidarität fördern die Gefahr, dass kurzfristige persönliche Vorteile weiterhin über langfristige gesellschaftliche Ziele gestellt werden. Entsprechend muss eine klare und verständliche Vermittlung der Notwendigkeit von Maßnahmen erfolgen, damit das Verständnis der Bürger erhöht wird. Sobald dies geschieht, wird sich eine breitere gesellschaftliche Akzeptanz entwickeln – eine Entwicklung, die angesichts aller Herausforderungen dringend erforderlich ist.

Sollte der Staat mehr private Initiativen fördern?

Von je 100 Befragten stimmen folgender Aussage zu:
„Der Staat könnte viel Geld sparen, wenn er private Initiativen aus den Reihen der Bürger aktiver unterstützen und fördern würde."

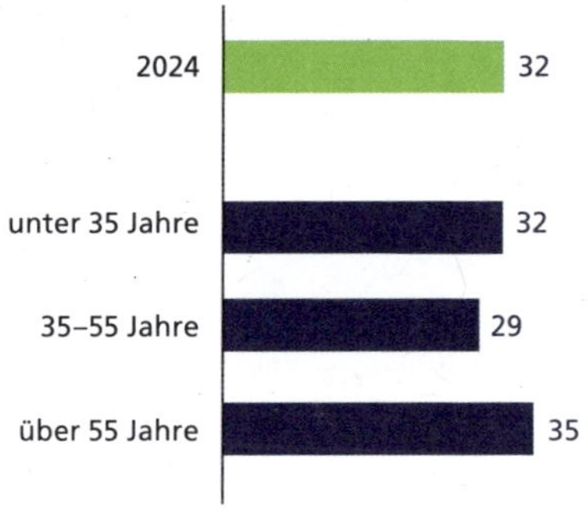

Staatliche Unterstützung privater Initiativen

MÖGLICHKEIT ZUR FINANZIELLEN ENTLASTUNG

Ergebnis

In Zeiten zunehmender finanzieller Herausforderungen und begrenzter staatlicher Kapazitäten wird die Frage nach neuen Möglichkeiten zur Begrenzung der Staatsausgaben immer drängender. Etwa jeder dritte Bundesbürger sieht in der stärkeren Förderung privater Initiativen eine Chance, die öffentlichen Finanzen zu entlasten. Die Kraft der Zivilgesellschaft soll genutzt werden, um Verantwortung auf breitere Schultern zu verteilen und innovative Wege für die Zukunft zu eröffnen.

KOOPERATION

Gründe

Private Initiativen können nicht nur Kosten senken, sondern auch gesellschaftliche Strukturen stärken und neue Lösungsansätze hervorbringen. Das Zusammenspiel von Eigeninitiative und staatlicher Unterstützung trägt wesentlich zur Bewältigung von Herausforderungen bei.

Ein zentraler Vorteil privater Initiativen liegt in ihrer Flexibilität und Anpassungsfähigkeit. Während staatliche Programme häufig durch langwierige Planungs- und Entscheidungsprozesse gebunden sind, verfügen private Projekte über ein besseres lokales Wissen und können schneller auf konkrete Bedürfnisse reagieren. Beispiele wie Bürgerbusse, Mitfahrbänke, Carsharing-Modelle oder Müllsammelaktionen zeigen, wie gezielte Maßnahmen mit begrenzten Mitteln große Wirkung entfalten können.

Ein weiterer Ansatz ist die Förderung von sozialem Unternehmertum. Diese Form privater Initiative ermöglicht es, gesellschaftliche Probleme unternehmerisch anzugehen und gleichzeitig finanziell nachhaltig zu arbeiten. Besonders in ländlichen Regionen können solche Projekte regionale Wirtschaftskreisläufe stärken und Abwanderungstendenzen entgegenwirken. Initiativen, die lokale Produkte und Dienstleistungen einbeziehen, fördern nicht nur die wirtschaftliche Stabilität vor Ort, sondern erhöhen auch die Resilienz gegenüber globalen Abhängigkeiten.

Darüber hinaus fördern private Initiativen das Verantwortungsbewusstsein der Bürger. Wer sich aktiv einbringt, übernimmt Verantwortung für konkrete Projekte und stärkt das Gemeinschaftsgefühl. Diese Form des Engagements erhöht das Vertrauen zwischen den Bürgern und hilft, gesellschaftliche Spaltungen zu überwinden – ein wesentlicher Aspekt in einer zunehmend polarisierten Gesellschaft.

Private Projekte ermöglichen zudem langfristige Prävention. Gesundheitsfördernde Programme wie Sport- und Ernährungsinitiativen können Krankheitskosten senken, während Bildungsprojekte wie Nachhilfeangebote oder Sprachkurse langfristig bessere Arbeitsmarktchancen

schaffen. Solche präventiven Maßnahmen fördern nicht nur die Eigenständigkeit der Bürger, sondern sind auch kosteneffizient. Die Finanzierung privater Initiativen bietet zudem eine hohe Hebelwirkung. Staatliche Förderungen können durch Spenden oder private Investitionen ergänzt werden, wodurch die finanzielle Basis solcher Projekte erheblich gestärkt wird. Dies mobilisiert nicht nur zusätzliche Ressourcen, sondern motiviert weitere Akteure zur Beteiligung.

Prognose

Private Initiativen werden in den kommenden Jahren eine zunehmend größere Rolle spielen. Die angespannte Haushaltslage des Staates und die Notwendigkeit, innovative Lösungen für gesellschaftliche Herausforderungen zu finden, machen privates Engagement unverzichtbar. Dennoch sind private Initiativen kein Allheilmittel. Komplexe und langfristige Herausforderungen wie die Pflege älterer Bürger oder die Integration Geflüchteter erfordern stabile staatliche Strukturen und verlässliche Ressourcen. Ohne diese Basis stoßen zivilgesellschaftliche Ansätze schnell an ihre Grenzen.

Neue Finanzierungsmodelle wie Social Impact Bonds oder öffentlich-private Partnerschaften könnten die Reichweite privater Projekte erheblich erweitern. Während Social Impact Bonds Investoren ansprechen, die bereit sind, in soziale Ergebnisse zu investieren, schaffen öffentlich-private Partnerschaften Synergien zwischen staatlichen Ressourcen und privatem Know-how. Solche Modelle bieten nicht nur finanzielle Vorteile, sondern erhöhen auch die Effizienz und Wirkung privater Initiativen.

Die Stärkung ländlicher Räume könnte ein zentrales Handlungsfeld für private Initiativen werden. Maßnahmen vor Ort fördern nicht nur den sozialen Zusammenhalt, sondern sind auch eine konkrete Antwort auf demografische Veränderungen.

Insgesamt liegt die Zukunft in einem ausgewogenen Zusammenspiel zwischen Staat und Gesellschaft. Der Staat bleibt verantwortlich für grundlegende Dienstleistungen und muss gleichzeitig Rahmenbedingungen schaffen, die privates Engagement fördern. Private Initiativen sind eine wertvolle Ergänzung mit eigenem Mehrwert, jedoch kein Ersatz für staatliche Leistungen.

KOOPERATION

Bremsen Parteiinteressen Veränderungen?

Von je 100 Befragten stimmen folgender Aussage zu:
„Die mangelnde Zusammenarbeit von Politikern unterschiedlicher Parteien bremst Veränderungen aus beziehungsweise verhindert diese sogar."

Parteipolitik verhindert Fortschritt

GROSSE MEHRHEIT BEMÄNGELT FEHLENDE ZUSAMMENARBEIT

Ergebnis

Die Mehrheit der Bundesbürger betrachtet die mangelnde Zusammenarbeit zwischen Politikern unterschiedlicher Parteien als Hindernis für Veränderungen. Neun von zehn Bürgern sind überzeugt, fehlende Kooperation bremse politische Fortschritte aus oder verhindere diese sogar. Besonders stark zeigt sich diese Meinung bei den über 55-Jährigen, während die Zustimmung bei den unter 35-Jährigen etwas geringer ausfällt.

KOOPERATION

Gründe

Die mangelnde Zusammenarbeit zwischen Politikern unterschiedlicher Parteien hat viele Ursachen, die sich in verschiedene Kategorien einteilen lassen: strukturelle, ideologische, soziale, externe und systemische Gründe. All diese Faktoren beeinflussen nicht nur die Interaktionsmuster zwischen politischen Akteuren, sondern auch die Wahrnehmung der Bürger hinsichtlich des politischen Handelns.

Ein zentraler struktureller Grund liegt in den parteipolitischen Interessen. Häufig besteht das primäre Ziel politischen Handelns darin, das eigene Profil zu schärfen und sich von konkurrierenden Parteien abzugrenzen. Hierdurch rückt die Kompromissbereitschaft in den Hintergrund, und die konstruktive Zusammenarbeit wird erheblich erschwert. Darüber hinaus stellen unterschiedliche Weltanschauungen und politische Überzeugungen eine wesentliche Barriere dar, um sich auf gemeinsame Ziele zu einigen. Besonders bei kontrovers diskutierten Themen wie Klimapolitik, Migration oder sozialer Gerechtigkeit treten diese Differenzen deutlich zutage. Populistische Strömungen verschärfen diese Problematik zusätzlich, indem sie gezielt auf Konfrontation und Abgrenzung setzen, um ihre Wählerbasis zu mobilisieren. Diese Strategie erschwert nicht nur eine sachliche Auseinandersetzung mit anderen Parteien, sondern verhindert häufig auch den notwendigen Konsens für nachhaltige politische Veränderungen.

Soziale und psychologische Faktoren spielen ebenfalls eine große Rolle. Ein Mangel an Vertrauen zwischen den Parteien lässt Kooperationen scheitern oder gar nicht erst zustande kommen. Politiker sehen ihre politischen Konkurrenten oft als Gegner statt als potenzielle Partner für gemeinsame Lösungen. Anstatt Brücken zu bauen, konzentrieren sich viele Akteure darauf, ihre eigene Position zu verteidigen oder die Schwächen der anderen hervorzuheben. Dies schafft ein Klima der Konfrontation, das konstruktive Zusammenarbeit nahezu unmöglich macht. Zudem liegt der Fokus vieler Politiker auf kurzfristigen Erfolgen, die schnell sichtbar sind und bei der Wählerschaft auf Resonanz stoßen. Langfristige

KOOPERATION

Veränderungen erfordern jedoch Geduld und eine kontinuierliche Zusammenarbeit über Parteigrenzen hinweg – etwas, das im politischen Alltag nur selten vorkommt. Auch externe Einflüsse tragen maßgeblich zur mangelnden Kooperation bei. Insbesondere die Rolle der Medien ist hierbei nicht zu unterschätzen. Polarisierende Aussagen und Konflikte erfahren in der Berichterstattung häufig eine größere Aufmerksamkeit als sachliche Debatten oder Kompromissfindungen. Dadurch setzen Politiker verstärkt auf Konfrontation, erhöht diese doch ihre mediale Präsenz. Zudem stellt die Komplexität vieler politischer Themen eine zentrale Herausforderung dar. Nahezu alle Problembereiche – sei es Bürokratieabbau, Steuerpolitik, Infrastruktur oder Wohnungsbau – sind hochgradig vielschichtig und lassen sich nicht durch einfache Lösungen bewältigen. Dies gilt umso mehr für besonders kontroverse Themen wie Migration, Klimapolitik oder Sicherheitsfragen.

Sie erfordern interdisziplinäre Ansätze sowie die Einbindung verschiedener Perspektiven. Ohne eine klare Strategie zur Bewältigung dieser Herausforderungen bleiben viele Initiativen stecken oder scheitern bereits im Ansatz.

Schließlich tragen auch systemische Faktoren dazu bei, die Zusammenarbeit zwischen politischen Akteuren zu erschweren. Eine strikte Fraktionsdisziplin reduziert die Flexibilität der Abgeordneten in ihren Entscheidungen und bindet sie stärker an die Parteilinie, wodurch Spielräume für Kompromisse eingeschränkt werden. Hinzu kommen kurze Wahlperioden, die den politischen Fokus oft auf kurzfristige Erfolge und die Sicherung der eigenen Wiederwahl lenken, anstatt langfristige und nachhaltige Lösungen zu fördern. Diese strukturellen Gegebenheiten erzeugen ein Umfeld, in dem Konsensfindung und Kooperation zusätzlichen Herausforderungen unterliegen.

Die Kombination der genannten Gründe führt in der Wahrnehmung der Bevölkerung zur Stagnation politischer Prozesse. Sie erleben diese als Stillstand oder Blockadepolitik und verlieren zunehmend das Vertrauen in die Kooperations- und Handlungsfähigkeit ihrer Vertreter.

Prognose

Die mangelnde Zusammenarbeit zwischen Politikern unterschiedlicher Parteien wird auch in Zukunft ein Hindernis für politische Fortschritte bleiben, wenn keine grundlegenden Veränderungen eingeleitet werden. Notwendig sind innovative Ansätze, die den politischen Diskurs konstruktiver gestalten und die Bereitschaft zur Kooperation fördern.

Ein zentraler Ansatzpunkt liegt hierbei in der Schaffung neuer Dialogformate. Mehr Parteigrenzen überschreitende Arbeitsgruppen oder ressortübergreifende Gremien würden dazu beitragen, den Dialog zu intensivieren und gemeinsame Lösungen in den Mittelpunkt zu rücken. Solche Formate bieten zudem die Möglichkeit, unterschiedliche Perspektiven einzubringen und innovative Ansätze zu entwickeln. Auch die verstärkte Einbindung externer Expertise sollte eine größere Rolle spielen. Viele politische Herausforderungen erfordern interdisziplinäre Ansätze und die Zusammenarbeit mit Wissenschaftlern, Politikern und den Bürgern. Bürgerräte oder Bürgerforen bieten die Möglichkeit, Meinungen aus der Bevölkerung in Entscheidungsprozesse einzubinden. Solche Formate fördern nicht nur den Dialog zwischen Politik und Gesellschaft, sondern können auch als Brücke zwischen unterschiedlichen Parteien dienen. Gemeinsame Arbeit an Vorschlägen aus der Bevölkerung würden den Fokus auf Sachthemen lenken und ideologische Differenzen in den Hintergrund rücken lassen.

Auch die Art und Weise, wie die politische Arbeit kommuniziert wird, sollte überdacht werden. Derzeit liegt der Fokus häufig auf Konflikten und parteipolitischen Differenzen. Eine stärkere Betonung von Kooperationen und gemeinsamen Erfolgen würde das öffentliche Bild von Politik positiv verändern. Medien könnten hierbei eine unterstützende Rolle spielen, indem sie Beispiele für erfolgreiche Zusammenarbeit hervorheben und weniger auf Polarisierung setzen.

KOOPERATION

Die Förderung von langfristigen Konzepten ist ein weiterer wichtiger Ansatz. Viele politische Projekte scheitern an ihrer Ausrichtung auf kurzfristige Erfolge. Themen wie Infrastrukturentwicklung oder Bildungsreformen erfordern jedoch eine kontinuierliche Zusammenarbeit über mehrere Legislaturperioden hinweg. Politische Akteure sollten daher stärker darauf hinarbeiten, langfristige Ziele zu definieren und diese unabhängig von Parteizugehörigkeiten voranzutreiben.

Die Umsetzung solcher Maßnahmen erfordert einen klaren Willen zur Veränderung sowie ein gemeinsames Verständnis dafür, dass Kooperation der Schlüssel für eine zukunftsfähige Politik ist.

KOOPERATION

Wer hilft bei der Integration?

Von je 100 Befragten stimmen folgender Aussage zu:
„Ich bemühe mich, aktiv bei der Integration von Geflüchteten und Zugezogenen mitzuhelfen."

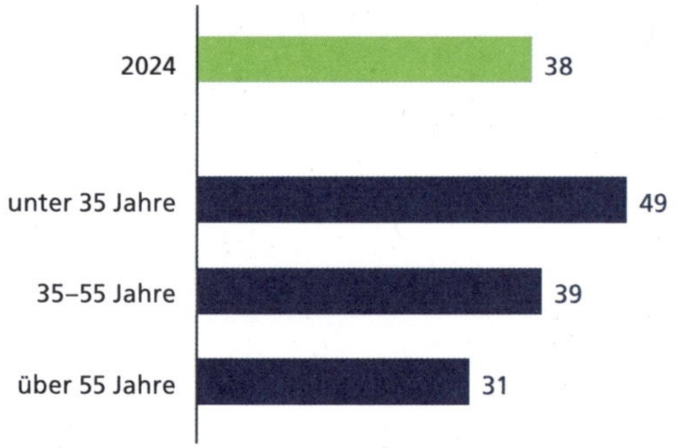

Integration durch Aktion

JEDER ZWEITE UNTER 35 JAHREN ENGAGIERT SICH

Ergebnis

Die Integration von Zugezogenen stellt eine zentrale gesellschaftliche Herausforderung dar, die sowohl politische Maßnahmen als auch das Engagement der Bürger und die Eigeninitiative der Migranten erfordert. Derzeit beteiligen sich 38 Prozent der Bevölkerung aktiv an der Unterstützung Geflüchteter bei ihrer Eingliederung. Im Gegensatz dazu übernimmt knapp zwei Drittel keine aktive Rolle in diesem Prozess. Dabei zeigt sich ein signifikanter Unterschied zwischen den Altersgruppen: Während sich jeder zweite Bürger unter 35 Jahren engagiert, liegt der Anteil bei den über 55-Jährigen bei weniger als einem Drittel.

Gründe

Die Gründe für oder gegen ein Engagement variieren erheblich und umfassen sowohl individuelle als auch gesellschaftliche Aspekte. Vorbehalte gegenüber Zugezogenen, Unsicherheiten im Umgang mit kulturellen Unterschieden sowie kritische öffentliche Debatten und Berichterstattungen über Migration und Integrationsprobleme wirken dämpfend auf die Bereitschaft, sich aktiv einzubringen. Zudem führen fehlende Berührungspunkte mit Zugezogenen, Zeitmangel aufgrund beruflicher und familiärer Verpflichtungen sowie unzureichende Informationen über konkrete Engagementmöglichkeiten zu einer Zurückhaltung. Sprachliche Barrieren, bürokratische Hürden und die emotionale Belastung durch die Auseinandersetzung mit den komplexen Herausforderungen Geflüchteter verstärken diese Hemmnisse zusätzlich. Viele Bürger betrachten Integrationsmaßnahmen als primäre Aufgabe staatlicher Institutionen, insbesondere wenn diese als ineffizient wahrgenommen werden. Dies führt oftmals zu Frustration und einem Rückgang der Motivation bei den Engagierten.

Auf der anderen Seite zeigen jene, die sich aktiv für die Integration einsetzen, ein hohes Maß an Verantwortungsbewusstsein und gesellschaftlichem Engagement. Neben altruistischen Motiven spielen die Freude am Helfen sowie die Sinnhaftigkeit des eigenen Handelns eine zentrale Rolle. Insbesondere jüngere Bürger weisen ein starkes Interesse an interkulturellen Begegnungen auf. Dies ist häufig auf ihre regelmäßigen Kontakte mit Zugezogenen in Bildungseinrichtungen und am Arbeitsplatz zurückzuführen, wodurch ein höheres Verständnis für deren Lebensrealitäten sowie persönliche Verbindungen entstehen. Die geringere Bereitschaft älterer Bürger könnte auf weniger Berührungspunkte mit Geflüchteten sowie auf eine stärkere Verwurzelung in bestehenden kulturellen Strukturen zurückzuführen sein, die zu Skepsis gegenüber Veränderungen führen.

KOOPERATION

Prognose

Die Integration Zugewanderter birgt ein erhebliches Potenzial, das über die Bewältigung gesellschaftlicher Herausforderungen hinausreicht. Sie fördert nicht nur die politische, soziale, kulturelle und wirtschaftliche Einbindung von Menschen mit Migrationshintergrund, sondern stärkt auch den gesellschaftlichen Zusammenhalt und ein harmonisches Zusammenleben. Besonders hervorzuheben ist das Potenzial auf dem Arbeitsmarkt zur Verringerung des Fachkräftemangels. Zugewanderte bringen spezifische Fähigkeiten und Qualifikationen mit, die in zahlreichen Branchen dringend benötigt werden. Durch gezielte Maßnahmen wie Sprachkurse, berufliche Qualifizierungsprogramme und die Anerkennung ausländischer Abschlüsse könnte dieses Potenzial effektiv genutzt werden. Dies würde nicht nur die wirtschaftliche Wettbewerbsfähigkeit Deutschlands stärken, sondern auch zur Bewältigung des demografischen Wandels beitragen.

Eine erfolgreiche Integration erfordert darüber hinaus die Schaffung von Begegnungsräumen, die den interkulturellen Austausch fördern. Kulturelle Veranstaltungen, sportliche Initiativen oder Nachbarschaftsprogramme könnten als Plattformen für Austausch und Zusammenarbeit dienen. Ein weiterer zentraler Schwerpunkt wird auf die Integration durch Bildung zu legen sein. Der Zugang zu Bildungseinrichtungen eröffnet Zugewanderten langfristige Perspektiven und befähigt sie, aktiv an der Gesellschaft teilzuhaben.

Um die Integration erfolgreich zu meistern, wird es zukünftig entscheidend sein, die vorhandenen Barrieren abzuschaffen und mehr Bürger für ein Engagement zu gewinnen. Niedrigschwellige Angebote sowie Erfolgsgeschichten gelungener Integration werden dazu beitragen, Vorurteile abzubauen und die Motivation zur Unterstützung zu erhöhen.

KOOPERATION

KOOPERATION

Wie hoch ist die Toleranz für kulturelle Freiheit?

Von je 100 Befragten stimmen folgender Aussage zu:
„Jeder sollte die Freiheit haben, seine kulturelle Identität und Religion auszuleben."

Religiöse Freiheit und kulturelle Vielfalt

DIE MEHRHEIT IST DAFÜR

Ergebnis

Im Jahr 2023 wiesen 25 Millionen der insgesamt 84 Millionen Einwohner Deutschlands einen Migrationshintergrund auf, was einem Anteil von 30 Prozent der Gesamtbevölkerung entspricht. Die kulturelle Vielfalt – 61 Prozent der Zugewanderten stammen aus Europa – prägt somit in den meisten Regionen das Alltagsbild. Viele Bürger betrachten diese internationale Diversität als eine Bereicherung. So befürworten drei Viertel der Bevölkerung, dass jede Person in ihrer individuellen Freizeit ihre kulturelle Identität und Religion ausleben darf. Diese Zustimmung zeigt sich unabhängig von Geschlecht, Alter, Bildungsstand und Einkommen.

KOOPERATION

Gründe

Das Recht auf freie kulturelle Entfaltung und Religionsfreiheit ist im Grundgesetz (Artikel 4 GG) verankert und spiegelt sich ebenfalls in internationalen Abkommen wie der Allgemeinen Erklärung der Menschenrechte der Vereinten Nationen wider. Ein signifikanter Teil der deutschen Bevölkerung sieht in diesen demokratischen Prinzipien Ausdruck von Pluralismus und individueller Freiheit und ist stolz auf diese Errungenschaften. Dieses Bekenntnis zur individuellen Freiheit wird allen Menschen zugestanden, unabhängig von ihrer kulturellen oder religiösen Herkunft. Dies erlangt besondere Bedeutung angesichts der in den letzten Jahrzehnten durch Migration verstärkten Herausforderungen der Integration und des Zulaufs populistischer Bewegungen. Dennoch betrachtet die Mehrheit der Bürger Toleranz als essenzielle Voraussetzung für ein friedliches Miteinander in einer pluralistischen Gesellschaft. Gegenseitige Akzeptanz wird dabei als Fundament für das Verständnis untereinander, die Stärkung des Gemeinschaftsgefühls und die Erweiterung individueller Perspektiven angesehen.

Diese Haltung wird durch Bildungsinitiativen und gesellschaftliche Diskurse gestärkt, die den Wert von Freiheit und Respekt gegenüber anderen Kulturen betonen. Dabei wird die Existenz religiöser und kultureller Konflikte nicht negiert, sondern stets im Kontext von Dialog und Zusammenarbeit betrachtet.

Über den individuellen Bereich hinaus wird kulturelle und religiöse Toleranz auch im größeren gesellschaftlichen Rahmen geschätzt, insbesondere in der Wirtschaft. Die kulturelle Vielfalt wird als Katalysator für Innovation, Kreativität und die Gewinnung globaler Talente betrachtet. Unternehmen mit diversen Teams profitieren von den unterschiedlichen Perspektiven und können Produkte und Dienstleistungen entwickeln, die internationalen und multikulturellen Märkten gerecht werden.

Zudem spielt die historische Erfahrung Deutschlands eine zentrale Rolle in der Betonung der Religionsfreiheit. Die Verbrechen des Nationalsozialismus haben die verheerenden Folgen

kultureller und religiöser Homogenitätszwänge deutlich gemacht. Dadurch ist in der Bevölkerung ein ausgeprägtes Bewusstsein für die Bedeutung von Vielfalt und Toleranz entstanden.

Prognose

Die fortschreitende kulturelle Diversität Deutschlands wird sowohl Potenziale als auch Herausforderungen mit sich bringen. Es könnten Vorurteile und Ressentiments in Teilen der Bevölkerung zunehmen, wodurch der soziale Zusammenhalt gefährdet und gezielte Gegenmaßnahmen nötig würden. Die Integration erweist sich weiterhin als komplex, da Faktoren wie Sprachbarrieren, die mangelnde Anerkennung ausländischer Abschlüsse und Diskriminierung auf dem Arbeits- und Wohnungsmarkt die gesellschaftliche Teilhabe vieler Migrantinnen und Migranten erschweren. Insbesondere geflüchtete Personen verbleiben häufig über Jahre in Gemeinschaftsunterkünften mit begrenzten Möglichkeiten zur Integration. Populistische Bewegungen und Parteien, die Ängste vor Überfremdung und wirtschaftlicher Unsicherheit instrumentalisieren, stellen eine Gefahr für demokratische Werte und die Willkommenskultur dar. Bildungsinitiativen und politische Programme werden daher verstärkt den interkulturellen Austausch fördern und Vorurteile abbauen müssen.

Die Chancen gelungener Integration für den Wirtschaftsstandort Deutschland sind jedoch erheblich. Unternehmen können von einer vielfältigen Belegschaft profitieren, die durch unterschiedliche Perspektiven Innovationen vorantreibt. Zudem erleichtert kulturelle Offenheit die Gewinnung dringend benötigter Fachkräfte aus dem Ausland und wirkt dem demografischen Wandel sowie dem Fachkräftemangel entgegen.

Für eine erfolgreiche Integration sind beidseitige Anstrengungen erforderlich. Die Aufnahmegesellschaft muss Offenheit zeigen und Strukturen schaffen, die eine umfassende Teilhabe ermöglichen. Gleichzeitig ist es essenziell, dass Zugewanderte Eigeninitiative ergreifen und sich aktiv in die Gesellschaft einbringen. Der Erwerb der deutschen Sprache bildet

hierbei eine Schlüsselrolle, um soziale und berufliche Teilhabe zu fördern. Die Bereitschaft zur Anpassung an grundlegende gesellschaftliche Normen sowie die Akzeptanz demokratischer Werte bilden weitere essenzielle Grundlagen für ein harmonisches Zusammenleben. Ziel sollte es sein, die eigene kulturelle Identität zu bewahren, ohne sich abzugrenzen oder Parallelgesellschaften zu bilden.

Wie wichtig ist Entscheidungsfreiheit?

Von je 100 Befragten stimmen folgender Aussage zu:
„Die Freiheit, meine eigenen Entscheidungen zu treffen, ist für mich ein wichtiges Gut."

Individuelle Freiheit und Gemeinwohl

SELBSTVERSTÄNDLICH FÜR DIE BÜRGER

Ergebnis

In einer Zeit, die durch globale Krisen, wirtschaftliche Unsicherheiten und tiefgreifende gesellschaftliche Herausforderungen geprägt ist, bleibt die individuelle Entscheidungsfreiheit ein zentrales Anliegen der Bevölkerung. Die Möglichkeit, selbstbestimmt Entscheidungen zu treffen, wird von neun von zehn Bürgern als unverzichtbar erachtet. Insbesondere ältere Generationen teilen diese Auffassung nahezu geschlossen. Auch unter jüngeren Bevölkerungsgruppen ist die Zustimmung hoch, wenn auch in etwas geringerem Maße.

Gründe

Die hohe Relevanz der Entscheidungsfreiheit lässt sich auf psychologische, soziale und lebensgeschichtliche Faktoren zurückführen. Die Gewissheit, über die eigene Entscheidungsfreiheit zu verfügen, vermittelt ein Gefühl von Kontrolle und ist ein fundamentaler Bestandteil der menschlichen Psyche. Autonomie fördert das Gefühl von Stärke, Widerstandsfähigkeit und Selbstwirksamkeit, indem sie das Individuum in die Lage versetzt, aktiv Einfluss auf persönliche und gesellschaftliche Umstände zu nehmen. Sie bildet zudem einen wesentlichen Bestandteil der sozialen Identität und der Wahrnehmung als mündiges Individuum.

In Krisenzeiten oder bei gesellschaftlichen Diskursen, in denen moralische Fragen – etwa nach Solidarität, Sicherheit oder Gerechtigkeit – vermehrt thematisiert werden oder individuelle Einschränkungen gefordert sind, streben viele Bürger danach, ihre Autonomie zu bewahren. Beispiele hierfür sind Debatten über Rauchverbote, Videoüberwachung, geplante Tempolimits auf Autobahnen oder den reduzierten Fleischkonsum. Selbstbestimmte Entscheidungen tragen wesentlich dazu bei, Gefühle der Fremdbestimmung oder Hilflosigkeit zu mindern, Stress zu bewältigen und aktive Handlungsspielräume zu schaffen. Sie symbolisieren somit nicht nur Autonomie, sondern auch Hoffnung und Resilienz.

Dabei dient Entscheidungsfreiheit keineswegs ausschließlich persönlichen Interessen. Vielmehr kann sie kreative Denkprozesse und innovative Lösungsansätze fördern, die sich positiv auf gesamtgesellschaftliche Herausforderungen auswirken. In der gegenwärtigen Gesellschaft ist es daher essenziell, auch unbequeme Meinungen äußern und Diskussionen anregen zu können. Gleichzeitig stärkt das Recht auf Unabhängigkeit das Vertrauen in Institutionen, was einen wichtigen Faktor für den sozialen Zusammenhalt darstellt. Umgekehrt können Einschränkungen individueller Freiheiten Misstrauen, Widerstand und gesellschaftliche Polarisierung begünstigen.

Die besonders hohe Wertschätzung der Entscheidungsfreiheit bei der älteren Generation lässt sich unter anderem durch deren Sorge vor einem Verlust der Autonomie im Alter erklären. Für diese Bevölkerungsgruppe ist die Möglichkeit, eigenständig handeln zu können, eng mit Lebensqualität verknüpft. Darüber hinaus verfügen sie über erprobte Strategien zur Bewältigung von Krisen, auf die sie auch in Zukunft uneingeschränkt zurückgreifen möchten. Ihre sehr hohe Zustimmung reflektiert nicht nur die hohe Wertschätzung für Selbstbestimmung, sondern auch die Befürchtung, diese verlieren zu können.

Jüngere Generationen zeigen hingegen eine pragmatischere Haltung gegenüber Einschränkungen. Sie sind tendenziell etwas eher bereit, persönliche Freiheiten zugunsten langfristiger gesellschaftlicher Ziele oder des Gemeinwohls einzuschränken. Diese Bereitschaft spiegelt sich in der Akzeptanz von Maßnahmen wider, die weniger stark als Eingriff in ihre Lebensqualität wahrgenommen werden. Beispielsweise unterstützen jüngere Menschen Maßnahmen zur Bekämpfung des Klimawandels stärker als andere Altersgruppen und sind bereit, dafür auf bestimmte Freiheitsrechte zu verzichten. Darüber hinaus leben viele junge Menschen noch in relativ abhängigen Strukturen – sei es im Elternhaus oder während der Ausbildung – und verbinden daher Entscheidungsfreiheit weniger stark mit ihrer sozialen Identität.

Prognose

Die Fähigkeit, eine Balance zwischen individueller Freiheit und kollektivem Gemeinwohl herzustellen, wird zukünftig eine entscheidende Rolle für den gesellschaftlichen Zusammenhalt spielen. Anpassungen und Einschränkungen werden nur dann breite Akzeptanz finden, wenn sie als fair und ausgewogen wahrgenommen werden. Die Herausforderung besteht darin, individuelle Freiheiten zu bewahren, ohne dabei das Gemeinwohl aus den Augen zu verlieren – ein „Sowohl-als -auch" statt eines „Entweder-oder."

Die Entscheidungsfreiheit bleibt auch in Zukunft nicht nur ein Symbol für Autonomie und Resilienz, sondern eine Grundlage für kreatives Denken und gesellschaftliche Innovationen. Besonders in Krisenzeiten zeigt sich: Freiheit bedeutet nicht nur Unabhängigkeit von externem Zwang, sondern auch die Übernahme von Verantwortung gegenüber dem Gemeinwohl.

FAZIT

Die vorliegenden Analysen haben die zentrale Bedeutung von Vertrauen, Verantwortungsbereitschaft und Kooperation für das Funktionieren unserer Gesellschaft herausgearbeitet. Dabei wurden sowohl die Voraussetzungen, Potenziale und positiven Auswirkungen als auch die Gefahren und Risiken thematisiert, die mit einem Schwinden dieser Werte einhergehen beziehungsweise wenn sie nicht mehr von allen gesellschaftlichen Akteuren vertreten und gelebt werden. Es lassen sich folgende zentralen Ergebnisse festhalten:

- Das Vertrauen der Bürger in die Relevanz staatlicher Organe ist weiterhin tief im gesellschaftlichen Bewusstsein verankert, wird jedoch durch zahlreiche aktuelle Entwicklungen zunehmend enttäuscht.

- Die Verantwortungsbereitschaft der Bevölkerung ist ausgeprägt, manifestiert sich jedoch primär im unmittelbaren sozialen Umfeld und wird in ihrem Potenzial sowie in Verbindung mit ziviler Eigeninitiative nur begrenzt ausgeschöpft.

- Alle verlässlichen Formen der Kooperation werden unter Wahrung der individuellen Freiheit von den Bürgern als unerlässlich zur Bewältigung von individuellen Krisen und gesellschaftlichen Herausforderungen angesehen.

- In allen drei Feldern sind mehr Anstrengungsbereitschaft und Reformwillen von den Entscheidungsträgern gefordert, insbesondere hinsichtlich der Kommunikation und Kompromissbereitschaft. Die Bevölkerung ist dabei durchaus bereit, auch unbequeme Entscheidungen mitzutragen und sich aktiv an der gesellschaftlichen Gestaltung zu beteiligen.

- Die Stärkung von Gemeinschaft, Vertrauen, Verantwortungsbewusstsein und Kooperation ist entscheidend, um eine breitere gesellschaftliche Basis für einen optimistischen Blick in die Zukunft zu schaffen.

Abschließend stellt sich die Frage, in welchem Verhältnis Vertrauen, Verantwortungsbereitschaft und Kooperation zueinanderstehen, um gezielt Einfluss auf deren Wechselwirkung und Effizienz nehmen zu können. Die Beziehung zwischen Vertrauen, Verantwortungsbereitschaft und Kooperation ist nicht als lineares Verhältnis zu verstehen, sondern als ein zirkuläres. Auch wenn Vertrauen scheinbar als Basis am Anfang steht, beziehen sich doch alle wechselseitig

aufeinander und können dem jeweiligen Kontext entsprechend als Voraussetzung oder Wirkung gesehen werden.

Vertrauen ist die Grundlage für Verantwortung. Um Verantwortung zu übernehmen oder auch zu übergeben, muss ein gegenseitiges Vertrauen in die Fähigkeiten des anderen vorausgesetzt werden. Dadurch entsteht ein Gefühl der Zuverlässigkeit und Sicherheit sowie die Möglichkeit, die Handlungen und Entscheidungen des anderen nicht ständig hinterfragen zu müssen. Gelichzeitig ist Vertrauen die Grundlage von Kooperation. Es schafft ein Gefühl der Sicherheit, eine positive Erwartungshaltung und ermöglicht offene Kommunikation. Ohne ein vertrauensvolles Verhältnis der Bürger zueinander sind sie nicht zu einer verbindlichen Zusammenarbeit bereit.

Verantwortung ist die Grundlage von Vertrauen. Wer Verantwortung übernimmt, zeigt damit seine Verlässlichkeit. Diese Eigenschaft ist entscheidend beim Aufbau von langfristigem Vertrauen. Gleichzeitig ist Verantwortung die Grundlage für Kooperation. Erst wenn die Bürger bereit sind, Verantwortung für sich und andere zu übernehmen, sind sie auch befähigt, gleichberechtigte Kooperationen einzugehen.

Kooperation ist die Grundlage von Vertrauen. Vertrauen ist kein statischer Zustand, sondern entwickelt sich über die Zeit durch wiederholte positive Interaktionen, transparente Prozesse und gemeinsame Vereinbarungen. Kooperation bewirkt eine Erweiterung der Perspektiven, einen Abbau der Unsicherheiten und eine Stärkung des Vertrauens. Gleichzeitig ist Kooperation auch die Grundlage von Verantwortung. Durch die Zusammenarbeit mit anderen oder den Wunsch, ein gemeinsames Ziel zu erreichen, ist der Bürger bereit, Verantwortung zu übernehmen.

Durch die wechselseitigen Beziehungen der drei Konzepte wird deutlich: Vertrauen, Verantwortungs- und Kooperationsbereitschaft bedingen, schwächen und stärken sich gegenseitig.

Eine Gesellschaft, die Vertrauen, Verantwortungsbereitschaft und Kooperation gezielt in den Mittelpunkt stellt, ist nicht nur besser in der Lage, die Herausforderungen der Gegenwart zu bewältigen, sondern kann auch eine nachhaltige und zukunftsfähige Welt gestalten.

ZUKUNFTSFRAGEN

PHILIPP AMTHOR

MdB (CDU)

Mit welchen Strategien oder Konzepten könnte das Vertrauen in Regierungs- und Unternehmerstrukturen gestärkt werden?

Um Vertrauen in unseren Staat zurückzugewinnen, müssen wir ihn grundlegend reformieren. Glaubwürdigkeit beginnt dabei damit, dass die Politik mit Reformen bei sich selbst anfängt: Die Arbeitsweise der Regierung und der Bundesverwaltung muss modernisiert werden und selbstkritisch auf den Prüfstand gestellt werden – im Hinblick auf Struktur, Personal, Digitalisierung und Verfahren. Deutschland braucht eine effizientere und schlankere Verwaltung mit klareren Zuständigkeiten. Die Aufgaben und Wirkungen sowie die personellen und finanziellen Mittel für die Bundesverwaltung müssen dabei wieder auf das Wesentliche konzentriert und zurückgeführt werden. Es muss aufhören, dass für jedes neue Problem immer wieder neue Posten und Strukturen geschaffen werden. Im Gegenteil: Ministerien und das Beauftragtenwesen müssen restrukturiert werden, und im Rahmen einer ressortübergreifenden Verwaltungsreform müssen der Personalbestand der Ministerien und die Rekordanzahl von mittlerweile über 950 Bundesbehörden auf ein adäquates Maß zurückgeführt werden. Ich bin davon überzeugt: Unser Staat muss mit besseren Arbeitsabläufen und mit weniger Personal bessere Arbeit machen. Dann wird er auch Vertrauen zurückgewinnen.

Wie sehen Sie persönlich das Verhältnis von individueller Freiheit und „Verantwortung für die Gesellschaft übernehmen" und wie setzen Sie das um?

Die Freiheit des Einzelnen und die Verantwortung für die Gemeinschaft sind für mich persönlich im besten christdemokratischen Sinne immer zwei Seiten derselben Medaille: Im Ausgangspunkt unserer Politik sehen wir immer zuerst den einzelnen Menschen mit seiner unantastbaren Würde und seinen individuellen Fähigkeiten, verbinden seine Freiheit aber immer auch mit seiner Verantwortung für die Gemeinschaft. Diese Gleichzeitigkeit von Freiheit in Verantwortung ist für mich Essenz unseres demokratischen Verfassungsstaates und zugleich Unterscheidungsmerkmal: Das Konzept von Freiheit in Verantwortung

immunisiert gegen einen überzogenen libertären Individualismus, bei dem allein der individuelle Freiheitsanspruch im Vordergrund steht. Es immunisiert aber ebenso gegen linke Identitätspolitik, die ein Gemeinwesen in konfligierende Gruppen aufspaltet und dadurch den Zusammenhalt der Gesellschaft gefährdet. Und es ist die richtige historische Lehre gegen sozialistisches, nationalistisches und völkisches Denken, das einem ideologisch begründeten Kollektiv den Vorrang vor den einzelnen Menschen gibt. Ganz in diesem Sinne ist das Verhältnis von Freiheit und Verantwortung für mich nicht nur Privatsache, sondern Systemfrage.

Braucht es dafür auch mehr Zusammenarbeit über Partei- und Wettbewerbsgrenzen hinweg und wie könnte das zu einem „Wandelwunder" führen?

Es braucht ganz sicher parteiübergreifende Anstrengungen, um das Zukunftsversprechen unserer Bundesrepublik zu erneuern: Freiheit, Frieden, Wohlstand und Sicherheit für uns alle. Dabei müssen – schon um der Demokratie willen – allerdings immer auch Unterschiede zwischen den Parteien klar erkennbar bleiben – und zwar nicht nur an den politischen Rändern, sondern gerade auch in der politischen Mitte. Und zum Stichwort „Wandelwunder" gilt: Wandel wird in der Regel weniger durch ein Warten auf Wunder, sondern besser durch beherztes Handeln erreicht. Bester Garant dafür ist eine kompetente Bundesregierung.

LAURA BORNMANN

Managing Director von STARTUP TEENS

Mit welchen Strategien oder Konzepten könnte das Vertrauen in Regierungs- und Unternehmerstrukturen gestärkt werden?

Mit ehrlichem Interesse, Authentizität und Menschlichkeit: Regierungs- und Unternehmensvertreter:innen müssen sich wieder stärker mit den Sorgen, Ängsten und Hoffnungen der Menschen auseinandersetzen. Nur so entstehen Lösungen, die echte Probleme in unserer Gesellschaft lösen. Vertrauen wird folglich nicht durch abstrakte Institutionen geschaffen, sondern durch die Menschen, die sie repräsentieren. Gefragt sind Führungspersönlichkeiten, die Haltung zeigen, transparent kommunizieren und zu eigenen Fehlern stehen. Damit ein solcher Kulturwandel gelingt, tragen wir alle Verantwortung: Besonders bei Politiker:innen sollten wir hinterfragen, ob die Forderung nach sofortigen Rücktritten immer gerechtfertigt ist – zumal es in der Vergangenheit oft um Sachverhalte ging, die weder die Kompetenz noch die eigentliche Arbeit der betroffenen Person betrafen. Denn wenn Offenheit immer wieder mit negativen Konsequenzen bestraft wird, wird sie eine Seltenheit bleiben.

Wie sehen Sie persönlich das Verhältnis von individueller Freiheit und „Verantwortung für die Gesellschaft übernehmen" und wie setzen Sie das um?

Freiheit und Verantwortung sind untrennbar miteinander verbunden: Je größer unsere individuelle Freiheit, desto größer sind unsere Gestaltungsspielräume – und desto größer auch unsere Verantwortung für die Gesellschaft. Für mich persönlich sind ein respektvoller Umgang mit anderen sowie ehrenamtliches Engagement in den Bereichen Gleichberechtigung, Bildung und Wirtschaft wichtig. Verantwortung bedeutet für mich, dass jede:r, der:die kann, etwas zurückgibt. Dazu gehört auch, klar Stellung gegen Unrecht und Diskriminierung zu beziehen. In einer Zeit zunehmender Polarisierung erfordert dies Mut. Viele schweigen aus Angst vor Anfeindungen, was ich nachvollziehen kann. Doch gerade jetzt dürfen die Starken nicht aufgeben. Wirtschaftsakteur:innen spielen hierbei eine Schlüsselrolle. Mit ihren Ressourcen und ihrem Einfluss können sie maßgeblich dazu beitragen, eine gerechtere Gesellschaft zu fördern.

Braucht es dafür auch mehr Zusammenarbeit über Partei- und Wettbewerbsgrenzen hinweg und wie könnte das zu einem „Wandelwunder" führen?

Ja, absolut. Die Herausforderungen unserer Zeit, ob Klimawandel, wirtschaftliche Transformation oder soziale Gerechtigkeit, erfordern ein grundlegendes Umdenken und ein gemeinsames Handeln. Ein „Wandelwunder" ist nur möglich, wenn Politik und Wirtschaft sich als Partner verstehen, die gemeinsam an einem Strang ziehen. Es ist an der Zeit, Gemeinsamkeiten in den Vordergrund zu stellen, Vielfalt als Stärke zu begreifen und Differenzen als wertvolle Bereicherung zu sehen. Vielleicht müssen wir auch unsere politischen und wirtschaftlichen Systeme grundlegend neu denken: Sind starre Parteistrukturen noch zeitgemäß oder sollten nicht vielmehr die Themen im Mittelpunkt stehen? Wie könnten Entscheidungsprozesse transparenter gestaltet und Bürger:innen sowie Mitarbeiter:innen direkter eingebunden werden? Sollten einzelne Unternehmen ihre Kräfte stärker bündeln, um gemeinsam innovative Lösungen zu entwickeln? Wäre es nicht auch sinnvoll, mehr Menschen aus Wirtschaft und Zivilgesellschaft in politische Systeme einzubinden? Und vor allem: Ist nicht mehr Mut die entscheidende Zutat für all das?

ZARAH BRUHN

Gründerin & CEO von Social-Bee

Mit welchen Strategien oder Konzepten könnte das Vertrauen in Regierungs- und Unternehmerstrukturen gestärkt werden?

Vertrauen ist die Basis für eine funktionierende Gesellschaft, ob im politischen oder wirtschaftlichen Kontext. Als Gründerin und Geschäftsführerin von socialbee erlebe ich fast täglich, wie entscheidend es ist, Transparenz, Glaubwürdigkeit und soziale Verantwortung in den Mittelpunkt zu stellen. Unternehmen und Regierungen können Vertrauen stärken, indem sie folgende Strategien verfolgen:

Transparenz und Kommunikation: Offene und ehrliche Kommunikation ist essenziell. Entscheidungen sollten nachvollziehbar und gut erklärt sein, damit Menschen sich abgeholt und integriert fühlen.

Partizipation und Einbindung: Menschen sollten dabei auch aktiv in Entscheidungsprozesse eingebunden werden. Sei es beispielsweise durch offene Dialogformate oder durch Mitbestimmung in Unternehmen.

Nachhaltigkeit und soziale Verantwortung: Unternehmen und Regierungen sollten langfristig soziale und ökologische Verantwortung übernehmen und keinesfalls auf kurzfristige Profite oder Wahlerfolge abzielen. Social Entrepreneurship beweist, dass wirtschaftlicher Erfolg und gesellschaftlicher Mehrwert sich nicht ausschließen, sondern einander verstärken können.

Vorbildfunktion von Führungskräften: Führungspersonen in Wirtschaft und Politik müssen selbst mit gutem Beispiel vorangehen, um langfristig Vertrauen aufzubauen.

Wie sehen Sie persönlich das Verhältnis von individueller Freiheit und „Verantwortung für die Gesellschaft übernehmen" und wie setzen Sie das um?

Ich bin der festen Überzeugung, dass individuelle Freiheit und gesellschaftliche Verantwortung keine Gegensätze sind, sondern sich optimal ergänzen können. Freiheit bedeutet nicht, egoistisch zu handeln, sondern die Möglichkeiten zu haben, Verantwortung zu übernehmen. In meiner Arbeit bei socialbee sehe ich tagtäglich, wie wichtig und auch schön es ist, individuelle Stärken für das Gemeinwohl einzusetzen. Freiheit bedeutet Möglichkeiten zu haben. Menschen sollten natürlich die Freiheit haben, ihr Potenzial

zu entfalten. Gleichzeitig bedeutet das aber auch, dass sie die Verantwortung tragen, diese Möglichkeiten sinnvoll zu nutzen. So kann jeder Mensch auf seine individuelle Art und Weise einen Mehrwert für die Gemeinschaft stiften.
Verantwortung zu übernehmen kann, dabei auch erfüllend sein. Es sollte nicht als Zwang, sondern als Chance verstanden werden, unsere Gesellschaft aktiv mitzugestalten und sich einzubringen für das größere Ganze.
Bei socialbee schaffen wir das sehr gut: mit konkreten Lösungen für gesellschaftliche Herausforderungen, indem wir Geflüchteten durch Arbeit und Qualifizierung echte Perspektiven bieten. Das zeigt, dass wirtschaftliche Freiheit und soziales Engagement vereinbar sind.

Braucht es dafür auch mehr Zusammenarbeit über Partei- und Wettbewerbsgrenzen hinweg und wie könnte das zu einem „Wandelwunder" führen?

Veränderung geschieht nicht isoliert. Wenn wir echten Wandel und langfristige Lösungen wollen, müssen Parteien, Unternehmewn und zivilgesellschaftliche Akteure zusammenarbeiten.
Branchen- und parteiübergreifender Dialog: Statt ideologischer Grabenkämpfe brauchen wir einen offenen Austausch. Die besten Lösungen entstehen oft aus einem Mix verschiedener Perspektiven.
Kollaborative Innovation: Wettbewerber können zusammenarbeiten, um größere gesellschaftliche Herausforderungen anzugehen. Kooperationen zwischen Start-ups, etablierten Unternehmen und der Politik können transformative Wirkungen entfalten.
Best Practices und Wissen teilen: Wenn erfolgreiche Ansätze offengelegt und nachahmbar gemacht werden, können sie schneller skaliert und auf neue Bereiche übertragen werden.
Gemeinsame Visionen schaffen: Damit Wandel nachhaltig ist, muss er von einer gemeinsamen Vision getragen sein. Der Fokus sollte nicht auf kurzfristigen Gewinnen, sondern auf langfristigen positiven Veränderungen liegen.
Ein „Wandelwunder" kann entstehen, wenn wir nicht in starren Denkmustern verharren, sondern gemeinsam neue Wege beschreiten. Social Entrepreneurship ist ein Beispiel dafür, wie durch kreative Lösungen und Zusammenarbeit echte Transformation möglich wird.

KIRA MARIE CREMER

Consultant, Gründerin von QUINGS

Mit welchen Strategien oder Konzepten könnte das Vertrauen in Regierungs- und Unternehmerstrukturen gestärkt werden?

Vertrauen entsteht nicht nur durch die besten Argumente, sondern vor allem durch konsequentes Handeln. Gerade die junge Generation erwartet heute von Unternehmen und der Politik eine klare Haltung, transparente Kommunikation und spürbare Veränderung. Mein Herzensthema „New Work" zum Beispiel ist nicht nur eine Frage von Homeoffice oder Vier-Tage-Woche. Es geht um eine neue Art des Arbeitens, die auf Eigenverantwortung, Sinnstiftung und Fairness basiert. Drei Faktoren sind dabei meines Erachtens entscheidend:

1. Glaubwürdigkeit: Unternehmen und Politiker:innen müssen das leben, was sie predigen. Wenn eine Firma Diversität auf LinkedIn feiert, aber intern immer noch gläserne Decken bestehen, ist das ein Vertrauensbruch.

2. Partizipation: Entscheidungen dürfen nicht mehr über die Köpfe der Betroffenen hinweg getroffen werden. Unternehmen müssen ihre Mitarbeitenden stärker einbeziehen, Politik muss ernsthaft den Dialog mit jungen Menschen suchen.

3. Messbarkeit: Lippenbekenntnisse reichen nicht. Fortschritte müssen sichtbar und überprüfbar sein – sei es durch unabhängige Audits, Gehaltstransparenz oder konkrete Maßnahmen gegen Fachkräftemangel.

Wie sehen Sie persönlich das Verhältnis von individueller Freiheit und „Verantwortung für die Gesellschaft übernehmen" und wie setzen Sie das um?

Freiheit bedeutet für mich nicht nur das Recht, Dinge zu tun – sondern auch die Verantwortung, sie sinnvoll zu nutzen. Als Dozentin und Autorin setze ich mich dafür ein, dass Menschen lernen, wie sie Arbeit aktiv gestalten können, anstatt in überholte Strukturen gepresst zu werden. Gleichzeitig braucht es ein Umdenken bei Arbeitgebenden: Es reicht nicht, nur über Fachkräftemangel zu klagen, während die Arbeitsbedingungen nicht stimmen. Freiheit im Job bedeutet nicht grenzenlose Flexibilität ohne Sicherheit – sondern einen fairen Rahmen, in dem Menschen ihr volles Potenzial entfalten können. Der deutsche Arbeitsmarkt steht vor einer Herausforderung: Während Unternehmen händeringend nach Fachkräften suchen, bleibt eine große Zahl an Ausbildungsstellen unbesetzt. Gleichzeitig finden viele junge Menschen keinen passenden Ausbildungsplatz. Um genau zu verstehen, wie

junge Menschen heute ihren Berufseinstieg wahrnehmen, habe ich gemeinsam mit dem Marktforschungsinstitut Appinio eine umfassende Studie durchgeführt. Wir haben untersucht, welche Erwartungen und Ängste die junge Generation beim Start ins Berufsleben hat, und daraus konkrete Handlungsempfehlungen für Politik, Schulen, Arbeitgebende und Eltern abgeleitet. Die Ergebnisse zeigen deutlich: Junge Menschen wollen Eigenverantwortung übernehmen – aber sie brauchen Praxiserfahrung, faire Bedingungen und echte Entwicklungsmöglichkeiten, um das auch tun zu können. Meine Verantwortung sehe ich außerdem darin, diese Debatte aktiv zu führen – sei es durch mein Buch, meine Vorträge, den FUNKE-Podcast „New Work Now" oder meinen Newsletter, in dem ich regelmäßig Best Practices vorstelle.

Braucht es dafür auch mehr Zusammenarbeit über Partei- und Wettbewerbsgrenzen hinweg und wie könnte das zu einem „Wandelwunder" führen?

Ja, und zwar dringend. Die Zukunft der Arbeit ist kein HR-Trend, sondern spätestens durch den sich weiter verschärfenden Fachkräftemangel auch ein gesamtgesellschaftliches Thema. Dass wir heute über Themen wie Remote Work, Vier-Tage-Woche oder KI am Arbeitsplatz diskutieren, zeigt: Wir stehen an einem Wendepunkt. Doch statt echter Kooperation erleben wir oft Blockaden – sei es durch politische Grabenkämpfe oder kurzfristiges Gewinnstreben. Echter Wandel wird nur passieren, wenn wir den Mut haben, Experimente zu wagen. Unternehmen und Politik müssen gemeinsam neue Modelle erproben. Was hält uns zum Beispiel davon ab, staatlich geförderte Pilotprojekte für mehr mentale Gesundheit am Arbeitsplatz zu starten? Branchenübergreifender Austausch ist außerdem entscheidend. Die besten Ideen entstehen oft nicht in der eigenen Bubble, sondern durch interdisziplinäre Zusammenarbeit. New Work muss raus aus der elitären Blase: Flexible Arbeitsmodelle dürfen nicht nur für hoch qualifizierte Büroangestellte gelten – auch Handwerk, Pflege und Produktion brauchen innovative Konzepte. Die junge Generation ist bereit für diesen Wandel. Jetzt braucht es Entscheider:innen, die nicht nur über die Zukunft reden, sondern sie mutig gestalten.

INTERVIEW

CATHARINA ENDERLEIN

Gründerin & CEO von ELSCP

Mit welchen Strategien oder Konzepten könnte das Vertrauen in Regierungs- und Unternehmerstrukturen gestärkt werden?

Die tiefer liegende Frage ist: Welche Kultur und Werte müssen wir dafür in uns genau jetzt wieder entdecken und erwecken, um uns als Menschen zu begegnen? Auf dieser Ebene entsteht echtes Vertrauen. Starke Unternehmen, starke Organisationen und starke Regierungen – sie entstehen in der Wahrnehmung vieler durch das Erlebnis von Menschen, die wahrhaftig und authentisch Werte wie Wünsche verkörpern und gleichzeitig in der Lage sind, aus diesen eine schöne, greifbare, realistische und nachhaltige Zukunft zu zeichnen. Fühl- und erlebbar. Am Anfang steht Mut. Und: Menschlichkeit, Empathie, die Gabe zuzuhören und aus Gehörtem etwas zu formen, in dem sich viele wieder erkennen können. Das vermittelt Sicherheit. Das vermittelt ein Wir-Gefühl. Daraus resultiert Vertrauen. Über kurz oder lang. In unsicheren Zeiten wird das Wie höher gewichtet als das Was. Auch höher als der Anspruch, perfekt zu sein oder die vollständigen Ergebnisse zu präsentieren. Das gute Gefühl steht im Mittelpunkt. Mit ihm der Teamgeist, die Natürlichkeit, die Leichtigkeit und die gemeinschaftliche Stärke – wissentlich hinsteuernd auf ein Ziel namens Zukunft. Speist sich dieses Gefühl aus einem Kreis vielfältiger Menschen, die Interessen gerade wegen Unterschieden bündeln und zusammenarbeiten, wiegt es umso schwerer. Hier geht es um mehr als um ein Einzelinteresse. Hier sitzen Menschen an einem Tisch, verbunden durch neutrale Zwischenräume, die sich – fernab von Rollen – zu höheren Themen als Menschen vernetzen wollen. Frei und ungezwungen. So entsteht ein starkes Kreislaufsystem voller Zuversicht, das uns trägt.

Wie sehen Sie persönlich das Verhältnis von individueller Freiheit und „Verantwortung für die Gesellschaft übernehmen" und wie setzen Sie das um?

Individuelle Freiheit bedeutet ‚selbst Verantwortung für die Gesellschaft zu übernehmen. Ich habe das selbst erlebt und aus diesem Gefühl heraus für die Zukunft in den letzten Jahren vernetzt gebaut. Als Gründerin und CEO des European Lab for sustainable companies & personalities für die Entstehung zukunftsfähiger Wirtschaftslösungen durch neue Teilhabeprozesse zwischen Wirtschaft, Wissenschaft, öffentlichen Institutionen, jungen Gruppierungen und Bürger:innen, zum anderen in meiner kommunikativen Nachhaltigkeitsberatung

meet MOMENTUM. Zum Dritten auch als Initiatorin der in 2020 gestarteten Bewegung „Sinnflut – Zukunft gesunde Stadt“ für einen gemeinsamen Wandel mit neuen Medien-, Community- und Bürgerformaten, digital und in ganz neuen, positiven Formen der Echtzeitkommunikation auf den Ströer-Screens in allen deutschen Städten. Als Partnerinitiative des „New European Bauhauses“ der Europäischen Kommission ist im Zusammenspiel mit der europäischen Mission „Beautiful. Sustainable. Together.“ bereits ein wunderbares Zukunftsgefühl voller Vertrauen entstanden, Gutes wie Gelungenes sichtbar zu machen, durch eine verbindende, verständliche Sprache Menschen in Einheit mitzunehmen, ein ganz natürliches Nachbarschaftsgefühl über Grenzen hinweg in Freiheit entstehen zu lassen – für diese Vision bringe ich viel in Bewegung.

Braucht es dafür auch mehr Zusammenarbeit über Partei- und Wettbewerbsgrenzen hinweg und wie könnte das zu einem „Wandelwunder“ führen?

Zusammenarbeit ist dafür der Kernbaustein. Basierend auf neuen Lab-Strukturen, Teilhabeprozessen, Co-Creations und Collaborations, um zu überraschen, Neues zu produzieren, ungenutzte Räume sichtbar zu machen und in diesen gemeinsam, ohne Vorurteile, für die Sache zu gestalten. Daraus bildet sich letztlich auch das Fundament für eine soziale und moderne Marktwirtschaft, die auf starke Werte baut und natürliche Ressourcen wie kreislauffähige Systeme von Beginn an zukunftsfähig mitdenkt. Wir werden dabei auch ein neues Gefühl des „Mehr“ erleben. Dafür gilt es ein Narrativ mit Leben zu füllen, das uns im Prozess erkennen lässt, dass in diesen neuen Formen von Zusammenarbeit ein wesentliches sinnvolleres, nützlicheres „Mehr“ steckt. Dieses basiert auf gleichbleibenden Bausteinen, in denen wir einfach durch Kreativität mehr Kombinationsmöglichkeiten als vorher entdecken und diese flexibel wie variabel ausschöpfen. Die Verbindung von scheinbaren Gegensätzen wird dabei die treibende Kraft sein. Dafür müssen wir nichts neu erfinden. Wir müssen nur das, was es schon gibt, sinnvoll miteinander verbinden!

FABIAN LUKAS GOSLAR

NGO-Gründer „Intergenerational Intelligence"

Mit welchen Strategien oder Konzepten könnte das Vertrauen in Regierungs- und Unternehmerstrukturen gestärkt werden?

Wir sollten auf verantwortliche Führungspersönlichkeiten setzen, diese suchen und aufbauen. Das öffentliche Vertrauen in Strukturen ist durch menschliches Versagen und mangelnde Führung geschädigt. Dazu gehört eine Fehlerkultur auf der obersten Ebene, in der Führungspersönlichkeiten Fehler eingestehen und aus ihnen Konsequenzen ziehen. Das fördert Authentizität und Glaubwürdigkeit. Gleichsam müssen Visionen und Ambitionen unserer Unternehmen und Regierungen vom Führungspersonal klar verinnerlicht und kommuniziert werden, verbunden mit eindeutigen kurz- und langfristigen Zielen. Orientierung und Vertrauen entstehen durch langfristige Pläne und holistisch, aber pragmatisch argumentierte Entscheidungen. Auch in herausfordernden Zeiten müssen wir uns auf einen klaren Rahmen einigen. Eine Vorstellung, wo wir als Gesellschaft, Regierung und Unternehmen hinwollen, was wir erhalten und erreichen wollen. All das muss durch starke, präsente und sichtbar authentische Führung mit Rückgrat untermauert werden.

Wie sehen Sie persönlich das Verhältnis von individueller Freiheit und „Verantwortung für die Gesellschaft übernehmen" und wie setzen Sie das um?

Gerade wir jungen Menschen sind mit verhältnismäßig großem Wohlstand, in Frieden und Freiheit aufgewachsen. Hier hilft es etwas weiter herauszuzoomen: Zwischen den Geburtsjahren meiner Großeltern und meinem liegen 58 bis 68 Jahre. In diesen Jahrzehnten hat sich Europa nach der Erschütterung des Zweiten Weltkriegs unglaublich gewandelt. Aus dieser Wandlung und dem Horror, den meine Großelterngeneration zu Beginn dieses Wandels in Europa erlebt hat, wächst für mich eine selbstverständliche Verantwortung, den Wert meiner individuellen Freiheit zu erkennen und wertzuschätzen. Für mich ist es selbstver-

ständlich, meine Fähigkeiten so zu nutzen, dass sie einen gesellschaftlichen Mehrwert entfalten. Bei mir sind das insbesondere verschiedene sozialunternehmerische Projekte und der Einsatz für politische Bildung über meine NGO. Wer in Freiheit geboren wurde, ist immer auch Verantwortungsträger, die freie Gesellschaft zu erhalten, zu pflegen und aktiv weiterzuentwickeln.

Braucht es dafür auch mehr Zusammenarbeit über Partei- und Wettbewerbsgrenzen hinweg und wie könnte das zu einem „Wandelwunder" führen?

In der Mitte der Parteienlandschaft brauchen wir mehr Kooperation. Die Kollateralschäden, die durch Konflikte innerhalb dieser Mitte entstanden sind, verursachen Missmut und stärken eine Abwendung von der Mitte hin zu den Rändern. Wir brauchen ein starkes gemeinsames Narrativ, das eine verbindende Kraft entfesselt: 80 Jahre nach dem Ende des Zweiten Weltkriegs bieten historische Lehren, die wir in die Gegenwart übertragen können, um unser Europa als Friedens- und Freiheitsprojekt voranzubringen, einen Ankerpunkt, an dem wir uns fragen: Was muss passieren, um nicht in Muster gesellschaftlicher Spaltung zurückzufallen, die uns einst in Fetzen zerrissen haben? Die Antwort liegt klar in einem geeinten, strategischen Vorgehen, einem pragmatischen Abbau von Bürokratie, der politische und unternehmerische Innovation entfesselt und Europa in einem Wandel weiterentwickelt. Eine Zusammenarbeit von Parteien und Wettbewerbern in einem agilen Thinktank - ein *European mind* – wäre ein erster Schritt.

MAX KLEMMER

Geschäftsführender Gesellschafter der Miss Germany Studios

Mit welchen Strategien oder Konzepten könnte das Vertrauen in Regierungs- und Unternehmerstrukturen gestärkt werden?

Um das Vertrauen in unsere Führungsstrukturen zu stärken, ist es essenziell, Transparenz und Integrität in viel mehr Prozessen zu gewährleisten. Entscheidend ist, dass Organisationen ihre Entscheidungsprozesse viel besser offenlegen und deren Auswirkungen transparent machen. Authentizität ist keine Schwäche, sondern vielmehr Stärke, um Verständnis und Vertrauen zu schaffen. Verantwortlichkeit muss gefördert werden, sodass Führungskräfte für ihre Handlungen einstehen und sich nicht hinter Fehlern verstecken – und sie dies auch nicht müssen, weil wir wieder viel mehr zu einer positiven Fehlerkultur finden müssen. Außerdem ist es von enormer Bedeutung, einen integrativen Ansatz zu etablieren, der diverse Stimmen berücksichtigt, insbesondere die der jüngeren Generationen und marginalisierten Gruppen, um Chancengerechtigkeit zu fördern und ein umfassendes Vertrauen aufzubauen. Wir dürfen jetzt keine Rolle rückwärts beim Thema Diversität machen – vor allem nicht wegen Amerika als Vorbild. Vielfalt ist ein Geschenk und keine Last.

Wie sehen Sie persönlich das Verhältnis von individueller Freiheit und „Verantwortung für die Gesellschaft übernehmen" und wie setzen Sie das um?

Individuelle Freiheit und gesellschaftliche Verantwortung sind komplementäre Aspekte unserer Demokratie, die zwingend in Balance zueinanderstehen müssen. Wir haben die gesellschaftliche Verantwortung, individuelle Freiheit zu fördern, um das wahre Potenzial ambitionierter Personen wirklich zu entfalten. Miss Germany fördert dieses Verständnis, indem wir Frauen unterstützen, die sowohl ihre persönlichen Ziele verfolgen als auch aktiv an der Gestaltung einer gerechteren Gesellschaft mitwirken. Wir schaffen Plattformen, die den Austausch von Ideen und die Vernetzung ermöglichen, und unterstützen Initiativen, die sowohl

individuelle Ambitionen als auch das Gemeinwohl fördern. Diese Balance von Freiheit und Verantwortung manifestiert sich in Projekten, die echte Chancengerechtigkeit vorantreiben und allen Beteiligten ermöglichen, auf Augenhöhe zusammenzuarbeiten. Andersherum darf individuelle Freiheit unser Zusammenleben als Gesellschaft nicht beschränken und unser aller Sicherheit nicht mit Füßen treten.

Braucht es dafür auch mehr Zusammenarbeit über Partei- und Wettbewerbsgrenzen hinweg und wie könnte das zu einem „Wandelwunder" führen?

Für nachhaltigen Wandel ist eine übergreifende Zusammenarbeit unerlässlich. Wir müssen bestehende Barrieren zwischen politischen, wirtschaftlichen und gesellschaftlichen Bereichen überwinden und ein Klima der Kooperation und des gegenseitigen Respekts fördern. Ein solches „Wandelwunder" erfordert kontinuierliche Dialoge und den Aufbau von Brücken, um gemeinsam innovative Lösungen zu entwickeln. Der Modus des Wahlkampfes muss nun vorbei sein. Es muss nun ein Klima der Möglichkeiten und Ambitionen in die Umsetzung kommen. Besonders wichtig ist es, als Europa enger zusammenzurücken und eigenständige, kontinentspezifische Ansätze zu verfolgen, anstatt externe Vorbilder wie Amerika zu imitieren. Dies stärkt unsere einzigartige Position und fördert Lösungen, die auf unsere spezifischen kulturellen und gesellschaftlichen Bedürfnisse zugeschnitten sind.

JAN KÖNIG

Mitgründer von ODALINE

Mit welchen Strategien oder Konzepten könnte das Vertrauen in Regierungs- und Unternehmerstrukturen gestärkt werden?

Authentizität. Alle unter 40 wurden mit Werbung zugeballert, seit sie Babies waren. Sie erkennen, wenn jemand ihnen Sh*t verkauft. Oder auch einfach lügt. So wie das unsere PolitikerInnen leider selbst in diesem Wahlkampf gezeigt haben. Der Glaubwürdigkeit tut ein „schnell vergessen" wie beim Thema Schuldenbremse der CDU nicht gut. Was es dann gebraucht hätte, wäre ein Video, in dem Merz die Fehler eingesteht und erläutert, warum man die Aufhebung der Bremse (jetzt doch) benötigt. Das hat in der Vergangenheit eigentlich nur Habeck mit Social Media Content geschafft – direkte Ansprache der Menschen. Fehler einstehen. Ehrlichkeit. Das Gleiche gilt auch für Unternehmen. Marken brauchen Gesichter. Gesichter müssen ehrlich sein. Fehler muss man eingestehen. Das Schlimmste ist „totschweigen" oder Kommentare abschalten. Ohne Nahbarkeit kein Erfolg.

Wie sehen Sie persönlich das Verhältnis von individueller Freiheit und „Verantwortung für die Gesellschaft übernehmen" und wie setzen Sie das um?

Freiheit und Verantwortung funktionieren zusammen. Freiheit bedeutet, Verantwortung zu übernehmen. Das gilt für Wirtschaft, Politik, aber auch in der Gesellschaft, zum Beispiel im Vereinswesen. Ich selbst bin dieses Jahr zum ersten Mal in meinem Leben einer Partei beigetreten und versuche meine Reichweite (sowohl im Freundeskreis als auch auf Social Media) einzusetzen für eine bessere Zukunft. Wir müssen alle lauter werden, denn die blauen Herzen der AfD werden immer mehr.

Braucht es dafür auch mehr Zusammenarbeit über Partei- und Wettbewerbsgrenzen hinweg und wie könnte das zu einem „Wandelwunder" führen?

Unser größtes Problem ist, dass wir nicht lösungsorientiert sind, sondern viel zu viel Energie ins Gegeneinander stecken statt ins „Vorwärts". Probleme stehen vorne, „die Meinung von dem gefällt mir nicht" versus „Anpacken". Wir legen die alten Denkmuster nicht ab und unser größtes Problem ist die fehlende Offenheit zur Digitalisierung. Wenn ich mir heute ansehe, wie viel noch gefaxt wird, dann ist das System in der Vergangenheit einfach gegen die Wand gefahren. Da bringt es jetzt auch nichts, das der CDU anzukreiden, sondern wir müssen jetzt verändern. Und von anderen Staaten lernen. Estland ist der digitale europäische Staat – wie managen die ihr System mit viel weniger IT-Power im Land? Auch unsere Unternehmen müssen daran arbeiten, dass unser Land wieder in den Vorwärtsgang kommt. Als Mitgestalter der Zukunft. Unsere Eigeninteressen müssen hintangestellt werden, wenn wir den Wohlstand unseres Landes verteidigen wollen.

INTERVIEW

ALICIA LINDNER

Co-CEO von ANNEMARIE BÖRLIND

Mit welchen Strategien oder Konzepten könnte das Vertrauen in Regierungs- und Unternehmerstrukturen gestärkt werden?

Vertrauen ist wie eine gute Naturkosmetikformel: Es braucht Transparenz, Geduld und den Willen, sich mit den „Inhaltsstoffen" auseinanderzusetzen. Für Unternehmen heißt das: weniger Hochglanzversprechen, mehr echte Haltung. Wer Vertrauen will, muss Entscheidungen nachvollziehbar machen – nach innen wie außen.

Wenn man nicht nur von Nachhaltigkeit spricht, sondern sie radikal lebt – von der Lieferkette bis zur Kommunikation –, dann entsteht etwas Stabiles. Dasselbe gilt für die Politik: weniger Spin, mehr Substanz. Und ruhig auch mal sagen: „Wir wissen es gerade nicht besser – aber wir hören zu." Vertrauen wächst nicht durch Perfektion, sondern durch Haltung.

Wie sehen Sie persönlich das Verhältnis von individueller Freiheit und „Verantwortung für die Gesellschaft übernehmen" und wie setzen Sie das um?

Freiheit ist für mich kein Freifahrtschein, sondern ein Privileg – und aus Privileg entsteht Verantwortung. Das beginnt bei Fragen wie: Welche Produkte biete ich an? Unter welchen Bedingungen werden sie hergestellt? Und das hört beim großen Ganzen noch lange nicht auf: Welche Haltung nehme ich öffentlich ein? Wir führen ein unabhängiges Familienunternehmen. Das heißt: Wir können Nein sagen – zu Greenwashing, zu kurzfristigem Denken. Und Ja – zu klarer Haltung, sozialem Engagement und ambitionierten Nachhaltigkeitszielen. Genau darin liegt für mich die schönste Form von Freiheit: gestalten zu dürfen – mit Verantwortung.

Braucht es dafür auch mehr Zusammenarbeit über Partei- und Wettbewerbsgrenzen hinweg und wie könnte das zu einem „Wandelwunder" führen?

Unbedingt. Wenn wir alle nur in unseren Silos denken – politisch, wirtschaftlich, gesellschaftlich –, wird das nichts mit dem Wandel. Wir brauchen Allianzen auf Augenhöhe, auch zwischen vermeintlichen Konkurrenten. Wenn wir gemeinsam an Lösungen arbeiten statt nur an Marktanteilen, kann tatsächlich ein „Wandelwunder" entstehen.

Bei Börlind glauben wir an Zusammenarbeit: Wir arbeiten mit Forschungseinrichtungen, Start-ups – und auch mal mit Unternehmen aus der Branche. Denn echte Veränderung ist kein Egotrip, sondern Teamarbeit.

Abschlussstatement:

„Verantwortung ist kein Trend, sondern unsere Pflicht. Wenn Wirtschaft, Politik und Gesellschaft den Mut haben, gemeinsam über den Tellerrand zu schauen, entsteht nicht nur Wandel – sondern echte Zukunft."

BRADLEY MUNDT

Gründer & CEO von PLAN-B NET ZERO ENERGY

Vertrauen, Verantwortung, Veränderung – ein neuer Blick auf nachhaltiges Wirtschaften

Vertrauen in Politik und Wirtschaft ist kein Selbstläufer. Es entsteht nicht durch große Versprechen, sondern durch nachvollziehbare Entscheidungen, Verlässlichkeit und eine klare Haltung. Als Unternehmer im Bereich erneuerbarer Energien erlebe ich immer wieder, wie skeptisch viele Menschen gegenüber politischen und wirtschaftlichen Institutionen geworden sind und das oft zu Recht. Zu viele Strategien bleiben Ankündigungen, zu wenige führen zu echten Veränderungen.

Wie können wir das ändern?

Für mich ist der Schlüssel eine Kombination aus Transparenz und Konsequenz. Unternehmen müssen klar kommunizieren, was sie tun, aber auch beweisen, dass sie es wirklich umsetzen. Vertrauen entsteht, wenn wir langfristig verlässlich sind und nicht bei der ersten Schwierigkeit einknicken. Gerade in der Energiewirtschaft sehen wir oft politische und wirtschaftliche Kurzschlussreaktionen, die nachhaltige Lösungen behindern. Statt mit wechselnden Subventionen und widersprüchlichen Regulierungen Märkte zu verunsichern, brauchen wir einen stabilen Rahmen, der Innovationen ermöglicht und Investitionen anzieht.

Freiheit und Verantwortung – kein Widerspruch

Viele sehen Klimaschutz als Verzicht. Weniger CO_2, weniger Ressourcenverbrauch, weniger Wachstum. Ich halte das für einen Denkfehler. Freiheit bedeutet nicht, möglichst viel von etwas zu haben, sondern die richtigen Entscheidungen zu treffen.

Wir bei PLAN-B NET ZERO denken in Fülle statt in Verzicht:

- Je mehr saubere Energie, desto mehr Umweltschutz
- Je mehr erneuerbare Energien, desto weniger CO_2
- Je mehr Nutzung, desto mehr Nachhaltigkeit

Klimaschutz ist für uns keine Einschränkung, sondern Teil eines nachhaltigen Konsums. Wir setzen darauf, dass der Zugang zu erneuerbarer Energie nicht teurer oder komplizierter sein sollte als fossile Alternativen. Deshalb entwickeln wir Geschäftsmodelle, die nicht nur ökologisch sinnvoll, sondern auch wirtschaftlich attraktiv sind.

Zusammenarbeit als Schlüssel für echten Wandel

Die großen Herausforderungen unserer Zeit lassen sich nicht durch Einzelmaßnahmen oder einzelne Akteure lösen. Wer wirklich etwas verändern will, muss über Unternehmens- und Parteigrenzen hinausdenken. Die Energiewende gelingt nur, wenn Politik, Wirtschaft und Gesellschaft an einem Strang ziehen. Ich bin überzeugt, dass wir mehr Kooperation brauchen, nicht weniger. Wettbewerbsfähigkeit und Zusammenarbeit schließen sich nicht aus. Wir sehen das täglich in unserem Wachstum: Jedes Unternehmen, das wir in unsere Gruppe integrieren, bringt Know-how, Netzwerke und Innovationen mit. So entsteht eine Dynamik, die mit Einzelmaßnahmen nie zu erreichen wäre. Der Wandel kommt nicht von allein. Aber wir können ihn aktiv gestalten: Mit klugen Entscheidungen, wirtschaftlichem Weitblick und einer Haltung, die nicht nur Probleme beschreibt, sondern Lösungen ermöglicht.

DR. CHRISTOPH PLOSS

Historiker, MdB (CDU)

Mit welchen Strategien oder Konzepten könnte das Vertrauen in Regierungs- und Unternehmerstrukturen gestärkt werden?

Wie sehen Sie persönlich das Verhältnis von individueller Freiheit und „Verantwortung für die Gesellschaft übernehmen" und wie setzen Sie das um?

Braucht es dafür auch mehr Zusammenarbeit über Partei- und Wettbewerbsgrenzen hinweg und wie könnte das zu einem „Wandelwunder" führen?

Nach dreieinhalb chaotischen Jahren der Ampelregierung hat die Bundestagswahl vom 23. Februar 2025 die lang ersehnte Möglichkeit ergeben, den dringend nötigen Kurswechsel in der deutschen Politik vorzunehmen. In den vergangenen Monaten haben wir hart daran gearbeitet, eine stabile und handlungsfähige neue Bundesregierung auf die Beine zu stellen. Ihr muss es gelingen, verloren gegangenes Vertrauen zurückzugewinnen. Dafür braucht es parteienübergreifend eine Politik, die nicht auf ideologische Kulturkämpfe setzt, sondern sich wieder auf die Themen fokussiert, die für die Zukunft unseres Landes wirklich wichtig sind – die Wettbewerbsfähigkeit Deutschlands und die Gewährleistung innerer und äußerer Sicherheit. Entscheidend bleibt dabei die Verantwortung jedes Einzelnen. Die wachsende Unzufriedenheit mit staatlichen Institutionen liegt erkennbar nicht an „zu wenig Staat" oder „zu viel Staat". Der Staat priorisiert falsch! Auf der einen Seite steht ein Sozialstaat, der immer häufiger nach dem Motto „Mehr Umverteilung gleich mehr Gerechtigkeit" vorgeht. Diese Politik hat vor allem Arbeitern und Durchschnittsverdienern geschadet. Konnte ein ordentlich bezahlter Arbeitsplatz in der Industrie früher eine ganze Familie ernähren, ist dies heute oft aufgrund von Steuern, Abgaben und Inflation nicht mehr möglich. Vor allem die breite gesellschaftliche Mitte darf nicht von Steuern und Abgaben erdrückt werden. Den Unternehmen wiederum entsteht durch immer neue Auflagen, Vorschriften und Dokumentationspflichten ein stetig wachsender Aufwand, der Kapazitäten bindet und zunehmend zu einem Wettbewerbsnachteil des Standorts Deutschland wird.

Demgegenüber ist der Staat bei der Gewährleistung innerer und äußerer Sicherheit immer wieder den Beweis seiner Leistungsfähigkeit schuldig geblieben. Die unzureichende Ausstattung der Bundeswehr wird angesichts der Bedrohungslage in Europa zu einem immer

größeren Problem. Die neue Bundesregierung muss sehr schnell und entschlossen, aber auch langfristig handeln, um die Bundeswehr wieder so auszustatten, dass sie die Sicherheit unseres Landes gewährleisten und ihre Bündnisverpflichtungen erfüllen kann. Auch im Inneren hat sich der deutsche Staat zu oft als zu schwach erwiesen. Viel zu lange schon hält sich der desaströse Eindruck, der deutsche Staat könne seine Grenzen nicht schützen. In einem Rechtsstaat ist es selbstverständlich, dass alle Menschen vor dem Gesetz gleich sind. Genauso zwingend ist es aber, dass der Rechtsstaat seine eigenen Gesetze umsetzt, inklusive des Schutzes seiner Grenzen.

Nicht weniger bedeutend für die zukünftige Wettbewerbsfähigkeit unserer Wirtschaft wird es sein, dass Unternehmen und Menschen in Deutschland auf eine moderne, gut ausgebaute und leistungsfähige Verkehrsinfrastruktur setzen können. Es darf nicht sein, dass Infrastrukturvorhaben wie die Hamburger Köhlbrandbrücke Jahrzehnte dauern. Schnelleres Planen und Bauen, etwa durch die Einschränkung von Klagemöglichkeiten sowie die schnellere Digitalisierung der Verwaltung, müssen ganz oben auf der Agenda stehen.

Es ist gut, dass die neue Bundesregierung es sich zu ihrer Aufgabe gemacht hat, diese Probleme anzugehen. Ebenso wichtig wird es aber sein, die Ausnahmeregelung der Schuldenbremse und das Sondervermögen nicht als unerschöpflichen Geldtopf zu begreifen, sondern gerade wegen der zusätzlichen Schuldenaufnahme umso energischer an Einsparungen und Effizienzsteigerungen zu arbeiten. Nur ein effizienter Staat und wettbewerbsfähige, profitable Unternehmen werden uns in die Lage bringen, die zusätzliche Schuldenlast tragen und auch wieder abbauen zu können. Dafür wird es auf jeden Einzelnen ankommen.

Kurzum: Um Vertrauen in den Staat und in die Politik zurückzugewinnen, braucht es ein neues Wohlstandsversprechen für die Bürger. An seiner Erfüllung wird sich die Politik messen lassen müssen.

VIKTORIA RENNER

Mitgründerin und Content-Strategin bei OZMOZE

Mit welchen Strategien oder Konzepten könnte das Vertrauen in Regierungs- und Unternehmerstrukturen gestärkt werden?

Vertrauen entsteht durch Transparenz, Nahbarkeit und konsequentes Handeln. In einer digitalen Welt erwarten Menschen direkte Kommunikation und nachvollziehbare Entscheidungen. Unternehmen und Regierungen müssen daher offener werden – durch interaktive Formate, in denen sie sich echten Fragen stellen, durch klare Wertekommunikation und durch den Mut, Fehler einzugestehen. Gerade Social Media ermöglicht es, Dialoge auf Augenhöhe zu führen und Nähe herzustellen. Wer sich als Marke oder Institution nur in PR-Sprache äußert, wird nicht gehört.

Ein weiterer Schlüssel ist Community-getriebene Partizipation: Bürger*innen oder Mitarbeitende sollten aktiv in Entscheidungsprozesse eingebunden werden – sei es durch Open Innovation, Co-Creation oder digitale Bürgerräte. Vertrauen wächst, wenn Menschen sich ernst genommen fühlen und sehen, dass ihre Perspektiven Einfluss haben. Dazu gehört auch eine verständliche Sprache. Politische und wirtschaftliche Akteure neigen dazu, sich in komplexen Formulierungen oder Fachjargon zu verlieren. Doch wer Vertrauen aufbauen will, muss verständlich kommunizieren – klar, direkt und ohne Umwege.

Zudem ist Verlässlichkeit entscheidend. Vertrauen entsteht nicht durch Ankündigungen, sondern durch das konsequente Einhalten von Zusagen. Gerade in Krisenzeiten zeigt sich, wie belastbar das Vertrauen in Institutionen wirklich ist. Unternehmen und Regierungen müssen in schwierigen Zeiten nicht nur reagieren, sondern proaktiv Orientierung bieten. Dabei zählt Ehrlichkeit mehr als Perfektion: Menschen vertrauen eher einer Institution, die Fehler zugibt und daraus lernt, als einer, die sich unfehlbar inszeniert.

Wie sehen Sie persönlich das Verhältnis von individueller Freiheit und „Verantwortung für die Gesellschaft übernehmen" und wie setzen Sie das um?

Freiheit und Verantwortung sind keine Gegensätze, sondern bedingen einander. Echte Freiheit bedeutet nicht, nur für sich selbst zu handeln, sondern auch die Verantwortung für das Kollektiv zu übernehmen. In meiner Arbeit bedeutet das, Marken dazu zu ermutigen, sich kulturell und gesellschaftlich relevant einzubringen – nicht aus reiner Imagepflege, sondern weil sie Teil der Gesellschaft sind. Verantwortung zeigt sich nicht in erzwungener Korrektheit, sondern in echtem Interesse an gesellschaftlichen Entwicklungen und einem authentischen Beitrag dazu.

Freiheit ist auch eine Frage der Perspektive. Sie darf nicht nur aus einer individualistischen Sicht betrachtet werden, sondern muss im größeren Zusammenhang gesehen werden: Was bedeutet meine Freiheit für andere? Welche Verantwortung ergibt sich aus meiner Position? In sozialen Netzwerken etwa trägt jede*r Einzelne Verantwortung für den Diskurs, der entsteht. Wir haben alle eine Stimme – die Frage ist, wie wir sie nutzen. Verantwortung beginnt dort, wo wir aufhören, nur zuzusehen. Individuell lebe ich das, indem ich mich bewusst in Diskurse einbringe, Wissen teile und mich für eine werteorientierte, progressive Markenkommunikation starkmache. Marken können gesellschaftliche Entwicklungen nicht ignorieren – sie sind längst Teil davon. Es reicht nicht, nur Marktführer zu sein, man muss auch Kulturführer sein. Unternehmen, die Verantwortung übernehmen, setzen Maßstäbe und inspirieren andere dazu, dasselbe zu tun.

Braucht es dafür auch mehr Zusammenarbeit über Partei- und Wettbewerbsgrenzen hinweg und wie könnte das zu einem „Wandelwunder" führen?

Ja, absolut. In einer Welt, die zunehmend fragmentiert wirkt, brauchen wir Kooperation statt Konkurrenzdenken. Besonders in Politik und Wirtschaft sollten alte Denkmuster aufgebrochen werden: Marken können gemeinsam kulturelle Trends prägen, statt isoliert um Marktanteile zu kämpfen. Parteien könnten in zentralen Zukunftsfragen an einem Strang ziehen, statt sich in kurzfristigen Machtspielen zu verlieren.

„Wandelwunder" entstehen, wenn unerwartete Kollaborationen neue Narrative erschaffen. Wir sehen das bereits in Bereichen wie Open Source, wo Wettbewerber kooperieren, um Innovationen voranzutreiben. Oder in branchenübergreifenden Nachhaltigkeitsinitiativen, bei denen Unternehmen gemeinsam an Lösungen arbeiten, anstatt sich in Einzelmaßnahmen zu verlieren. Es braucht aber auch eine neue Erzählung des Wandels: Wir müssen weg von der Vorstellung, dass Fortschritt immer das Ergebnis einzelner Held*innen ist. In Wahrheit sind es Netzwerke, Allianzen und interdisziplinäre Teams, die die großen Veränderungen unserer Zeit ermöglichen. Kollaboration bedeutet nicht, die eigene Identität aufzugeben, sondern sie durch Austausch zu stärken. Wenn wir beginnen, Vertrauen als gemeinschaftliches Gut zu begreifen – eines, das gepflegt, geschützt und aktiv gestärkt werden muss –, dann kann echter Wandel entstehen. Eine Gesellschaft, die sich als Team versteht, kann Großes bewirken.

CATARINA DOS SANTOS

MdB (CDU)

Mit welchen Strategien oder Konzepten könnte das Vertrauen in Regierungs- und Unternehmerstrukturen gestärkt werden?

Vertrauen entsteht und bleibt für mich dort, wo Zusagen gemacht werden, die auch eingehalten werden. Ich erlebe immer mehr, dass Menschen genau diesen Zusagen nicht mehr glauben. Sie haben das Gefühl, dass Regierungsstrukturen ihre Sorgen und Nöte nicht hinreichend ernst nehmen. Im Vergleich dazu: Die interessantesten Austausche habe ich mit Unternehmen erlebt, in denen großes Vertrauen zwischen Leitung und Mitarbeitern besteht. Sie haben es geschafft, ihre unternehmerische Motivation genauso wie ein Wertekonstrukt vorzuleben, es zusammen mit den Mitarbeiterinnen und Mitarbeitern zu entwickeln und aktiv zu gestalten. Diese Betriebe, oft alte Familienbetriebe, waren in der Regel auch sehr erfolgreich. Natürlich funktioniert beides aber nur, wenn Institutionen einen Freiraum haben oder ihn für sich schaffen – auch um letztendlich die eigene Struktur zu hinterfragen. Gerade Letzteres sollten wir auf Regierungsstrukturen übertragen, denn die Stärkung von Vertrauen ist im politischen Betrieb eine der Kernaufgaben.

Wie sehen Sie persönlich das Verhältnis von individueller Freiheit und „Verantwortung für die Gesellschaft übernehmen" und wie setzen Sie das um?

Die individuelle Freiheit aller Bürgerinnen und Bürger bildet das Fundament unserer Gesellschaft, das essenziell für unseren Wohlstand, individuelles Wachstum und Fortschritt ist. Wir Menschen brauchen diese Freiheit, um uns entfalten zu können. Freiheit ist für mich aber auch aktive Gestaltungsmöglichkeit von Gemeinwesen. In der menschlichen Natur liegt das Bedürfnis, anderen zu helfen, was sich bei vielen durch ehrenamtliche Tätigkeit ausdrückt. Tagtäglich engagieren sich Menschen in Deutschland in Ehrenämtern und als Helferinnen und Helfer für ihre Mitmenschen. Eigenverantwortung und Gemeinsinn gehören zusammen, denn wir alle halten einen Verantwortungskompass in unseren Händen, dessen Pfeil stets in unsere Gesellschaft lenkt. Persönlich setze ich dabei als Bundestagsabgeordnete auf politische Bildung, etwa durch Informationsarbeit in den sozialen Medien, und den Dialog.

Braucht es dafür auch mehr Zusammenarbeit über Partei- und Wettbewerbsgrenzen hinweg und wie könnte das zu einem „Wandelwunder" führen?

Kompromissfähigkeit und Kooperationsbereitschaft sind die Quintessenz des erfolgreichen Handelns in der Politik. Unterschiedliche Wertvorstellungen zwischen den Parteien können die Vereinbarkeit von politischen Interessen erschweren – umso wichtiger ist es deswegen, auch hier Chancen zu ergreifen und mögliche Potenziale der Zusammenarbeit zu nutzen. Daher müssen nicht nur Parteien oder Fraktionen untereinander zusammenarbeiten, sondern gerade auch Wirtschaft und Gesellschaft einbeziehen. Wir können einen Wandel erreichen, wenn wir zusammenhalten. Das klingt wie die nächste Sonntagsrede, füllt sich aber gerade für mich dort mit Leben, wo ich bereits sehe, dass es funktionieren kann. Es geht nicht darum, möglichst viel vom eigenen Willen durchzusetzen, sondern darum, das Ringen um die bestmögliche Lösung in der Sache hart anzugehen und sich dann hinter einen Kompromiss zu stellen, mit dem alle leben können. Vielleicht müssen wir wieder lernen, Kompromisse einzugehen. Lassen Sie uns mutiger sein.

VALENTIN STALF

Mitgründer & CEO von N26

Mit welchen Strategien oder Konzepten könnte das Vertrauen in Regierungs- und Unternehmerstrukturen gestärkt werden?

Ich bin davon überzeugt, dass Deutschland eine Strategie braucht, um im globalen Wettkampf um digitalen Wohlstand und Technologieführerschaft mithalten zu können. Innovationen sind der Schlüssel dazu. Innovative Digitalunternehmen sind besonders auf Zuwanderung von Fachkräften aus dem Ausland angewiesen. Die Zuwanderung von hoch qualifizierten Menschen muss deshalb deutlich erleichtert werden – unter anderem durch einfache und schnellere Visaverfahren.

Gleichzeitig haben internationale Arbeitskräfte hohe Erwartungen an Deutschland, gerade mit Blick auf den Grad an Digitalisierung in der öffentlichen Verwaltung. Die Expertise ist längst im Land. Vorsprung durch Digitalisierung bedeutet nicht nur einen Standortvorteil, Deutschland würde zudem massiv Kosten sparen.

Zudem müssen die Anreize für Spitzenkräfte verbessert werden, beispielsweise durch Mitarbeiterbeteiligungen. Gewinne aus Employee Stock Ownership Plans (ESOP) sollten, wie in den USA oder Frankreich, nicht als Einkommen, sondern als Kapitalerträge und damit niedriger besteuert werden. Zudem sollten Steuererleichterungen für ausländische Spitzenkräfte in Deutschland eingeführt werden.

Wie sehen Sie persönlich das Verhältnis von individueller Freiheit und „Verantwortung für die Gesellschaft übernehmen" und wie setzen Sie das um?

Für mich als Gründer und Unternehmer ist individuelle Freiheit ein extrem hohes Gut. N26 ist das Ergebnis schöpferischer Freiheit. Natürlich haben wir als Bank viele regulatorische Auflagen zu erfüllen. Aber in diesem Regelsystem gibt es sehr viel Freiheit, Dinge radikal neu zu denken und das Bankgeschäft zu modernisieren. Es motiviert mich jeden Tag, bessere Produkte zu entwickeln und N26 zu einer Bank zu machen, die unsere Kunden lieben. N26 ist dabei mehr als nur eine erfolgreiche Digitalbank. N26 soll den Menschen den Zugang zu Finanzdienstleistungen erleichtern. Das Bankgeschäft soll Menschen nicht daran hindern, ihre Ziele zu erreichen, sondern die Erreichung ermöglichen und zu beschleunigen.

Insbesondere im Bereich der Altersvorsorge, dem Zugang zu fairen und transparenten Konditionen für Sparpläne, aber auch beim täglichen Bankgeschäft erfüllt N26 eine riesige gesellschaftliche Verantwortung. Durch unsere Produkte ermöglichen wir den einfachen digitalen Zugang zu Bankprodukten, die davor oft intransparent, teuer und nur einem ausgewählten Kundenkreis zugänglich waren. Wir leisten dadurch einen enormen Beitrag zu einer effizienteren Lebensgestaltung, die es jedem Einzelnen, unabhängig vom Vermögensstand, ermöglicht, das Beste aus seiner finanziellen Situation zu machen und dadurch den persönlichen Impact zu maximieren. Die Gesellschaft wird dadurch insgesamt produktiver und effizienter.

Braucht es dafür auch mehr Zusammenarbeit über Partei- und Wettbewerbsgrenzen hinweg und wie könnte das zu einem „Wandelwunder" führen?

In einer Zeit, die wir gesellschaftlich, politisch und technologisch zu Recht als disruptiv beschreiben, braucht es nicht nur eine bessere Zusammenarbeit zwischen Wirtschaft und Politik, sondern vor allem eine andere Haltung zu neuen Technologien. Innovationen wurden in der Vergangenheit zu oft als Risiken verstanden, die erst einmal gründlich reguliert werden müssten, bevor sie sich entfalten können. Diese Haltung müssen wir überwinden, wenn wir die Chancen nutzen wollen, die neue Technologien uns bieten.

Neben dieser positiven Haltung zu Innovationen braucht es ein gezieltes Streben nach Größe und Tempo. Tesla, Amazon und Google sind vor allem deshalb zu globalen Tech-Giganten aufgestiegen, weil sie in kurzer Zeit sehr stark wachsen konnten. Der Wunsch, möglichst schnell etwas möglichst Großes zu schaffen, ist Teil der amerikanischen Kultur. In Europa ist diese Kultur nicht besonders ausgeprägt. Die Chancen für Challenger-Unternehmen wären in Europa noch größer, wenn sich die Politik insgesamt zu innovationsfreundlichen Rahmenbedingungen verpflichten würde. So könnte die Chance auf ein digitales Wirtschaftswunder in Europa zumindest gewahrt werden.

INTERVIEW

JENS TEUTRINE

MdB a. D. (FDP)

Mit welchen Strategien oder Konzepten könnte das Vertrauen in Regierungs- und Unternehmerstrukturen gestärkt werden?

Es ist eine große Respektlosigkeit, die man Menschen entgegenbringen kann, wenn man ihnen durchweg paternalistisch signalisiert, dass sie keine Ahnung von der eigenen Lebensführung haben und man selbst alles besser weiß. Aus einer solchen Misstrauenskultur des rechthaberischen Gängelns, des argwöhnischen Bürokratisierens und der staatlichen Erziehung entsteht nicht gegenseitiges Vertrauen, sondern eine Spirale des Misstrauens. Ich bin davon überzeugt, dass, wenn wir das Vertrauen in Regierungsstrukturen wieder stärken wollen, Regierungen zuallererst wieder den Menschen etwas zutrauen müssen. Dass die besten Ideen nicht beim Staat, bei Politikern und Behörden entstehen, sondern durch die Schaffenskraft der vielen Individuen. Wenn wir die Eigenverantwortung stärken, anstatt dass Politiker sich Besserwisserei anmaßen, dann stärkt das auch wieder Vertrauen in Institutionen. Denn jedes Mal, wenn ein Politiker sich anmaßt, etwas besser zu wissen und in der Folge zu regulieren, zu bürokratisieren und zu subventionieren, aber es in Wahrheit schiefgeht, sinkt selbstverständlich auch das Vertrauen. Stärken wir also wieder den Glauben der Menschen an sich selbst, so stärken wir auch das gegenseitige Zu- und Vertrauen.

Wie sehen Sie persönlich das Verhältnis von individueller Freiheit und „Verantwortung für die Gesellschaft übernehmen" und wie setzen Sie das um?

Das Zutrauen in individuelle Freiheit stärkt die Bereitschaft, selbst Verantwortung für die Gesellschaft zu übernehmen, anstatt jegliche Verantwortung an den Staat zu delegieren. Beispielsweise als Unternehmer für Arbeitsplätze und Wertschöpfung, in der Fürsorgearbeit in der eigenen Familie oder durch soziale Initiativen. Ich nenne hier gerne die Hospizarbeit in Deutschland, die insbesondere auch durch ehrenamtliche Strukturen getragen wird. Mein politisches Engagement begann bei den Jungen Liberalen, wo wir jungen Menschen, un-

abhängig von Herkunft und Elternhaus, nicht nur die Möglichkeit politischer Partizipation ermöglichen, sondern auch Bildungsarbeit leisten und einen Ort schaffen, an dem man sich selbst weiterentwickeln kann. Außerdem engagiere ich mich in persönlichen Mentoring-Partnerschaften für Jugendliche, die mit Hürden und Herausforderungen zu kämpfen haben. Dabei geht es um Austausch, Ansprechbarkeit, Gespräche und persönliche Unterstützung.

Braucht es dafür auch mehr Zusammenarbeit über Partei- und Wettbewerbsgrenzen hinweg und wie könnte das zu einem „Wandelwunder" führen?

Demokratie lebt vom Wettbewerb der besseren Ideen. Es mangelt nicht an Zusammenarbeit im klassischen Sinne, sondern an Respekt vor anderen Meinungen. Unsere Diskussionen sind häufig geprägt von bewusstem Missverstehen, Zerrbildern und einer empörten Shitstorm-Kultur, in der es mehr um gefühlte Moral geht als um sachliche Auseinandersetzung. Hier braucht es einen kulturellen Wandel. Mich besorgt es, dass sich im Land der Aufklärung immer mehr Menschen nicht mehr trauen, ihre Meinung frei herauszusagen. Das schwächt den Wettbewerb der besseren Ideen und ist ein zivilisatorischer Rückschritt, der umgekehrt werden muss.

CAROLIN VOGT

Stellv. Vorstandsvorsitzende von VOLT – Deutschland

Mit welchen Strategien oder Konzepten könnte das Vertrauen in Regierungs- und Unternehmerstrukturen gestärkt werden?

Meiner Meinung nach entsteht Vertrauen in den Staat und die Demokratie durch spürbare Ergebnisse, die den Alltag der Menschen verbessern. Deshalb setzt Volt auf massive Investitionen in Infrastruktur, die konkret zeigen, was der Staat leisten kann: grüne Städte mit sauberer Luft, sichere Radwege und Plätze für Begegnung, stabiles und schnelles Internet sowie ein digitaler und effizienter Bürger*innenservice. Ein Beispiel ist die Schaffung einer digitalen Verwaltung nach estnischem Vorbild, die Behördengänge vereinfacht und Zeit spart. Im Unternehmensbereich ist Transparenz entscheidend: Ich finde es wichtig, dass Unternehmen, die nachhaltig und fair handeln, steuerlich gefördert werden, während Steuervermeidung konsequent bekämpft wird. Solche sichtbaren Ergebnisse – ob im öffentlichen Raum oder in wirtschaftlichen Strukturen – schaffen Vertrauen und zeigen den Menschen, dass Veränderung zu ihrem Vorteil geschieht.

Wie sehen Sie persönlich das Verhältnis von individueller Freiheit und „Verantwortung für die Gesellschaft übernehmen" und wie setzen Sie das um?

Für mich sind Freiheit und Verantwortung keine Gegensätze, sondern bedingen einander. Freiheit gibt uns die Möglichkeit, Entscheidungen zu treffen, Verantwortung bedeutet, diese Entscheidungen so zu gestalten, dass sie der Gesellschaft zugutekommen. Vertrauen in die Demokratie entsteht dann, wenn die Menschen sehen, dass ihre Verantwortung sichtbar wirkt – sei es in einer klimafreundlichen Mobilität, nachhaltigen Stadtplanung oder barrierefreien digitalen Services. Ich wünsche mir, dass Verantwortung nicht als Last, sondern als Möglichkeit gesehen wird, gemeinsam eine bessere Zukunft zu gestalten. Volt setzt sich dafür ein, diese Rahmenbedingungen zu schaffen: zum Beispiel durch Investitionen in spür- und sichtbare Veränderungen wie digitale Bürger*innenservices oder die Förderung von urbanen Grünflächen und Fahrradwegen. So können Bürger*innen unmittelbar erfahren, wie ihr Engagement und ihr Vertrauen in den Staat zu echten Verbesserungen führen.

Braucht es dafür auch mehr Zusammenarbeit über Partei- und Wettbewerbsgrenzen hinweg und wie könnte das zu einem „Wandelwunder" führen?

Absolut. Ich bin der Überzeugung, dass echter Wandel dann geschieht, wenn wir über politische und nationale Grenzen hinweg zusammenarbeiten, um sichtbare Ergebnisse für die Menschen zu schaffen. Denn nur mit europäischen Lösungen können wir die Herausforderungen unserer Zeit, allen voran die Klimakrise, bewältigen. Volt adaptiert die besten Konzepte aus ganz Europa – etwa die digitale Verwaltung Estlands oder die nachhaltige Stadtplanung Dänemarks – und setzt sie in Deutschland um. Solche greifbaren, positiven Beispiele wie grüne Städte, bessere Luft, sichere Radwege oder ein digitaler Bürger*innenservice schaffen Vertrauen und zeigen, dass Fortschritt möglich ist.

Ich bin der Meinung, dass parteiübergreifende Zusammenarbeit der Schlüssel zu einem Wandelwunder ist. Eine „Koalition der Willigen", die progressive Themen wie Klimaschutz, Infrastruktur und soziale Gerechtigkeit gemeinsam anpackt, kann den Menschen zeigen, dass Politik Ergebnisse liefert. Mit Investitionen in eine lebenswerte Infrastruktur – sei es durch nachhaltige Mobilität oder moderne digitale Dienste – machen wir den Wandel konkret und erlebbar.

EMILY VONTZ

MdB a. D. (SPD)

Mit welchen Strategien oder Konzepten könnte das Vertrauen in Regierungs- und Unternehmerstrukturen gestärkt werden?

Wie sehen Sie persönlich das Verhältnis von individueller Freiheit und „Verantwortung für die Gesellschaft übernehmen" und wie setzen Sie das um?

Braucht es dafür auch mehr Zusammenarbeit über Partei- und Wettbewerbsgrenzen hinweg und wie könnte das zu einem „Wandelwunder" führen?

„Wieso sind es eigentlich immer die gleichen Gesichter in der Politik, egal, was die schon angerichtet haben?" Diese Frage stellte mir eine Besucherin im Bundestag vor wenigen Wochen. Nur wenige Minuten später fragte ein weiterer Gast: „Wieso machen sich die Politiker gegenseitig runter und werden auch so persönlich? Müssten die Parteien nicht enger zusammenarbeiten, statt immer nur gegeneinander zu sein?" Beide Fragen haben mich seitdem sehr beschäftigt, denn sie spiegeln den Eindruck vieler Bürger*innen wider, dass Politiker*innen zerstritten und selbstbezogen seien und ihr Handeln nicht nachvollziehbar. Einen Eindruck, der weit entfernt ist von dem, was Politik eigentlich sein sollte – ein gemeinsames Bemühen um Lösungen für die Herausforderungen unserer Zeit. In meiner Zeit als Bundestagsabgeordnete habe ich viele Kolleg*innen aus unterschiedlichen Parteien kennengelernt. Menschen, die für ihr Mandat alles geben und oft viel aufgeben, um dem eigenen Anspruch und den Erwartungen von Partei und Gesellschaft gerecht zu werden. Und dennoch bleibt oft der Eindruck von Streit, Stillstand und Eigennutz zurück. Wie kommt das? Unsere Demokratie steht unter Druck. Die großen Krisen unserer Zeit – sei es der Klimawandel, die Transformation unserer Wirtschaft oder die sozialen Herausforderungen – erfordern Lösungen, die komplex sind und Zeit brauchen. Populisten bedienen sich dieser Unsicherheiten, propagieren vermeintlich einfache Antworten und provozieren so letztlich gesellschaftliche Spaltung. Wir als Gesellschaft tragen in dieser Situation eine zentrale Verantwortung. Für eine lebendige Demokratie ist es essenziell, dass Bürger*innen sich nicht nur über Politik beklagen, sondern sich aktiv engagieren – sei es in Vereinen, in Initiativen oder bei Wahlen. Politik kann nur dann besser werden, wenn wir uns darum bemühen, einander zu verstehen. Politiker*innen sind Menschen, die Fehler machen, unter Druck stehen und oft schwierige Abwägungen treffen müssen. Im Sinne eines neuen Miteinanders bedarf es mehr Nachsicht und weniger Pauschalkritik. Doch die zentrale Frage bleibt: Wie kann Politik Vertrauen zurückgewinnen? Ich bin überzeugt: Es braucht einen neuen Politikstil, der von Ehrlichkeit, Mut und Zusammenarbeit geprägt ist, der den Dialog mit den Bürger*innen auf Augenhöhe sucht und sich zum Beispiel durch folgende Ansätze auszeichnen könnte:

1. Einfache Sprache und klare Kommunikation – auf allen Plattformen: Politik muss verständlich sein. Komplexe Entscheidungen müssen so erklärt werden, dass sie nachvollziehbar sind – ohne Fachjargon und ohne Phrasen. Das würde auch jungen Menschen helfen, Politik besser zu verstehen. Deshalb ist es gut, dass sich die Formen der politischen Kommunikation langsam wandeln und Politik mittlerweile auch auf Social Media stattfindet.

2. Normalisierung von Schwäche: Politik braucht mehr Menschlichkeit. Niemand hat alle Antworten, und es ist in Ordnung, das zuzugeben. Es schafft Vertrauen, wenn man offen sagt: „Das weiß ich gerade, ehrlich gesagt, nicht, aber ich nehme Ihr Anliegen ernst und kümmere mich darum." Mehr Ehrlichkeit bedeutet in diesem Zusammenhang auch, Fehler öffentlich zuzugeben und möglicherweise Konsequenzen zu ziehen.

3. Überparteiliches Handeln – vielleicht ein „Wandelwunder": Die Herausforderungen unserer Zeit erfordern Lösungen, die über Partei- und Ideologiegrenzen hinausgehen. Bürger*innen beklagen zu Recht, dass Debatten sich häufig in parteipolitischem Klein-Klein verlieren. Stattdessen sollte konstruktiv und gemeinschaftlich an Lösungen gearbeitet werden. Wenn Politiker*innen parteiübergreifend an einem Strang ziehen, kann das zu einem echten „Wandelwunder" führen.

4. Mehr Bürgerbeteiligung: Bürger*innen müssen zu mehr Engagement und Partizipation ermutigt werden. Niedrigschwellige Beteiligungsmöglichkeiten, etwa in Form von Bürger*innenräten oder lokalen Dialogformaten können das Vertrauen in die politischen Institutionen stärken und ermöglichen, dass Entscheidungen gemeinsam statt von oben herab getroffen werden.

5. Weniger Inszenierung, mehr echte Begegnung: Anstatt den zehnten typischen Politikertermin mit langer Begrüßungsrede abzuhalten, dann noch schnell ein Foto für Social Media zu machen, um anschließend gleich zum nächsten Termin zu eilen, sollte sich mehr Zeit für echte Gespräche genommen werden. Ein Politikstil, der sich dem Zuhören, dem Nachfragen und dem Ernstnehmen verschreibt, wäre glaubwürdiger Beweis dafür, dass Politiker*innen im Dienst der Gesellschaft handeln und nicht für die persönliche Profilierung.

Vertrauen entsteht nicht über Nacht. Es braucht einen Wandel, der von mehr Ehrlichkeit, Mut und Zusammenarbeit geprägt ist. Ein neues Verständnis dafür, dass Politik und Gesellschaft gemeinsam Verantwortung tragen und auch nur gemeinschaftlich ein solches „Wandelwunder" vollbringen können.

INTERVIEW

AMELIE M. WEBER

Freie Journalistin

Mit welchen Strategien oder Konzepten könnte das Vertrauen in Regierungs- und Unternehmerstrukturen gestärkt werden?

Viele junge Menschen fühlen sich von politischen und wirtschaftlichen Institutionen nicht ausreichend gehört oder ernst genommen. Vertrauen entsteht, wenn Beteiligung und Transparenz in den Fokus rücken. Es reicht nicht aus, junge Menschen nur als Zielgruppe zu betrachten – ihre Perspektiven müssen aktiv eingebunden werden.

Authentizität ist dabei unverzichtbar. Insbesondere die jüngere Generation erkennt schnell, wenn Greenwashing betrieben wird oder Versprechen nicht eingehalten werden. Statt symbolischer Gesten sind konkrete, überprüfbare Maßnahmen erforderlich. Fehler einzugestehen und klar zu kommunizieren, schafft Respekt und zeigt Verantwortungsbewusstsein.

Gleichzeitig ist Bildung zentral, um Desinformation entgegenzuwirken. Je besser politische und wirtschaftliche Prozesse verstanden werden, desto eher entsteht eine fundierte Basis für Engagement und Vertrauen.

Wie sehen Sie persönlich das Verhältnis von individueller Freiheit und „Verantwortung für die Gesellschaft übernehmen" und wie setzen Sie das um?

Es geht darum, bewusst Entscheidungen zu treffen, die sowohl der eigenen Selbstverwirklichung als auch dem Gemeinwohl dienen. Das zeigt sich beispielsweise im Umgang mit Klimaschutz. Viele verzichten auf Flüge, ernähren sich nachhaltiger oder engagieren sich politisch. Nicht aus Zwang, sondern aus Überzeugung, dass das eigene Handeln Auswirkungen auf die Zukunft hat.

Diese Haltung lässt sich im Alltag umsetzen: durch bewusstes Konsumverhalten, den Einsatz für lokale Initiativen oder durch das Nutzen der eigenen Stimme – zum Beispiel in sozialen Medien. Verantwortung wird dabei nicht als Einschränkung erlebt, sondern als Chance, aktiv die Welt mitzugestalten.

Braucht es dafür auch mehr Zusammenarbeit über Partei- und Wettbewerbsgrenzen hinweg und wie könnte das zu einem „Wandelwunder" führen?

Die großen Herausforderungen der Gegenwart erfordern neue Formen der Zusammenarbeit. Einzelne Parteien, Unternehmen oder Institutionen stoßen an ihre Grenzen. Statt Konkurrenzdenken sind deshalb Kooperation und Austausch notwendig.

Ein „Wandelwunder" wird möglich, wenn verschiedene Akteure ein gemeinsames Ziel verfolgen. Das erfordert Mut, neue Ansätze zuzulassen, Macht zu teilen und zuzuhören – gerade auch jungen Perspektiven, die oft unkonventionelle, aber zukunftsweisende Lösungen bieten.

Hoffnung spielt dabei eine entscheidende Rolle. Sie ist nicht naiv, sondern der Motor für Veränderung. Mit Hoffnung beginnt jeder Wandel – und sie ist es, die Menschen, Generationen und Ideen verbindet.

WOLF CHRISTIAN WEIMER

Gründer & CEO von ARTICLY

Mit welchen Strategien oder Konzepten könnte das Vertrauen in Regierungs- und Unternehmerstrukturen gestärkt werden?

Vertrauen entsteht durch Transparenz, Mitsprache und eine gemeinsame Vision – Prinzipien, die sowohl in der Politik als auch in Unternehmen gelten. Menschen wollen nicht nur informiert, sondern auch einbezogen werden. Das bedeutet, Entscheidungen nachvollziehbar zu machen, Beteiligung zu ermöglichen und ein gemeinsames Ziel zu formulieren.

Gerade in Zeiten wachsender Unsicherheit braucht es eine gleichzeitige Kultur der starken Führung und des offenen Dialogs. Wenn sowohl Regierungen als auch Unternehmen auf Augenhöhe mit Bürgern und Stakeholdern kommunizieren, entsteht nicht nur Vertrauen – sondern auch eine gemeinsame Verantwortung für die Zukunft.

Wie sehen Sie persönlich das Verhältnis von individueller Freiheit und „Verantwortung für die Gesellschaft übernehmen" und wie setzen Sie das um?

Freiheit ist für mich ein zentraler Wert – und genau deshalb habe ich mich persönlich für die Selbstständigkeit entschieden. Als Unternehmer steht fest: Verantwortung zu übernehmen ist keine Option, sondern eine Grundvoraussetzung. Das gilt nicht nur für große Unternehmen, sondern auch für kleine Strukturen. Selbst in einem Start-up kann jede Entscheidung Mitarbeiter, Partner und die Gesellschaft insgesamt (positiv) beeinflussen.

Braucht es dafür auch mehr Zusammenarbeit über Partei- und Wettbewerbsgrenzen hinweg und wie könnte das zu einem „Wandelwunder" führen?

Wettbewerb belebt das Geschäft. Ebenso belebt der Austausch mit Wettbewerbern den Markt. „Coopetition" ist hier das Stichwort. In unserer Arbeit erleben wir regelmäßig, wie wertvoll der faire Austausch mit Mitbewerbern ist. Konkurrenz bedeutet nicht Abschottung – im Gegenteil: Gerade in der Start-up-Welt profitieren wir davon, Wissen zu teilen und voneinander zu lernen.

INTERVIEW

HAMZA R. WÖRDEMANN

Geschäftsführer von Soziale Dienste und Jugendhilfe gGmbH

Mit welchen Strategien oder Konzepten könnte das Vertrauen in Regierungs- und Unternehmerstrukturen gestärkt werden?

Während bei vielen älteren Menschen das Vertrauen in Regierungs- und Unternehmerstrukturen gesunken ist, haben junge Menschen ein angemesseneres Vertrauen. Weniger hohe Erwartungen reduzieren potenzielle Enttäuschungen. Sie sind insgesamt mit den Vorzügen eines demokratischen und rechtsstaatlichen Gemeinwesens zufrieden. Die Strategie der Regierungsstrukturen sollte darin bestehen, einerseits weiterhin bürgernah und fair zu agieren und andererseits Verständnis dafür zu wecken, dass auch staatliches Handeln nicht frei von Fehlern sein kann.

Schwieriger sieht das bei dem Vertrauen in die Unternehmensstrukturen aus. Weil die meisten jungen Menschen nie in einer Zeit gelebt haben, wo eine langwierige, zum Teil lebenslange Bindung an den Arbeitgeber bestand, sind sie verständlicherweise weniger loyal und emotional kaum gebunden. Als Strategie wird empfohlen: Die Stärkung der Gestaltungsmöglichkeiten erhöhen, Mitarbeiterkapitalbeteiligung, viel Transparenz und längerfristige Sicherheiten bringen mehr als kurzfristige und künstliche Personalmarketinginstrumente, die in schwierigen Zeiten ohne nennenswerte Vorwarnung über Bord geworfen werden. Die jungen Menschen sind aufgeweckt genug, echte Loyalität zu erkennen und nur dann eine tragfähige Bindung aufzubauen.

Wie sehen Sie persönlich das Verhältnis von individueller Freiheit und „Verantwortung für die Gesellschaft übernehmen" und wie setzen Sie das um?

Das Streben nach individueller Freiheit und die Bereitschaft, selber Verantwortung für die Gesellschaft zu übernehmen, stellen keinen Widerspruch dar. „Individuelle Freiheit" hat ja nichts mit dem Wunsch zu tun, sich alleine oder außerhalb einer Gemeinschaft zu verwirklichen. Es geht lediglich darum, sich seine Gemeinschaft selber auszusuchen und dort möglichst ungebunden die eigene Individualität ausleben zu können. Aber: Die zunehmende Individualisierung bedeutet: Junge Menschen möchten nicht mehr „irgendwas" für

die Gemeinschaft machen und die Ausgestaltung ihres Engagements den dortigen Regeln unterwerfen. Sie streben ein Maximum an Wahlfreiheit und Gestaltungsmöglichkeiten an. Deshalb werden „freiere" Engagement-Modelle wie zum Beispiel Patenschaften, bei denen sich die Zeit frei einteilen lässt, auch heute noch gut nachgefragt. Die Strategie sollte darin bestehen, den Zugang zur Verantwortungsübernahme „barrierefrei" zu gestaltet und auch für komplexere mentale Belohnungssysteme zu werben (ein menschliches „Danke" anstelle eines Social-Media-„likes").

Braucht es dafür auch mehr Zusammenarbeit über Partei- und Wettbewerbsgrenzen hinweg und wie könnte das zu einem „Wandelwunder" führen?

Die Bereitschaft, selber persönlich Verantwortung für die Gemeinschaft zu übernehmen, hängt davon ab, wie positiv diese empfunden wird. Extremisten versuchen, „den Staat" und die Demokratie als negativ und „dem Untergang geweiht" und den Einzelnen als hilflos darzustellen. Eine die Demokratie schützende Strategie besteht darin, die Zusammenarbeit über Partei- und Wettbewerbsgrenzen hinaus auszubauen. Diese Zusammenarbeit muss aber so gestaltet werden, dass Vielfalt und Widersprüche ausgehalten werden und auch weiter sichtbar bleiben dürfen. Eine Polarisierung, wie sie während der Coronapandemie erlebt wurde, muss vermieden werden.

ULRICH REINHARDT

SO GELINGT DEUTSCHLANDS ZUKUNFT

VERTRAUEN STÄRKEN
VERANTWORTUNG TEILEN
KOOPERATION LEBEN